THE COLLECTED TALES OF
A LAKELAND LAD

by

LEN HAYTON

To Sheila — in appreciation of a long and happy friendship and in honour of your father Tom who sold me my penny farthing.

Best Wishes

Len & Jean

This book is dedicated to my wife Jean, my late wife Joy, and my first wife Sandra; to my children: Jacqueline, Ingrid, Martin, Peter, Penelope and Nicholas Paul who died in 1978; to my grandchildren: Gareth and David, Millie and Jennie; Sarah, Nicholas, Kayleigh and Michael; Oliver, Toby, Mollie and Beatrice; Christopher, Michaela, Rebecca and Kieran; and to my great granddaughter, Isabelle; to their spouses and partners: Gordon, Mossop, Richard, Claire, Mark Raven, Mark Lee and Nicholas Hall; and to all the wonderful people I have met on my journey through life to date, who have brought work, love, friendship and good humour, so enriching our lives together.

Published by Leonard and Jean Hayton

ISBN 978-0-9570942-0-8

Printed by Titus Wilson, Kendal
2011

ACKNOWLEDGEMENTS

It is a pleasure to express my thanks to the people who have been so helpful in the preparation of this book and those who have generously given their consent to the use of existing research papers and documents.

I particularly wish to thank Norrie Davies-Shiel for generously allowing me access to her late husband Mike's research files on Anglo-Saxon and Viking settlement in Lakeland and permission to include his maps, figures 8.12, 8.13 and 8.14. Likewise, I am grateful to Paul Robinson in kindly agreeing for me to include his "Report of Bird Sightings" on and around Kentmere Tarn.

My grateful acknowledgement is due to Professor James Graham-Campbell and his publisher, Francis Lincoln, for permission to include the pictures of Viking ships, figures 8.7 and 8.10, his maps of Scandinavian settlement and Viking trade and towns, figures 8.8 and 8.9, as well as the Viking long-ship picture on the book cover. My sincere thanks go to Robert Ridley A.R.C.S. for his help and the use of his Kentmere Commons map, whereon I have noted some Viking evidence of settlement in Kentmere. Likewise, I wish to gratefully acknowledge Dr John Clegg and Dr Elizabeth Haworth and the Microscopy Journal for permission to use the article, "Diatoms of the Kentmere Diatomite Deposits". I am grateful to Ken Clarke for the information on the Brunskill photographers, who photographed my great great grandfather, the Reverend Gerard Hayton, and to Philip Taylor and the Lake District Planning Board, who produced the ecological report on Kentmere Tarn at my request in 1982. I thank the Westmorland Gazette for consent to use the extracts which appear in the book and for their support.

Particular thanks are due to my daughter, Penny, for early encouragement and typing all my old notes, finding family photos and improving my knowledge of the day-to-day use of the computer. She has done a marvellous job. I am grateful to my wife, Jean, for her unflagging energy and determination in collating the usable material I have written over the last 50 years, for her advice to celebrate the happy aspects of my life in a positive way and for the attention to detail in editing and correcting my faults, all done in a most agreeable way. Together we have relived my life through the writings in this book – and despite all my short-comings we are still on cloud nine!

I am grateful to Jean's good friend, Christine Denmead, who created some of the illustrations. She has succeeded in catching the spirit of Willie, the satisfied farmer, as well as the alcoholic, the burglar, "Dew Drops on a May Morning", the bank voles and all the birds: the kestrel, kakapo, peregrine falcon and the albatross!

I am pleased to acknowledge the artistry of the late Christine Birchall, who conceived the advertising cartoons for the Poll Charolais Cattle Society, and likewise to "Christopher", who drew the cartoon presented to me by Helme Lodge residents on Independence Day, which is reproduced in the book.

For all their help and work in the production of this book my grateful thanks go to Shaun Drummond for type-setting, Bryan Harper for picture settings and plate preparation, and to Steve Edwards and the administrative staff and printing team at Titus Wilson in Kendal. My thanks are also due to David Rigg, the proprietor of Titus Wilson, for his advice that the book needed to be more than a collection of my verses. It has been a privilege to work with the skilled people at Titus Wilson and to broaden our knowledge and understanding of their expertise.

To print this book in England with a long established local firm is very pleasing indeed, for it is only by using the skills of our local industry that such expertise lives on in our country and can be passed on to the next generations.

To Triarom of Windermere I wish to express my appreciation for their help with computing and the excellent after-sales service and support from Marion Kenyon, Daniel Shaw and Kim Burrows.

For special encouragement and enthusiastic support I would like to thank John and Carol Beckett and Andrew and Rona Bromley, and in particular for reading parts of the the text and giving helpful and constructive comment.

Thank you to our friends, Robbie and Jean Ellis, for their enthusiasm, pleasant cooperation and good work in recording my verses, as well as giving consent to include the advertisement of their studio website.

For photographs and pictures I acknowledge and thank Peter and Juliet Townsend for the use of the monochrome photographs of Kentmere by Juliet's father, the late Geoffrey Berry. Acknowledgement and thanks are due to my friend, Jack Loan, for the colour photographs of Kentmere, as well as for developing the photograph of the Reverend Gerard Hayton from the glass slide loaned by Mrs Diana Matthews. I also wish to acknowledge my mother, the late Evelyn Mary Hayton, who took the pictures of our early family life at Brow Top with her Kodak Box Brownie camera. She certainly had an eye for photography, as is shown in the book.

Special thanks are due to Annabel Williams, my niece, for her wedding photography in May 1997 and July 2010, when with her usual cheerfulness and professional skill, she created a living memory of two very happy days in my life.

For the loan of photographs to reproduce in the book my thanks go to: my son, Martin Hayton; my former wife, Sandra Johnston; Gloria Montague, the daughter of our wartime landgirl, Eva Kinchin, who has remained a friend ever since she first visited us as a little girl at Brow Top; our good friend, Christine Sutton, who provided me with some photographs of the Poll Charolais Cattle Society; Christine Knipe and her team at the Westmorland County Agricultural Society; and Nigel Wilkinson, MD of Windermere Lake Cruises. Where any photo picture or drawing is not acknowledged it has been made by me or every effort has been made to contact the relevant persons to ask permission to print them.

I am grateful for all the helpful information readily given by friends, Will and Val Duffield, Andrew and Pat Taylor, Colin and Margaret Tyson, and Jeff and Rose Walker.

For their help, advice, "leg-pull" and support my thanks are due to: Bill and Jenny Bewley, Peter and Joan Matthews and Tony and Jen Sansom, as well as to Reg and Finn Ashworth, Gordon and Pat Atkinson, Jean Cowling (now Mrs Lear), Roger and Heather Gardner, John and Rachel Geldard and their sons, Richard and Charles, and their daughter Victoria Hodgson, Ron Gerrard, Reg and Elizabeth Gifford, Zoe and Paul Gibson, Tony and Sheila James, Annie Mawson, Dr Samuel and Gil Murphy, Stephen Read of the Levens History Society, Colin and Pauline Sandy, Bernadette Tomlinson of Bay Farm Tours, Malcolm and Elsie Tyson, and Kate Winkley and her sisters, Sue Robinson and Roz Everitt.

There are many other friends who have helped along the way, too many to record here, but you know who you are and my appreciation is equally intended for you. As to errors and omissions, they are entirely mine and my responsibility.

CONTENTS

9. MUSINGS AND AMUSINGS

10. TWO WHEELS & FOUR WHEELS

11. THE MAGIC OF THE INTERNET

12. APPENDICES
1. DIALECT AND VIKINGS

2. Kentmere Tarn

Robbie Ellis' website can be found at www.wix.com/meadowsuite/
albums Also on Facebook – Robbie Jenny Ellis

FOREWORD

Len has kindly asked me to write this foreword.

He and I met through Guardian Soulmates on the internet in March 2010. Len's former wife, Joy, had sadly died in 2007 and I was single. Little did we think when we first met that our lives would lead to a whirlwind romance and our marriage within four months. My professional background was first in teaching and then in nursing. I always loved the study of literature and my hobbies were in music, as in choral singing, and I was lucky to enjoy travelling in this country and abroad during my holidays.

I have found Len's family and friends and the people of Levens to be delightful, and I am grateful to them for their warm welcome and support. Len's niece informed me that "life with Uncle Len would never be dull." And that is just as I have found it to be! The 18 months since we met have been the happiest time of my life and full of fun and interest. It is amazing what opportunities life can hold in store. I never imagined that one day I would become a pillion passenger on Len's motorbike! Nor did I ever envisage helping my husband to publish a book! Len and I feel very fortunate to have met in the autumn of our lives and to share our appreciation of living in this beautiful part of the world, the English Lake District.

Very soon in our relationship I realised what a man of many interests and talents Len is, and I discovered a treasure trove of his writings. He has written poems and stories for friends and for his own amusement for many years, and his themes cover a wide range of subject matter. For me, hearing his lovely warm Westmorland accent reading his own verses, and other poets' verses that he loves, has been a great joy. One of Len's poems, "After a Ceilidh on Islay", is hilarious and has everybody in tucks of laughter when he recites it with a Scottish accent! Readers having access to the internet can hear Len reading his poem on the Meadowsuite website: see the end of the contents list in this book for more information.

I find Len's writings amusing, informative and often profound as well as poetic. He has a great compassion for humanity and wildlife and this is expressed in his writings as a deep concern for the people of our local community, the natural world and the state of our own beloved nation.

Len's roots are the small hill farm in the Kentmere Valley in the South Lakes where he was brought up, but his profession took him out of this "Shangri-La" and led him into the wider world as a Lakeland lawyer in many varied areas of work, both country-wide and abroad, earning him the Outstanding Achievement Award at the Cumbria Business Awards in 2007.

Len loves the local dialect which he heard and spoke as a boy, and he is enthusiastic in his support of the Lakeland Dialect Society and its intention to keep the various forms of Cumbrian dialect alive. He wants to encourage others to enjoy the character, lovely lilt and humour of its colourful vocabulary and turns of phrase.

This book is a patchwork of Len's life and interests including many of the verses, stories and songs that he has written. He has been well-known in South Cumbria for his entertaining after-dinner speeches as well as talks on various other occasions, although he is now enjoying a rest from those activities.

I have encouraged Len to publish this book so that people who have heard him speak, either in person or on his CD, 'Tales of a Lakeland Lad', can now enjoy his verses and stories in print. I hope that many readers, who do not know Len, will enjoy dipping into his writings and receive as much pleasure as I have.

Jean Hayton
November 2011

INTRODUCTION

This is a book for browsers and I don't expect anyone to read it all, but you can pick and choose what interests you. Although in places it may appear so, I have not set out to write an autobiography. My verses and stories are a hop, skip and jump through a life full of variety – successes and failures – joys and sorrows – as well as much love, laughter, fun and fellowship along the way. There are some historical notes and snippets which appear here and there like currants in a fruit bun.

The best advice came from my Father as we sat side by side in our "Kentmere College" in the 1940s – *Truth – Love - Honesty – Straight dealing - and - Get up in a morning!* Throughout my life there have been many people who have helped me forward. The love and support of my family, my wives, my law partners and the firm friendships I have made have sustained me and been my inspiration

There are references to my growing up through the 1940s and 50s in the cocoon of Kentmere valley, followed by the shock of realising that there was a wider world out there, when I started at Windermere Grammar School in 1951.

My interest in the old dialect words used by my parents and the local folk in Kentmere has spawned some verses in dialect. There is a small glossary attached to each dialect poem to aid interpretation, plus the main glossary in the appendix. The Viking timeline and my Viking trail provide a light-hearted trawl through the history of the Northmen in Lakeland.

There are verses and stories about my work. I was articled (apprenticed) to John Kenneth Jackson, a Solicitor practising in Kendal and Milnthorpe, from 1957 to 1962. He and my late brother, Jack, gave me a good practical training in country legal practice. It was also character building, as were my college days at Blackpool Law School and the College of Law in Guildford. I had been fairly average in most subjects at school but the English Common Law and its history inspired and interested me so much that I performed more successfully. I enjoyed my studies and qualified as a Solicitor at the age of twenty two.

In the book I celebrate my family years with my wife, Sandra, and our children. We married in 1964 and brought up our family together – doing our hobby farming in Kentmere and discovering the Hebridean island of Islay along the way. There are poems and notes about this period, which give a flavour of Kentmere life, as well as some nature poems and songs about Islay.

There are historical notes about the date of draining the original Kentmere Tarn and how the existing tarn was created. The appendix contains a paper on diatoms and one on the botany around the tarn. Paul Robinson has kindly included his bird sightings in the area since 1978 to the present day, as my own notes have been mislaid during house moves.

Joining the Windermere, Ambleside and District Round Table in 1965 opened my mind further and established firm and lifelong friendships. I learned how to work with young men from all walks of life, not only socially, but in service to the local community and internationally. Our successful project in building the Marchesi Centre for senior citizens in Windermere involved using all our skills, resourcefulness and perseverance. The Round Table was a wonderful organisation for getting things done, but I doubt if the authorities today would allow Round Tablers to dredge the lower stretch of the River Gowan through the village of Staveley, in order to cure the flooding of the houses, as we did!

The book includes some early court and other legal stories, where it is possible to relate them. I am unable to reveal some of the funniest cases in the life of a country lawyer, because much of my work was confidential and the information belonged to the Client. Some stories have the Client's consent and others are already in the public domain. Though I spent time in court as a young solicitor, I was also expanding our practice in Windermere, dealing with the hotel and tourist trade, buying and selling guesthouses and hotels for Clients, as well as doing domestic conveyancing. We developed a broad-based practice and dealt with company law and partnerships, wills, estates and successions. We also had to keep up with the changes in tax, divorce and family law and all the human problems which came our way.

As our Solicitors' practice grew, I specialised more in the law relating to agriculture, tourism and taxation. Amongst other work I was instructed to form a new Pedigree Cattle Society in 1984 and as a result my work took me to Texas, Canada, France, Belgium and Hungary when the latter was still behind the Iron Curtain. See "Teeth, Testicles and Tattoos" for more information. The work also took me to many farms, auctions and shows around the UK and I met some very interesting and talented farmers.

As a result of my interest in agricultural and commercial work, I was asked to act for the Westmorland County Agricultural Society. I have enjoyed a happy relationship for many years with this wonderful Society, which achieves so much for our rural and urban communities.

In September 1990 I left Kentmere because our marriage had broken down and my health with it. This is not the place to recite cause and effect. Suffice it to say that I accept 50% of the cause but it was a great sadness for both of us and our five children, who were then all grown up, three of whom were married. It became our mid-life crisis which has taken time and patience to heal, and even now I have no contact with one branch of my family despite all attempts at reconciliation. It remains a deep sadness that four of my grandchildren have had no access to me, but I hope that one day they may read this book with an open mind and make their own judgement of their grandfather. Meantime I take comfort from hearing good reports of the family and the children's progress. As to the rest of my family, we are all on good terms and I am proud of them all. I have lovely grandchildren and now a great grandchild, Isabelle, in the USA.

Glimpses of my path through life since then will become apparent as these pages progress.

Over the years I have been invited to speak at many dinners and other functions. As I could rarely remember the punch lines of jokes, I tended to put something for each occasion in rhyme. I talked about my upbringing in Kentmere, sometimes in dialect, with a variety of legal stories, which for some reason appeared to amuse folk.

It meant I had to do some research about my hosts and I hoped that some inspiration would come to me. I preferred rhyme to blank verse, but often got bogged down if I tried to follow scholarly rules of prosody. After many years of 'doing my own thing', I took a short course for writers.

The course was run at Ambleside through Lancaster University with Professor Macpherson. She was encouraging and helpful, but perhaps because of my roots in the Lakeland dialect, spoken during my formative years, I still had bad habits in spelling and construction! It was a delightful learning experience with up to twelve would-be writers having a go and reading our efforts to each other. The following was a plea to the Professor for help!

PLEASE PROFESSOR TELL ME

Am I such an ignoramus
When it comes to writing verse?
I just get a funny feeling
It's a kind of rhyming curse.

I warm with inspiration
It excites me through and through
I don't know why I feel that way
It's just something that I do.

The technicalities escape me
Be it couplet or quatrain
Perhaps stanzas I should study
To measure my refrain.

To divide my verse in sections
Inhibits me a lot
I get bogged down in length and meter
So I lose the blooming plot.

My life is full of deadlines
And things that I MUST do
So must I be disciplined
And punctuate my verses too?

Please Professor tell me
If my heart has things to say
Should I set its beat to a pattern
Or let it have its way?

Should I study forms of verse
In measured feet and time
Learn the art of composition
Scheme my rhythms and my rhyme?

Please Professor tell me
How my study should proceed
How to learn the art of prosody
What knowledge do I need?

Your teaching made me realise
The little that I know
About the craft of writing
Or the way that I should go.

So please Professor tell me
What apprenticeship I need
To learn the art of poetry
Whose wisdom should I heed?

It's clear I'm an ignoramus
Some writers leave me cold
I cannot find the lilt in it
Perhaps I am too bold.

So please Professor tell me
In the workplace of my soul
What tools of verse to polish
What forms of words my goal?

LH 14.8.99

I still do not profess to be a poet but I have had many requests to put my verses and stories in print: so here goes! My "musings and amusings" are difficult to classify in any pattern or order. *"Variety is the spice of life,"* my father used to say. I have certainly had variety in my family and home life, my work and my interests.

Having lived on my own for two and a half years following my wife Joy's death in 2007, and after the sudden death of my law partner and friend, Michael Winkley, in January 2010, I felt very unsettled. It was at such times in life that I recalled my Granny Hayton (figures 1.9 and 1.12) singing beside the piano:

"When upon life's billows you are tempest tossed
When you are discouraged thinking all is lost
Then count your many blessings,
Name them one by one
And it will surprise you what the Lord has done."

Thus in March 2010 I decided to try internet dating with Guardian Soulmates. That was how Jean and I met and a wonderful change in our fortunes began. Since then there is a skip in our gait and sunshine in our smiles! I have called this new awakening: "The Magic of the Internet." If you are interested – read on!   5th October, 2011

INDEX OF FIRST LINES OF VERSES

MAPS INDEX AND MAP NOTES

Robert who assisted Steve Dickinson on the Bryants Gill dig states:

"There is an extensive Viking era settlement at Bryants Gill which comprises a longhouse situated amongst an extensive field system. There are two squarish sheepfolds integrated diagonally into the wall lines and evidence for a possible separate washfold (although being separate, one can be less sure of the dating for this structure). Below the well defined fields there is evidence of two areas of clearance cairns. The longhouse itself was of a typical Viking pattern seen at Jarlshof in Shetland. The Bryants Gill longhouse has one stretch of internal paving. This paving characteristically stretches down the spine of the building or across the building between two opposing doors. Some buildings have both types of paving. Other Viking remains include a Viking spearhead which was found in 1969 just above the Nan Bield Pass between Kentmere and Mardale, and a spearhead which was dredged from Kentmere Tarn in 1942 and which conformed to an 11th century Norwegian pattern.

On the higher stretches of the fellside in upper Kentmere, there are many Medieval longhouses which probably date back somewhere between 1200 AD and 1500 AD. They seem to form a coherent landscape. It is possible that they pre-date the arrival of the Black Death in 1349 and were subsequently abandoned. Alternatively they may have been built during the subsequent reorganisation of medieval society which took place after the Black Death. Their existence probably reflects the profitability of the successful Wool Trade in the local area during the Medieval period."

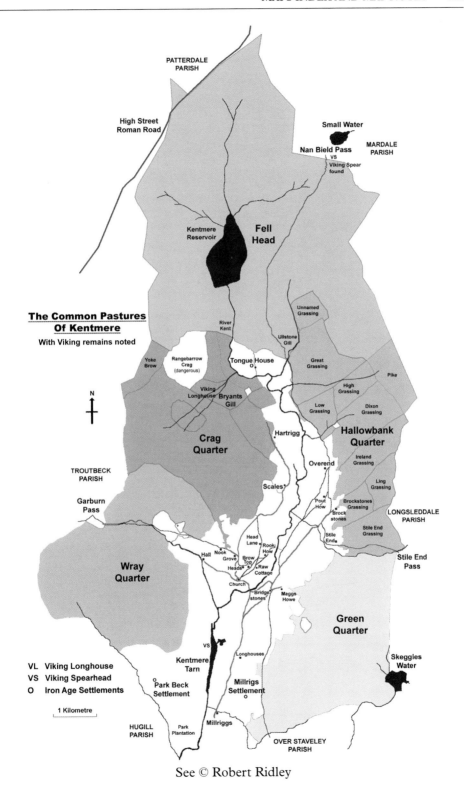

**The Common Pastures
Of Kentmere**

With Viking remains noted

PATTERDALE
PARISH

High Street
Roman Road

Small Water

Nan Bield Pass
VS
Viking Spear
found

MARDALE
PARISH

Kentmere
Reservoir

Fell
Head

Unnamed
Grassing

River
Kent

Ullstone
Gill

N

Yoke
Brow

Rangebarrow
Crag
(dangerous)

Tongue House
O

Great
Grassing

Pike

Viking
Longhouse Bryants
Gill

High
Grassing

Crag
Quarter

Hartrigg

Low
Grassing

Dixon
Grassing

Hallowbank
Quarter

Ireland
Grassing

Overend

TROUTBECK
PARISH

Scales

Ling
Grassing

Garburn
Pass

Pout
How

Brockstones
Grassing

Brock
stones

LONGSLEDDALE
PARISH

Stile End
Grassing

Stile
End

Head
Lane

Rooki
How

Hall Nook

Grove

Brow
Top

Stile End
Pass

Wray
Quarter

Heads

Raw
Cottage

Church

Bridge
stones

Maggs
Howe

Green
Quarter

VS

Skeggles
Water

VL   Viking Longhouse
VS   Viking Spearhead
O   Iron Age Settlements

Kentmere
Tarn

Longhouses

Park Beck
Settlement

Millrigs
Settlement

1 Kilometre

HUGILL
PARISH

Park
Plantation

Millriggs

OVER STAVELEY
PARISH

See © Robert Ridley

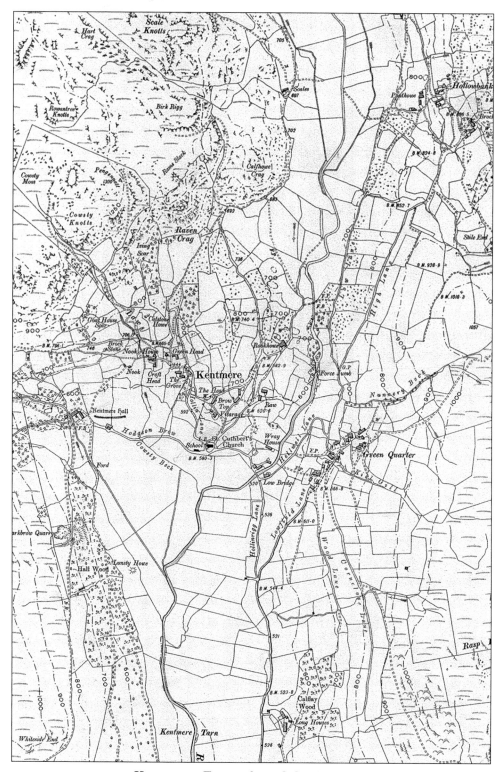

Kentmere – Extract from O.S. Map 1899

1

___

A LAKELAND CHILDHOOD

KENTMERE: THE LAKELAND VALLEY
WHERE I GREW UP

Kentmere is an idyllic and peaceful valley community which lies nine miles north of Kendal in the south east of the Lake District. The valley has remained largely unspoiled because it lies off the main tourist route with only one access road by car.

Like the sheep which are heafed or hefted to a particular part of a Lakeland fell and nurtured there, my family has lived in Kentmere almost continuously since 1844. My great great grandfather, the Reverend Gerard Hayton, came as curate to Kentmere in 1844 and in 1851 he purchased Brow Top Farm. The farm has been the family home ever since. I was born at Brow Top and brought up there and I lived in Kentmere for fifty years. My male line ancestors lived in the Westmorland parishes of Kentmere, Grayrigg, Orton and Asby from before 1660 and my mother's ancestors came from Levens in Westmorland, where I now live.

The Kentmere valley is margined by a range of beautiful fells and crags sloping into stone-walled enclosures, pastures and meadows on the valley floor. To go through the valley to Troutbeck in the west, Haweswater in the north or Longsleddale in the east, one must walk over Garburn, Nan Bield or Stile End passes respectively. These passes were in times past pack-horse tracks and communication routes before turnpike roads were constructed from Kendal to Appleby and Ambleside in 1762. The houses and farms scattered about the valley are built of stone and slate in the traditional Lakeland style. One can often find a spring as the source of water and a small quarry near at hand, where the stone for the dwelling has been hewn from the rock.

An old Roman road from Galava camp at Ambleside to Brougham follows a route over the range of fells behind the summits of Yoke, Ill Bell and Froswick and crosses High Street above the head of the valley basin. In the 1870s my great-grandfather, Richard Mattinson, a

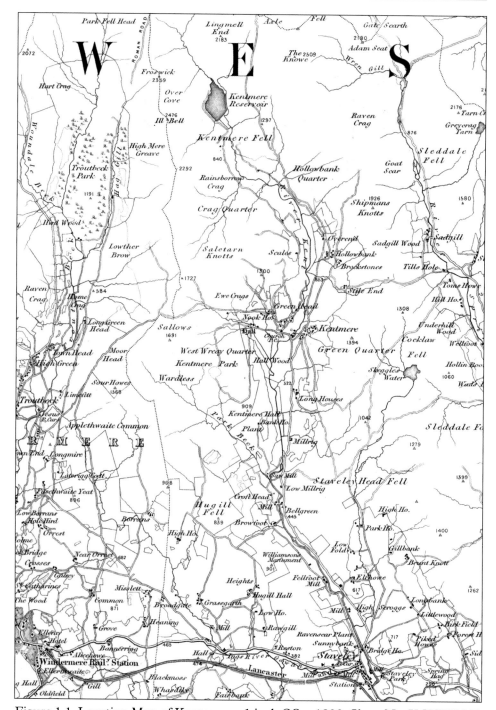

Figure 1.1. Location Map of Kentmere – 1 inch OS *c.* 1899. Sheet No. XCVIII N.E.

gamekeeper on Kentmere Hall Estate, used to collect dotterel feathers on High Street to make his flies for fishing. He fished from a boat on "Kentmere Broadwater", now known as Kentmere Tarn.

It seems odd to us now that sporting occasions, including traditional wrestling and horse racing and "shepherds' meets", were held so high in the fells on High Street. However, when we look at the topography we see that High Street is mainly level on the top and is a central meeting point for the people of the valleys of Kentmere, Longsleddale, Mardale, Martindale and Patterdale with access to Hartsop and Howtown. Lakeland folk were used to walking fair distances to country dances and "merry neets" in those days! Frank Garnett in "*Westmorland Agriculture 1800-1900*" tells us that the last shepherds' meet (a meeting to exchange stray sheep) was held on High Street fell in 1835.

Figure 1.2. Kentmere Dale Head in winter by Geoffrey Berry

In recent years the "Kentmere Horseshoe", which includes High Street, has become a favourite circuit for fell-walkers and fell-runners. The annual fell race has generated more interest in Kentmere and increased the number of visitors. Walkers and cyclists as well as bird watchers, wildlife enthusiasts and local history buffs can all find something of interest in Kentmere.

It is thrilling to watch a pair of majestic golden eagles, easily identified by the length of their wings and primaries, circling high above Kentmere or see a peregrine falcon dive at wondrous speed out of the sky. Equally, to sit at peace with binoculars near the re-made Kentmere Tarn or the plantation and observe the wonders of nature around you is a joy in itself.

When I was born at Brow Top Farm in 1940, the houses and land in the valley were mainly occupied by farmers and their workers. In addition there were quarrymen working at the quarries in Dale Head and workers extracting diatomite from the site of the old Kentmere Tarn.

The Kentmere form of Lakeland dialect was spoken by my parents, grandparents and neighbours. Hopefully, the verses and stories which follow give a flavour of the period.

View of Kentmere, looking south from the fells, with the quarries in the foreground

A LAKELAND LAD
Reflections on growing up in Kentmere

To lie on your back on a beautiful day in a meadow and smell the grass and wild flowers or to sit on a steep fell-side under the dome of a Lakeland sky is a simple luxury which costs nothing. I used to sit and look around marvelling at the wonders of creation. All nature seemed in tune, albeit in the raw.

Following a concert in January 1999 held at Levens Hall with Annie Mawson singing and playing so beautifully on her Celtic harp, I wrote this song for her the following morning. It recalls my feelings as a boy and as a man lying on the grass in Kentmere among the fells of Lakeland with the dome of the sky above me.

She sang it the following year at her Millennium concert in Levens Hall.

UNDER LAKELAND'S DOME OF SKY
The Millennium Dome of Lakeland

O the Lakeland hills are calling
And the bonny mountain streams
This loveliest part of England
Fills all my waking dreams.

Chorus:
Where the Herdwick sheep are grazing
And the falcon circles high
I am part of Mother Nature
Under Lakeland's dome of sky.

When I walk those fells of Lakeland
Then my worries fly away
And freedom: I can touch it
On a glorious summer's day.

Chorus

There are mighty rocks and pinnacles
Which attract the mountaineers
Inspiring youth and aged alike
To explore like pioneers.

Chorus

Our lakes and tarns of Lakeland
Mirror mountains rising high
To the dome of blue up yonder
Where cirrus paints the sky.

Chorus

O it's there at the Millennium
I'll awake as comes the dawn
To walk my favourite fells of Lakeland
On a "hasky" winter's morn.

Where the Herdwick sheep are grazing
And the falcon circles high
I am part of Mother Nature
Under Lakeland's dome of sky.

Hasky: A Lakeland dialect word meaning a sharp, frosty morning, clear and bright.

c. LH: 20th January 1999; revised 15th January 2000

★ Annie Mawson is the founder of and runs the wonderful Sunbeams Music Trust. She creates so much happiness and inspiration for disabled adults and young folk alike with her music therapy. Annie put my verse to music and she plays and sings it on the CD which I published in 2005. See figure 1.4 in colour section of Annie playing her Celtic harp. Readers having access to the internet can hear Annie singing and playing "Under Lakeland's Dome of Sky" on Robbie Ellis' website, Meadowsuite, on CD album "Tales of a Lakeland Lad" 2005. See colour section for more information on Meadowsuite website.

LH: A WAR BABY

It must hev bin se-an on in August
Back in nineteen thirty-nine
Joseph mi Fadder was forty-fower
And Mudder was thurty-nine.

T'hay moo must hev been gay comfy
Sae pleasing en smellen sae sweet
That Fadder persuaded oor Mudder
Ta hev a lile cuddle en treat.

I was telt I was nobbut an efter-thowt
Mi brothers were upwards of ten
When pre-war on t'hay moo up Kentmer
Mi parents created lile Len.

Figure 1.5. September 1944 – Wartime agricultural regulations required us to plough a specified acreage on each farm. Picture shows us picking potatoes in Cross Howe, Kentmere. Left to right: Father, L.H., landgirl Eva Kinchin and brother Gerard. Mother took the picture with a box Brownie.

Then Chamberlain lan't back fre Munich
Wid Hitler's promises worth nowt!
Fer it wasn't lang til poor Poland
Fell under his Panzers' clowt.

Lile Len was born se-an on in April
Just afoor Winston took o'er in May
What wid him en t'brave Battle of Britain
We're safe en we're o' here today!

LH 5.11.06

Thank you to those men and women from all nations
who fought for our freedom.

Glossary

Afoor = before
Clowt = clout
En = and
Fadder = Father
Fre = from
Hay moo = haystack in the barn
Hev = have
Lan't back = landed or came back

Lile = little
Mudder = Mother
Nowt = nothing
Sae = so
Se-an on = early on
Ta = to
Telt = told

THE 1940s and 1950s

I was born a month before Winston Churchill took over the conduct of the Second World War from Neville Chamberlain. The War was almost over by the time my memory was recording war planes flying over the valley to bomb the shipyards at Barrow-in-Furness (although the bombs never reached their targets but fell on the houses instead). I remember seeing the glow in the sky at the time of the bombing and being told that a plane had crashed on Garburn between the Kentmere and Troutbeck valleys. The British Army also practised manoeuvres with tracked Bren gun carriers over Garburn Pass, which caused long-term damage to the old road.

For me 1945 recalls picking "spuds" (potatoes) with our land girl, Eva Kinchin, in Cross Howe, a fertile field which the War Ag had requisitioned my father to plough.

During those years I went to church most Sundays with my grandmother. Like Queen Victoria, she always dressed in black after her husband, Gerard Albert Hayton, died in 1941 before I could form any memory of him.

Figure 1.6. LH's grandparents Gerard Albert Hayton and Mary Lib with my mother Evelyn and brothers Gerard and Jack. *c*.1935

At that time Brow Top was the home of my parents, Evelyn Mary Hayton and Joseph Hayton, my two brothers, Gerard and Jack, plus Granny, our land girl Eva, a farm man and a maid. The farm produced sufficient to sustain us and also produced butter from fourteen pedigree dairy Shorthorns. Father delivered the butter each Saturday in an old Singer van to our butter-round customers in Staveley, Burneside and Kendal.

In addition Mother did bed and breakfast and we had regulars who came year after year. Mum was a wonderful cook. Her casseroles and redcurrant and raspberry pies were delectable – sadly the visitors never

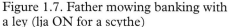

Figure 1.7. Father mowing banking with a ley (lja ON for a scythe)

Figure 1.8. Eva, our landgirl, and my mother Evelyn with farm dog

left any! My first wife Sandra was also an excellent cook and her red currant and raspberry pies were famous too!

When in later years I read the annual edition of Giles' cartoons at Christmas, his sketch of Grandma Giles always reminded me of "Mary Elizabeth" – my granny. She took me to church because I am sure she wanted me to be a parson like my great great grandfather, Reverend Gerard Hayton. He was the parson at Kentmere from 1846 to 1880. I had to blow the organ but sometimes I forgot to blow for the psalms. Then the notes yawned to a stop until I woke up! I got a toffee for blowing the organ but not if I missed blowing on time!

Granny was a curious mix of puritan and woman of the world. She was realistic about procreation. It was all around us on the farm but she would not have any truck with feminism. She was the matriarch anyway. The farmhouse and how it was run was her domain and God help any male who thought otherwise! My mother, Evelyn, was a delightful, kindly and loving lady. She got on well with Gran most of the time; I fancy it was because she respected and appreciated her mother in law's ability and loving care and so she was happy to wait her turn to be the boss, as was the custom in those days.

Outside was the male domain but the "womenfolk" expected the same standards of cleanliness and order outside that applied in the house. There was no toilet in the house until 1952. The closet: "thunderbox" or "t'lile hoose" (dry soil toilet) was up the yard. It was a solid stone and slated lean-to on the end of the old barn or hoghus (animal shed in old Norse). The hoghus was then used as a workshop and store.

There was a lovely view across the valley from the open door of the closet as the sun rose over Green Quarter fell.

Our closet had a long wooden seat with a large hole for Father and Mother and a small one for me. I would sometimes join my parents at the closet where we chatted and I learned about the basics of life from them. Later I likened the debates we had there to consultations with the Oracle at Delphi! They call it "bonding" nowadays. The closet was my first college for I'm sure the bonding of love and respect for my parents and the sound basis of life they gave me had its origin there.

It was cleaned out from below each spring through a "hog-hool" (hole) which was

Figure 1.9. Granny Hayton in the porch at Brow Top. Mary Elizabeth Hayton (née Mattinson)

behind a large stone slab leaning against the wall. The south-west wind whistled through the gap between the slab and the wall and acted as a giant extractor fan. There was no necessity for air fresheners and no time was wasted on the closet in cold weather!

The kitchen fire rarely went out in winter. Each morning my mother would rake the ashes, set the kindling and stir the fire to life before her first visit to the closet. Nothing was wasted, not even the daily paper – toilet rolls were a luxury. Food scraps went to the pig and in due course we ate the pig! There was no need to segregate waste – it was used or re-cycled through the pig or the closet!

I remember Mother getting agitated in the morning if the kindling was damp! Her closet routine was sometimes delayed when the fire wouldn't light. She needed the "black nanny" (kettle) to be ready and boiling and the fire ready to cook the porridge when she returned from the closet. She had a graphic expression which she used when the fire was not taking hold. When the fire refused to light, she would be heard to say and repeat under her breath:

"Aye, I will hev ta ga; I will hev ta ga; a short-nebbed sparrow wod touch it!"

You see time could not be wasted on the toilet. *"Ye hed ta lowse doon garn tul t'closet and fasten up yer gallases (braces) as ye cem away."* Today we take for granted a warm bathroom and toilet. It was different then with the wind howling up the valley. Going to the toilet up the yard last thing at night and first thing in the morning was a bracing experience!

Figure 1.10. View down the valley from the closet

After the war, as well as running the small mixed farm, my parents did bed and breakfast to augment their income and made teas for the dozens of cyclists who came with touring clubs and the National Cyclists' Union, whose plaque was displayed on the outside wall of the farmhouse. Cycling was all the craze after the war as it is today. The wheel has turned full circle!

One day a large fancy car arrived with a well-to-do couple. *"Do you do Bed and Breakfast?"* asked the posh lady. *"Yes,"* said Granny. *"Do you have a **bathroom en suite**?"* requested the lady. Granny had not heard of this expression *en suite* before and enquired what she meant. *"Well, a toilet in the bedroom and a bath,"* said the lady.

"Nay nay, noo Missus," Granny said. *"We don't mek stinks in oor hoos, let alane in t'bedroom. T'closet is up t'yard yonder."* She pointed up the hill. *"O' t'stink blaws away in t'wind up theer. It's a turble deal mair healthy ye knaa. I reckon nowt of mecken stinks in t'hoos.*

"Oor hoos is as clean as any thoo'll find. But if oor spot's nut fine enough for ye falderen fancy folk and thou wants this

Figure 1.11. LH with pet lamb on wall at Brow Top – July 1949

"en suite", well ye mun gang ta Bownuss. T'Ald England or Bellsfield – I believe they hev these new-fangled watter closets but I don't hod wi mekken stinks in t'hoos missel."

T' KENT'MER COLLEGE

My education started
On the day that I was born
In oor white-weshed Kent'mer farmhouse
On a bonny April morn.

I can't remember howling
Or t'hippins oot to dry
But I do recall correction
At the hint of any lie.

"Speak nobbut truth mi lad," they said
"Cost it what it will.
He that hides the wrang he dew-eth
Doth the wrang thing still."

These words cem doon fre t'elders
Etched upon mi varra soo-al
As Dad and I sat side by side
Upon the closet hoo-al.

Oor se-at of early larnin
Was oor closet in the dale
Which had stood through many centuries
Withstanding ivvery gale.

T's e-at was smooth en polished
With countless years of wear
And we didn't need de-odorants
In oor healthy Kent'mer air.

The wood was warm as we sat doon
Cald plastic yet unknown
Nor were we interrupted
By t'discord of t'mobile phone.

There was allus a gurt hoo-al fer Father
En allus a lile hoo-al fer me
We sat side by side on the closet
As he passed on his wisdom ta me.

Mainly-what we'd hev doo-er opp-en
As t'sun com up o'er t'hill
"Git thisel up in a morning lad"
I can remember mi first lesson still!

LH – 19th February 1982

Glossary

Allus = always
Cald = cold
Gurt = great
Hippins = baby's nappies
Hoo-al = hole.
Larnin = learning or study
Lile = little, small.
Mainly-what = usually or most times

Nobbut = only
O'er = over
Oor = our
Soo-al = soul
Varra = very
White-weshed = white-washed in traditional Lakeland style
Wrang = wrong

T' KENT'MER KIDS' HUNT AT KIRK SCHOOL

A fun lunchtime at Kentmere Church of England School circa 1948.
Miss Jessie Braithwaite from Staveley was our long-suffering teacher.

★   ★   ★

Hev you ivver hard o yon Kent'mer Kids' Hunt
Yance hunted fre t'school up Kent dale?
We ran through Crag Quarter en up o'er t'Yoke
Then doon o'er t'crags en pas t'Scale.

Oor hunt allus started just efter hey noon
When t'school-missus sent us ta dine
But we'd miss oor dinner en git that bit thinner
Ta ga hunten when t'weather was fine.

Scholars of all ages would join in the chase
Loup woes, scale hedges en hill
Then baying like hoonds,
Would mak all hunten soonds
Like a pack ga'en in fer t'kill.

Well yan sick time, I remember it weel
Lile Ben was t'fox that day
We'd count up ta fifty, ta give him a start
En mak sure he gat on his way.

Generally what humans don't stink like a fox
En hounds hev a sensitive nose
We're disadvantaged: we run on two legs
En oor nostrils don't track, I suppose.

Now oor huntsman that day
Shouted, "Hark hark away!"
Young Ben to the Garburn did steer
Up o'er sheep knotts en Sid Leyland's front lots
Us hoonds did bark at his rear.

Then doon by t'Scale en across t'mid dale
To Stile End en Green Quarter fell
T'fox it med out ta Maggs Howe or nowt
En t'chase was beginning to tell.

Ben scrammelled up a gurt wo', too hey en too tall
Like a Swardle that's lost its he-ad
En he dived fre the top, far too late fer ta stop
En sank like a gurt lump of le-ad!

Deep in the dipping tub he fell through green slime
En surfaced gasping wi fright
Us hoonds in the chase were flummoxed by his face
Which was covered with sheep wool en sh... (sheep trunlins!)

We laughed off our socks at this ill-fated fox
But stinking he quickly climbed back
Then to oor surprise wi wild flashing eyes
Our quarry turned on the attack!

Pursued by his stink we had nay time to think
We fled down the lane back ta school
Ben in a state, hoonds half an hour late
We were in fer a "touch of the rule".

Jessie walloped us all as we went through the hall
Save the fox with the terrible pong
Then we suffered that reek fer darn near a week
That sure was fox hunting gone wrong!

LH c.1975

Glossary

Crag Quarter = North West Quarter
 of the Valley
See Index Ref. to Border Tenure &
 Kentmere Quarters
Garburn = Garburn Pass, Kentmere
 to Troutbeck
Generally what = usually
Green Quarter = South East Quarter
 of the Valley
Hey = high

Ivver = ever
Knott = small, peaked hill
Loup = jump
Scale = Scale Farm
Scrammelled = scrambled
Sheep lots = enclosed sheep fields
Swardle = Swaledale sheep
Trunlins = sheep droppings or muck
Wo' = dry-stone field wall
Yance = once

NOBBUT A COUNTRY LAD'S VIEW

Written for a Lakeland Dialect Service in Kentmere Church

Glossary

Aboot = about
Afoor = before
Boggles = ghosts
Boo = bow
Bumly = bumble bee
Doon = down
Flayt = frightened
Freet = fright
Gurt = great
Hoo = how
Kirk = church

Larn = learn
Laiked = played
Leet = light
Likesear = likewise
Lile = little
Lish = agile
Loup = jump
Marra = friend
Mudder = mother
Neet = night
Nebbers = neighbours

Nobbut = only
Noo = now
Poddish = porridge
Reet = right
Sarved = served
Sae = so
Sen = since
Stane = stone
Thur's = there is
Varra = very

When I was lile en nobbut a lad
Mi Mudder said to me
Git off ta t'kirk wi Granny lad
Larn Christ-ian-ittee.

I larn't aboot ald Moses' Law
En his gurt slabs of stane
I memorised t'Commandments
While I laiked aboot doon t'lane.

But Jesus seemed to git it reet
Least sae't seemed ta me
"Just treat thi nebbers nicely like
As thou'd like em ta treat thee."

"Gentle Jesus meek and mild"
Was t'prayer we sed at neet
Then agen afoor t'poddish
In t'mornin at first leet.

Thur's nay need to be flayt aboot boggles
Ner loup up in t'air wi freet
If thoo tells o' thi troubles ta Jesus
En says a lile prayer at neet.

Sen then oor world hes altered
En likesear oor country talk
But not oor simple faith in Thee
T'faith o country folk.

Varra lile wi boo en scrape noo
But mebbe mair we shud
But we sense oor God aroond us
In ivverything that's good.

We praise Jesus fer o' t'seasons
His sunleet en his rain
Wild roses in oor hedgeraas
En blossoms doon oor lane.

Deep in oorsels we find Jesus
If nobbut we wod see
Hoo his luv is o' aboot us
Hoo wondrous it wod be.

In sunbeams on a fell he-ad beck
In the peace of a woodland glade
We can feel the livin' Jesus
In ivverything he's me-ad.

That feelin' of joy in a job weel done
T'skill in a craftman's hands
We can see hoo the love of Jesus
Hes spread through many lands.

When we're thrang as a bumly in Springtime
En as lish as a gurt March hare
When we're riven at life like a beaver
We're nobbut happy when Jesus is theer.

What a Marra we've gitten in Jesus!
He was nobbut a country lad
He sarved his time as a joiner
En he loved folk good en bad.

His spirit of life is within us
His love through joy en pain
Hoo great er the blessin's of Jesus
Lang may his teachin's reign.

LH. 19.6.1988

Figure 1.12. Granny and I, back from church

T'MILKEN

Figure 1.13. Our landgirl Eva Kinchin milking

My "Milken" verse recalls life on our Lakeland family farm in the 1940s and 50s. It was my first attempt at writing in my family's form of Lakeland dialect.

So have a go! Read the verses out loud a few times to savour them and get the feel of the words handed down to us by our forefathers.

Glossary

Atween = between
Ba-eth = both
Be-us = beasts or cows
Byre = shippen, shuppen or cow house
Black nanny = kettle smoked black over the fire
Coo band = rope neck collar for tying up a cow
Copy = three legged stool
Coves = calves
Cravacked = stiff backed
Gallasses = braces or suspenders
Gang = feeding passage or gangway between two rows of skell-boose

Gay = rather
Gloo-ered = looked around hard to see
Greap or gripe = channel where dung and urine dropped.
Guss = grass
Gussins = grassings or pastures
Hurpl-en = limping, stiff with age
Kine = cows
Laiken = playing
Laa groond = low ground or bottom fields
Liggen = lying down
Lile = little
Loosed doon mi galasses = unfastened my braces

Lowped = jumped
Milk be-us = milk beasts or milk cows
Milken side = space between cow and rud-stake where there is room to sit to milk
Nobbut = only
Pap = teat
Poddish = oat porridge
Pow = wooden pole
Ring widdy = a ring swivel ring to which the cow band was attached
Rough brat = apron made from sackcloth

Rud-stake = pole in centre of skel-boose between two cows
Sarra t'coves = feed or serve the calves
Se-an = soon
Settlestean = bed where cow lies down.
Shippen or shuppen = cowhouse or byre
Skel-boose = cow stall for a pair of cows
Sowked en eased ut ivvery pap = squeezed and eased milk by hand from every teat
Thowt = thought
Yan = one

T'MILKEN

I gat up gay early
Yan fine summer's morn
Mi he-ad hardly wakken
It was nobbut just dawn.

I lowped oot of bed
En I gloo-ered oot ta see
If o' oor milk be-us
Wer waiten fer me.

There was some craa-ken in t'hen hoose
En t'cockerel he sang
While doon Foxthwaite gussings
T'mornin chorus fair rang.

I thowt it was se-an
Fer ta wakken up t'wife
Cos she helps sarra t'coves
She's a gay busy life.

So I went oot ta t'closet
In t'fresh mornin air
If thoo looks ta t'priorities
Thoo hessent a care.

I loused doon mi gallasses
En gat on wi mi job
While I whistled fer t'farm dogs
Either Lassie er Bob.

But it was oor auld Tom
That com hurplen aroond
So I whistled en sent him
In t'laa ground.

While Tom brought be-us
Up in t'byre
I went in t'kitchen
En kindled up t'fire.

I picked up t'Black Nanny
And hinged it on t'crane
Then I mixed oor poddish
En went oot again.

O' t'coos in each skel–boose
Wer chowen thur cud
Divided bi t'rud-stake
A gurt pow o wood.

I clattered up t'shuppen
Wi mi copy and pail
En I lowped inta t'gang
O'er t'skel-boose rail.

I gev em some cake
En a lile bit o hay
'Cos they let doon their milk
Far better that way.

At milken side on mi copy I sat
While I held mi pail atween mi rough brat
I soaked en I eased at ivvery pap
En t'coos stood content while some hed a nap.

Yer can git turble cravacked
Sitten milken a coo
Thur wer nay fangled machines
Sick as farmers hev noo.

But I'll tell o' you fell-as
Who sleep in til nine
Ta git up at five
En then milk o' thi kine.

It's better than liggen
En laiken wi wife
'Cos it stengthens thi muscles
En calms o' thi strife.

En while I'd been milken
Oor hens hed been fed
En t'Missus hed gitten
Oor oat poddish weel med.

Ham en fresh eggs
We ba-eth can enjoy
What! It's allus been t'same
Sen I was a boy.

★   ★   ★

This verse was put to music in the 1970s and is sung by Robbie Ellis on his CD and also later by Craig Duggan on his CD: "Songs of Cumbria".

I have also recorded reading T'Milken in dialect for visitors to the Museum of Lakeland Country Life at Abbot Hall in Kendal.

NANCY

My favourite cow

After my father or my eldest brother, Gerard, had finished milking, it was my job as a small boy to walk the cows half a mile up the lane from Brow Top through Rook Howe yard to our meadows further up the valley before going to school. The cows would only walk at their own speed. "Old Tom", my collie dog, kept them in line when need be. Our old dog Tom, intelligent and loyal, was my pal and companion as I grew up in the valley.

It was all a very relaxed pace and procedure. I had time to watch the birds and marvel at the spring flowers, look for tadpoles in the boggy ground behind the water-hole while the cows stopped for a drink. Then I would open the gate for them to walk past the footbridge and along to the meadows.

Nancy, my favourite cow, usually walked along chewing her cud towards the rear of the herd. I would lean against her and pull her in to the lane-side and stop close by the wall. There was an ideal mounting block which enabled me to climb on her back. Then she would amble on in a leisurely fashion, seemingly unconscious of my seated presence. She was a docile and kindly animal and she holds a special place in my childhood memories.

My parents farmed a small hill farm
Near the Church up Kentmere Dale
And Mother churned on Thursdays
To make butter pats for sale.

The butter was so tasty
It was always in demand
Dad said, "It comes fre t'Shorthorns
It's the finest in the land!"

My favourite cow was Nancy
When I was just a boy
She was quiet, cuddly and tender
And always rather coy.

We walked in step each morning
So far along the lane
Her thighs she wiggled as she walked
She felt warm in wind and rain.

Her skin was soft like velvet
Underneath her lovely chin
And often when I stroked it
I'm sure I saw her grin!

I rode on her back some mornings
And sometimes home at night
Her back felt smooth like a camel
So it was hard to sit her right.

She plodded home beneath me
But her belly was so wide
I did the splits upon her
I could hardly sit astride.

Her spine was hard and notchy
Her hide as soft as silk
Her "bag" four-square beneath her
Was bulging full of milk.

Unlike a horse she held her head
More closely to the ground
Precarious it was to say the least
No cow's saddle to be found.

Nancy was a pedigree Shorthorn
I wish you could see her now
I trained her to act as my pony
For she was an intelligent cow!

GARN A' BULLIN

Glossary

Garn a' bullin = going with or taking a cow to the bull when it is on heat
Gay happy = quite happy
Kytle = a smock or loose jacket worn by farmers
Yam = home

Each year the cows were put to the bull when they "cem a bullin". It was not economic for smaller farms in the valley to keep a bull all year round just to service fourteen cows – as in our case. So it was that my first sight of real sexual intercourse occurred when Father asked me to help him walk Nancy to Millriggs Farm. I would be six or seven years old.

Millriggs was a large farm, a mile down the valley, where Jim Iceton kept a fine bull. Father had an arrangement with him to use his bull to service our cows. That morning Nancy didn't seem herself. She was frisky and unsettled and would have nothing to do with me. Father walked behind Nancy and my job was to run forward, stand at road ends and gateways and keep her heading south. I ran in front but she still tried to pass me. We were soon there. And this is my recollection of what occurred.

My face drained white with astonishment
As it rose before my eyes
Like the mighty horn of the unicorn
It pointed to the skies.

I had trotted a mile with Nancy
For she was my favourite cow
She seemed in a hurry to get there
She was eager and frisky somehow.

Then I was six or seven
Grown up in my father's cap
A walking stick higher than I was
"Just William" my favourite chap!

I goggled at this mighty bull
Its thighs like limbs of oak
I held my breath, my eyes were wide
Tension, no one spoke!

Taurus reared in silhouette
Against the morning sky
And I knew in my heart that this was the start
But I had no inkling why.

For you have to see it was new to me
This need for copulation
Naïve lile Len, I didn't know then
How to renew the population.

Nancy quivered as the bull rose high
Her legs began to quake
I feared for Nancy and grabbed Dad's arm
I was sure her legs would break.

"Poor Nancy!" I cried and buried my head
Under my father's kytle
He stroked my hair and said "Noo lad
Thou'll find this sort o thing is vital.

"We need good semen fre a bull
A bull with conformation
With powerful muscles in its legs
To achieve that penetration.

"Well noo lad, just dry thy eyes
Fer Nancy looks quite snappy
Her eyes are bright, her head held high
She'll set off yam gay happy."

That primeval thrust, the spark of lust
Had died away in Taurus
Charmed by the balm of post–coital calm
He joined in the morning chorus.

As we turned for home, I could not have known
How another large bull one day,
Would cause me to study the pedigrees of
The famous Poll Charolais.

The experience with Nancy's courtship was to prove useful. A case which involved some contention between breeders of horned Charolais and hornless Poll Charolais cattle arose in 1984. As a result I became the secretary of a new cattle breed society for five years, which involved a diversion from my ordinary legal work. I had an interesting time travelling to farms in England, Wales, Scotland and Northern Ireland – also to the USA, Canada, Hungary and France.

DIVING IN T'BECK ON OUR FORDSON TRACTOR, *c.*1955

Jane Meadow was divided from High Meadow by a deep cut or stream. High Meadow was between the cut and the river. The field surface came close to the top of the river wall with a 10 feet drop into the bottom of the river.

Figure 1.14. My father driving the Fordson tractor with my brother Gerard, landgirl Eva Kinchin and LH going to the hay field

★   ★   ★

"Hand me that spanner oor Len," brother Gerard said.
As from under the tractor
He popped out his head.
"But it's black and it's oily, it's horrible!" I said.

Gerard was my brother, ten years older than me
Fetching and carrying was my job, d'you see?
But he loved all his engines and mechanical toil
And our lovely old Fordson needed a change of oil.

There was 'hay-time madness' in the air
T'hay grass needed scaling, we'd nay time to spare
The clutch and brake lever were as one combined
The foot part was broken, the lever difficult to find.

"Weld me that brake lever Giddy," I said.
"We heven't time for that, it mun do," he said.
"Nay damn it, oor Len, thou'll hev ta be garn
That maa-en guss needs scalen, we need it in t' barn.

"T"weld woddent hod, it's high-tensile steel
Just be careful wi thy be-ats, thou'll se-an git the feel
Keep t' lever on thy instep so t'spike will work fine
Now let's mak some hay while t'weather is fine.

"This knotter on t' baler I've ta stop here ta adjust
So thee git up ta Jane Meadow, thou really must!
Clumps of coloured clover all purple and white
Will o' tak some drying afoor taneet."

As I drove through t'lanes fer varra near a mile
I was sae amused by mi brother, I had ta smile
Any problem mechanical would always come first
For puzzles perplexing he sure seemed ta thirst.

As I hitched up the scaler I saw a lapwing fly
Her chicks in the hay grass I couldn't let die;
Flailing in the wind the peewit screamed at me
As I drove her young forward safe under a tree.

Then back and forth I scaled the grass
My run getting shorter with every pass;
For the field, you see, was nowhere square
But tapered in shape more like a pear.

With the sun boiling down and a gentle breeze
The throttle wide open with all speed I could ease
My mechanical movements became routine
As from stream to beck I coursed between.

With a deep cut at one side and the beck at the other
I'd to de-clutch and brake as I swung the wheel over;
My muscles were working like those of a fighter
As each time on my turning the angle grew tighter.

Hay fluttered from the scaler in the breeze gently drying
While between cut and beck I seemed to be flying;
I was young, I was headstrong, perhaps only fifteen
The Fordson the best tractor I ever had seen.

But just in such moments when free of all care
Some danger is waiting so cruelly there;
My mechanical movements had become so routine
Concentration had lapsed as I viewed the scene.

As I declutched and braked on approaching the river
My ankle was tired and was starting to quiver;
My foot missed the brake spike and the tractor roared on
The split seconds for turning were exhausted, all gone.

I was half on the turn as I mounted the beck wall
Where the drop into the water was over ten feet tall;
As if God lent a hand I turned straight for the splash
On full open throttle I was going at a dash.

Both the tractor and scaler with the hay flying high
Went deep in the water and far from the dry;
I held onto my "bronko" but knocked it out of gear
Then shock overwhelmed me, I felt decidedly queer!

As the splash subsided and the water ran clear
The peace all around me abated my fear;
The sturdy old tractor was ticking over just fine
No damage, no injury: was it intervention Divine?

The fan belt in the water threw a mist of fine spray
Refreshing and cooling as I wondered what way
What way I could drive the machine back up the bank
And where in the fools' register Leonard would rank?

And so to big brother I had to walk back
Fearing the worst: the belt or the wrack?
But when I had walked home for nearly a mile
"Was I unhurt, no damage?" he broke out in a smile.

An adventure, a challenge, I could see in his face
My misfortune not treated as any disgrace!
But a problem to solve we could still beat the weather
If we hitched up two tractors we'd both pull together!

So I drove down the river bed with the scaler behind
To the lowest slope of banking that we could find;
In harmony with Gerard as he pulled from the field
Our Fordson reared upwards before the banking would yield.

Then I shot out of the river and soon back to the hay
Where we rowed it and baled it and got it that day.
And many's the time that I've wondered since then
What today's "Health and Safety" would have said to "Our Len"!

★   ★   ★

Figure 1.15. Grandfather Hayton mowing with horses in High Meadow

BLUEBELL WOOD

One of my Father's sayings was the well known adage: "Variety is the spice of life".

So some weekends after I had taken the cows to the meadows in spring and summer, I used to get diverted. I sat either by the river Kent or on the footbridge watching the brown trout and crayfish. Sometimes I saw a white-throated dipper searching for mayflies and caddis larvae.

Just up "Low Dote", the rocky field between the river and the lane to Pout Howe, there is a lovely view of the upper valley from near the stile and split rock. Dote or Dalt was the name given originally to a specified share in an open field. Following the Inclosure Acts of 1757 to 1830 for the improvement of agriculture, many of such areas were enclosed or walled off, as in this case. When I was a lad the Low and High Dotes belonged to my father.

Sometimes I went across the footbridge, up the path through Low Dalt and along the lane to Bluebell Wood on the east side of the River Kent. It was a lovely peaceful place. I felt like Saint Francis of Assisi with nature all around me. I used to wander down the "lonnin" (lane) under a canopy of hazel trees and into Bluebell Wood which slopes down to the river.

★   ★   ★

BLUEBELL WOOD

There's a picture in my memory
Of a wonderful woodland glade
Where sunbeams shone through the canopy
In a sprinkling of light and shade.

Before I grew to manhood
I used to wander in the wood
To observe and savour nature
As every human should.

Hazel, silver birch and alder
Seemed to gossip in the breeze
But oak stood firm for England
The monarch of English trees.

A red squirrel dashed for cover
Song birds sounded the alarm
But my disturbance was soon forgotten
When I lay down in the woodland calm.

I stayed in that dell for hours
In a sea of bluebell blue
While below the bank beneath the brow
The busy beck splashed through.

And from the dappled water
A dipper would appear
Then bob upon a mossy rock
And as quickly disappear.

Where aconites and snowdrops
Had seen late winter snow
When the warmth of vibrant springtime
Made oxlip and primrose glow.

In spring the woodland butterflies
Fluttered in the sun
The brimstone and the orange tip
On their annual nectar run.

While still I lay, the woodland birds
Were busy all around
Wood pigeon, wren and woodpecker
With their distinctive sounds.

The nuthatch and the blue tit
The great tit and the thrush
The blackbird, finch and bunting
Building nests in tree and bush.

But always there was a reason
That I could no longer stay
So I promise and I promise myself
I'll return to that glade one day!

★   ★   ★

TO BE OR NOT TO BE … A PARSON?
The Youngest Son!

Mary Elizabeth Mattinson, known in her early days as "Mary Lib", was born at Sawmill Cottage, Kentmere, on 6th July 1871. Her father, Richard Mattinson, was then the gamekeeper for the Kentmere Hall Estate. She used to tell me that her father collected dotterel feathers on High Street fell, which is the mountain across the head of Kentmere, where the old Roman road runs. He used the feathers for fly-making to fish on Kentmere Tarn from a boat. Mary Lib always averred that the lake was drained when she was small by a Mr Wilson, owner of Kentmere Hall. Her parents were still living at Sawmill Cottage in the Kentmere valley at the time. The contractors had lodged with her parents.

There was a whisper in the family that Mary Lib's father, Richard, had been hit over the head with a post by a poacher, which left him a changed and melancholy man. He had later taken his own life. The Mattinson family moved to a small farm, Cote-o-West in Lambrigg, but it is not clear whether this occurred before or after the tragedy.

Mary Lib was my grandmother on my father's side of the family. Her brother had joined the police force, much to the chagrin of her mother and Mary Lib, leaving them to make a living in Lambrigg. It had caused a rift which was only mended a generation later. Mary Lib attended Grayrigg Church as a girl and sang in the choir. She had a good singing voice and she sang in the Methodist chapel also.

Sitting in her rocking chair years later before a roaring fire and knitting seemingly endless pairs of socks for her grandchildren, she regaled me with tales from her youth, much of it to do with her church and chapel-going. She wanted me to be a parson!

We would sit in the farmhouse living-room at Brow Top in the evenings, my father reading, my mother pegging a rug and Granny (Mary Lib) knitting and reminiscing. The floors were flagged with Westmorland green stone laid straight on to gravel, or so it seemed, because the draughts coming up through the cracks cooled my back, whilst my face and front were roasted. The house, being well-positioned for lovely views down the dale, was nevertheless exposed to the wind, no small part of which blew through the floor cracks and crazed the fire with what seemed pure oxygen! That is why my mother was continually pegging rugs to keep out the draughts – all made from old clothes. Nothing was wasted.

"Sedbergh, Middleton, Barbon, Kirkby Lonsdale: all change," Granny would suddenly sing out, mimicking the old station master. She had lived in Lambrigg, not far from the railway station. She used to enjoy watching the steam trains chuffing up the line and the comings and goings of the passengers at the little country station. The railways had been in their heyday and she would have loved to travel but got little opportunity to do so. Her growing up centred round the church and chapel.

The Reverend Dwire was apparently the Vicar at Grayrigg Church where she sang each Sunday in the choir. He admonished her for going to the chapel, telling her she could not sit on two stools. "No," said Mary Lib, "and you cannot preach a sermon like I heard!" She enjoyed hearing the lay preachers perform: old farmers and country folk who felt they wanted to "spout" as she put it.

"Jack Sedgwick was there," she said. "He was tight and swaying about on the stand. He kept shouting and repeating the same words: 'Whish't lads! Whish't lads! Lile Jack Sigzick oot o Howgill. Lile Jack Sigzick oot o Howgill! Whish't! Whish't! When t'Holy Ghost touches t'third button hole, that's time, lads! That's time, lads!'"

Just then someone she called Charlie, sitting at the back of the chapel, "Let out the loudest fart I ivver hard in mi life! It echoed through the Chapel. Even the candles and the oil lamp lights seemed to quiver!" "And did Jack say from which button he started to count?" asked the Reverend Dwire. I was never sure whether it was his waistcoat buttons or his fly buttons she was referring to, but Mary Lib always had a twinkle in her eye when she related this tale.

Anyway it was many years before anyone touched my third button hole but when it was touched, it had a lasting effect! Whether it was the Holy Spirit or Mother Nature I cannot say but I have always been puzzled as to what all this had to do with religion or being a parson. However, it was often the youngest son in the family who was landed with being the parson and I was the youngest of three sons!

Granny also claimed in support of her proposition that my great great grandfather was the Reverend Gerard Hayton, who had gone to Kentmere as Curate in 1846 and succeeded the Reverend Greenhow, when he died. The Reverend Gerard had later married his widow, Jane, and brought up their son, John Greenhow, and with Jane had a further six children, of whom five survived. He was the Vicar at Kentmere until his death on 1st November, 1880. The rest of the family appear to me to have been artisans: joiners, wheelwrights and farmers. Even the parson's parents had been farmers and innkeepers at the farm beside the A6 road at the bottom of "Huck's Brow". He had bought the family farm, Brow Top, in Kentmere in 1851. His descendants are still there today.

After the Second World War when I was old enough to walk down the lane with Granny, I had to go to church. Granny was dressed like 'Giles' grandmother' in black, with me reluctantly dragging along behind. So the weekly pilgrimage began – but no old farmers got up to rant, no-one seemed to break wind at the back of the church – certainly the oil lamps never flickered more than usual! But in St. Cuthbert's Church, Kentmere, during the reign of the 'Countess' such weaknesses, like the verb to fart, were taboo. As I grew stronger, I was assigned to pump the organ. Anyway I could not sing like Mary Lib! I got a toffee after the service for blowing the organ. I could sit out of sight round the corner but I had to be alert to pump for the psalms and the wailings, which punctuated the progress of the service.

The organist and general organiser, Mrs Robinson, whom we called the Countess of Kentmere, got agitated if the organ ran out of wind. She was nimble with her toes on the foot pedals but began to run desperately if the wind failed – because I had missed pumping for a minute, perhaps to recover a marble or my collection or maybe I had rolled it round the corner to my friend, Martyn Wrathall, in the choir!

The Countess had no children of her own. She was rather prim and strict. But later in my teens, I had much to thank her for. I did practical maintenance work for her at her home, Greenhead, the remuneration for which enabled me to run my motorbike. I used to mow her lawns and trim the hedges. I painted all the windows of her house inside and out twice and re-roofed the porch! She had standards, style and intelligence, but little tact. My mother never altogether forgave her for looking at me in my pram shortly after my birth and saying, "He's no bigger than a runt rabbit." 'Just Willliam', often unwittingly, and certainly absent-mindedly, levelled the score, when my concentration lapsed, by forgetting to pump the organ so the wind failed and the hymn with it! Nevertheless, I grew to respect her and her husband, Arthur, a retired solicitor from Liverpool.

Before I graduated to organ blowing, I used to sit with Granny in the front pew. This was the Hayton pew, where the old Parson's wife, Jane, would have sat; so we had to keep up the tradition. It was the worst pew in the church – right under the pulpit! As the sermons droned on, my attention was lost, but from my seat immediately below the parson's chin I could see his epiglottis quivering like a pelican's. At evensong an oil lamp bathed him in a warm glow, which seemed to clothe him in avuncular benevolence. I wondered if God looked like the parson and whether God had an epiglottis!

It did nothing to further Granny's grand design! I had no wish to occupy the pulpit.

Yet that childhood experience was valuable. In retrospect, I would not wish to have missed it; I would not have had it any other way. Those weekly visits instilled the basic tenets of Christianity: "To love thy neighbour as thyself; to do unto others as you would be done by; to forgive and be forgiven."

But Granny added to the commandments the following words which have stood me in good stead throughout my career. When circumstances tempt, her command rings in my ears. She burned and branded my soul with these words:

> "Speak the truth and speak it ever
> Cost it what it will.
> He that hides the wrong he doeth
> Doth the wrong thing still."

From my mother, Evelyn, I learned the value of peace and forgiveness. To kneel with her, so gentle and loving, at the bedside most evenings and hear her say in her soothing way the children's prayer, "Gentle Jesus meek and mild, look upon this little child ..." left a lasting impression of joy, contentment and stability. She taught by example. She was loved by her family, all the friends who knew her, and likewise in her later years as the postmistress at Kentmere.

So it was the gentleness of my mother, Evelyn, the practical instruction and support of my father, Joe, and the firmness of Mary Lib, which moulded my growing years. My parents were patient and left me to grow up on the farm, helping me and allowing me time and space to learn the ways of growing up. My two brothers, Gerard and Jack, who were almost ten years older, generally spoiled me but sometimes got tough. They thought "Loo Lant", as they called me, would make a good parson and teased me about Granny's stated intentions for me. Mary Lib did not get all her way.

In 1950/51 when my brother, Jack, was doing his National Service, he was stationed in Egypt in the Royal Army Service Corps legal section. In the period leading up to my 11 plus exam, he wrote many letters to me from Egypt with facts he thought might be helfpul. I learned much about the Suez Canal, the Pyramids and the Sphinx. Jack also enjoyed poetry and introduced me to Rudyard Kipling, Robert Service and Laurence Hope (the latter was Amy Nicholson, who wrote romantic verse under the pseudonym).

Jack was my mentor and my inspiration at that time. When I had visited Jack at T.O. and J.K. Jackson Solicitors' office, where he had worked since 1946, the variety of matters with which Jack dealt fascinated me. I used to look in the big, heavy law books and find all sorts of interesting cases to read. Jack and Gerard had not had the chance to go to a grammar school but Jack had always encouraged me to study and do my homework. He was determinted that I should pass the 11 plus. I have much for which to thank Jack because he inspired me and I wanted to live up to his expecations.

Thus my grandmother, Mary Lib, did not persuade me to be a "clerk in holy orders". Instead in my teens I decided to be a clerk of law and order! I followed my brother Jack into the offices of T.O. and J.K. Jackson to do five years of articles in Kendal and Milnthorpe with Kenneth Jackson – a true gentleman.

Only then did Granny tell me before she died that one of the Mattinson ancestors had been a Queen's Counsel. But that was Mary Lib – no one really got the better of her and her genes live on after her!

Figure 1.16. My brother Gerard's wedding to Alice (née Bingley) at Sedbergh Parish Church: Front row, left to right: my brother Jack, my father Joseph, LH, bridesmaid Betty Stowe, my mother Evelyn, Gerard and Alice, Mrs Alice Bingley behind little Ann Rycroft, bridesmaid Jean Bland, Audrey Bingley, Mrs Ann Rycroft and Leslie Bingley 2nd row: Mrs Dawson, Mary Bell, Edith O'Connor, Dorothy and Tony Dixon in church doorway, Margaret Coward behind GH, Thomas Bingley, Harold Bell, Thomas Bland and Thomas Rycroft

A LAST LESSON AT KENTMERE SCHOOL

When I was about eight or nine years old, our teacher, Miss Jessie Braithwaite, who lived in Staveley, was teaching us to do weaving and knitting. The boys had to do what the girls did and we did not think knitting was a "man's job"!

We were given a choice of what to knit and I chose to knit a scarf but as usual my idea was different. I only had some red and grey wool at home, so I wanted to knit one row across and back in red and the same in grey, making alternate stripes.

I knitted and I knitted during each knitting class until I was thoroughly fed up of the monotony! We kept our knitting in a long, deep drawer under our teacher's unusually large table. I decided to

Figure 1.17. Back row (left to right): Teacher – Miss Jessie Braithwaite, Ann(e?) Stow, Tony Marshall
Middle: Bobby Brunskill, Audrey Bingley, Carolin Wrathall, Ben & Richard Dickinson, Victor Cousins
Front: Martyn & Penelope Wrathall, Keith Leyland, Peter Marshall?, Jimmy Brunskill, Peter Chilton, Ivan Dickinson
(Leonard Hayton off school that day.) The Marshall boys lived at "Crows Nest" Elf Howe, the Brunskills at Kentmere Hall, Peter Chilton at Crofthead

Figure 1.18. Four generations of the Hayton family: my brother, Gerard, Granny with my niece, Heather, on her knee, and my father, Joseph

push my knitting to the very back so it was lost when the next knitting class began. Miss Braithwaite gave me another task which I seem to remember being a relief from knitting!

However, towards the end of my last term at Kentmere, Miss Braithwaite came to me with a brown paper parcel. I recall her facial expression which seemed stern but amused. Her eyes twinkled and she was having difficulty restraining a grin. She unwrapped the parcel and there before my eyes was the dreadful half-finished scarf!

"Now," she said, "you have just time to finish this before you leave! Let it be a lesson to you. Your sins in life will always find you out. Remember: procrastination is the thief of time!"

I did finish the scarf and her message still rings in my ears – particularly when the exigencies or pressures of life prevent one from finishing the current task or … one just feels bored or lazy!

NEW FRIENDS AND NEW HORIZONS
At Windermere Grammar School
1951 to 1957

Before attending the 11-plus examination at Windermere Grammar School (WGS) in 1951, Windermere was miles away: a foreign land!

I attended Kentmere Church of England School from 1945 to 1951. There were approximately sixteen boys and girls ranging from five to eleven years of age, taught by one teacher. It was like leaving a happy family and being exposed to a whole new world beyond Staveley when I started at WGS.

My recollection is that WGS was said to be a bilateral school for boys. It was the forerunner of a comprehensive school because the L-stream was for those who had passed the 11-plus and the N was for those who had not. The good thing about it was that the N-scholars who had failed the exam, but were found afterwards to be capable, could transfer to the L-stream and vice versa.

We had a full range of subjects, both academic and practical. We even had gardening, horticulture, wood and metal work. All the teachers seemed excellent to me and Henry Hiley seemed to be able to teach all kinds of subjects including Maths, Latin, English and German, and still have time to run the school's Young Farmers' Club, teach horticulture and keep pigs in the gardens!

Desmond Hartley taught economic history in a splendid way, which was helpful to me later in my law studies. Michael Davies-Shiel made geography and local industrial history fascinating because of his hands on approach. Michael carried out valuable field studies and research all his life, as later references in my book show.

The L-stream could also do woodwork, so I made myself a desk and a stool with the guidance of Alf Henderson. Alf must have been a young teacher then, because he is still lively and active as I write. Alf took up gold-prospecting and in his 80s he is as enthusiastic as ever to teach and encourage his friends to go panning for gold. All the teachers were male except one formidable mistress named Eleanor Carter. She taught Physics and Maths which were out of my league, but she also taught Current Affairs for the General Paper exam. She was very capable and inspiring, as were all our masters. On reflection how blessed we were.

I recall Eleanor Carter in one lesson in the 1950s prophesying that the country we would have to watch was China. She said when China woke up, the world should beware! How right she was.

Our headmaster, Sydney George Lewis, was a fine principal of our school, combining a reliable, rock-like character with a kindly and avuncular nature. He did administer the cane, however, if one got too many bad marks. Yet the system was fair and balanced because it also provided us with the option of earning stars to avoid the ultimate punishment.

Fortunately I avoided the cane but I did receive the mightiest of slaps across my bottom from Patrick Gibbs, our gym master. I can feel it still. It did no harm but it really stung. I cannot remember what I had done wrong but he told me years later, when I was doing some legal work for him, that he had an agreement with the Head that where necessary he could, if need be, administer one slap to each of us during our time at school. The problem with his slap was that he swung round as if he was throwing the discus and we were only dressed in thin gym pants!

The ultimate deterrent, however, was Roland Robinson, the Deputy-head. When he came into assembly, you could hear a pin drop. Some scholars have said they were frightened of him and were upset by the discipline he promoted, yet for my part I found him firm but fair. He had the respect of staff and scholars alike. There was a balanced

Figure 1.19. Harold Auty   Head: S. G. Lewis   Deputy-head: Roland Robinson
WGS production of Gilbert and Sullivan's "The Mikado"

blend of authority and goodwill. Between the Head and Roland, they displayed good sense, whilst driving our education forward by example with firmness and kindness.

I cannot claim a classical education or any great success but I have much for which to thank Roland Robinson. He ensured I got my Latin O' level, which I needed along with six other O' levels, in order to get exemption from the Law Society preliminary exam.

Roland also took part in the Gilbert and Sullivan operas which WGS produced each year between 1949 and 1967. The operas were produced by Reg Griffiths, head of music, and Harold Auty, our art master.

Harold was my form master and he became a client and a friend in later life. He was a gifted artist and teacher. I was pretty average in most subjects and pitiful in maths! Surprisingly one year I did manage to come top in art! My pal, Geoffrey Braithwaite, usually beat me in art most years because he had a great imagination and sense of colour. He went on to become an inspiring art teacher himself.

Some years later, after Elsie Robinson, Roland's wife, died, I found her husband's copy of a Gilbert & Sullivan book by Leslie Baily in a Windermere bookshop. There painted within the fly leaves front and back are sketches by Harold Auty of the parts played by Roland, a terrific actor, which appear in tribute to them both (Figure 1.18 colour section).

Figure 1.20. WGS 1956 production of "The Gondoliers" at the Royalty Theatre, Bowness

Unfortunately, living in Kentmere and having to catch the school taxi at Staveley, which was four miles from home, as well as allowing time to do homework each night, I could not take part in the operas. I did, however, learn the tunes and the lyrics when my friend, Ian

Johnston, was learning his part walking to and from St John's Church room, where the school dinners were served each day.

My new wife, Jean, is a chorister and she is much amused by my amateurish renderings in the car, as we sing along through the lyrics in The Mikado, Patience, The Pirates of Penzance and The Gondoliers. I enjoy music but I am not a musician.

My friends and fellow lawyers, Richard Holloway and Tony James (both of whom became very competent judges), took me off to Glasgow and happily introduced me to the Scottish National Orchestra productions, which widened my interests. So now in later life, Jean and I can enjoy her interest in music and go to concerts, musicals, plays and even ballets together.

I cannot say that I excelled in sport at school either. I enjoyed rugby to a degree, but I needed spectacles and even when I got them, having to take them off for sports meant my focus on the ball and the players was deficient.

Likewise in cricket, I rarely saw the ball until it hit me! I ran out of breath in athletics and high jumps but, funnily enough, the longer the cross-country set run over hill and fell, the nearer the leaders I became. Still none of my efforts really ended in glory and I had to accept my limitations. My attitude was not enhanced either by my parents and family telling me that anyone who needed to "punch a ball of wind about" was short of work!

Nevertheless I grew quite strong because I was also becoming the shepherd on our farm. My best friend at first was my dog, Tom, the farm dog. He used to ride on my bogey or sledge with me. Later when I learned how to ride my brother's Panther motor cycle, Tom sat in front of me with his back feet and bottom on my thighs. He put his front feet, one on the advance and retard lever and the other on the air control lever on the

Figure 1.21. LH with his intelligent dog, Tom

handle bars. He was eager to get on the motorbike when we went for the cows in Low Meadow. Quad-bikes had not been invented then!

Because he was really a one-man dog, Tom was not keen on working for my brother, Gerard, who tended to shout at him. Thus I did more of the sheep work on the farm as I grew up. With the help of Tom I had to gather the sheep on Nook Farm allotment at Kentmere, which my grandfather and father had rented since 1913. I used to take the sheep up the steep "intacks" – walled in pastures – after lambing or shearing times to the allotment. There is a small crag within this allotment called Pengennet, one of the few Celtic names in Kentmere. All this experience on the farm was good. Having to clean out calf-hulls (pens) by hand with a fork after winter and tugging at the packed straw manure in spring strengthened my back muscles and made me a man.

For some reason I never got involved in Cumberland and Westmorland wrestling but sometimes I used to go with my uncle, Mother's brother, Jack Jackson, who farmed at Orchard House, Preston Patrick, to watch the wrestling at Morecambe. Watching Bill Coverdale, an Australian wrestler, must have subconsciously imprinted some self-defence mechanism in me because it came to my aid in the school gymnasium some time later.

One day while waiting for our gym master to come, it must have been my turn to be "scragged". A certain member of my class with his henchmen came to attack me. By some strange impulse, perhaps recalling Bill Coverdale's technique, I dropped onto the floor in a ball on my back with my knees on my chest as he came at me. He was thrown in the air and landed on the hard floor, out cold. We were all shocked but fortunately he was only winded. No-one ever attacked me again. The odd thing was that Patrick Gibbs arrived on the scene just as it was happening and he could not believe that this "quiet Kentmere lad" could do such a thing. At the time, I think, he accepted it was self-defence and I did not get the "discus power slap"!

My classmates in 1L in 1951 at WGS are shown in the picture with Harold Auty, our form master. Our names are shown in Figure 1.22.

On Speech Day each year we were encouraged to take our hobbies to school and put them on display. Once I took my one year old pet lamb to school. He was fully grown by then. He was an ebullient, castrated tup-lamb, used to following me about and full of energy. Nevertheless, I got him in the school taxi and on to the school bus at Staveley. The bus driver, who later became a client, always recalled the morning when I took "Buster" on the bus and brought him home at night. He was an unusual passenger!

Our neighbours at the Old Vicarage in Kentmere were antique dealers. Mrs Wrathall, my good friend Martyn's mother, allowed me to learn to ride her Penny Farthing bicycle. When I was about fifteen, I

Figure 1.22. LH's classmates in Class 1L at Windermere Grammar School in 1952:
Front row, left to right: Christopher Robinson, Septimus Cooper, Alan Wilson, Ian Johnston and Tony Dobson
Middle row, left to right: Richard Whitton, John Beckett, Melvyn Jeffrey, David Clarke, Samuel Murphy, Tony Norbury and Tilly Pearce
Back row, left to right: Geoffrey Braithwaite, LH, Carol Graham, our form master Harold Auty, Graham Dixon, Tony Gibson and Alan Martindale

asked if I could ride it to Windermere for Speech Day, which I did. All was well on the way to school but coming back down to Ings, just as I got a good head of speed, the solid tyre came off, whipping my legs and posterior as the wheel went round. Happily I managed to slow down as the road levelled and got off by the wall somewhat bruised and bloody – but it was fun. I succeeded in getting the tyre back on and slowly rode home. Later in life I bought a Penny Farthing from my friend, Tom Potter of Kirkby Stephen, which I used for charity fund-raising.

Before the end of the summer term we had "house climbs". The houses were named after the mountains: Scafell (red stripe on school cap), Wetherlam (blue stripe) and Fairfield (green stripe). I was in Wetherlam. The tradition was that members of each house climbed their own mountain every other year, so in my case I climbed Wetherlam one year, then Fairfield the next, then Wetherlam, then Scafell, and so on.

In 1955 we climbed Fairfield on a very hot summer's day. I well recall it because as we reached the top of the mountain, the sky was turning inky black and the mightiest cumulo-nimbus cloud-burst occurred that I have ever seen.

There was sheet lightning, rope lightning and flashes of all descriptions. The sky appeared very threatening, riven by almost constant flares of tormented lightning, as if all the Earth's fuses were sparking and blowing at once. Large hailstones battered us through our summer shirts. The rain came down in deluges and flowed across the ground in deep torrents. This was the year when the road above the Queen's Head Hotel in Troutbeck was washed out for ten feet down to the graphite seam then exposed. Rocks were washed down in Langdale.

When we eventually got down into Ambleside, the lower town was flooded. Water lapped over the bottom step of our bus as we edged along towards Windermere, torrents still flowing across the road and into the lake.

During the summer holidays in 1955 my friend, Sam Murphy, and I had a cycling holiday. We made our own panniers to carry food on the bicycles and we cycled ninety miles the first day, laden with our tent and sleeping bags, to Sam's granny's house in Dumfries. The second night near Airdrie, south of Glasgow, we could not find anywhere to camp, so we asked a farmer. We offered to help unload bales from a trailer and ended unloading two more large trailers for him until it was almost dark. We were weary but we had a good supper and a free breakfast, plus a site to camp.

On Rannoch Moor we woke with our sleeping bags full of earwigs but they did us no harm. We enjoyed our journey along the banks of the Scottish lochs and got to Pitlochry before we turned for home. One morning on our way back we were awakened by myriads of tiny, biting midges. In desperation we submerged our entire bodies in the coldest loch I ever have known! I bought my first haggis in Callander and I was eager to see a true Scottish haggis. I half expected it to have two long legs and two short ones: the Scots like to tell us the haggis can only run round a hill one way because it uses its long legs on the low side and would roll down the hill otherwise!

It was a memorable adventure which cemented a lifelong friendship. Sam has always been full of energy and enthusiasm in all he does. When his mother had to leave Windermere to nurse her own mother in Dumfries, Sam came to live with us for a year at Brow Top, so as not to interrupt his schooling. We both enjoyed motorcycling and after his degree at Sheffield University, Sam became an accomplished metallurgist and worked in Zambia for a time.

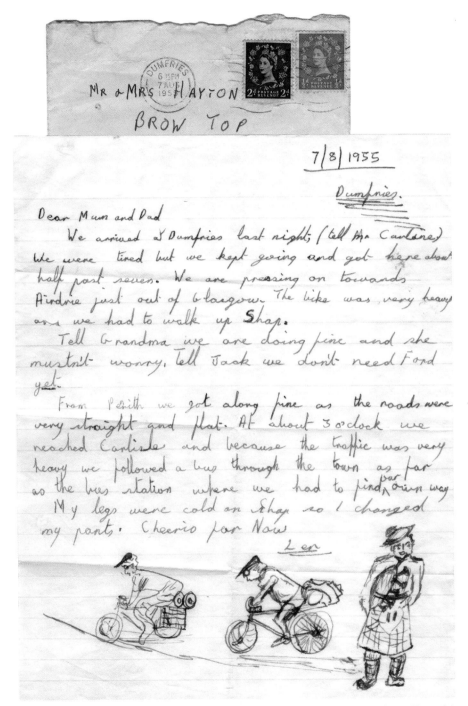

Figure 1.23. Sam Murphy & LH, cycling holiday, 1955. LH's letter from Dumfries. I was beginning to doubt my recollection of this holday until I found this letter amongst my mother's papers!

My brother Jack died of cancer in December 1967 leaving Gillian, his widow, and my nieces, Annabel and Lucinda, and my nephew, Robin. Some years later Sam and Gil were happily married. The family moved to Tanworth–in–Arden to be near Aston University where Sam was Reader in Metallurgy. Since his retirement Sam and Gil have returned to the Lakes and he is still pursuing his interests as enthusiastically as ever.

I made lots of friends at WGS who have gone on to lead interesting lives both in our local community and further afield. Many have done good work for me in their chosen occupations and others I have acted for over the years.

I was always rather shy at school but Colin Barton, our English teacher, said in his deep, clear voice, "I want you to play a small part in Arnold Ridley's play, 'The Ghost Train', Hayton." He used to castigate me: "Far too many long, rambling sentences – you'll make a good lawyer one day!" He was right. It is still a weakness!

In 1957 I did not think I would get sufficient A' levels to go to university, so I chose to start my career with the law firm in Kendal and Milnthorpe, where my brother Jack had become managing clerk: now there's a long sentence! Colin would smile.

And so to work ....

Figure 1.24. Miss Bourne, dressed in Granny's old church-going attire, in "The Ghost Train" with a parrot in a cage. I look as though I have fallen asleep!

2

A COUNTRY LAWYER'S TALES

My legal career in Lakeland and afar spans the period from October 1957 to October 2008 which commenced with 5 years' Articles of Apprenticeship. I shall explain the initial guiding influence of my late brother, Jack, who died in 1967 and my Principal, Kenneth Jackson. My friendship and legal partnership with Michael Winkley, which lasted 36 years, was the basis from which the practice expanded, taking in Tony James and Malcolm Whiteside followed by Peter Briggs, Andrew Bromley, Keith Wood, John Oldroyd and Naomi Fell. We also employed some talented assistant solicitors and we trained articled clerks also.

As the practice expanded, so did our wonderful team of support staff at each office. Having started as an office boy myself at the beginning of my articles I had some idea how they felt when later the pressure was on and my priorities changed during the day. I could also be tiresome, as Jean Cowling so colourfully portrays in her verse to me on my 60th birthday!

I was a general practitioner and dealt with a wide variety of human problems and aspirations. Conveyancing was the bread and butter of the practice then but I

Figure 2.1. LH working on a case at home.

acted for an increasing number of hoteliers and tourist businesses as the practice grew in Windermere. This involved work connected with the re-development in the 1970s of Bowness Bay, and legal work for businesses based on Lake Windermere and in the southern lakes. This work continued and expanded throughout my career and brought me in contact with a variety of entrepreneurial clients. These are the people who create work and employment for others, seeing and taking opportunities. I enjoyed being an adviser to them but I always remained independent.

The planning legislation of 1947, while desirable to protect visual amenity, had an effect partly similar to the Scottish clearances. Though very necessary to protect the visual amenity of Lakeland, it created a frustrating and unbalanced system. This brought me into contention, on behalf of clients, with the Planning Board. There was no "Use Class" for holiday homes. House prices rocketed when outside buyers of holiday homes outbid the locals.

If it had been necessary under a special 'Use Class' to apply for planning consent for holiday use, the Board could have looked at each community and kept a balance.

We welcomed new people coming into the communities because they often brought energy and new ideas. They also brought capital and created work, which was good for Lakeland, but there was no mechanism to keep a balance in each area or to consider the needs of the local economy in the planning process. It was the lack of balance and blinkered thinking which created the more recent "Homes for Locals" campaigns, none of which have really remedied the problem.

During the crucial early years when young families were moving out of the villages and could not afford homes there, planning consents for small workshops were also very difficult indeed to obtain. All this made work for me but the policies caused me heartache when I saw local people having to buy houses in Kendal only to travel back to work in the Lake District villages. Short-term and short-sighted policies have done nothing for "Global Warming" or the preservation of fossil fuel!

As a local businessman I was asked to address "The Future of Rural Cumbria Conference" in November 1989. I intended to include a copy of my paper in the appendix but lack of space prevents. In part it was a lament for the loss of our customs and usages but I also made some positive suggestions. Some have come to pass while other problems remain.

Until Tony James took over most of the Magistrates' Court work to allow me to do more commercial work, I dealt with the court work. I appeared in Windermere, Kendal, Shap, Hawkshead and Ambleside Magistrates' Courts. Yes, there were Courts in all those places and the Magistrates served their communities well because they had local knowledge. They looked for ways to help offenders to solve their problems rather than send them to prison, which often proves to be a college for further crime. However, they could also be tough. The Magistrates' Clerks were sticklers for ensuring any solicitor appearing in their courts had done their homework and prepared the cases properly. Some of my stories come from that period.

In 1964 I also joined Windermere, Ambleside and District Round Table and got involved on the steering and fundraising committee, when we decided on the ambitious project of building the Marchesi Centre. This gave me my first involvement with charity law in drafting the constitution and dealing with the connected legal issues. I learned much from my days in Round Table, working with an excellent group of capable and enthusiastic young business and professional men, who wanted to give something more to their community.

The life of a country lawyer is never dull, neither is it always easy. All sorts of conflicts of interest can arise between clients and friends. My genial boss, Kenneth Jackson, used to say: "You have to have a hide like a rhinoceros and the wisdom of Solomon to be a solicitor!" I am not sure I achieved either but I know what he meant.

Being a farmer's son and enjoying some hobby farming with my first wife, Sandra, I developed a degree of specialism in agricultural law. This widened my experience, took me abroad and later involved me in the work of the Westmorland County Agricultural Society.

In later years I dealt with inheritance and estate planning, capital taxation, probate and administration of wills – many of which I had drafted for clients years before.

I have been blessed with partners and colleagues who have been a pleasure to work with. I have had many interesting and loyal clients who became good friends. You all know who you are. This book cannot include or do justice to all of you but it is a celebration of the happy times we have had in work and play together. Thank you.

After my apprenticeship years, what follow are some of my experiences along the way. I have deliberately changed the names of the people and places involved, where necessary, to maintain confidentiality. Client privilege and confidentiality rules prevent me from disclosing many of the fascinating and amusing cases with which I have dealt. Some cases have been in the public domain and in others consent has been given by the client.

WHAT DOES A LAWYER DO?
Justice or hearsay?

All professions are criticised at one time or another but lawyers are often blamed for the ills of the world; yet the same folk will tell you: *"My lawyer is a grand chap".* To have a friend who is a lawyer can be a benefit in life.

One question which often comes up is: *"How can you defend in Court someone whom you know is guilty?"*

In answer to this I usually ask the questioner to imagine him or herself accused, arrested and placed in custody for a crime of which he or she has no knowledge and is innocent. You will need help from a trained lawyer whom you can trust.

Everyone under English law is presumed innocent unless and until proved guilty. Trial by the media is not just; neither is trial by a mob.

My job as a lawyer is not to be the judge and jury but to ascertain the facts from the accused, check the evidence against the accused and make necessary enquiries as to the facts surrounding the case. My duty is to place those facts truthfully before the Court. I must not mislead the Court.

If in the investigation the accused admits his guilt, then I would advise the accused to plead guilty and put all mitigation available before the Court. However, there are all manner of difficult cases where an innocent person admits to a crime, believing it is simpler to do so or because he/she thinks no one will believe him or her. There may also be outside influences and fear of reprisals. That is why under a fair system of justice we all have a part to play in the process. *"What does a lawyer do?"* touches on the role of lawyers in society.

Not all cases involve crime. Many civil disputes also come before the courts and the work of lawyers is to present cases properly to the Court for a decision. Again we have to dig for the facts and present them according to mainly sensible rules of procedure, honed from many years of experience in dispute settlement. We are expected to understand and follow those rules on a client's behalf. It all takes time and costs money.

★   ★   ★

WHAT DOES A LAWYER DO?

You ask me what does a lawyer do?
I sigh: where to begin?
Law libraries are full of legal tomes
That encompass human sin.

Where two or more folk come together
Some rule they will devise
While one means this, another that
Disputes will soon arise.

The law of the wild and nature's law
Have endured since time began
While we attempt to civilise
In the written words of man.

Such words may be enacted
Authorised by Royal nod
To some such acts are sacrosanct
As if the words of God.

While others heed them not at all
Transgress the common law
As greed, aggression, sex and hate
Are pursued by tooth and claw.

All shades of such behaviour
Appear in the book of life
From the worthless pursuit of materialism
To the marriage with a wife.

Well someone drafts the rules we need
Someone must say what they mean
For a mob will condemn on the words of another
Who says what a third has seen.

Someone must care for freedom
See fairness and justice done
Let fair play shine in the affairs of man
Like the warming rays of the sun.

Someone must hear the prisoner's tale
Someone must put his case
Even if he is guilty
The judge must see his face.

Someone must know what his rights are
Those rights we all assume
The justice our forefathers fought for
The equality we all presume!

That someone may be your lawyer
That someone may be you
Sitting as one of the noble twelve
Jurors good and true.

Solicitor, Barrister, Judge and Clerk
Magistrate and Jury-man
All of these folk are just folk like you
Balancing JUSTICE the best they can.

© LH 1982

FIVE YEARS APPRENTICESHIP
1958 to 1963

Having signed my 'Articles of Clerkship' deed in December 1957, the term started on 1st January 1958. It was a very happy period in my life, learning and meeting new friends. I thrilled with the realisation that at last I had found my feet and a future which appealed to me. Every day we had interesting people coming for a variety of reasons – some who had transgressed, some with family problems and others with ideas and drive who needed commercial advice and documentation to record their agreements. I rejoiced in my new world and my exams at last came easy to me.

At Blackpool College of Law I met my lifelong friends, Reg Ashworth and Mike Winkley. Together we argued and debated about case law and statute and memorised hundreds of cases where the Courts had interpreted this or that point of law. It was said we had to know and understand the 'ratio decidendi' (reason for the decision) in 6000 cases to be fit to pass the final exam! Our triumvirate mental boxing, as we

Figure 2.2. Mike Winkley with my parents, Joseph and Evelyn Hayton (standing) and Uncle Jack and Aunty Agnes on the white cliffs of Dover

drove the 30 miles to college each day, proved to be really beneficial as the results of our monthly tests put us ahead of the rest. So we all passed the Intermediate Exam followed by Trust Accounts and Book-keeping.

During this same period I learned about life and the thrills and spills of courting. Reg Ashworth had a photographic memory and was bright with it, so he had more time to spend with "Flower" as he called his then girlfriend. Mike Winkley and I were a bit slower in getting started with the fairer sex but happily we both made progress along the way. Our priority was to pass the exams and qualify. This we did successfully. I passed the final exam which was held in London in November 1962 and after my articles expired I was admitted to the Roll of Solicitors on the 1st March 1963. I will spare you the details because some of them emerge in my toast to Mike on his 60th birthday.

In learning how to handle difficult situations and sometimes awkward folk, I have to thank my brother, Jack, and my wise and amusing Principal, John Kenneth Jackson (JK), both sadly long since passed away. Drafting documents, interviewing, getting the facts of a case down, finding the answers and researching the law applicable are the skills I learned with them. Their motto was, likewise mine as a result of their teaching: "Dig deep for the facts, play fair and bite hard- but only if the opponent will not negotiate." This may seem obvious but often the real issues can be obscured by emotion and an erroneous client's presentation of the problem. The real facts, when the law is applied to them, usually point to the solution.

JK was Secretary of the Milnthorpe Angling Association, so John Garnett, the river bailiff, called quite often – a jocular man. JK also ran the British Legion Poppy Day Appeal, so one room was full of poppies each year. We were awash with them!

We had a great variety of country folk as clients from landed gentry to little old ladies and pompous individuals. JK kept a tight control on wages and expenses in the office but if one had the pleasure of his company outside the office, perhaps as on an archaeological field trip, he was most generous. I never really understood why but if he was buying a meal or a drink he would say: "To hell with the expense, Leonard, give the cat another goldfish!" A kind of genial exuberance seemed to come over him but it did not happen often!

JK was small in stature in his 60s but a wise and well respected man. He had a lovely rapport with people and could calm a prickly situation without anger or fuss. He got on well with staff and clients

Figure 2.3. My elder brother Jack in his M.G model TF at the time of my Articles

alike without the heavy hand of over- regulation. We enjoyed our work, inspired by his grin and personality.

Though he was also Secretary of the Westmorland Law Society, JK was perhaps slow to accept the winds of change which were blowing through the profession. Shortly after I qualified, he persuaded the Committee to appoint me as Secretary of the Westmorland Law Society instead.

On reflection JK probably felt, as I do now, that society has lost more than it has gained by devaluing trust and friendliness in everyday business. Commercialisation and over-regulation has made access to sensible advice, when needed on the spot, more difficult.

Many times friends and clients have telephoned me at all times of day and even in the night for help or a word of advice. We did not send bills for that advice or have file opening procedures that drive you mad. There was also client loyalty and we knew that when they had some business our clients would come to us. It was called goodwill! Before advertising became lawful, a legal practice grew from the good work of the partners and staff and by recommendation from satisfied clients.

STARTING IN PRACTICE AND MARRIAGE

It is beyond the scope of this book, nor is it my intention, to record a fully detailed autobiography of my personal life or of the full range of matters I have dealt with in practice, but I will set the scene to start with and put sections in context from time to time. With hindsight, I was clearly in a hurry as a young solicitor, bent on "going forward" as my friend John Geldard would say.

Suffice it to say that when I qualified in 1962 there was a demand for young solicitors but JK rather disappointed me at first with his offer of salary and prospects. Thus I decided to look further afield. After some interesting and successful interviews, I was in the happy position of having secured offers of four good jobs all with good starting salaries, two fairly local and the other two from companies in Ipswich and Darlington, both of which were very tempting.

This surprised JK and as a result I was offered a better salary and a partnership from 1964 on the terms that we would open an office at Windermere. I was at a crossroads in life like most young people at that age but being heafed to Lakeland and in loyalty to Jack and JK, I decided to accept his offer and to stay.

With the backing of our friend, James Nicholson, a retired timber merchant and local benefactor in Staveley, Jack and I bought the freehold of 17 Crescent Road, Windermere, and got planning permission to turn it into an office. James Nicholson took pleasure and pride in helping young people to start in business by providing capital at a reasonable interest rate. He had helped a number of young craftsmen to get started and in a few years, when they got established, he would be repaid and find another person to help.

There used to be a number of benefactors like that before the government brought in credit control restrictions. Sadly society has lost most of this useful grass roots finance which relied upon trust and the recognition of capable, young people. Now in 2011, having lost the real local bank managers, who could assess their customers well and had the authority to lend, it is small wonder that new entrepreneurs have difficulty in getting started. We all lose as a result. Perhaps I, and folk like me, have lived in "The Golden Age".

Eric Laycock, a lovely man, then Manager of the Bingley Building Society in Kendal, (before the amalgamation of the Bradford and Bingley) together with Jack and me, got our jackets off and removed the shelves and clutter of the shop and prepared the walls and decorated it. We "set our stall out" as the saying was.

We then opened our Solicitors' office and the first Building Society branch-type agency in Windermere. I have much to thank James, Jack and Eric for their backing at the beginning of my career. It helped us to get started and establish good working relationships with the banks and business men in the area.

My first secretary was Janet Hayton (no relation) who proved to be an excellent secretary and building society clerk. Friends whom I had met at Windermere Grammar School and their families came as clients. The practice seemed to grow quickly at all three offices in Kendal, Milnthorpe and Windermere. With Court appearances, appointments at each office and site visits etc., it was a busy life: so much so that we needed an assistant.

On 26th September 1965 we employed my college friend, Michael Winkley, who wanted assurance he could join us in partnership. Michael became a worthy partner with me for 35 years and also with the other partners who joined later. The rest is history. You may pick up glimpses of my professional journey through life as the pages unfold and perhaps read my toast to Mike on his 60th birthday.

In the meantime, the years 1963 to 1965 were very formative years because after our courtship in 1963, Sandra and I got married in March 1964. We had our first child, Jacqueline, followed by Ingrid less than a year later. So with Sandra's little boy, Nicholas, we had a family of three by the end of 1965.

To begin with we lived in a fairly large caravan in the garden at Pumple Syke in Kentmere, while we extended

Figure 2.4. Sandra and I on our wedding day: 21.3.1964

the bunglow, which my brothers and I had built for my parents and me before my marriage. We got planning consent to extend the bungalow in which my parents lived and the mutual support of the family proved invaluable. Again my brothers, Gerard and Jack, helped but we also engaged joiners and plumbers whom I had come to know in business.

The experience of running a building contract, doing the practical work on site and liaising with an architect was useful, because I understood what builders were talking about when I came to draft building contracts later in my legal practice. I could tailor-make a building contract to the job and I developed a formula in respect of extras, which when followed, eliminated building disputes. We acted for some very capable builders who had served real 'hands on' apprenticeships with experienced artisans. They knew their job.

Sandra's son, Nicholas, was approaching three when we married. He was a fine boy and fully part of our family. With the arrival of our daughters, Jackie and Ingrid, in quick succession, I had a real incentive to work and develop the practice, which we did. Sandra had her hands full with the children. She was an excellent wife and mother and a good cook. Her redcurrant and raspberry pasties became quite famous later. She also got on well with my parents. The following picture of Nicholas, Ingrid and Jackie encapsulates the happiness we all enjoyed as a family at the time.

Figure 2.5. Nick, Ingrid and Jackie

THE BURGLAR
and
Courage in the Moonlight!

My first case prosecuting for the Police – long before the CPS (Crown Prosecution Service) was formed – concerned a burglary at a house just out of Windermere on the Crook road.

Two elderly spinsters lived alone on a smallholding out of town. One bred pedigree goats – she had a large Billy goat on stud to which we later took our goats. The other sister bred fell ponies. Both of them were self-reliant and courageous ladies with the strong spirit of country folk, as I will relate.

★   ★   ★

The moon shone bright through the window
The house was cold and still
As the silhouette of the Burglar
Slid over the window sill.

His car was parked on the country road
As the Police patrol went by
So our constable noted the number
It was good policing – that's why.

The fibres from his coat on the drain pipe
Were found the very next day
But there he was in the bedroom
Where the sleeping old lady lay.

She rose from her bed as a warrior
Would rise on a night attack
But her armour was only her nightwear
With nothing to shield her back.

The sheets of the bed in the moonlight
Exploded before his eyes
As her courage and dauntless spirit
Took the Burglar by surprise.

He leapt over the bed and took to his heels
With the old lady in hot pursuit
And such was his haste he dropped the lot
And escaped without his loot.

Her sister was also awakened
And she joined in the hue and cry
She launched herself at the Burglar
As the dark-clad thief sped by.

But he escaped into dark shadows
Cast over the country lane
A car engine roared in the distance
The Burglar was free again.

When at half past two in the morning
The Police knocked upon his door
"He's been in bed with me all night"
Said his wife of common law.

"So who's been out in the car then?
For the engine still is hot
And I've the number on my clip board list
So you're talking Tommy Rot!"

In the end at the old Quarter Sessions
He pleaded guilty to his crime
Justice was done, no violence
But he had to serve his time.

The ladies lived on with their animals
But their windows and doors were barred
For crime is a cancer of freedom
Which leaves all humanity scarred.

SHEEP TRESPASS OR WAS IT?

Look for the evidence before it goes cold

Glossary

T'Bobby = Policeman
Cam stanes = wall topping stones
Caps langcrown = is beyond belief or very puzzling
Crack or good crack = a chat or good conversation
Hubbyshoo = trouble or controversy, a commotion or noisy gathering
Laiken = playing

Lile lasses = little girls
Lowp = jump
Maaen guss = mowing grass.
Meedas = meadows
Proven or proggin = animal food
Stown = stolen
Swardles = Swaledale sheep
Woes = walls
Yows = ewes

"Fotty five of mi best swardles hev bin hijacked," said Willie. "What mun we dew aboot it? T'Bobby rang me first thing this mornin ta tell me that them new folk at caravan site hed gitten mi yows. I exed him, 'What dust ta mean? Hev they stown them or what?'

"Well t'Bobby tells me they've ivvery reet, under some damned Animals Act that oor daft Parliament hes passed, ta tak em and hod em up, provided they give em proven and watter. Is that reet?" asked Willie.

"Yes, the Animal Act has introduced a new remedy for animal trespass," I told him. "They can take them away and hold them until you pay the cost of any damage caused, provided they notify the police and give them food and water.

"Worse than that, they can claim damages and there is no straight forward way under the Act to defend their action. Challenging the amount of the claim is also difficult. We can start an action to recover goods but it will take too long. They can charge you the cost of the damage to their trees and the cost of keeping the sheep. It is a very effective remedy for sheep trespass if it is genuine. You are in a weak position. How did the sheep get into the site?" I asked. "What are they claiming? What happened?"

"Well," said Willie. "They tell me that mi sheep hev itten a turble deal o young trees which they'd hed ta plant as a screen fer o' thur damned caravans en sick-like. They've telt ma that t'claim will be aboot a thoosand pund. Well thoo knaas, it's a gay cheek. I've nivver bin against folk comen inta t'country ta relax, but there's nay give en tak wi these folk.

"Yer knaa t'visitors lowp o'er mi woes. They knock cams inta mi maaen-guss and trample o' o'er meedas and nut by mi leave. They chuck beer tins en bottles aboot en kids laik in t'pastures. Well I put up wi that en o' sick-like. Noo I don't mind t'lile lads en lasses enjoyen thursels en laiken aboot in oor fields but this cap's langcrown!

"Many a time I've stopped en hed a crack wid em. Aye, en I've laiked a bit o football, kicken t'bo aboot wid em, just ta mek em welcome. En this is t'thanks I git. Well noo Leonard, thoo mun dew summat aboot it. I want mi ald yows back!

"I can't think where t'yows have gitten oot," said Willie. "Mi woes en fences er o' in good order. I've always believed in fencen weel against mi nebbers. It maks fer good nebbers. O' t'cam stanes er on t'wall tops. I can't think hoo this hes happened. It's a mystery ta me.

"I've allus minded mi arn business en I've nivver hed a hubbyshoo like this afoor."

It turned out that the land next to the caravan site was some distance from Willie's house and Willie had been away a few days at the time. I suggested that we arranged to meet on site at once and check the walls and fences with the Claimant. I invited the Claimant's solicitor and his Client to join us in the field from which the sheep had escaped.

Willie was right. There was no sign of walls down or poor fences. There was no place for the sheep to have escaped. We walked the boundary wall towards the far end, over a knoll and on towards a copse.

I had been looking for sheep trods in the grass and as we rounded a bend in the wall there was a concentration of feet marks behind the wall which led on round the corner. Some yards further on, out of sight to the normal view of the field, was an old gateway. This had connected the fields before the caravan site was developed. The gateway was blocked by a fairly new hurdle-type gate which was chained and padlocked.

It was then I noticed that the sheep trods converged and ran under the gate. There was a clear concentration of sheep foot marks showing clearly the path taken by the sheep into the caravan site. I said nothing. I had walked ahead of the rest. They were arguing with Willie about the extent of the tree damage as they followed me.

I climbed over the gate and immediately saw a long mark in the grass behind the wall. It was a yellow mark. I measured its length with my feet. I looked up as the opposition looked over the gate, their faces full of confidence.

Then I pointed to the yellow mark in the grass. The colour in their faces drained away and faded to a pale ashen hue. The yellow mark was the length of the bottom rail of the gate where the gate had been leaned against the wall! It was clear that the gateway had been open and the gate propped against the wall while Willie was away. It appeared to have been done to allow the caravan site visitors to gain easy access to the fell as a short cut across Willie's land. The colour of the mark in the grass indicated the gate had rested there for a few days. The caravan site owner or his employees had forgotten to put the gate back and the sheep had got in as a result! The truth was written fair on the Claimant's face. It was a try-on.

I addressed the Claimant's solicitor: "You can return our sheep now please at no cost to Willie. I will send you a bill for my fee.

"I suggest Willie, if you want to let them use this gate for access to the fell, that you have me draw up a licence agreement and that they pay an annual licence fee. Furthermore they must accept responsibility for keeping the gate shut and the sheep out." The tables were turned.

Figure 2.6. Willie, a happy and satisfied client

Willie said nothing but lit his pipe; thick smoke enveloped him and when it cleared he was grinning from ear to ear. His old sheepdog sat with eyes only for Willie. It seemed to know that all was well again.

The sheep were returned that day. It had paid well to look for the evidence before it went cold. The yellow line in the grass and the sheep trod would have disappeared in a few days.

My five years of legal apprenticeship in articles in a country practice with John Kenneth Jackson, Solicitor of Kendal and Milnthorpe, served me well. His approach to any problem was not to assume or presume but check the facts. He said: ***"Dig deep for the facts my boy, play fair and bite hard only if you have to."*** It is a good guide for a solicitor. Sometimes one needs to be firm and litigious, but you rarely need to bite folk if you get at the facts because the solution to a problem often stares you in the face.

AMBLESIDE MARKET CHARTER
29th June 1688
A summons for obstruction – How could this be?

Ambleside had a market and sheep fair with farmers and folk coming from the valleys and areas around to buy, barter and exchange. At the sheep and tup fairs they bought and sold stock, which before transport and railways arrived, had to be walked to the market in Ambleside. A major link between the town and farming was lost, together with some town trade which went with the market, when it became easier to transport stock to the Kendal Auction Mart.

In time past the Ambleside market traders had ceased to bring their stalls but an interesting change occurred in the summer of 1969. I had a call from Robin Anderson, known to me from schooldays, clutching 'The Royal Commission on Markets and Fairs' and a Summons he had received for obstruction.

I sought and obtained an adjournment whilst I investigated the law and history of the matter. He and colleagues had erected market stalls in the Market Place in front of Malcolm Tyson's shop where the old market used to be. Robin had researched the history and was sure they had the right to stand the market there.

I discovered the old Market Charter was lodged with Barclays Bank at Ambleside. The Charter was written in Medieval Latin, so I arranged for

Figure 2.7. Robin Anderson with Sergeant Barras and a police constable looking on and a picture of Robin at his stall in the old market place

Peter Dover, the deputy head and Classics master at the Lakes School, to translate it.

Meantime I argued that a grant from the Crown, which had not been revoked by statute, gave the market traders every right to do what they were doing. Case law supported this argument in principle. I applied for adjournments until we had the translation completed.

The Court and Police, who prosecuted in those days before the Crown Prosecution Service was set up, agreed to adjourn the hearing until the Market Charter had been translated and copies supplied to all parties.

At first shop-keepers felt put out but when they realised that there were more people coming into in Ambleside on the Wednesday market days and takings were going up, opposition started to melt away. As Malcolm Tyson reminded me recently, Robin and his fellow traders tidied up and left the area cleaner than the Council. Malcolm has always set the standard for cleanliness and the cleanest car in Ambleside, so the area must have been clean!

Whilst our preparation for the Court hearing was going on, a public meeting was held in Ambleside. It was decided that the market traders should be encouraged but that the site of the market should be moved. It was moved to a temporary site and then to the car park opposite the library where it is held today. The translation of the Charter confirmed the right to hold the market in Ambleside with all the usual arrangements.

As everyone was happy with the outcome, I persuaded the police to withdraw the summons. Our very sensible Magistrates on the Windermere Bench agreed. Thus thanks to Robin and his pals, Ambleside market was revived and has been held there ever since. Robin emigrated to South Africa and returned recently to live in Kendal.

Before the advent of the breathalyser a lady (long since gone to her Maker) had been caught driving her car and smelling of drink. She was charged with driving under the influence. She came to me for help.

THE ALCOHOLIC

Through the door came an elegant lady
Refined, clearly well brought up
When I offered her tea to calm her nerves
She looked chic as she held her cup.

"My dear Mr Hayton I'm dreadfully worried,"
She uttered as she started to cry
When she passed me the charge sheet
I got my first whiff
So that was the reason why!

The breathalyser had not been invented
The charge sheet alleged: driving in drink
"But oh Mr Hayton I've given it up
Will they withdraw do you think?"

The facts when I checked them
Could not be denied
But she insisted she'd given up drink
"My reformed situation; please plead mitigation
Will I lose my licence do you think?"

She was a widow who grieved for her man
She drank to soothe her pain
Medical help I arranged for her
Lest she did it all over again.

In the Court she looked so elegant
She faced the charge with style
As she walked into the witness box
She wore a charming smile.

She took the oath with dignity
She could have been a Queen
Looked straight in the eye of the Magistrate
The most convincing I had seen.

Her sadness in bereavement
Alcohol became her prop
Now medical help had taught her
Not to touch another drop.

I cannot remember her punishment
But still clearly I recall
How outside the Court just afterwards
As she stood there proud and tall

She fumbled in her handbag
Then looking sheepish in her sin
She produced and drank from a bottle
Long slugs of London Gin!

★   ★   ★

© *LH c. 1970.*

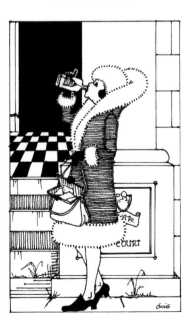

SMILEY LIGHTFINGER
AND THE BRIEFCASE

One cannot generalise about crime or criminals, but in the years between 1963 and 1973 I dealt with criminal cases. I represented people who came from the cities: Liverpool, Manchester, Leeds and Glasgow, as well as some locals. Often they took work during the season in the tourist industry. They brought their habits and idiosyncrasies with them. Some kept the Police, the Courts, the Probation Service and the likes of me busy. However, I met very few criminals whom I would regard as truly evil. Most cried out for a relationship with someone whom they could love and respect; but sadly fate is not always so kind.

Smiley Lightfinger was an inadequate. The Probation Service tried hard and I was often able to persuade the Magistrates to help him .We had a very good bench of fair and sensible Magistrates at Windermere along with a very enlightened Clerk who served them. The Magistrates in Kendal and South Lakeland were equally as fair-minded and did a good and valuable service to the community.

Alas, the police houses in towns and villages, where the local policeman lived among the community and knew what was going on, were later sold. Local Magistrates' Courts have since been amalgamated: a short-sighted policy I believe. They knew their communities and were the first to assess whether there was a case to answer. They showed compassion but could be tough when the occasion demanded. The accused also had an early opportunity to have legal representation.

I tried to help Smiley in many ways but sooner or sometimes much later he repeated the same kind of petty thefts. He had no family background. Always he spent his money buying "friendship" and always he wanted a companion; yet no relationship lasted any length of time.

★   ★   ★

SMILEY LIGHTFINGER

Smiley Lightfinger was a likeable crook
With a pallid complexion and a friendly look
He was "educationally sub-normal"
Or so it was said
Certainly juvenile thoughts
Mainly filled his head.

His mother had left him alone at birth
So he had no family on Mother Earth
He tried to buy love and he craved for affection
But was always cast down by hurtful rejection.

In children's homes and borstals
He had spent his formative years
On the ladder of self-preservation
He acquired his criminal's spurs.

He never did anything violent
He worked well, was helpful all day
But on buying his friendships each evening
He had to spend more than his pay.

Yet friendship purchased with money
Is rarely sincere or fair
Sadly when Smiley had spent all his earnings
Bought "friendships" were lost in the air.

He wished to stand well with his peers
His behaviour reflected that fact
But somehow something was missing
What was the spark that he lacked?

Smiley had the same views as a poacher
Jewellery and cash were fair game
His crimes opportunist and simple
The clues always suggested his name.

At Court he made frequent appearance
And though he led Probation a dance
As he always seemed a bit better
His progress earned him a chance.

But the last time I heard of Smiley
His light fingers had led him astray
With his manager's best coat, cash and briefcase
He was heading for the motorway.

With the briefcase and rolled umbrella
He strode out like an office clerk
Thumbing for a lift quite gaily
Singing as cheerfully as a lark.

But when the Police patrol car passed him
He dropped the case and ran
Had he just kept walking onwards
They would never have noticed their man.

He told them he was a solicitor's clerk
And the briefcase was borrowed from me
Sadly his lie precluded any help I could give
So that was the end of his spree.

★   ★   ★

In the happy days when banks still did banking and didn't want to do everyone else's job, they invited their customers and other professionals to their annual dinner.

I was invited by Ron Gerrard, the well-respected Manager of the Midland Bank at Kendal, who was then the President of the South Cumbria Branch of the Institute of Bankers, as guest speaker to reply on behalf of the guests. Ron was a well-liked and popular bank manager and a real character.

When I conferred with Mrs Gerrard, she was much amused by his latest scheme for cutting the lawn. He had put a temporary fence around their sloping lawn and borrowed some geese from a farmer client to eat the grass. The problem was that the geese converted the grass into slippery green … excrement! They also took off and flew out of the enclosure; so the scheme wasn't a success. Nevertheless, Ron took the leg-pulling in good heart.

At the time of the dinner the Bank of England rate was high as were interest rates also. Bank customers generally were being squeezed and were feeling the pinch, so at the end of my address, Sally, my imaginary bank customer in this poem, reverses the experience.

A BANK SQUEEZE!

Nut lang sen, ya Cursmass time
It was Cursmass mak o weather
Ald Joe Scrooge fre Turnip Howe
En his wife ligged doon en de-ed tagither.

Noo Joe left nowt but land en wark
En didn't leave a will
But he hed three dowters
O' on em endowed with brains and skill.

Sally wod be t'eldest
A bonny lass was she
Her backside fair, it med men want
Her brusts a sight ta see.

Well Sally saw t'solicitor
He said there's tax to pay
Thoo'd better see yon bank man
En see what he mun say.

Now Sally was a wily lass
She dressed up fine for Ron
This healthy comely country lass
How her blue eyes shone!

Her hair was clean and silken
Her cheeks were in full bloom
As Ron behind his massive desk
Arose from banking gloom.

He said, "I'm sure that I can help
But the interest will be high."
It was then that Sally fidgeted
And deftly moved her thigh.

Ron sensed beneath his testicles
A gentle grip but firm
As Sally reached beneath the desk
He lengthened then the term!

(Sally) "Now thee and me are equal
The security's in hand
We'll be gentle with each other
One percent above base will be grand!"

ALIBI FOR BONFIRE NIGHT

The Lake District National Park attracts visitors and tourists from all over the world. Seasonal workers from different parts of the country work in hotels as well as local staff. In my working days in Court some of these workers kept our local Magistrates' Courts busy, usually with petty offences, but sometime serious crimes came before the Bench. In this case a hotel worker had been arrested initially for possession of an illegal firearm.

For about ten years or more after qualifying as a solicitor, I spent at least two and sometimes three days a week working in the local Magistrates' Courts or briefing a barrister at the Assizes Court in Carlisle – before the Crown Court was formed. Murder charges were less common in those days than they are now.

The gun, which was later proved to have killed a mother and seriously wounded her daughter at a crime scene in the south of England, was found in a mattress in a flat just 100 yards from my office in Windermere. But the Accused had an alibi.

I got a telephone call from the Detective Chief Inspector because the Accused had asked for a solicitor to represent him. I was assigned to his case and the Court granted him legal aid. I investigated his alibi as described later. I represented the Accused at the preliminary hearing in the south of England and prepared the case for trial with the Counsel who was to conduct the defence at the hearing.

At that point the legal aid authority, to minimize expense, required me to appoint an agent firm of solicitors local to the Court to deal with the trial hearing in the south of England. The agent firm then attended Court with Defence Counsel who conducted the Accused's defence at the trial. I kept in touch with my agents. The case is outlined in my own words below. Where the narrative begins, the trial is nearing its close and in my 'summary' the Judge is reaching the end of his analysis of the evidence and addressing the Jury…

★   ★   ★

"Members of the Jury: I have almost completed my summing up. It is now over three weeks since Counsel for the Prosecution opened this trial of the Accused and outlined how the club owner's wife was shot dead and her daughter severely injured on Bonfire Night over two years ago. You have heard that another man has already been tried twice for these murders and acquitted on both occasions, possibly because the accomplice at the scene of the crime had not then been found nor identified.

"In addition, one important piece of evidence was missing at those trials: the gun which was used to kill and injure. It is common ground between the Prosecution and the Defence that the gun, found sewn into the Accused's mattress in Windermere over 250 miles from the scene of the crime, was the gun used to shoot the victims of this crime. Forensic evidence is clear on that. The Accused has told you why he bought the gun and who from, but he cannot provide any other details as to the identity of the man who sold him the gun.

"The mother and daughter were shot in their home on the outskirts of London. Their home was, as you have heard, across the yard from the husband's nightclub. Two men walked into their home and forced the two ladies to summon the husband, the club owner. It is alleged that when the husband arrived, he refused to comply with their demands, despite the evidence you have heard that the keys to the safe were in the house and that one of the men was holding the gun at his wife's head threatening to shoot her.

"If the accomplice is to be believed, it was the Accused who shot the wife dead and then shot the daughter, gravely injuring her. Both were shot in the back through a cushion to muffle the sound. The club owner told us that he was made to lie down and he also was shot but the bullet only grazed his head. He lay still bleeding and feigned death. He lived and his account of the events agrees with the evidence of the accomplice. After this, the accomplice tells us that they made their escape, taking with them only some small items from the room, which they later buried while taking shelter in a wartime pillbox.

"Why the crime was committed may always remain a mystery. Members of the Jury, you are here to decide whether the man who stands accused in the dock before you was at the scene of this cold-blooded crime that night. You must also consider whether the evidence of the accomplice, who has identified the Accused as the gunman, can be believed.

"The Accused has denied that he was ever at the scene of the murder and avers that he is being framed. He has explained how and why he purchased the gun. Defence Counsel has produced evidence of an alibi supported by documentary proof that the Accused purchased a bicycle in Leeds and went on a cycling holiday. It is clear that the

Accused purchased the bicycle in Leeds on the 6th November and stayed overnight there. But was he at the scene of the crime at midnight on the 5th? He says he recalls seeing bonfires in Yorkshire on Bonfire Night but not all bonfires are lit on the 5th November. The accomplice says they got a lift into London in the early morning of the 6th and parted company. Where was the Accused in the early hours of the 6th? His alibi does not cover beyond doubt the crucial time when these shots were fired on the 5th November.

"Members of the Jury, you have to weigh the evidence. You will recall that in the jacket left by the Accused at his grandmother's flat in Leeds there was a London hotel booking-in card for two people to stay there, which was booked on the morning of the 5th November. Why did the Accused and the man who was with him not stay in that London hotel on the night of the 5th November when they had booked a room for two? The Accused's signature was in the hotel register. Did the Accused not stay there because he was in Yorkshire that night or was it, as the accomplice alleges, because the Accused was at the scene of this crime with his accomplice?

"You have before you the evidence of the self-confessed accomplice. The Accused says that this man is lying. The Accused has told you that he has been framed. He has been open with you about his background.

"You have to be very careful and very wary about the evidence of an accomplice. If that evidence is to have any bearing on the guilt or innocence of the Accused, it should be corroborated in some material particular by independent evidence. You may think, Members of the Jury, that the items found in the wartime pillbox, located after the police helicopter search, do show that the accomplice was in the wartime pill box, because how could he have known that those items from the scene of the crime were there?

"You may think that points the finger at the Accused. Was the Accused with the accomplice? You may think the accomplice was at the scene of the crime because he has said he was and because of his detailed evidence. How, otherwise, would the accomplice know the details of how the shooting took place? How would he know that the items stolen from the scene of the crime had been buried in the pillbox if he was not there? You may think this is corroboration of the accomplice's statement in a material particular. But does that prove that it was the Accused who was with him? The Accused denies any knowledge of this and avers that he is being framed. I have already examined with you his reasons for this belief at the beginning of my summing up but you must decide what weight you give to it.

"It is now for you, Members of the Jury, to weigh the evidence placed before you during this trial. I have reviewed that evidence with you and now will you please retire and consider your verdict."★★

When the Jury had retired from Court to the Jury room and while it was deliberating, I reflected upon the events of the previous six months beginning with the telephone call that had come one evening from the Detective Chief Inspector. "I have a prisoner in the cells who needs a solicitor," he had announced bluntly. "It is a serious charge but I won't discuss it on the phone. Can you come?"

When I got to the police station, it emerged that a petty offender, a flat mate of the Accused, who was in custody for an unconnected offence, had bragged that he had a friend with a gun, who would "see his arresting officer off" if they prosecuted him. Drawing the youngster out, the police had elicited the fact that there was a gun sewn into his flatmate's mattress. The young offender had reported a conversation with the Accused which put the police on to the enquiry. The young offender had spoken about women being shot through a cushion and this reference rang a bell with the detective. He remembered reading of the crime in a national newspaper. It appeared that the person accused had been acquitted in that case mainly because the evidence of identity had been unreliable and the second man had not then come forward.

The Kendal police had obtained a magistrates' search warrant and found the gun, which they sent for forensic testing. When the result was positive, they had arrested the Accused.

I was introduced to the Accused in the police cell at Kendal. He was lean and tall and of pale complexion. His eyes were hooded and hawk-like and he seemed unusually calm and still. At first he was rather cold and unfriendly. It was clear the man had little respect for lawyers or the police. He gave me the impression that he was hardened to the system and had seen the whole process before.

He had the kind of background that often leads into crime, but he was forceful in his denial of responsibility for the murder. Yes, he had served a previous gaol sentence and was in fact on parole at the time when the murder took place. But no, he could not have been at the scene because he had been in Yorkshire on a cycling holiday. He remembered the bonfires in Yorkshire on Bonfire Night, which was the night when the killing had taken place. Yes, he was sure he had been in Yorkshire on Bonfire Night and he could prove it. He said that he recalled reading about the brutal nightclub murder in the papers while he was on holiday. He said he had bought a bicycle in Leeds, visited his grandmother and had paid for accommodation there.

I explained to him about the law relating to alibis, which at that time had only recently changed. It had become necessary to give details of an alibi to the police in good time before a trial. I informed him I would need to check it and get the evidence.

He and I passed a long evening locked in the police cell while I took his statement and the details of his wanderings after leaving prison in the South. Sometimes his eyes stared intensely and his steady, predatory look seemed more menacing and disturbing when my questions probed his story too closely. I decided to check the alibi myself and to take Peter, who was then my articled pupil, with me. I noticed the detail of his alibi seemed to grow in successive interviews. Was it because of slow recall or pure fabrication?

Peter was keen to get started. He likened us to the 'Two Ronnies' as Charley Farley and Piggy Malone! When we knocked on the door of a seedy apartment beside a night-club in Leeds, we were met by a giant of a man, dark skinned, with the appearance of a bouncer. As he opened the door he was restraining two large Alsatian dogs on short leashes which snarled at us aggressively. We kept our nerve but I couldn't help thinking that the Charley Farley and Piggy Malone types could have the job for me! In today's world we would probably send a detective to check the alibi.

Yes, we found the Accused's signature in the visitors' book. Yes, we found the bicycle shop where he had bought a bicycle. We got a copy of the invoice and his signature on the purchase slip. We found his grandmother's flat also – but she did not tell us the police had visited the day before and taken his jacket – as it happened an important find for the Prosecution. All the dates we found were from the 6th November onwards – not the 5th. So when did he leave London and how did he get to Leeds?

We followed the trail as outlined in his statement and retraced his steps to London. He had worked for a while on parole in a factory but he was not working there on the 5th November. We called on his landlady to check when he had last slept there. She was non-committal. It could have been the 4th or the 5th but she thought it might have been the 4th November. She could not be sure. She had no records. So where was he on the 5th of November? The Jury would have to decide.

When a prisoner in Winchester Jail read that the nightclub murder was being re-opened, he made a statement in the hope of getting a lighter sentence by giving evidence. When that statement was put to the Accused, he gave a convincing explanation of how and why he was being framed for the crime. It was plausible but what was the truth?

★   ★   ★

Suddenly the waiting is over. The tension rises. A whisper spreads round the Court. The Jury is coming back and is filing into the jury box. The Courtroom is tense and all the pomp and ceremony is stripped away. Everyone stands as the Judge returns to resume his seat. The focus flicks between the Accused and the Foreman of the Jury. The Accused is ordered to stand.

The Judge asks the Foreman of the Jury, "Are you agreed upon your verdict?"

There is a pause. The Jury has been out for several hours. The Court is now as silent as the grave.

"Guilty," says the Foreman.

The Accused shows no emotion. He stands motionless and stares coldly at the Judge as he is sentenced to life imprisonment.

Then the Prisoner is taken down to the cells below. The Court rises with the Judge and all disperse.

★   ★   ★

My mind's eye then focussed on the hotel booking-in card and the Prisoner's signature in the hotel register. The evidence presented to the Court was that two men had booked in on the morning of the 5th November but did not return to sleep in the reserved bed. That was the evidence which had destroyed his alibi.

But why on that Bonfire Night was such a brutal crime committed? We may never know. Was he framed? The Jury clearly thought not.

**Note: the above address to the Jury is not in the actual words of the Judge trying the case but it is my own outline-summary as to how a Judge in the circumstances might have addressed the Jury.*

SMILEY MOTHERSON'S PROBLEM

The booming voice of an hotelier Client had forced me to hold the phone away from my ear. He shouted down the wire, "One of my chaps has got himself into a bit of bother. He's a good skin really but a bit simple. His mother has never told him about the facts of life and he's a bit shy, poor lad."

"What's his problem?" I enquired.

"Well, I'd rather not say on the phone, old lad; bit private you know. I'll bring him in. Don't bother about legal aid and all that. Send the bill to me, lad."

When he brought Smiley in, the hotelier introduced him to me and turned to go. He did everything at a gallop. "Tell them the tale, lad, tell them the tale," he said. "Smiley's a good worker, real good worker, lad; honest as the day is light. Needs a good lass, he does. Swinging sixties you know. You should be able to help him. Surprised he needs to do that in these times. Well, must be off. Tell them the tale, lad, tell them the tale." He disappeared, almost running, and shut my door as he went.

Flushed with embarrassment, Smiley beamed at me from a large, round, well-weathered face. He had a ruddy complexion and his hair was beginning to recede. I guessed he was around forty and worked out-of-doors. He was not the usual criminal type, imported to work as back-up staff from faraway cities. He was a countryman born and bred. Sitting beside him was a Lakeland sheepdog, obedient and watchful.

"Are you married?" I enquired. "No, I live with my mother. She keeps the house and we live on my wage and her pension. She's a good cook, my mother, and she irons and does for me. There's just me, Mother and our old sheepdog, Meg. Meg's my best pal. She goes everywhere with me." He stroked her head and smiled down at the dog.

I looked at the charge sheet. His composure left him and tears came into his eyes. Then his head bowed in misery, he blubbered uncontrollably, "Mother will be heartbroken when she finds out. Does she have to know? Why did I do it? What came over me? Can you help me?" He broke down in a convulsion of sobs and misery and I had to go round the desk to comfort him.

"Don't get this out of proportion," I said. "Have you been in trouble before or been warned about this?" He hadn't. I put my arm over his bowed shoulders and gave him a gentle re-assuring hug. I comforted him as best I could in his distress until his sobbing subsided and he could talk again.

I took my chair round the desk to sit beside him and confer quietly with him. The dog licked my hand. One gets an inkling of a man's nature from his dog. To make any progress, Smiley had to see me as a friend and confidant. It needed time and patience. He was a shy, retiring man with a gentle, caring nature but he had a problem.

We talked of his interests: wildlife and horticulture. His knowledge of birds, flowers and trees was encyclopaedic. On these subjects and about his work, which occupied most of his time, he was authoritative, confident and a delight to converse with. He was a very interesting and amiable man.

I asked who his doctor was. I was pleased with his reply for his old doctor was a tower of strength in the community, a man respected by everyone for sound judgement and common sense. I was sure the doctor and I could help Smiley. But how would the Bench view the matter? This was a country Court with the Bench from his own community. This was long before cost-saving amalgamations centralised court sittings in the bigger towns. For my part, I was wet behind the ears: a new solicitor breaking new ground in the area. How would the Bench take to me?

Quietly we went through the facts and his background. Later I arranged for his doctor to help him broach the subject with his mother and then I joined them to explain his dilemma and agree the best course of action with them.

On the day of the hearing I met Smiley, his doctor and mother outside the Court. In those halcyon days doctors were allowed more time for their patients and we could make arrangements with the Magistrates' Clerk to deal with matters early in order to let a professional witness give his evidence and get off on his rounds.

"Stand, please," said the Court usher in his black gown as the door opened and in filed four members of the Magistrates' Bench.

Licensing applications were dealt with first. These mainly concerned transfers of public house licences or extensions of permitted hours and usually only took a few minutes each. It was a useful opportunity to gather one's thoughts and to gauge the mood of the Magistrates. It gave me time to think how best to pitch what I would have to say.

The Court occupied a large room, which could have been the village institute. It was fenced off in sections with the Magistrates' area at a higher level, as was the witness box and the dock. The public and the advocates were at floor level and we had to look up to the Bench, to the witness stand and to the dock area which the accused would occupy when the charge was put to him. All the wooden structures could be removed when the building was needed for other functions.

"Smiley Albert Motherson, please stand. You are charged that ....."

The Clerk read out the charge.

"How do you plead?" asked the Magistrates' Clerk?

Smiley looked at me for reassurance. I nodded and he seemed to relax. With the hint of a pleasant smile he turned his honest, weathered face to the Magistrates. His sincerity and pleasant approach to life was revealed to them in that simple act. He seemed to cast away his awkwardness like a morning mist driven from a Lakeland valley by the rising sun. His problem was now in the open.

Nonetheless, Smiley replied in an embarrassed tone, "Guilty sir."

"Please sit and listen to the Inspector."

At that time there was no separate Prosecution Service. The local Police Inspector normally conducted the case for the prosecution unless it was a serious matter, in which case it was passed on to a local solicitor who specialised in that work. The system was criticised, often unfairly, because the police did both the investigation and prosecution. However, on the whole it worked well because the prosecuting Inspector made sure that cases were properly investigated and prepared. Police were on the beat and knew their area. Community policing is not a new invention. At the time it was a reality. The Inspector was the one who had to face the Magistrates, and they were not slow in putting him right if he got anything wrong.

Smiley was allowed to sit. The Inspector outlined the facts supporting the charge. The incident had taken place in the local park near a path frequently trodden by the senior girls from the local school. The Inspector explained what had happened and what the witnesses would have said. He summarised the facts fairly. He sat down.

That was the pregnant moment when all eyes turned on me. I was a new solicitor to the area. How was I going to perform? I could see it in their eyes. What line will he take? I could feel the expectation as I rose to address the Court.

"Your Worships," I began. "You have heard the outline of the facts which have been put fairly. My Client, whom I will, with your approval, call Smiley, has admitted this charge and co-operated with the Police from the beginning. As you will hear, he is a simple but honest, hardworking man, admired by all who know him for his honesty and reliability. But he has a problem.

"He very much regrets what has happened. It is a first offence and I sincerely believe from what I have learned that it will be the last. I wish to address you in mitigation of the penalty later but first I want to call Smiley's family doctor."

Smiley had told me about the background and events that led up to the incident on that day in the "swinging sixties". He had often seen pretty lasses in the park laughing, joking and engaging in horse play, as teenagers do. He had seen them looking at the "Health and Efficiency" magazine and giggling about it. He had taken a train excursion to Blackpool. He managed to buy some "girlie books" away from his village where the newsagent wouldn't know him. He had looked at a few magazines in a shop and felt very self-conscious and confused. He kept his purchases in his potting shed. When he went to read them, he always kept an eye on the path to give him time to hide them when Mother brought his tea.

He had always been able to talk to girls about things he was interested in but he could never pluck up courage to ask them out. Once, on the only occasion when he had done so, he didn't turn up for the date because Mother had wanted him to do something else. It always seemed that his mother found something which got in the way. He had never dared to ask anyone again. He was frightened to upset his mother whom he loved deeply. So he had got to the age of forty and had never had a real relationship with a girl friend. He felt shy and inadequate. He could never bridge the gap. The older he got, the worse it seemed to be.

Yet from time to time he had this feeling. It was a feeling that tempted him with its urgency. His skin tingled with excitement so much that he could burst. He had this warm excitement in his loins and he had had to relieve himself. He had seen his peers excite themselves at school and he had tried it, but it didn't give him any real fulfilment or satisfaction. Still it was the best he could do and it relieved the pressure from time to time. He always wondered what it would be like with a woman. How he had missed out! All his contemporaries had married and had children. He loved children and animals. He had such a gentle nature, yet he convinced himself he was a failure.

Smiley developed an overwhelming urge to make contact, to bridge the gap: but how? He did not know. But he just had to do something!

On the day of his offence he told me he was in a kind of dream. He just went to the park and waited in the rhododendron bushes with Meg. When the girl he saw as the loveliest girl in the world came laughing along with another friend, he could hold himself back no longer.

He dropped his trousers round his ankles and exposed his manhood to her! She and her friend had frozen in astonishment. The dog, looking quizzical, sat quietly beside him. He did not touch the girls or attack them. He just stood there in pathetic bewilderment as his erection withered before their eyes.

Then the worst thing for him happened. They broke into hysterical laughter, called him a dirty old man and sped off to tell their mates. It was later that their parents had taken them to the Police Station.

The doctor gave evidence of Smiley's condition and his family background. He explained to the Court how he could be helped to overcome his problem and that he had already had some useful co-operation from Smiley. The family doctor spoke with conviction and honesty and the Bench clearly weighed his evidence carefully because they asked him some intelligent questions very relevant to the issues involved.

Next I asked Smiley to take the stand and the oath. I wanted the Bench to see for themselves the man as he was. I wanted them to relate to him and understand him. He was a sad but honest and sincere, middle-aged "mother's boy". He needed help, not any draconian measures. He apologised to the Court and to the girls and their families for his unseemly behaviour. He promised to follow his doctor's advice. His mother, "whose eyes had been opened", had written a helpful letter with my assistance. I handed the letter up to the Bench. She was too frail to call as a witness but she did manage to attend the hearing. I gave them a sound, no-nonsense but helpful testimonial from the hotelier.

My preparatory work, the doctor's evidence and the probation report, which supported our line, meant that I needed to add little in my final address. However, it was with some concern that I asked for a conditional discharge and sat down. The Court rose and the Magistrates filed out. A few minutes later the door opened and the Clerk was summoned to advise them on some point of law. My heart sank.

Five long minutes later the Magistrates returned.

The Clerk addressed Smiley, who rose smartly to attention. "Stand, please, and listen to the Chairman."

The Chairman began, "Smiley Motherson, you have wisely pleaded guilty. It was a foolish thing which you did. You caused embarrassment to the girls and upset to their families. Fortunately, we have heard that you intended no harm to them. We accept the advice of your doctor and the evidence of good character and honesty as well as your hard work. These facts persuade us that your Solicitor's request for a conditional discharge is entirely appropriate." The Chairman went on to explain the meaning of their decision. They discharged Smiley and turned to their next case.

Smiley's relief and that of his mother was evident for all to see. His round, honest face beamed as he bowed in respect to the Bench, turned and walked slowly to the door.

Outside the Court in the yard the old, experienced Police Sergeant, who came out with us, approached us and quietly took Smiley and me on one side.

He had spent most of his career in the country districts of Westmorland. "Young lad," he said to me in his strong dialect accent. "Thoo's done a good job fer Smiley. Thoo knaa's wi git a gay deal of these lousen-out jobs in summer. I hev a feelen that t'blood gits o'er hot. Thoo knaas it happens ivvery year when it gits a bit warm. We git o' maks of nebber disputes en sae on."

Then quietly he said to Smiley, "Well mi lad, thoo's a lucky fella. I'll be watchen them bushes en thou mon't ga lousen-oot agen in t'park. Lile school lasses hev to be protected til they git o' mack a graan up. Thoo mun git up t'dale ta yan o them hunt balls. There's many a gurt country lass like thee that gits ta wanten en can teach thee what to do. So thoo mun shape up lad!"

Smiley was never in trouble again and he became a worthy and respected member of his community. I sometimes wonder, when I hear of sex offenders being hounded out of a community, how he would have been treated today. The Bench was local. The Police had authority and respect and lived in the community. His background and family were understood and accepted with their strengths and weaknesses in their known locality. The locals could be hard and dismissive but they looked after their own and did not expect everyone else to solve their problems.

Smiley kept in touch with his doctor and kept on good terms with the Sergeant. He always waved when I saw him in the street.

Smiley learned the art of courting but never married. I fancy the old Sergeant and the doctor gave him a few tips. In his latter years Smiley became the heart throb of the old people's sheltered housing where he retired. As a male he was in the minority. He would do shopping for his lady friends and make their breakfasts. He was kindness itself.

Later in my career when I visited other clients there to make their wills or attend to their affairs, I enquired as to Smiley. Always I had glowing reports of his good works. But with one or two of those elderly ladies, I thought I perceived a knowing smile, mixed with a contented wistfulness!

Sadly Smiley died some years ago but I know he had overcome his difficulties and was a happy, well-respected man in the community.

© LH c.1966.

DRAMA AT THE AUCTION

"Thee garn see oor Len," was the advice given to Cheery Farmer by my eldest brother, Gerard, who ran the family farm in Kentmere and who was a man of many parts. When I first became interested in Agricultural Law, most of my farmer and agrarian clients in the north of England seemed to be sent by Ger; but more about my genial and good-hearted brother another day.

Cheery now sat four-square opposite me at my desk. Rightly named, his weather-worn face was swathed in smiles, which played in greater intensity round his eyes. I took an instant like to this kindred spirit of my big brother. He just looked so honest and reliable – but a little embarrassed.

I wondered why he needed a solicitor?

Cheery spun his cap nervously round on his head and began with an apology. "I don't tek mi cap off, well varra rarely Len, so happen thoo'll understand that I feel better keepen it on like. I allus hev it wid ma. If I hev ta pick up summat o'er hot I might just use mi cap, or mappen if a coo hes gitten some shit on it's pap at milken time, I might clean it off wi mi cap for hand milken. I can collect eggs in it as weel. Aye en oor lass might, odd times like, mak me tek it off when I git inta bed. I feel rayder lost widoot mi cap. Noo she does insist when I hev mi weekly bath on a Sunday, mappen! Otherwise I nivver ivver tek mi cap off, so thoo will understand, waint ta?

"It's like Nell, mi ald dog, I woddent be widoot her either." I realised that a black and white sheep dog must have followed him in unnoticed, because it was sitting at his feet, its coat shining and eyes alert, watching every move that Cheery made.

I enquired politely why he had come, but he seemed reluctant to come to the point. He did not answer my question at first, but told me all about his farm, his stock, and market prices. I realised he was weighing me up, deciding whether indeed I was the right man for the job. Finally, when he had drawn me out, he seemed to pause. Then he leaned forward with a serious expression.

"Well it's like this, thoo knaas, I hev a nebber Joe next doo-er – well aboot a mile away – but his grund is reet inta t'middle of mi farm. He telt ma that he wants to sell t'main on his land to me. Well him en me, what we've allus bin gud friends but he hes been in turble laa watter lately. He gat louked oor t'heed with a post by a poacher last eer. He's nivver bin same sen. But Jessie, Joe's wife, is a grand body, en well, we're rather bothered aboot Joe.

"Well, Joe wants me ta buy his grund privately, but I want him ta git a proper value fer it, en I've telt him ta put it ter auction en I'll tak mi chance," said Cheery. "I couldn't leeve wid missel if he thowt I'd gitten mi ald friend's land through t'back doo'er or o'er chee-ap. I'd rather I bowt t'land fair en in t'open market."

At this point, Cheery rather startled me by spinning his cap round in a full circle on his head and at the same time stretched and leaned back in the chair, drawing in a deep breath. His boots banged under my desk. I was puzzled. The dog never moved. It was not surprised. It was clearly used to Cheery and loved every facet of his character.

Now this really was new to me: Cheery, a farmer, wanting land and still prepared to see it sold in auction to help a friend! Land to a farmer is like gold to a prospector on the Klondyke!

"Noo, I'se nut garn ta say that I don't want his land but I don't want it fer nowt. I want o' ta be reet, thoo knaas. But there's nobbut yan snag!"

Cheery went on to tell me how some time previously he had been in dispute with another adjoining neighbour called Digger Grub over land encroachment and boundary problems. It appeared that no love was lost between them. They exchanged insults frequently, yet also in accordance with farming custom they exchanged stray animals. It was clear they disliked each other intensely.

Cheery hadn't helped by questioning Digger Grub's parentage. In the heat of one exchange he had been heard to shout across the dike, "What is ta anyway? Thou's oot of nowt, gitten by nowt, so hoo the hell can ye be owt?" You will appreciate that pedigree to a farmer is everything and he applies it to his neighbours as well. So Cheery had weaknesses too, I thought.

Well the snag was clearly Digger Grub. Even if Grub didn't want the land, he would bid it up to get at old Cheery.

Joe wanted Cheery to have the land but he felt relieved that Cheery was letting him get the market value. Joe kept worrying about Digger Grub. Doubtless Grub would do Joe no harm by bidding, but he couldn't sleep with the thought that Grub might outbid Cheery.

Cheery leaned further across my desk. He fixed me with a quizzical look. He spun his cap a full circle on his head again. It was a puzzling idiosyncrasy. All I could think of was him getting into bed with his cap on, but he brought me back with a jerk. "Hesta ivver bowt owt ut auction?" he asked. I assured him that I had and outlined the various approaches to the problems that can arise at an auction.

He seemed satisfied with my answer and then he asked if I would bid for him at the auction of Joe's land. I said he should consider his limit carefully and give me details on the morning of the auction, as I would need a written authority with the limit he would set. In the meantime, although he was familiar with the land, I advised that he should instruct me to check the terms of the contract with Joe's solicitor and do the local search. I would need to look for reserved rights as Joe was retaining the house and some land to keep a few sheep in his retirement.

The auction day arrived and I travelled to meet Cheery in the village institute where the sale was to take place. We agreed we would sit together. It can be unwise to sit away from your client as sometimes they can become impatient and bid against their solicitor, wasting their money in doing so. But Digger Grub would see us together and know I was bidding for Cheery. He might "run" us. Well we would take that chance. I had done what I could to protect Cheery.

All the neighbours and local farmers were there. I could feel the tension in the room and an air of expectation. There were other solicitors, no doubt with instructions to bid, and a gaggle of land-agent types, in yellow fustian trousers and hacking jackets, leaning round the walls and at the back.

Joe noticed a mysterious-looking fellow with a beard in a Barbour jacket. Nobody he asked had seen this chap in the district before and Joe eyed him with a worried expression. He wished he had never agreed to an auction. It was a real strain. "Why didn't we just sell it to Cheery without all this fuss?" he thought. "Cheery is not going to get this, you know, Jessie. Grub is here as well. Oh, I don't want Digger getting it!"

His wife could hardly console Joe. He was beside himself. Beads of sweat appeared on his forehead. He got up from the table and paced around behind the auctioneer's rostrum. The auctioneer had placed Joe and Jessie with their solicitor on the top table facing the audience. Joe would rather have been anywhere but there.

"Good afternoon, ladies and gentlemen. It is two o'clock, the advertised time for the auction of 'Laa Gussins fields', being seventy-five acres of productive meadow and pasture land." The auctioneer went on to describe the land and extol its virtues and then asked Joe's solicitor to read the contract and conditions of sale. After answering a few questions and clarifying certain points, the solicitor sat down.

The auctioneer rose again. The tension in the room was palpable. Now it came home to Joe that his land, his lifetime's work, was really on the market for sale because his agent was asking for bids. There was a pause … and then a silence which seemed to Joe to go on forever.

I waited. If possible, I like to let the bidders value the land first before I start to bid. No one moved a muscle. No bids.

"Now come on, ladies and gentlemen, we are here to do business. Shall I say £100,000 to start?"

There was no movement or sign of any bid.

"75,000 then. No? Who will start me at £50,000? Yes sir, £50,000 on my left. £60,000 … £70,000 … £80,000. It's against you, sir," the auctioneer pointed to the last bidder. "£85,000 shall I say? Yes, £85,000 and £5,000. £90,000 and five … and £100,000." The bidding climbed to £120,000 and slowed.

At that point I bid £125,000. Then I saw Digger Grub perk up. "£130,000" he shouted! He was in. I bid £135,000 and Grub, clearly against his wife's wishes, for she was striking him across the chest, bid loudly, "£140,000!" Grub was making us pay. He ignored his wife; he enjoyed seeing the smile die on Cheery's face.

"£150,000." I stepped up the bids. Grub shouted immediately, "£151,000!"

The auctioneer turned to me. I paused and deliberately shook my head. I could see Digger Grub's smile disappear. He was starting to sweat too. The bidding had stopped. The auctioneer waved his gavel round the room. No movement. Joe's face had turned through white to an ashen grey. Cheery had not got the land. What was happening?

Cheery had his head bowed, looking at the floor. He was spinning his cap again but in a more controlled manner than usual. I wondered if he had any hair under it!

The auctioneer stepped down from the rostrum. He huddled in the corner with Jessie, Joe and the solicitor.

The £151,000 bid was over the reserve. Joe should have been happy but he felt downright sick. "But Grub is last in," he said. "I don't want him buying it. The land comes right to my yard."

"Well, Cheery's solicitor may be waiting until we confirm it is in the market," said the auctioneer. "What have I to do?"

Joe's solicitor pointed out that they were selling subject to a reserve but he had, nevertheless, included a clause that Joe could still withdraw the property before the hammer fell. The strain on Joe was immense. What should he do?

Jessie took his arm and whispered something to him. He seemed relieved and nodded. "Put it in the market," he said.

The auctioneer climbed back on the rostrum.

"I can tell you, ladies and gentlemen, the property is in the market to be sold. The bidding stands at £151,000." Looking at me, he said, "The bidding is against you sir, shall I say £155,000?" I shook my head. "I'll take £1000 to get started." I shook my head again.

Grub's face said it all. He had run me and was left with it. Everyone was looking at Digger Grub. Then the auctioneer, pointing all round the room and having got no further bids, raised the gavel and started the time honoured ritual:

"Going once – it is with you, sir," pointing at Digger Grub. His wife was hitting him harder in the chest now and shouting, "Tell him 'No', tell him now," she said. "Going twice – for the thir…," – his gavel was in the air. I was starting to get worried myself.

"One hundred and fifty two thousand," came a clear voice from the tall man with the beard.

The auctioneer turned and started again. Digger Grub subsided with relief, his wife purple with rage that they had made such fool of themselves. Joe was still looking grey, sad that Cheery had not bid any further. Joe's decision to sell by auction had been wrong. He had lost his lifelong friend. No money was worth it. How could he face Cheery? He felt greedy and tainted. But why had Cheery not bid again? Clearly, Grub was over his limit. Why?

Cheery was holding the sides of his cap down to his ears with both hands and wearing an expression that puzzled both Jessie and Joe.

Joe's heart sank lower as the auctioneer's ritual began again. Joe was in a daze. He couldn't mouth or say anything.

The gavel was in the air. "To you, sir," pointing at the tall man with the beard, "For the third and last time." The gavel came down with a bang.

The bearded man smiled and walked to the table where Joe's solicitor had the contract ready for his signature.

Jessie and Joe both looked sick. Honest country folk that they were, they looked Cheery straight in the eye. They had to face it: he had lost it. Cheery was coming to the table with Nell at his heels. Their disappointment was evident for all to see. As the room was emptying, I got up and followed Cheery to the table.

A broad grin came over Cheery's face. He pushed his cap to the back of his head like a trailer "kekking" stones. He took both Joe and Jessie's hands in his and pressed them fondly.

"Don't thoo worry Joe. I've bought thy land, Joe lad," he said. "Thoo's gitten t'reet price for certain, and we've rather rubbed Digger's nose in it this efternean.

"This bearded fella here that med that last bid for me is Mr Hayton's partner in oor solicitor's firm. Gerard telt me that Leonard wod hev some wease up his sleave ta ootwit yon fella Grub. We hed Mr Bromley, Leonard's partner here, primed up ta buy it but I couldn't let that oot, could I?

"I'se varra sorry that thou gat sae worried but I was nivver garn ta buy thy land fer less than it was worth. Thoo has allus been a good nebber en friend ta me."

The sight of the two relieved old couples, standing with tears running down their cheeks in mutual relief and eyes twinkling as grins spread across their faces, is an abiding memory of mine.

The inherent decency of Cheery and his strong character always shone through all the dealings I had with him over the years. Even Digger and Cheery continued to co-operate in exchanges of strays, but both had a wry smile on meeting.

So it is that the farming cycle goes on through the years, following the customs and usages of farming folk. When I met Cheery afterwards, we would often have an amusing conversation and always I felt better for the exchange of good humour. He would say, "Well dew look in fer a crack when thoo's garn by, 'cos thoo knaas, *a good crack, it's worth o' thy physic.*"

Whether Cheery still wears his hat in bed I can't say but the last time I saw him his wife had bought him a new one; at least that is what he told me, as he spun it round and round on his head, smiling cheerfully as ever!

AN ENJOYABLE WORKING LIFE

Figure 2.8. LH in the Windermere office of Hayton Winkley

Over most of my practising career I worked mainly from our Windermere office. We employed some delightful and intelligent staff during that time. They came from all kinds of backgrounds but many had attended the Lakes School and came from families in South Lakeland. Those who came straight from school we trained ourselves from junior upwards and they attended night school or were released for day courses. Our senior members of staff were happy to train and pass on their skills, so most of the time things went smoothly.

Usually they stayed until marriage and babies arrived but they often popped in to see us and sometimes came back to work when their children started nursery. In those halcyon days we had time for tea breaks and biscuits – ice creams in the summer! We had flexible part-time arrangements which worked well. Many of our staff learned business skills in the office just by observing what entrepreneurs and business people could achieve by seizing opportunities and pursuing them. Some ex-staff later joined their husbands or friends in business, using the experience gleaned in our office to make successful businesses themselves. This is another way that the "green shoots" of enterprise can increase the prosperity of an area.

Other members of staff came to live here in South Lakeland and brought professional skills with them. I was lucky to have some very competent staff, some of whom were certainly brighter than me and could make a real contribution to the resolution of any problems which might arise.

Before money became God and the strait-jacket of strict time-recording replaced trust and natural responsibility, I believe we had an enjoyable working atmosphere in our office. We nevertheless produced good work and had satisfied clients, who in turn trusted us, which to me is the priority.

Our happy and sometimes hilarious Christmas parties were held at various hotels and venues over the years. The Kendal, Windermere and Ambleside offices arranged them from year to year in a rota. In the summer I liked to surprise the staff occasionally with a lunch at the Langdale Chase Hotel or the like. We usually arranged it at a client's hotel as it maintained goodwill both there and in the office. The Windermere partners and staff would organise no appointments between 12.30 and 3.30 pm that day. One of the staff would volunteer

Figure 2.9. Windermere Office Staff outside the Langdale Chase Hotel
Front row, left to right: Mrs Dinal Salisbury, Lisa . . . . , Myra Huddlestone, Jean Cowling, Caroline Astle, Liz Sarginson, Pamela Boyes and LH
2nd row: Jane Wrobel, Sarah Taylor, Mrs Barbara Willan, Hazel Turner and Marilyn Helsby
Back row: Keith Wood and Andrew Bromley

to cover the switchboard for emergencies or a partner's wife would come in. I would arrange with my friend, Bill Bewley, for a boat to pick us up at the Langdale Chase Hotel pier after lunch. We would then have a short sail and return happy and refreshed to finish our work.

We also arranged our area Bradford and Bingley Building Society (BBBS) meetings at the Wordsworth Hotel in Grasmere with the kind attention of our good friends, Reg and Elizabeth Gifford, the proprietors.

This was in the happy times when the BBBS was a mutual society with agents around Cumbria. In those days banks were banks and building societies were building societies. Each had a local manager in the community, who supported businesses and young people starting out in life. Managers were in competition but had discretion and could make sensible judgements without being fettered by computer tick boxes from on high.

Bank managers were still managers of their local bank and did not want to do the work of all professions. They knew their customers and had discretion on site to lend. They exercised judgement in lending and helped our grass roots businesses expand and grow.

Unfortunately banks grew greedy, the members of the building societies voted and, like the BBBS, some became banks. People accepted shares and money incentives, as I did at the time, but I bitterly regretted doing so when I saw the changes which occurred as a result.

We seem to have lost the quality of life in business, when there was time to think long-term. In our modern world of instant communication and reply, there is no time to think or make an objective judgment after due consideration, and thereby make the right decisions.

I often wonder how our senior government ministers can make important policy decisions for us when they are constantly hounded and criticised by the media, who seem interested only in sensationalism and instant analysis. The media can do more in five minutes to destroy business confidence and create panic than we can do in a lifetime to create the business enterprises and wealth on which our wellbeing and our pensions depend.

It seems to me that we have lost a great deal in trying to express everything in money's worth and in over-regulation, which assumes we are all fools with no common sense or understanding of risk! We need to reward and encourage development and manufacturing in our own country so that we are more self- reliant and can provide a long-term future for our young people.

Over the years I have been blessed with wonderful secretaries and "PA"s. Jean Cowling, who has worked for me and the firm for over 25 years, probably expresses the kindly frustration felt by her and all her predecessors in her poem "IF" on my 60th birthday.

Figure 2.10. Miss Joyce Leach is presented with an engraved silver drinks tray and a crystal decanter and glasses to mark her retirement after 29 years service, from Hayton and Winkley Solicitors, Kendal. Making the presentation to Miss Leach, who was office manager is Mr Len Hayton and looking on, from left are Mr John Oldroyd, Mr Peter Briggs and Mr Michael Winkley

In March 1986 Miss Joyce Leach retired after 29 years of service as office manager. She worked mainly at the Kendal office and Joyce was originally my brother Jack's secretary. She came to the firm at the same time that I started as an office junior at Kendal in October 1957.

Long-serving members of staff who worked with us at Windermere include: my first secretary/cashier, Janet Hayton; the late Mrs Dinah Salisbury, cashier; the late Irene Spencer; Mrs Linda Parker (nee Caley); Mrs Barbara Willan, cashier; Mrs Marylyn Helsby; Mrs Christine Sutton and Mrs Kate Ainsworth.

Still with the firm at Windermere are: Myra Huddleston, 29 years; Jean Cowling, 25 years; my daughter, Penny Hayton, 22 years and Zoe Gibson, 15 years.

At the Kendal office: practice manager, Alison Hine, 25 years; Lynne Wharton, 25 years; legal executive, Susie Fisher, 25 years; Judy Walker, 22 years; Emma Irving, 16 years and Tracy King, 14 years.

Many other members of staff have worked for us over the years and I take this opportunity to thank you all. You know who you are and how much I valued your good work for our many clients and for the benefit of the firm and the staff as a whole.

While playing my part in the firm, I was also Secretary of the Westmorland Law Society from 1964 for a few years and later President of the Society in the 1980s.

There followed an interesting six year stint, first as Vice-President and then as President of the North Western Association of Law Societies, which covered the area from Carlisle to South Lancashire,

Figure 2.11. Westmorland Law Society Annual Dinner at Shap Wells Hotel on 5th April, 1984:
Front row, left to right: Recorder John Rowe, Q.C., LH (President of the Westmorland Law Society), Bert Newman (Mayor of Kendal), Sir Christopher Hewetson (National President of The Law Society)
2nd Row: His Honour Judge A. A. Edmondson, Frank Stainton (entertaining Guest Speaker), B. D. K. Price (Chief Constable of Cumbria Police)
Other guests were: District Judge Richard Holloway, Solicitors Rowland Hart-Jackson and Paul Millet, together with representatives of other organisations.

excluding the cities of Manchester and Liverpool.

I enjoyed the work, which involved meetings in London with the leaders in my profession, but I will spare you the full details. I did a survey of the North Western Law Societies to determine the needs of the profession in their areas and of the public they served. Prior to this the representatives from Manchester and Liverpool tended to hold sway but it became clear that the legal practices in the towns and cities in our area had different needs and problems from the Manchester and Liverpool areas.

The North West area needed a clear voice. This culminated in the appointment of a full-time representative for the North West with direct contact with London. The North West representative revitalised us with better communication and channelled information to us and the Law Society effectively. He and his worthy successors also arranged the law courses for continuing professional education in accessible venues around our area. I passed on the results of our feed-back and findings when I gave evidence to the Lady Marr Commission on the future of the legal profession.

In 1996 when Michael Winkley was President of the North Western Association, we organised a delegation, of which I was a member, to visit the EEC headquarters in Brussels on a fact-finding mission. This revealed the shortcomings on the part of British companies in making applications for EEC funding for projects in the UK. We learned from the EEC Commissioners, whom we met, how other member states operated and were more successful. I like to think that we brought

Figure. 2.12. Michael Jackson, John Batty, Gwen Broadbent, Andrew Thornley, Michael Winkley, LH, Edward Smethurst and Andrew Meachin

back some useful knowledge and hints for our members who dealt with such matters. But again a wind of change was blowing and is still blowing. Control of the housing market has moved to the banks and building societies with standard conditions, new fees and financial services systems for providing money. I ask myself: what advantage has been achieved by putting so much control of the housing market in the hands of the money men?

For example, could a client safely buy a property at short notice when finance is needed? Could I safely act on an assurance by telephone from a building society or bank manager today and secure finance for a client one hour before an auction of property is due to take place? Some time ago an existing client had been away and came into the office one hour before an auction. He asked me to bid for him with a written authority. I rang the Building Society Manager in Kendal and secured finance on his reliable word. You may think that was a risk but it was a calculated risk, made on the word of a man in a system one could rely upon.

I walked round to the auction room and examined the searches and title documents before the auction. It was then the practice to have the contract and the search documents ready and available for inspection. I bought the property at the auction, the client signed the contract and we returned to the office soon after the purchase had been secured. The client was a grafter whom I trusted. He went on to build a business employing others. It is much more complicated these days and I would suggest more expensive and unlikely to be achieved in time.

While all my work on Law Society matters was going on, I had to make a living and have time for my family.

As in most walks of life, keeping the balance is not easy. A country lawyer's work involves helping people with a variety of needs and problems at different stages of their lives and sometimes in an emergency. In a true profession a client's interest must come before your own and that ethic, as in many people's callings, creates pressure on family arrangements as well as on staff. Most of the time we achieved the balance at work and home but I now wonder how we managed to achieve all the things we did in the time available.

★   ★   ★

DON'T FORGET THE ENCLOSURES PUELLA★

We all have our little faults! Sometimes I had to make a plea to junior staff who occasionally erred. Here I expressed my concern in verse. It seemed to work!

> If you give me your attention
> I will tell you what I am
> I'm a patient old employer
> All other kinds I sham.
>
> But I really go quite scatty
> About this continuing forget-ful-ness
> The absence of enclosures
> Is becoming quite monotonous!

I've gently said, "Enclosures
Should be listed at the end
And checked before they're sent
Lest we lose another friend."

So perhaps I should express myself
Before your memory gets much worse
And hope a polite reminder
Will be effective expressed in verse.

We all have faults and weaknesses
I surely have my own
I know you have to suffer me
I hear the sigh and groan!

But oh dear fair Puella!
I pray you will take heed
Enclosures are meant to be enclosed
Let this now be your creed.

This note I hope you will receive
With your bonny country smile
And hang it to remind you
On your wall a little while.

You are a super secretary
We must keep this in proportion
I only ask you check much more
And apply a little caution!

*Puella = a maiden in Latin

LH February 1996
With a nod to Gilbert and Sullivan

★   ★   ★

"CONTRACT RACE!
WHAT IS A CONTRACT RACE?"

A charming couple, near retiring age, approached my desk and I greeted the new clients with courtesy and anticipation. Both were smiling from ear to ear: the kind of smile which thinly overlays a desire to jump for joy and pour out a pent-up enthusiasm. They restrained themselves long enough to identify themselves and go through the preliminaries. Then it all came out.

He was a civil engineer and his wife a linguist. They had never really managed to settle anywhere as the job of building roads, bridges and large civil engineering works around the world, had taken them to a variety of countries. "But now we are going to settle in the Lake District. We were both born in Westmorland and we are coming home. We have just agreed to purchase this."

He dropped a glossy estate agent's brochure on my desk. It described a large 'gentleman's house' in fifteen acres of gardens, woodland, out-buildings and all the facilities we lesser mortals might dream of owning. It was a gem. They were justifiably delighted. They were both keen gardeners, ornithologists and lovers of wildlife in our area.

As with all property transactions, big or small, the lawyer needs to take basic steps to protect the clients' interest. So began the questions. There was no house to sell but how was the purchase to be financed? That was easily dealt with. Was it to be bought in joint names and how, as between them, was it to be held? We discussed the description, boundaries, services, access and all the usual matters which have to be checked. We agreed to meet on site when the draft contract was received. Normally it might be expected in about a week from the initial negotiation.

They were not in a hurry to move in. It seemed at that point a straight forward 'run of the mill' job. All appeared normal and we could make progress in a sensible and orderly way. But just as the clients stood up to go, the question came!

"WHAT IS A CONTRACT RACE?" It hit me like a brick in the face. "Why do you ask?" I replied rather abruptly. "Well," spluttered the client, "Is it important?" "Why do you ask?" I repeated.

"Well, it was just the agent said there was a contract race and I wondered what he meant."

I said, "Why didn't you tell me that first?" I suggested that they sit down again. I quickly picked up the phone and spoke to the agent.

"Yes, there is another offer for this property. The seller has been mucked about by a previous prospective buyer. Now there are two more prospective buyers who want it and your client is one. He's not going to choose the wrong one this time. The seller has decided to issue two contracts, one to each prospective buyer. The first to exchange contracts and pay the 10% deposit will get it." So now I knew the seriousness of our position.

We had no contract in hand to sign. This was an unregistered title and searches needed to be done in the Local Authority Charges register and in the Land Charges registers. This process would normally take about two weeks. The property needed to be surveyed. The title or ownership had to be verified.

Fortunately my clients had the money available to buy the property. I did not need to worry about that as I would in some cases. I needed to check the boundaries and services against the plan and the deeds. I needed to check the title and make sure we would be paying the purchase price to the true owner and that we were not buying subject to a mortgage or a prior overriding interest. Being an unregistered title, the deeds would need to be examined and checked carefully. Normally such investigation would take between ten days and a month, depending on whether information is available and on the local authority's response time.

"Who is the seller's solicitor?" I asked . The agent gave me the name of a firm in Cardiff, South Wales! "That's a hell of a way," I thought, but said nothing. My brain was already working on a strategy for the race which was to come. How does the seller's solicitor intend to be fair to both parties? Has he already issued the other contract? Is the contract ready? When will the seller complete? Where is the other party's solicitor?" I shot these questions at the agent over the phone in staccato.

"Well," said the agent, "I believe the solicitor is preparing a contract as we speak and is going to post two copies to each of the two prospective purchasers' solicitors tonight. They will be issued at the same time in the post and the first contract to be signed on the seller's solicitor's desk will get the property. I believe the other solicitor is in Manchester. It's a big firm."

Then the agent started to pull my leg. "You haven't a hope, Len. He got started two days ago on the preliminaries and he's got a head start. They are a big firm. A lile country lad like thee? No chance!"

The agent was well known to me and was enjoying himself. I had often acted the slow country lad approach to my advantage in the past but here he was putting me on my mettle. There was a good commission in it for him and he wanted to see the contract signed. It was a seller's market, but the seller had been put to a lot of trouble by a previous would-be buyer who had said he was a cash buyer – when it was not so.

The clients had listened to this exchange with puzzlement and rising alarm. I put the phone down and appraised them of their position. I rang the firm in Cardiff. It was 10.30 a.m. Yes the contract was being typed. It would be in tonight's post. I asked if he was keeping a copy to make sure he would have one to sign. "Of course," he replied, rather haughtily.

The contract could not be faxed because fax machines had not been invented then. So how was I to do all my searches and get the signed contract on to his desk ahead of our rivals?

While my clients looked on bewildered, I gave instructions to my secretary to prepare the search forms for Keith Wood (my very able articled clerk and trainee solicitor) to attend and make a personal search of the registers at the council office in Kendal. I made the necessary arrangements with the registries to expedite the search. I despatched Keith with instructions to report to me by phone that afternoon.

I gathered the necessary forms of enquiry into my brief case. The clients were warming to the competition and were highly motivated. The property was empty, the previous owner having died. We left the office, attended on site with the sale particulars and plan. We inspected the boundaries, services and appearance of the property. I then despatched an efficient surveyor with instructions to inspect at once and to report on the condition of the house and outside buildings later that day.

I arranged with the seller's solicitor to have a copy of the contract and title available at his office in Cardiff and indicated that my clients would pick it up later in the day, in case the posted copy went astray or did not arrive in time. I did not at that stage say I was accompanying the clients. The solicitor had not heard from our rival. I asked him if he felt obliged to inform our rival's solicitor of my request. He said that all they had undertaken was to issue two contracts in the post at the same time, and whoever signed and exchanged a contract first would be the buyer. It was up to each party how they undertook the race. That seemed fair to me.

I explained my plan to my anxious clients and they readily concurred. We resolved to drive to Cardiff at once.

I shall always remember that drive. I am a bad passenger but the husband drove like a man inspired to win the Formula One world championship! A quiet, competent but determined driver, he had the bit between his teeth. He clearly intended to win that race. For my part I always assume my rival is ahead and the driver had the same thing in mind. If our opposition had the same idea then we knew they had a head start. They would be starting from Manchester while we had started from Windermere.

The clients' car was a large Ford Granada estate and I fancy we were flying most of the way. Certainly we were in Cardiff long before the office closing time with no stops.

We were ushered into the senior partner's empty room, which was the only room available for our use. The senior partner was, we were told, "in the House". He was a Welsh M.P., rather famous for his oratory and colourful clothing.

I sat judge-like in his sumptuous leather chair while my clients and I perused the title deeds. We checked the plan against the deeds, followed the devolution of ownership through the title documents down to the seller and checked that he had a good right to sell. We checked the enforceability of covenants, rights and easements.

We then checked through the contract and its terms, all of which were acceptable. We could not alter any basic terms because that would have been unfair to the other prospective buyer and it would have obliged the seller's solicitor to inform him of the change. That would have given him notice that we were ahead.

I telephoned the surveyor who provided a useful and satisfactory report. Keith telephoned and reported positively on his search enquiries. Only a control of advertisements order (common to most of the Lake District National Park) was revealed by the search. There were no charges in the register. There was nothing risky about the property.

We had been through all the pre-contract enquiries and my clients were eager to get signed up. They signed and we exchanged contracts late that afternoon. With our part of the signed contract in my briefcase we began a relaxed journey home. We had agreed a month to completion so that entry and removal arrangements could be made in an orderly way.

The following day when the Manchester solicitor discovered the property was already sold, his client made an enhanced offer to ours to release the property; but to no avail. Our clients were delighted with their purchase and nothing would have tempted them to sell for a profit.

For years now the house and its surrounding woodland have been not only their home, but also home to the birds, animals and all the creatures of nature which they have encouraged to live in peace and harmony with them.

Shortly afterwards I faced a similar challenge for an hotelier. On that occasion I used a similar action plan and I drove overnight to Wiltshire. I secured the property for him by exchanging contracts when the seller's solicitor opened his office at 8.30 the following morning.

My father's first advice, when seated side by side in my "Kentmere College",* was: "Get up early and get started in a morning." It has stood me in good stead!

So it was that my clients learned by practical experience the nature of a "contract race" when there is competition in a seller's market.

* See my Kent'mer College verse.

CRISIS AT CHRISTMAS
"This injunction threat could put me out of business!" said Smiley

Some years ago Smiley Distributor rushed into my office twelve hours before we were due to close for the Christmas holidays. He had received a High Court Writ claiming damages and an injunction for breach of the copyright/patent in a design. I had to sit up and take notice, Christmas or no Christmas. There was a short time limit to enter an appearance to the Writ. The Plaintiff was a large national corporation with considerable resources and legal clout. There was no time to waste.

Smiley owned a number of wholesale and distribution companies in different parts of the country. They held large stocks of machinery spares for equipment used in the construction and transport industries. The value of the stocks ran into huge figures. Most of the stock was manufactured by Stubborn Strongwill's company. His manufacturing company was the first Defendant named in the Writ. Smiley's companies, as distributors, were the second Defendants.

"Elizabeth, by the grace of God, we command you." These peremptory words, which prefaced the Writ of summons in those days, struck fear in many a defendant.

The Writ claimed an injunction against all the companies to cease manufacturing the spares and to stop distributing them or selling them at once. The Writ also claimed substantial damages. It would be a serious blow to Smiley if the Plaintiff were to succeed in putting a stop to his sales. It would put Smiley out of business and how would he avoid losing the value of his stock? Nevertheless, it seemed to me that Smiley was rather easy-going about it.

"Just thought, Len, I should pass this in front of you. I've talked to Stub Strongwill. He is the managing director of my suppliers and he says there is nothing in this; not to worry. He says I have to send him the Writ and he'll deal with it. What do you think? Stub has been a good friend and reliable supplier for years."

I enquired as to the background and read through the particulars of the claim. The allegation was that Strongwill's company was manufacturing the equipment in breach of the copyright and patents which the Plaintiff owned. The allegation, if true, was serious.

"But Stub say's there's nothing in it and he can prove it. It's his problem and I don't want to get involved with lawyers and legal fees."

I probed the facts a bit longer and felt very uneasy about Smiley's easy-going attitude and his faith in Stub. I could see a real conflict of interest if things went wrong and we did not have the facts.

Copyright and patent cases arise only occasionally in country practice and one cannot be an expert on every area of law. However, this is where the benefit of the two branches of the legal profession works to a client's advantage.

Solicitors in general practice are like doctors in general practice. They are able to examine the facts, diagnose the problem and have access to specialists with particular expertise. I immediately rang my London agent, a solicitor and friend of long standing. I asked him to recommend a firm with the best expertise in copyright and patent law. This turned out to be not only excellent advice but involved an amazing coincidence, as you will learn.

While Smiley nodded approval, I discussed the outline of the problem with the expert London solicitor and got a recommendation from him as to the most able barrister specialising in copyright litigation. I rang the specialist barrister's clerk and retained him. I confirmed the retainer in writing and sent him a copy of the Writ in that evening's post. There were no emails or fax machines then.

Smiley still wanted to let Strongwill deal with it himself in order to avoid legal fees. It emerged that Strongwill had employed a designer from the Plaintiff's company. My antennae were quivering now. I did not like the sound of that.

I advised Smiley that his own company was in direct line of fire. If his supplier was to take on Smiley's defence, I recommended that at the very least he should get an indemnity from the manufacturing company and an agreement to take back the stock at cost if his supplier lost the case. In the event that they failed in defending the action, the indemnity needed to cover Smiley against damages, loss and costs, if that could be negotiated.

Despite my advice Smiley still seemed happy to put his trust in Stubborn Strongwill. I was concerned. I had seen friendships dissolve so often where conflicts of interest arise. It is especially so when it comes to money and one's livelihood.

"At least," I said, "let us arrange a meeting with Stub Strongwill and get to know what has been happening." After some reluctance Smiley agreed to arrange a meeting shortly after Christmas. We agreed that I would travel with him to the manufacturing company's headquarters. We still had time to enter an appearance to the Writ to prevent judgement being entered. We had retained an expert barrister. Christmas carols were being sung and the coloured lights flickering in the street below reminded us it was Christmas.

Smiley clearly intended to enjoy Christmas. He had an instinct for self-preservation which had brought him to me, yet outwardly he preferred to be the cheerful optimist. "Come for a drink, Len," he said. "A new day and a New Year are coming. Have a drink, Len, and stop worrying!" Christmas came and went. We then made an early morning start to see Stub and his co-directors.

We were ushered into an oak-panelled board room by a very shapely personal assistant: a lovely greeting if ever there was one! Belinda showed us to our seats.

There, sitting foursquare on oak captain's chairs around a vast, solid, oak table were the board members of the manufacturing company. All smiled a half smile simultaneously and nodded as if programmed together. It was clearly a 'them and us' situation. That was my clear impression.

At the head of the table, commanding immediate attention, was the Managing Director, whom I took to be Stub Strongwill. His huge, muscular frame rose from his seat, hand outstretched in a gesture of half-greeting and half-reluctance. He had a large cranium, a thick, bull-like neck and he thrust his head forward with a determined expression. He stopped short of leaning forward to shake hands. The half-gesture was all we deserved.

I got the impression he did not like solicitors and particularly one who was not prepared to do as he was told. He was used to being the boss.

I smiled, thanked him for his welcome and came to the point: "Can you tell us the background to this claim? I understand one of your designers once worked for the Plaintiff Company. It would help if I could get the feel of the matter."

"This is a b......waste of time. Thou just let me have Smiley's Writ and we'll deal with it," said Stub.

"But what happens if they win and Smiley can't sell his stock?" I asked.

"That will not happen. There is nothing in their claim. They won't win. Smiley is in no danger and neither is his stock," he said.

"Sorry, I am just a simple country solicitor and as I see it they have issued a Writ against Smiley also. He has to defend that Writ. You have the facts. If you want to handle the case you will need to make us aware of the background." I repeated my observation. "I believe you employ a designer who was previously employed by the Plaintiff. Has he anything to do with this claim?"

"Damn and blast, does thou think I am a fool? Our designs are original designs. He has designed our equipment with our design team. He assures me our design is original. There is no basis for their allegation that he has used his knowledge of their designs to help us.

"I have given him a reet grilling and I am satisfied he is straight; so thou hand over that Writ and git thysel back to Windermere! Thou wants to stick to a country solicitor's work. Thou knows nowt about copyright or patents law."

I could see no employee of his would dare to admit to Stub Strongwill that he was wrong or had been influenced by someone else's design. His insult stung me. I was familiar with the main principles of that field of law but was no expert. I knew enough to protect my Client.

I replied, "I know enough to realise that if there is substance in the detail of this claim that you are facing a real fight. They allege you have copied their design. I'm not going anywhere until I know what has gone on in your design department. If you are so sure of your case, then it is no skin off your nose to give Smiley an indemnity. There could be a hefty claim and it could put you and Smiley out of business. We have to put in an appearance to this Writ and prepare our defence."

"Thou's not gitten any indemnity from me! There's no need for any indemnity. We'll look after Smiley. He's been our customer for years. We look after our customers. There's no need for any indemnity. There is nothing in their claim."

"Well then," I said, "If there is nothing in their claim, there is no harm in giving the indemnity. You are not taking any risk in signing my indemnity if you are sure you are right. As it happens I have prepared an agreement for you to sign. If you want to conduct the whole case and Smiley's defence, then the simplest thing is to sign it. I have a copy of it here. It might be wise to ask your solicitor to look at it first."

"I want no solicitor," said Stub. "I know what an indemnity is. It means I cover the costs and any of Smiley's losses."

I handed it down the table. Stub's face was purple and all eyes were on him. I thought he would explode.

Smiley's face, coloured by years of his favourite whisky, was tense but the makings of a smug smile played around his mouth. He winked at me which I took to be encouragement. He was beginning to see my point. Stub saw the wink. An ugly scowl spread across his face but he spluttered, bit his lip and said nothing. He picked up my draft agreement and began to read.

There was a long silence while Stub read the indemnity.

I broke the silence. "As you will see, all we are saying is that in consideration of our releasing the conduct of Smiley's defence into your care, your company agrees:-

a) To conduct the defence professionally and supply us with copies of all pleadings and documents and correspondence as the case proceeds, so that we may comment if necessary.
b) To take back the stock at cost if they win.
c) To pay all legal costs of both Writs and to cover my firm's costs.
d) To cover the cost of any award for damages against Smiley or his companies.
e) Smiley will not claim damages for loss of profit against your company if you lose but will be happy if you pay for the stock. You will appreciate that if they win...

"They are not going to b...... well win," exploded Stub. "They have no case and we have got a good team to work for us but for your damned interference."

"What do you mean my damned interference?" My hackles were beginning to rise. Smiley was grinning and he seemed to be enjoying the exchanges.

Stub Strongwill exploded and swore at Smiley, accusing him of grinning, winking at me and interfering. I then saw the blood rising up Smiley's neck like the neck of a turkey jock in a mating display. Smiley suddenly realised Stub could turn on him. He saw at last the importance of my advice: the need for the indemnity. He could see it very clearly now.

Smiley addressed Strongwill: "If they have no case Stub, why are you so reluctant to sign? It's a simple agreement. I am not asking you to cover more than the return of stock and the legal costs. You have all the facts. You know your designer man. I'm in your hands."

Stub went ballistic, cursing and swearing. Even his docile board, who until then had watched in silence, began to gesticulate for him to calm down.

"This bugger here," said Stub pointing at me, "has put a retainer on our man. Our London solicitor says we should have our usual top copyright barrister man, and this upstart solicitor from the backwoods at Windermere has put a retainer on our top man. Damn your hide!" he exclaimed, glaring angrily at me.

I looked at Smiley. His anger had subsided. He was grinning from ear to ear. He realised at last that we had given him the right Christmas present. When I had secured the retainer on the specialist Patent and Copyright barrister, I had by sheer coincidence engaged Stub's usual adviser and by chance had got in first.

"Give me a pen, Belinda!" Stub addressed his order to the shapely personal assistant who had ushered us in. She sat at a side table, dutifully taking notes during the meeting. Her face glowed. It was rare that anyone got the better of Stubby Strongwill and she couldn't help enjoying the moment, but in a protective sort of way.

Stub signed his name to the agreement, holding his pen like an iron bar and striking the paper with an angry flourish.

Belinda stood beside Stubby and leaned over him as she witnessed his signature. Her long nylon-covered legs were topped by a neat mini skirt. Her presence seemed to calm and mellow him. Having made the decision, his anger dissipated. I noticed Belinda sway slightly against him. She certainly had a calming influence. She smiled at Smiley and the board and looking sheepishly at me, she added, "I'll just make a photocopy." The board members nodded their assent to Belinda without saying anything. None of them had contributed a word to the proceedings.

Each of them nodded farewell but said nothing as Smiley and I took our leave. Stub, having recovered his composure, smiled engagingly and came out of the board room with us. He shook our hands in a most gentlemanly fashion, assuring us all the time that the Plaintiff had no case.

"Safe journey home," he said as we parted company. I wondered if he meant it!

Thereafter the case dragged on with procedures and negotiations through the High Court for almost two years, while the parties to the dispute argued in pleadings and in correspondence. It became clear that the former employee of the Plaintiff Company, who had subsequently worked for Stub's company, had indeed used the knowledge he had gained with the Plaintiff in designing the components for Stub.

Finally, Stubborn Strongwill's company had to compromise. Thus Stub had to cover my Client and indemnify him. Much of Smiley's stock, affected by the disputed copyright design, had to be returned at Stub's expense.

Our emergency action at Christmas had been successful in the end. The Indemnity Agreement had proved its worth and had also given Smiley time to re-source materials and protect his own businesses.

I wondered what crisis would happen next Christmas!

IF

A Sixtieth Birthday Leg-pull by Jean Cowling
5th April, 2000 – Pip Pip!

If you can lose your files while all around are finding theirs
In places occupied by you;
If you can trust yourself when secretaries flout you
And make allowances for their sulking too;
If you can watch your weight although you're tired of dieting
And eat at Renoir's, meet with countless friends;
If you can drive a Jag, a bike and Penny Farthing
And know all about the geometry of bends;

If you've got a laptop that is hard to master,
If you can drink and still not spoil your aim;
If you can meet with Jean and Marilyn
And treat those two imposters just the same;
If you can rise at dawn and not be shirty,
Start dictating ere your legs have reached the floor
And often phone us up at seven thirty
To see what joys the diary holds in store;

If you can make one heap of all your earnings
And risk it all upon a new extension
That grows and grows but fulfils all your yearnings
With rooms and views that are all your own invention;
If you've got heart and nerve, when even in a tizzy,
To whom all turn when life is just a bummer,
And always want to know with what we're busy (!)
And buy ice creams for all of us in summer;

If you can talk in dialect, write verse and funny stories
That hold us all in sway;
If you like cows and selling cattle semen
And wonder where your in-tray is today;
If you can please the unforgiving Kendal
And fill your time sheets each and every one,
Yours is Hayton Winkley and all that's in it;
And, which is more, you'll be **LEN** my son.

Figure 2.13. Andrew Bromley, Patricia Sanderson, LH and Keith Wood, partners in the Windermere firm of HWBW (2000) with our visiting ex-partner, Judge J. Anthony James in my garden at Quarry Foot, Levens

THE WESTMORLAND COUNTY SHOW
The Option Agreement and Twenty Years on

Although much of my work is normally confidential, this story had a lot of publicity at the time. It is also mentioned in Roger Bingham's "History of the Westmorland County Show".

In 1989 I was approached by John Geldard with a request to meet the officers of the Westmorland County Agricultural Society to give advice on the form of an option agreement which they had received from a development company wanting to secure a site for a client. Their client was Morrisons, who were looking for a place to build their supermarket in Kendal. At the time it was a controversial issue among the members of the Society: between those who wanted to sell and move the show-field and those who wanted the show to stay in Kendal. The controversy was reflected in the local politics of the time.

Roger Bingham, in his excellent bi-centenary history of the Society from 1799 to 1999, "*From Fell & Field*", between pages 138 to 143, records the background situation: problems of rising numbers at the shows, diminishing car parking areas, congestion in the town, creeping development, which would have destroyed our car parking etc.

My task was to look at the draft option arrangement under discussion. I remember explaining at the time that I always view draft option agreements with the utmost caution! Signing one is like getting on a train and having to go where the driver takes you - I like an option to get off the train if the journey does not prove to my liking. That was the principle I adopted in 1989.

My new society client was represented by some very shrewd and sensible men, well experienced in the way the show was run and the needs of the Society. As I worked with them I grew to respect them very much.

I had also worked with John Geldard in my office over the previous 4 years, when he was chairman of the Poll Charolais Cattle Society, which I ran as Secretary from there. The Chairman and Officers of the Westmorland Agricultural Society were forward thinking and well aware that if they missed the opportunity to move, possible development on the fields used for car parking could severely restrict the future of the County Show. It was a worry at the time.

I like to get "the feel of a matter" before giving my advice and settling on a course of action. Chis Lambert, the Society's very able and experienced Secretary, Fred Martin, the Chairman, and Henry Willison, Vice Chairman, Brian Ellis, Tony Duckett, John Geldard and members of the Management Committee all gave me a comprehensive analysis of the relevant facts, issues and aims of the Society.

It was clear to me that the Society needed to set out in a schedule to the option agreement a specification for any new show-field and list all our priorities: the access, car parking requirements, suitability of the ground, grandstand, toilet facilities, services, limited planning conditions and many other requirements.

Importantly, I also negotiated a "get out" clause if the developer could not meet the specification, because we did not wish to be left without a show-field upon which to hold the show. We also retained the right to do our own survey of possible sites within a suitable radius from Kendal. We did a feasibility study on seven possible sites but none were ideal and all had snags.

We hired a plane on the County Show Day to obtain aerial pictures of the show at Kendal. Peter Thornton, who had his photography business in Kendal and is now a local councillor, did the aerial photography. I flew with him and we got some good pictures which clearly showed the traffic congestion in Kendal, the fields full of cars and the show-ground itself packed. We also took pictures of the others sites in my feasibility study on the same day; we flew back to Blackpool airport and returned to the show. It was useful evidence and an interesting day.

As the Society had not settled on a particular site, the developers were getting impatient and negotiated their own options for a show-field on land at Endmoor, south of Kendal. There were some problems with the site but they were convinced they could provide all the requirements in our specification schedule, so the Society went along with their efforts.

The application to the planners at South Lakeland Council for a new show-field at Endmoor was turned down and an appeal was lodged. The planners wanted conditions not really acceptable to the Society, which would add costs to the specification. There was strong opposition from many Endmoor residents and the surrounding district.

The developers paid for the appeal as our option agreement put all such burdens on them. The preparation for the appeal required that a full costing of providing the facilities had to be done. There was a public hearing of the appeal but the proposed development was turned down by the Inspector. The developers had to go back to the drawing board. The Society's right to terminate the option agreement could have been exercised at that time but it was decided to look for another site and let the Society's right to terminate run on. We had purposely made the Society's right flexible in our negotiation.

We looked at other sites already included in the feasibility study but then "out of the blue" the present site at Lane Farm, Crooklands, in the parish of Preston Patrick, was offered to the Society. Lane Farm, together with other land which we negotiated to buy next to it, was the best site we had found. There were issues about access but the Society believed they could be overcome, which has proved to be the case.

Rather than go for a full-scale, new show-field application with all the scheduled facilities, it was decided to proceed step by step with planning for roads, services and necessities and let the development evolve as the Society gained experience and knowledge of the best way to run the new site.

Because the Society had the right to withdraw from the Kendal site option and the developer was under pressure to make progress at Kendal, the developer agreed to pay an additional sum over and above the original option price. The additional sum was based on the equivalent to what they would have had to pay at Endmoor to provide our scheduled facilities. This, in effect, with the costs involved more than doubled their original option purchase price and provided useful capital for the Society.

It is gratifying to know that along with Chris, Fred, Henry, Brian, Tony, John and all who were instrumental at the time, I played a part in putting the Society on a sound footing when the show-field moved to Lane Farm in 1991.

Nevertheless we should always remember that without the negotiation by Alan Thompson, who was the Westmorland County Show Secretary from 1949 to 1964, and his colleagues at the time when they very sensibly bought the Kendal site, we would not have been able to realise the development value in the Kendal show-field.

Sensibly, the Society's Planning and Development sub-committee organised a tour of other show grounds and over a long period we gleaned information about the experience of others in developing show ground facilities. We noted that in some cases the show ground trustees had taken on long-term commitments, which obliged members to be constantly running what amounted to a trade, with all the complications that arise under charity law as a result.

Rather than spend millions and get into debt with on-going commitments, which would become a long-term burden on our Charity Trustees and members, the Planning and Development Committee recommended a policy of more gradual development. Thus the show-field has been and is being improved each year.

Though the move from Kendal was controversial at the time, it has brought substantial benefits, namely:

a) The financial stability which flowed from the move has enabled the Society to employ full and part-time staff throughout the year, not only to produce and organise the show but to widen the scope of the Society's work for the community.

b) Everyday management of its affairs, including an income stream from grazing rentals when available through the year, promoting and managing the lettings of the function rooms, which are very popular and well located, as well as taking proper investment advice on the Society's assets.

c) The provision of a computer training centre at Lane Farm where tuition with courses in accounting for farming families and local

Figure 2.14. **Management Committee – 13 January 2011**

Front Row: O Clarke; S Procter; C Knipe; J Mason; J Buckley; J Dewhurst; J Park; D Galbraith; J Geldard

2nd Row: C Hodgson; J Clark; L Bennett; R Rigg; B Ellis; J Dixon; D Galbraith; I Grisedale; B Bond; B Clarke; B Gorst

3rd Row: C Postlethwaite; D Martin; P Duckett; P Gibson; C Briggs; N Dowker; A Duckett; B Willison; H Robinson; T Gorst; T Mason; R Sedgwick

4th Row: A Pratt; G Capstick; P Broomby; T Wilson; D Knipe; G Robinson; J Barton; G Procter: R Taylor; C Wildman; B Barnes

Back Row: R Waller; S Lambert; N Buckley; A Smith; J Dickinson; J Bennett; J Garnett; C Geldard; J Alexander; S Rayner

Not Pictured: H Barnes; J Bland; W Case; C Davies; C Dennison; D Fell; R Gardiner; C Gibson; L Hayton; M Johnson; D Knowles; D Lawrence; F Martin; C Mason; R Mason; R Park; M Robinson; Harold Robinson; N Sharp; J Stott Jnr; J Todd; G Wadsworth; C Whittaker; H Willison; A Nicholson; E Lord; I Taylor

businesses takes place. The centre is open to anyone to join the classes. One to one training can also be arranged.

d) The provision of practical training courses run at Lane Farm: for example, tractor driving, trailer handling, machinery handling, etc.

e) Specialist training in the use of chainsaws, sprays and pesticides etc.

f) Courses on understanding new government regulations: for example, the regulations governing the transport of live animals.

g) The development of the very successful "Rural Links" programme which inter alia arranges farm open days for children from town and village schools to visit the farms.

h) The establishment of the Chris Lambert Bursary in his memory and in recognition of his excellent work as Secretary of the Society for over 26 years. The bursary usually sponsors two people, drawn mostly from the Young Farmers' Clubs, to attend the Oxford Farming Conference (OFC). It is also possible for farmers who fit the criteria to apply. The OFC is held annually in early January. It is a conference which attracts national and international speakers, leaders in agriculture, as well as political leaders from abroad, government ministers, industrial leaders and scientists on global warming, food security and alternative forms of energy production. It always has papers from practical and resourceful farmers who have made a success of their business and are invited to share their experience. The delegates usually return inspired and well pleased with the experience.

i) Roger Read, who succeeded Chris Lambert, and Christine Knipe, our Chief Executive, have been able to take the Society forward on a full-time basis, developing the show facilities and pioneering new ideas. They have developed improved methods of communication with the public on behalf of our farming and our wider community. Christine and her staff at Lane Farm are an enthusiastic and dedicated team who are recognised nationwide for producing one of the best "One Day Shows" in the UK.

3

IN CELEBRATION OF
OUR FAMILY YEARS

THE GROWING YEARS 1964 TO 1990

By the end of 1970 our family had grown in number to six with the births of Martin in 1967, Peter in 1969 and Penny in 1970. Kentmere School had been closed in 1958*, so our children were transported in the school bus, driven by my brother, Gerard, to Staveley Church of England Primary School. When each of our children reached eleven they attended the Lakes School at Troutbeck Bridge, again transported by Gerard to Staveley, then by public transport to the Lakes School. We attended the parents' evenings and gave support where we could. I was a governor of the Lakes School as well as chairman of the governors for a few years. It was an enlightening and productive experience.

Figure 3.1. Our children watching the photographer's bubbles
Front row: Penny and Peter
2nd row: Ingrid, Martin and Jacqueline
with Nicholas standing behind

Sadly, my brother Jack became ill in 1967 with cancer and died in December of that year. He had been my mentor and guide. Cures for cancer were not so advanced as today and we spent a lot of time looking for ways to help, but in vain. So 1967 was a difficult year both in the office, helping to cover Jack's

---

*As to the closure of Kentmere School, my friend, Jeff Walker, a first class joiner and craftsman, who still lives in Kentmere, provided me with the picture of the last pupils taught there. See figure 3.2.

work, and with the aftermath of his death. The needs of our family at such a time and the needs of clients are sometimes incompatible. The professional ethic, which often requires us to put the clients' interest first, could lead to frustration for both my family and me.

Figure 3.2. Pupils in the final year of Kentmere Church of England School:
Front row, left to right: Jan Coles, Richard Coles, Jeff Walker and Kath Marshall
2nd Row: Nicholas Pighills, Maurice Cousins, Annis Leyland and Philippa Wrathall

Still demand for our services grew and the following years saw the partnership of Hayton Winkley expand to a three town practice with seven partners, assistant solicitors and a wonderful support staff of around forty in number.

Before advertising was allowed, clients came by recommendation and our practice grew steadily. We were lucky in getting Tony James to join us as an assistant in 1971 and as partner from 1973, which enabled us to open an office in Ambleside. The practice continued to grow and we took on more partners: Malcolm Whiteside, Andrew Bromley, Peter Briggs, John Oldroyd, Keith Wood and Naomi Fell, all capable in their areas of law. Solving people's problems and helping others in commerce meant, as in all walks of life, that we needed recreation to occupy and clear the mind.

Michael and Tony's recreations were golf, Round Table and Rotary. Tony was also a hockey referee. My interests outside the practice were Round Table, hobby farming, bird watching, motor cycling and my old car. We all had varied fields of interest and even our hobbies brought new contacts and new clients.

However, this is not a history of Hayton Winkley but a summary of the background in those years. My work in the firm underpinned what we as a family were able to do.

Islay became our place for family holidays in the summer and we had lots of jolly times there. In spring and autumn it was my opportunity to step off the world for a long weekend on Islay with my chums. Between bird watching, walking and beachcombing we used to cut peats for the fire on our spring visits. We laid them out to dry, "dessed" them up at the beginning of the summer holiday and carted them down from the moor in autumn. The glow of a peat fire and the peat smell in the evening air were lovely.

This section is a celebration of those family years, a hop, skip and jump through the period, picking up some of the events and areas of interest as we progress. Many friends have helped us along the way, too many to mention by name but their contribution to what was mainly "The Good Life" is much appreciated. You know who you are.

★   ★   ★

Building our home and raising our children, Round Table years, building the practice, hobby farming, goats, visits to Islay, Kentmere Tarn, historical snippets, verses and stories

★   ★   ★

Becoming an equity partner, opening a new office in Windermere, getting married and starting a family in 1964 was a tall order and meant that we had to get cracking. Happily, my brothers and our families, as well as good friends, were in full support and I seemed to have boundless energy in those halcyon days. My father's first lesson – "Get up in a morning" – helped and 5 a.m. was my getting up time and still is.

Sandra and I began married life by living in a caravan in the garden at Pumple Syke. As already stated, the bungalow was built manually by my brothers, Gerard and Jack, and me in 1959/60 as a home for our parents and myself. Sandra started a garden at Pumple Syke and grew fresh vegetables and flowers. She really seemed to have green fingers. The children enjoyed the freedom with plenty of space in the garden and field to play. When Nicholas, Jacqueline and Ingrid were small, my parents enjoyed having them nearby, as the next three pictures show.

By the time our daughter, Penny, was born in October 1970, we had built and extended Pumple Syke three times. My brother, Jack, assisted us before his untimely death, and he gave a great deal of encouragement and of his time when we built our first extension. With the help of friends in the building trade we were soon able to move from the caravan into our new home.

The bungalow was given the unusual name of Pumple Syke because

Figure 3.3. My mother and father with Jackie and Ingrid

Figure 3.4. Jackie looking cute with Nick   Figure 3.5. Sandra with Jackie and Nick

my grandfather always referred to the stretch of road from Low Bridge House to the bottom of Church Hill as the "Pumple Syke" (his pronunciation of Pinfald Syke). The Kentmere village pound was situated just outside the gate to Pumple Syke. It was a boggy place with a stream flowing through, which never seemed to dry up, even in a drought.

The stages of building Pumple Syke

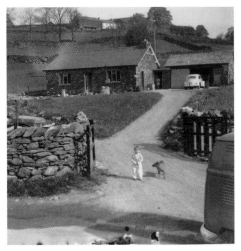

Figure 3.6. Nicholas and Cammy, the dog, at the gate to Pumple Syke before the building of the extension started

Figure 3.7. My brother, Jack, at work on the building site at Pumple Syke

Figure 3.8. Our son, Nicholas, and my nephew, Edwin, helping to carry bricks

Figure 3.9. The extension ready for roofing before winter, 1964

Pumple or Pumfald was my grandfather's pronunciation of Pinfald, the Westmorland spelling of the name for a village pound, where stray cattle or sheep were penned until the owner recovered them. A syke means a small stream or a wet or hollow area. In fact this stream was the place where my family had watered our cattle from Brow Top for generations. Our water supply at Brow Top came from a well which my father dug on Bell Hill behind the farm in the 1920s. In the winter or during a drought, when the cows were inside and the water ran out in the well, we sometimes had to carry water 250 yards uphill from a spring near Rawe Cottage. When I was growing up, if there was a drought, I used to take the cows to water in the stream at Pumple Syke. My father always told me that Brow Top Farm had the ancient right to water cattle in the stream there.

I was informed by Granny and Father that in his last years my grandfather used to stand outside at Brow Top and watch for the milk cows coming from his fields at Cross Howe and Low Meadow. When they got to Low Bridge, he would shout: "T'coos er cummen alang t'Pumple Syke! Yer mun be gitten milken tackle ruddy!"

When my parents and I moved to Pumple Syke, my brother, Gerard, and his wife, Alice, took over Brow Top Farm in 1960. Before that they lived at Pout Howe, Hallowbank in Kentmere following their marriage.

With the business expenditure of opening the Windermere office and building our home, holiday costs had to be carefully budgeted. So we bought a second-hand Sprite Musketeer caravan. I got to work making more bunk bed space inside for the children. That enabled us to visit our friends, Martyn and Pam Wrathall, in Argyll. Martyn, who has been my pal ever since we met at Kentmere School 66 years ago, had by then done his practical farming apprenticeship with Ken Dawson at Hartrigg in Kentmere and Frank Salkeld at High Fold. He got his degree at Durham (where he met his wife, Pam) and then secured a post as an adviser with the Scottish Agriculture College.

Martyn was based at Campbeltown on the Mull of Kintyre and lived with Pam in a lovely cottage on Ardnacross Bay. It was there in a field on the edge of the sea that we took the children for our caravan holidays. One year we went to the

Figure 3.10. Caravan holiday at Ardnacross Bay

Isle of Arran with the children and stayed in the caravan at Glen Rosa. Thus began a lifelong love of Scotland. At that time there were a number of old dwellings standing in ruins on the Kintyre peninsula. I thought we might try to buy one to restore it and I placed an advertisement in the Oban Times. It became clear that we could not afford the prices on the mainland but I received a postcard picturing Portnahaven on the tip of the Rhinns of Islay. On the card was a large arrow pointing to a cottage on the edge of the harbour. Thus began a love of Islay which I shall describe later in these pages.

Meantime I had joined the Windermere, Ambleside and District Round Table (WADRT) and Sandra later joined the Ladies Circle. After our home was completed, Sandra had more time, my mother was happy to babysit and Sandra was able to take a more active part in the Ladies Circle. We also had help from Sandra's family from time to time. She became Chairwoman

Figure 3.11. Martyn and Pam Wrathall with Sandra, Nick and Jackie at Ardnacross.

of the Ladies Circle in 1978/9, the same year that our friend, Bill Bewley, became Chairman of the WADRT. The Round Table and Ladies Circle brought us new friends, many of whom have remained friends ever since. A sketch of my early years in the Round Table follows.

Sandra and I had a succession of golden retrievers for the children. They were gentle, good-natured dogs and they were all called "Amber". (See Figure 3.12 colour section)

Figure 3.11b. Sandra with Peter, Penny on her knee, Martin and Amber our family dog

FUN, FELLOWSHIP AND SERVICE
IN ROUND TABLE

Early years, the Marchesi Centre, a Penny Farthing Ride and a Deep Sea Rescue

I was invited to join the Windermere, Ambleside and District Round Table after having attended the requisite three meetings as a guest of my proposer. In the Table Year 1963-64 when Ted Rothwell, a director of Windermere Lake Holidays Afloat, was Chairman, he inducted me into the Table.

On my prior visits to the Table meetings I had been impressed with the energy and fellowship of the members, both in the social and in the energetic community service activities in which they were engaged.

Figure 3.13. Sketch of the proposed Marchesi Centre in Windermere, our most challenging and successful project

The aims and objects of the Round Table movement are:

1. To develop the acquaintance of young men through the medium of their various occupations.
2. To emphasise the fact that one's calling offers an excellent medium of service to the community.
3. To cultivate the highest ideals in business, professional and civic traditions.
4. To recognise the worthiness of all legitimate occupations and to dignify, each his own, by precept and example.
5. To further the establishment of peace and goodwill in international relationships.
6. To further these objects by meetings, lectures, discussions and other activities.

I also found the Round Table Grace inspiring as it expresses succinctly the ideals which one tries to live up to.

THE ROUND TABLE GRACE

May we O Lord adopt thy creed,

Adapt our ways to serve thy need,

And we who on thy bounty feed,

Improve in thought and word and deed.

WINDERMERE AMBLESIDE & DISTRICT ROUND TABLE No. 584.

The first Round Table, No. 1, was formed in Norwich on the 25th May 1928 and Louis Marchesi is acknowledged as the founder. He was a member of Norwich Rotary Club and perceived a need for an organisation of young men between 18 and 40 years of age. The age limit was 40 during my years in table but is now 45. The Windermere, Ambleside and District Round Table (WADRT) was the 584th Table to be formed. It was sponsored by Kendal Round Table and received its Charter Presentation in 1958.

The members are drawn from all walks of life and in my time no more than two of the same profession or calling could join a Table.

Members came from all walks of life but had to retire at 40 unless they were given an honorary year. Ex-members usually joined the 41 Club, which is a club for ex-Tablers.

Thus began a very happy experience, making new friends and getting involved in all sorts of projects with like-minded, young business and professional men. We were not just a social club, we did things to raise funds, assist with projects and help needy folk in the community. We collected items and raised funds to provide Christmas parcels, which we distributed during the festive season. We also arranged a Christmas party for the elderly and the housebound, providing the necessary transport and the entertainment. People asked for our help and we had fun and fellowship doing so.

Figure 3.14. Members of WADRT, Christmas 1974 preparing the Christmas parcels
Front row, left to right: John Wood, Bill Bewley, Mike Dawson, LH and Derek Tebay
Back rows, left to right: Tony Sansom, Jim Holden, David Wood, Jim Nelson, Tony Lowe, Tony James, Colin Tyson, Ron Perrygrove, Mike Hynes, Keith Taylor, John Sergeant, Neil Harris, Alec Edmundson, Mike Holt and Bill Jackson
A full list of the WADRT chairmen and the membership list in 1974/5 when LH was chairman appear in the appendix.

Most of our wives joined the Ladies Circle. As well as following their own pursuits in the community, the members of the Ladies Circle were always helpful and encouraging and supported us where need be.

Among many projects we built a Wishing Well in Bowness-on-Windermere, which provided a regular income for the Community Service Committee to allocate. We had a members' rota to empty it each night and count the cash – it was a chore but worthwhile because all the money was used to help needy folk or projects of benefit in the area.

When several houses beside the River Gowan in Staveley were flooded, we dredged the river from the confluence with the Kent opposite the Eagle and Child pub up towards Reston, allowing time for the fish and crayfish to move upstream. It certainly cured the flooding but I doubt if the authorities today would allow us to do such a project! We had members who owned wagons, diggers and other useful equipment. We also got into the beck ourselves with shovels and tools to help the process. We learned to work together as an effective team.

Above all we learned to respect the skills and strengths of each other and discovered how working together with good fellowship and enthusiasm could achieve amazing results. Between us we had wide resources of expertise and equipment to draw on.

Although I was at the time appearing in Court and learning skills in advocacy, I still felt embarrassed when I had to stand up and speak in meetings. Advocacy was quite different. One has the facts of a case, the issues of law at hand and the focus. I had been on an advocacy training course but I was still shy and avoided having to speak in public.

Unfortunately I had not been in a Young Farmers' Club where speaking competitions were held, nor had I been taught the skills of public speaking from an early age. I did not have confidence so I tended to feel inadequate. My joining Round Table was a great help in overcoming the natural shyness which I seem to have inherited from my mother. She was lovely, capable and amusing. Mother was all one could wish for in a parent but she preferred being in the background doing practical things. I felt the same.

Then came an experience which galvanised me into action. On the 20th May 1965 my Round Table friend, Gordon Atkinson, and I attended the Lancaster Round Table Charter night at Lancaster Golf Club. It was expected that members from neighbouring Tables would send delegates to such events and we were the representatives of the WADRT on this occasion.

On arrival we found that the guest speaker had given back-word at the last minute and our hosts in the course of the evening announced that, in place of the speaker, each Table should nominate a representative from their Round Table to tell a funny story of some kind – in good taste, of course! Gordon flatly refused because he said he did not tell jokes and anyway I was a solicitor, so I must be able to stand up and speak. I knew no jokes either and I had never spoken to an audience. There were at least 150 people there! In desperation I asked my pal, Reg Ashworth, who was then in the Lancaster Table, to tell me a joke which I tried to memorise.

When it came to my turn, I stood up and related the opening of the joke, then promptly forgot the punch-line. I heard a mighty roar of laughter but it was not the joke at which the audience was laughing! Thus I did not become a teller of jokes but started to put my experiences into rhyme. That way I could remember them better and, when recited in my form of dialect, it seemed to amuse a gathering.

★   ★   ★

BUILDING THE MARCHESI CENTRE

Our most ambitious community service project was the raising of the funds to build the "Windermere Old People's Community Centre". It is now named "The Marchesi Centre" in honour of the founder of the Round Table movement.

In June 1967 when Geoff Robson was our Vice-Chairman and also at the time the Treasurer of Windermere Urban District Council, he brought to our notice a report from the Medical Officer of Health for the County of Westmorland. The report drew attention to the problem of loneliness for a growing number of people of pensionable age. There were 700 people in Windermere over the age of 65 who were living alone or were otherwise in need. A total of 28% of the population was over the age of 65.

In August the same year we formed a small working party to examine the possibility of building an up-to-date meeting place for the over 60s, which could meet the needs of the various activity clubs in Windermere. The W.R.V.S. meals-on-wheels service would also be based there. We concluded that such a centre was needed and the Table decided, after a very short debate, to embark on the project. The projected cost first suggested was £12,000, but with all the various needs and expenses it finally came to nearly £20,000 including the furnishings.

We had an initial donation of £2000 promised from a lady who wished to remain anonymous, but when it arrived she actually gave us £5000. This gave us an enormous boost to start. Her enthusiastic support of our Table arose, unknown to us at the time, because we had made a grant from our Wishing Well fund to a charity with which she was deeply concerned and to which we had given practical help in the past.

We had an enjoyable time raising the funds for the Centre over the next three years. We began with a Spring Fair, contributions from our Wishing Well at Bowness and a 200 Club, all of which proved very profitable each year. The Social Committee had a "Blackpool-night" type of entertainment evening and a "Roaring Twenties" dance, all to raise funds.

The Community Service Committee had major fundraising events over the following three years. These included Gala Weeks in 1968 and 1969, a Donkey Derby held at the Rugby Club and a Sponsored Walk in 1970. We had sales of surplus bric-a-brac, a concert, a Gilbert and Sullivan evening, a Caribbean dance, a wine and cheese evening and a Flag Day.

In addition I served on the project finance sub-committee with Colin Tyson and John Curtis. After negotiating with the Windermere Urban District Council, we obtained a 99-year lease on a site in the gardens of Ashleigh at a peppercorn rent. Our anonymous donor made suggestions as to who to approach and gave further support as the building progressed.

We also arranged a special loan with the directors of the Bradford and Bingley Building Society at their head office in Bingley to cover any shortfall if, when the building was complete, we should not have raised sufficient funds to pay the builder. In the event the loan was never needed but it was a safeguard when we, the Trustees, signed the building contract on behalf of our Table.

At the same time we drafted a constitution which was approved by the Charity Commission and adopted at a meeting of the members of the W.A.D.R.T. on the 31st January 1969. The original members of the Charity comprised all the 30 members of the WADRT. The four original Trustees appointed to hold the land were John Curtis, who was Chairman at the time, myself as Secretary of the Charity, with Colin Tyson and Tom Gorst as the joint Treasurers. We then registered the constitution with the Charity Commissioners. The Centre was to be used by people over 60 years of age who lived within the urban

THE WESTMORLAND GAZETTE, MAY 15, 1970

WALKERS leaving Ashleigh, Windermere, at the start of a 20-mile sponsored walk on Sunday, the proceeds of which will go towards the Windermere, Ambleside and District Round Table Old Folk's Community Centre Appeal. Below, members of the Round Table, in front of the partially completed centre. About £14,000 has now been raised towards the target of £20,000.

Sponsored walk raises £500 for old people's centre

A sponsored walk, organised by the Windermere, Ambleside and District Round Table on Sunday, raised £500 for the Old People's Community Centre.

In the region of £14,000 has now been raised for the Centre, towards the target of £20,000. It is hoped that the Centre will be finished by August.

Approximately 50 people took part in the walk which was a 20-mile circular route around Crook and Winster. Two members of the Windermere and Bowness Old Folk's Club, Mrs Pearson and Miss E. Wilson, took part and the youngest to complete the course was nine-year-old Timothy Youdell.

Figure 3.15. Report from the Westmorland Gazette, 15th May 1970
Top: Sponsored walkers setting off on the 20-mile walk
Bottom: Windermere, Ambleside and District Round Tablers outside the building of the Marchesi Centre with a poster advertising the fundraising appeal target of £20,000, left to right: ? , John Curtis, ?, ?, LH, Tony Lowe, Bob Pennington, Keith Taylor, Derek Clark, Neil Harris, Peter Dover, Gordon Atkinson, ?, ?,

district of Windermere, but the age range has now been extended to the over-50s.

While we in the Round Table were raising the funds, we recognised that a Management Committee to represent the likely users needed to be formed. We therefore invited Mrs Elsie Robinson, the widow of the late Roland Robinson, former Deputy-head of Windermere Grammar School, to chair the Committee and agree a programme with the users for the running of the Centre.

Over the three years 1967/68 and 69/70, the WADRT raised £6246 through Round Table activities, galas and fun days. We went personally to see potential private donors and grant-making trusts and raised £8,800 by this means. We had, in the main, enthusiastic support and as a result received donations which, with the interest on our accumulating deposits, raised a further £3000, bringing the total to £19,046 by the end of 1971.

Originally, as I recollect, the organisations which came together and were represented on the Management Committee included among others the old folk's club, dance club, bridge club, chess club, art club, Scottish country dancing, whist and dominoes clubs. The Centre was also equipped and used as the distribution centre for Meals-on-Wheels.

An Open Day was held on Tuesday, 9th February 1971, when the Windermere Old People's Community Centre, as it was then called, was completed and ready for use. The day proved a great success and it was announced that the Centre would be open on Mondays, Wednesdays and Thursdays each week commencing the following day, 10th February 1971.

It was decided to rename the Charity the Marchesi Centre in honour of the founder of the Round Table, Louis Marchesi, who had died in 1969.

The official opening of the Marchesi Centre took place the following year on the 14th February 1972. It was opened by Mr Paul Perry, President of the World Council of Young Men's Service Clubs, who handed the keys to Mrs Elsie Robinson, Chairman of the Management Committee, and unveiled a plaque, carved by one of our members, Brian Johnson, to mark the occasion.

We also received a national award for the National Table of the

A top-award project

The Windermere, Ambleside and District Round Table has been presented with a national award, for the Marchesi Centre at Windermere.

The award is presented by the East Kilbride Round Table, usually annually, to the Round Table which has distinguished itself during the year in some form of community service. In previous years it has been given to the Merthyr Tydfil Round Table for their work for the Aberfan Disaster Fund, and to Leicestershire Round Table for their fund raising efforts for victims of the Yugoslavia earthquake.

The award was presented to the Windermere, Ambleside and District Round Table at their meeting at Ambleside on Friday evening. Mr T. Todd, chairman of the East Kilbride Table made the presentation and Mr B. Pennington received it on behalf of the Windermere, Ambleside and District Table.

Year: *A Top Award Project from East Kilbride Round Table.*

Since its opening the Marchesi Centre has flourished and it became necessary to extend the building, first with the Cecil Reed Room and later with the Millennium Lounge. The latter was opened by the Lord Lieutenant of Westmorland, Sir James Cropper.

★   ★   ★

During my years in the Round Table and Sandra's years in the Ladies Circle we enjoyed a great deal of fun, not only at social events, but also when raising funds and doing practical things together.

In 1973 I offered to ride my "Ordinary Bicycle," more commonly known as a Penny Farthing (made circa 1860s), from Bowness Pier to Ambleside Pier at Waterhead – the distance was five miles. That summer at weekends we sold a large number of tickets for people to guess the time it would take. I did demonstration runs around the Glebe car park and the tennis courts at Bowness. The reaction from the public was hilarious. The guesses ranged from 20 minutes to 17 hours! Some no doubt were joking but thought because of the age of the machine it would take a very long time. After each demonstration we sold more tickets and the guessers would return to revise their estimates and buy more tickets!

Figure 3.16. Ticket for guessing the time taken for the Penny Farthing ride

When it came to the Saturday for the Penny Farthing ride, it happened that I had been up all the previous night. I had been asked by friends to act as a liaison for the wife of my friend, Roger Mallinson, who with Roger Chapman, was stranded 1575 feet below the Atlantic Ocean 150 miles off the coast of southern Ireland.

The two Rogers, sub-mariner engineers, had been laying a telephone cable under the sea, when the Pisces III mini-submersible in which they were working became entangled with the towing cable attached to the mother surface ship. This damaged the back end of the submersible, which filled with water, but the crew's quarters remained sealed. The mini-sub sank to the bottom of the sea. The accident occurred on the Wednesday lunchtime but the search party did not locate the submersible on the sea bed until the Friday. By then this terrifying drama had become of national and international interest. The operating company, Vickers Oceanics at Barrow-in-Furness, needed time to organise a rescue and it was known that the oxygen supply was limited. Fortunately the two Rogers were able to communicate with the surface ship, which helped their morale, but they had to conserve their energy and ration the oxygen.

On the Friday afternoon I received a call from my friend in Round Table, Tony Lowe, our local jeweller, who was concerned about the harassment of the Mallinson family by the press and cameramen surrounding their home in Windermere. He had managed to help them escape the pursuit of the press by taking them on a circuitous route down country lanes and had hidden the family in his own home. I was asked to join them to deal with the communications between the Vickers Oceanics' representatives and the Mallinson family. Because the media at one stage were speculating and giving information on the television and in the newspapers which was inconsistent with the information we were receiving, it was both confusing and alarming for the family. At one stage there was a news blackout so that the rescue work could get the priority it needed. It was a terrible experience, but we did our best to remain calm and obtain reliable and trustworthy information, which is so important in such a situation.

In the event when it was 8 a.m. on the Saturday morning it was agreed that I should do the Penny Farthing ride and afterwards return to my task.

Thankfully, the submersible was located and lifting cables were attached later that morning. The logistics of getting equipment to the site to effect the rescue had taken time. The two Rogers were rescued from the seabed with only 12 minutes of oxygen left! At 1575 feet down they held the record for the deepest successful sea rescue.

As to the Penny Farthing ride, it took 32 minutes and 8 seconds to complete the 5 miles. I only had to get off once and walk up the hill near the famous Miller Howe Hotel. Then I rode the rest of the way at a gallop! I was timed cycling at 26 miles an hour on my ancient steed down the hill from Troutbeck Bridge past White Cross Bay. We raised a princely sum of several hundred pounds for the Community Service Appeal.

Figure 3.17. Chairman John Curtis at Waterhead seated on my Penny Farthing after I had completed my five mile run on September 1st 1973
Round Tablers left to right: Peter Matthews, LH, John Curtis, Bill Bewley, David Wood, Richard Bell, Jim Nelson and Keith Taylor with children

★   ★   ★

In the Round Table year 1974/75, I was Chairman of the WADRT, David Richardson was Vice-chairman, Bill Bewley was Secretary and Derek Tebay was Treasurer. We enjoyed another year of fun and fellowship. The Charter night dinner that year had a Lakeland dialect theme rather like a "Merry Neet". The guest speakers delivered their good old Lakeland Dialect in amusing and traditional form. We had a jolly evening with a goodly number of representatives from other Tables.

I smoked a pipe at that time and smoking after meals was allowed in those days. Guests who wanted them were provided with clay pipes for the evening. Such conduct we have since learned is not beneficial to health, and indeed from the moment I had heart failure in 1990, I have not smoked since!

As well as fundraising, we had an interesting social programme of events for the year 1974/75. These included:

i)   a Wild West evening at Pumple Syke,

ii) a Burns Night Supper near Paisley at Glasgow Queen's Park Round Table Number 772 held on the 18th January 1975,

iii) an outside demonstration of a mountain rescue on Loughrigg Fell at Lanty Scar Crag.

The Wild West evening was held in the barn which Sandra and I had built at Pumple Syke. It is a large bank barn with double doors at the back to allow access for trailers of hay.

Alec Edmundson, Bill Bewley and John Sergeant brought a large horse box with three horses to Kentmere and unloaded them and saddled them up out of sight behind the church.   Bill was dressed as a Mexican bandit in a sombrero, leopard skin waistcoat and leather chaps. Alec and John were also dressed in full cowboy outfits, with chaps, Stetson hats, checked shirts and neckerchiefs over their faces.

Figure 3.18. LH with pipe addressing the Round Table Charter night dinner

At this point, when they unloaded the horses, they realised that the animals needed water. Not thinking of their appearance, they knocked on the door of the Old School House Cottage. When the lady opened the door and saw the three of them, she screamed with fright because she thought it was a hold up! However, Alec and Bill, as always diplomatic and good natured, calmed her fears – and they got their water!About 10 minutes later, our barn doors burst open with the three of them mounted on horseback, surprising us all and scattering all the dancers! The arrival of the Mexican bandit and the two cowboys heightened the enjoyment and set the tone for the Wild West evening.

On the occasion of the Burns Night Supper Alec, who had a PSV licence, drove us in Brown's coach from Ambleside to Paisley in Scotland. It was a Round Table charter night in the form of a Burns Supper and about 25 WADRT members, including some friends, decided to attend.

On the way through south Glasgow we ran into a "pea-souper" fog. You could not see much more than a couple of yards in front of the bus. Alec was an excellent driver and we had great confidence in him, but he couldn't make a comfort stop in the fog. He had to keep going. Bill & I both needed to stop for a wittle.

We were in very slow-moving traffic but Alec was always resourceful.

Figure 3.19. Burns Supper Programme

So he pressed the button to open the bus door and advised Bill and me to stand on the bottom step and relieve our pressure into the fog. The problem was that when we were in full stream, it happened that the bus was just travelling very slowly past a bus queue, which was no more than two feet from us!

The Burns Night itself proved to be a hilarious and memorable occasion, not only because of the bus incident but also the good time that we had with Alec and friends. The Reverend Dow's address to the immortal memory of Robert Burns, though expertly crafted, went on for well over one and a half hours, by which time the band was too intoxicated to play!

An unusual adventure for me was the mountain rescue demonstration by the Langdale and Ambleside District Mountain Rescue team, when

I was the guinea pig, trussed up on the stretcher and lowered down Lanty Scar Crag on Loughrigg Fell. I usually get a touch of vertigo when I look down from heights but I didn't let on. I saw that the team at the top of the crag had the ropes properly anchored, and I was very relieved to know this when the stretcher tipped up vertical as we went over the edge! I saw the top of a tree a long way below as the "Barrow Boys" at each side lowered and guided the stretcher down the face of the crag in a series of jumping motions. The tree got closer and I realised it was growing out of the crag and the drop went down a long way below that. It was all very exciting at the time.

Later, in 1989, I was asked by the Langdale and Ambleside Mountain Rescue team to help celebrate their Christmas dinner and dance with my dialect tales of a Kentmere Lad. I referred to the above experience in my toast to them at the end of the evening, a copy of which follows this section.

The picture of climbers on Calf Howe Crag in Kentmere reminds me of the demonstration on Loughrigg Fell, but Lanty Scar Crag was much higher. (See Figure 3.20 colour section)

In the years which followed up to leaving the Table at the end of my honorary year in 1982, we enjoyed many events both in community service and socially. There were many members who became excellent Tablers giving of their time, energy and expertise.

Sandra was Chairwoman of Ladies Circle in the same year as Bill Bewley was Chairman of Round Table and Bill asked me to be the Secretary of the WADRT in his year. See Figure 3.21.

Figure 3.22. LH and Judge Richard Holloway, guest speaker, at Tony Sansom's Charter Night in 1983

On the 24th February 1989, I was invited to the Annual Dinner of the Langdale and Ambleside Mountain Rescue Team at the Waterhead Hotel in Ambleside to entertain them with my "Tales of a Kent'mer Lad". The team and their supporters were in fine fettle and we had some laughter that evening.

Many people have much for which to thank them. The team does excellent work, all on a voluntary basis, often under very difficult conditions. They used to get lots of leg-pulling from the locals, who said that it was easier to see a doctor on the mountains than in the surgery! However, having been the guinea-pig on one of their training demonstrations for the Round Table, I saw at first hand the wonderful competence and expertise of the team – an occasion I shall always remember with admiration and pleasure. I concluded my address on the evening with the following toast.

LANGDALE AND AMBLESIDE MOUNTAIN RESCUE

★   ★   ★

Do you remember the gentlemen climbers
We saw on the box camera snaps
Dressed in their Sunday-best outfits
Knee breeches, plus fours, keppin caps?

Contrast these with grandfather Hayton
A fell farmer with gurt shepherd bee-ats
Riven rocks oot off t'hills ta mak pasture
En pullen up whin-bushes by ree-ats.

He hedden t'time ta ga glooeren aboot
Ner carten ropes en harness in bags
T'fell was fer githeren his yows up
He'd nay time ta ga scramblen up t'crags.

★   ★   ★

So deep in the psyche of locals
Was a feeling of rustic disdain
For the fool with no gumption or knowledge
Of the mountains in storm, snow or rain.

I remember the pompous young fellow
Who lant inta Kent'mer ya day
Sayen he'd walked many miles with his compass
And was certain he'd not lost his way!

"I am in Mardale now this is certain
My compass and map I can read
I am safe in my own satisfaction
I have the sense of direction I need."

Then there's the one who fell off Ill Bell
He rolled down the fell in the mist;
His rucksack, it surely had saved him
But he broke both his legs and his wrist.

Granny was sure he was puddled
"Ta ga climmen aboon six foot ten!"
There wasn't a mountain rescue
And helicopters weren't available then.

Now your customers come in their hundreds
Some sensible, some well prepared;
But some in their pumps and their high heels
Can soon get in trouble and scared.

What a wonderful service you've set up
You're like the lifeboat men of the hills
Stretching your nerves and your sinews
Testing your training and skills.

I remember when I was the Chairman
Of Round Table you gave me a thrill
Strapped into a stretcher you lowered me
Vertically down Loughrigg Hill.

Roped between you I hung there
Suspended high on the crag
Like a smoked ham in a farm kitchen
Trussed up and hung in a bag!

That night I overcame vertigo
And the fear that I had of height;
I was terrified but dared not tell you
I did what was British and right!

Vivid it is in my memory
Your competence and your skill
As between those ropes you lowered me
Down and down to the bottom of the hill.

But I was thankful, hale and hearty
Descending safely, fit and well;
So how great must be your succour
To the really injured on the fell.

That careful demonstration
I remember still so clear
The competence and professionalism
The safe return, the fun – the beer!

You train in all kinds of weather
Through mountain, dale and stream
Good humour, dedication and jobs well done
Have moulded this famous team.

TOAST TO THE TEAM

FAMILY ADVENTURES AND WE DISCOVER ISLAY

Having sold my MG in 1962, when we had got the house built and the children were old enough, I yearned for an open car. I looked for one which had enough room to carry all of us and occasionally to visit the lovely beach at Silecroft on the west Cumbrian coast.

I had fond memories of my occasional trips to Silecroft with the Wrathalls, who were our neighbours at Kentmere. When Martyn Wrathall and I were young boys together in Kentmere, his father, Donald, and mother, Jane, would occasionally invite me to join them. They had an antiques shop in Kendal and an open-backed Austin 12 car. We sang "Going round the corner, yippee!" as we whirled along through the bends to Silecroft. I suppose I wanted our children to have the same happy experiences.

So when in Cheshire I came

Figure 3.23. Studio family portrait circa 1972: Ingrid, Peter on my knee, Martin with Nicholas behind, Penny on Sandra's knee and Jacqueline

Figure 3.24. LH with our children and the Lagonda

across a Lagonda, a spacious, four-seater, open tourer at a very reasonable price, I bought it and brought it home. I was never quite sure whether Sandra approved of it at first, but I think it grew on her later when our children enjoyed the fun and freedom of the open car.

Anyway we had some good trips out in it. On one occasion we drove over Wrynose and Hardknott passes to Silecroft. The brakes were good and the car had enormous brake drums but I really had to tread hard on the pedals going down the steep hills. The Lagonda had a fine long bonnet and a long wheelbase. It was hard to handle on some of the tight bends on the passes, so we came back on the main roads via Keswick!

We kept the Lagonda about 18 months and enjoyed occasional spins out in it. It was really a luxury we could not afford and it was difficult to find room for it. So reluctantly we sold it, together with our bulging family car, to buy a second-hand Range Rover which gave us more space and versatility.

The Range Rover was one of the first series with washable seats, not the luxury of today. It had plenty of room for 6 children, a dog and all the panoply of family things plus – it could tow a caravan or a large flat trailer. This allowed us to cart hay bales and keep the children safe in the car at the same time. We had adventure trips over Stile End and up our high pastures above Longhouses in Kentmere. We also went exploring in places we had never been able to reach with the family. Amber, our golden retriever, went too.

The Range Rover proved ideal later on for bringing down the peats from our peat moss on Islay. We sometimes brought peat home for burning at Pumple Syke but eventually I rented a peat moss from the Farrer estate at Witherslack for home use.

Earlier I referred to our holidays with a caravan on the Mull of Kintyre and how I advertised for an old cottage to renovate. Among others I received a reply from a man who had had a similar thought and had bought a cottage in Perthshire and one on the Isle of Islay. At that time I had never heard of Islay but the picture he sent, with an arrow pointing to the cottage in Portnahaven on the southern tip of the Rhinns of Islay, attracted me. At the same time he sent a large key for the front door mortice lock and suggested that we went to view the property. He said he had paid £400 for the cottage and £25 in legal fees and if I reimbursed him the £425, we could have the property.

Sandra and I decided that I should take a friend with me to inspect the property before buying it. The journey from Tarbet on Loch

Figure 3.25a. Our children helping to load hay bales on the trailer

Figure 3.25b. Sledging

Figure 3.25c. Ice sliding in Kentmere

Figure 3.25d. Our family at the Islay Show

Lomond to Tarbert on Kintyre is a delight in itself, travelling over the 'Rest and Be Thankful' Pass and along the length of Loch Fyne. The journey to Islay felt like an adventure to us.

In 1970 the ferry went, not from Kennacraig as it does now, but from the head of West Loch Tarbert. The cars were loaded on to the ferry in a net, a whole new experience for us! When the car was lifted off after a sail of two and a half hours at Port Askaig, we found ourselves on a completely undeveloped island with very narrow roads and passing places. After following the beautiful ribbon of road along the coast of the Rhinns and passing through Bridgend, Bruichladdich and Port Charlotte, we came over the brow of the hill above Portnahaven.

The view which opened out before us of the old harbour and across the bay to the lighthouse on the tiny island of Orsay was breathtaking. At least half the houses in the village were in ruins, but the cottage arrowed in the picture had a sound roof with a large dormer window and was only a few feet from the sea.

Figure 3.26. Picture of Portnahaven with arrow pointing to the cottage

The cottage had been used as an artist's studio but to get upstairs one had to go round the next house and up the outside steps. It was an oddity but in a lovely situation. What follows is my account of our first visit and the poem I wrote some years later called *"After a Ceilidh on Islay"*. It usually raises a laugh!

ISLAY – MY FIRST VISIT

"You're no going ta build the new Nessy there er ye?"

My first visit to Islay in the spring of 1970 was to view a cottage in the village of Portnahaven on the south end of the Rhinns of Islay, just 30 miles or so as the crow flies from the coast of Northern Ireland. Islay is the most southerly island of the Inner Hebrides. It is a two and a half hours' sail west from Kennacraig on the Mull of Kintyre.

⋆   ⋆   ⋆

"You're no going ta build the new Nessy there er ye?" We stood up from our measuring. The question had come from a pearshaped, apron-clad old lady, standing on Queen Street above us, looking down like a rather genial emperor-penguin with her white apron.

The back garden, or more precisely the wilderness, at 10 Shore Street in Portnahaven on the island of Islay, dropped steeply from Queen Street above, from where Bella McEwan was watching us, down to the cottage in Shore Street which we were proposing to buy. The view south over the old abandoned fishing port out across the open sea to the lighthouse on Mackenzie Island was breathtaking.

"Are you from the Bureau? "Bella asked. "I hear we're having a new Nessy in Portnahaven. I hope you're not going to build it there." She had mistaken us for officials from Argyll County Council. I discovered later that the existing Nessy (community toilet) stood roofless on the shore, still in use, but mainly as a shelter from the wind to consume whisky after the pub had shut! The empty bottles round the pan told their own story. (See verse: "This Thing We All Need")

My companion and I had been measuring the boundaries of 10 Shore Street which included a long strip of steep ground rising directly to the front of the McEwan's house in the street above. Bella was greatly

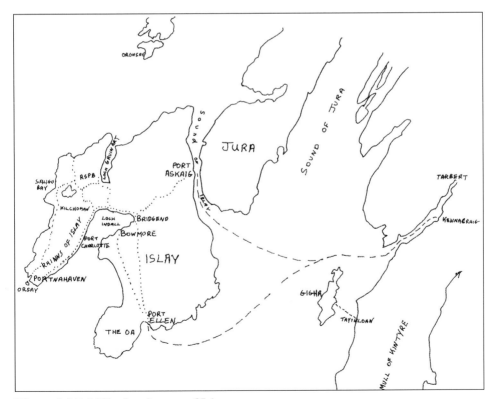

Figure 3.27. LH's sketch map of Islay

relieved when I told her that I had advertised in the Oban Times for a holiday cottage needing repair. An Englishman in the south of England had responded, sending a postcard of Portnahaven with the cottage arrowed, together with a very large key for the mortice lock on the front door. The postcard and key were so intriguing that I had decided that the two and a half hour trip by sea from West Loch Tarbert on the Mull of Kintyre would be part of a real adventure. So it was that I found myself meeting Bella and her husband, both then well into their eighties. They were the first of many warm and friendly folk we grew to respect and love on this beautiful Hebridean island.

Bella was greatly relieved that we were not measuring up for the "Nessy" and invited us to afternoon tea: "When you have finished your surveying." Her soft Gaelic accent was warm and melodic .We accepted at once and a little while later she reappeared in her Sunday apron and announced that tea was ready. It turned out to be Grandad McEwan's birthday tea!

The table was laden with scones, jam and cakes. Beside our place mats stood a pint glass of beer and the largest dram of pure malt whisky that I had ever seen. It was an evening of stories, good humour, drams and genuine Islay hospitality. Finally, with the warm, cosy feeling that is peculiar to good Gaelic company and Islay malt, we persuaded them to let us go and find some accommodation.

"Och Len–art! There's nowhere in Portnahaven ye can find a bed and breakfast the noo. Number 10 Shore Street will be damp and there's no beds. We'll hev ta see if we can persuade Maureen McKinnon at the Pub ta give ye a room. We hevna a spare room the neet, for our daughter Wendy is commen!"

It was very late but Bella used all her charm and arranged for Maureen to give us a room. There were not many tourists on Islay at that time. It was a sparsely furnished room but it had the most wonderful, uninterrupted view of the lighthouse and the ocean. We went to sleep that night listening to the roar of the mountainous waves boring through between the islands at the mouth of the harbour inlet.

It was the first of many nights I would spend on the beautiful island of Islay, where the lighthouse flashed its beam on seals basking only a few feet from us and illuminated our bedroom walls as we slept. So it was that thirty years of lasting friendships were formed on Islay.

Bella and her husband have long since been laid to rest in the windswept cemetery on the Rhinns of Islay facing the sea they loved. Over the years we took part in evenings of singing and live accordion and bagpipe music at various celebrations and ceilidhs. Days were spent talking and walking the cliffs and shoreline with family and friends.

Although we were holiday visitors, the Rhinns folk seemed more hospitable than most. Many of the Islay folk and their children had to spend their working lives at sea or over on the mainland and were used to folks coming and going away for long periods. They would say when we returned to the cottage: "Och Len-art, you've come home then!" We entered into the fun and enjoyed real Islay ceilidhs which seemed to us a mix between a "Lakeland Merry Neet" and a Highland Romp!

But one story of a ceilidh still tickles me concerning the McEwans. It was following a ceilidh in the Rhinns Hall at Portnahaven. It had been a night of dancing highland flings, songs and stories. The kilts and the lasses had been swinging to the wild antics of the Islay men! The bagpipes, the accordions, the fiddles and the songsters had all played their part – young and old. What a night! Afterwards it was the practice for the islanders to return with friends to their homes where they would continue their enjoyment in songs and stories. Of course, there were more of the drams. We were invited back also. It was just such a night which prompted me to embellish a true story told to me by Wendy, the Mc Ewans' daughter, of what occurred at their home after a ceilidh.

There was a glowing peat fire which lit up the bare boards and floor joists of the bedroom above. Grandpa McEwan went to bed. Meanwhile Gilbert, who was I believe a relative, lay snoozing on the hearthrug below. Everybody seemed to be related to each other in some way on Islay.

I have taken some poetic licence and embellished the story a little in my poem "After a Ceilidh on Islay"

★   ★   ★

AFTER A CEILIDH ON ISLAY

★ ★ ★

'Twas after a ceilidh on Islay,
The folks came home for a chat.
There was drinking and singing in Gaelic,
As round the peat fire we sat.

Grandad was tipsy,
So he went to bed.
His bedroom was sited
Just over our head.

Poor Gilbert McWhatsit
Was having a snooze,
Half paralytic
On whisky and booze.

He lay on the hearthrug
Full length on his back,
Directly beneath
A bedroom floor crack.

Grandad upstairs
Undressed to his skin,
Searched under the bed
For the pot to piss in.

Unsteady, unstable,
He slowly took aim,
But whatever he tried,
The result was the same.

For Grandad was bursting
On drams and whatnot,
And his sight was impaired
For locating the pot.

While some found its target
A great deal went by,
And ran through the crack
Where Gilbert did lie.

Now Gilbert was dreaming
Of a land fresh and fair,
Where the drink was all free,
And the girls were all bare.

He lay in the shade
Of a coconut tree,
And dreamt that the nuts
Were full of whisky.

The sun through the fronds
Seemed to glint on the juice,
As a crack in the coconut
Let the whisky come loose.

Gilbert drank of the nectar
Tasty and sweet,
For it came clean through Grandad
Pure and neat!

★   ★   ★

Figure 3.28. The Hector Torrie on Kennacraig pier waiting to
be ferried to Islay – boat built by friends, Richard Holloway
and Gilbert Bainbridge – not the Gilbert in the poem!

GOATS
The trials and tribulations which attend them!

Our friends and neighbours, Gordon and Barbara Fox, of the now famous Fox Pottery at Sawmill Cottage, Kentmere, advertised their goat called Sherry for sale. My wife, Sandra, wanted to buy the goat and we did so. And so began our bitter-sweet experience of rearing goats.

At that time we only had a small field available for use. We later purchased Kentmere Tarn and the marsh area from the mill owners and from Mrs Connie Logan, the former owner of Kentmere Hall. Most of the best land to the east of the tarn was tenanted by our friends, Colin and Mary Iceton, formerly of Millriggs but then living at Ambleside.

The rough area on the west of the tarn was in hand: not tenanted. It had run wild. In the years which followed we were used to rising early at 5.30 a.m. to tend to our goats before breakfast. On the way to work at about 7.30 am, I used to take our herd of goats in a cow-trailer each morning up the back of the tarn. I left the trailer open as a shelter for them. Gradually we acquired more land and had a small flock of Rough Fell sheep and a few calves.

The goats could feed happily on the abundant grass and vegetation including the rose-bay willow herb which grew in abundance behind the tarn. Unfortunately they also barked some of the willow trees. It is easy to see how vegetation is lost in developing countries if goats are allowed free range. I collected the goats in the trailer on the way home from work at night and we milked them in the evening before supper. Sandra enjoyed milking but when the herd increased in number, I bought a milking machine and made a dairy and pens especially for the goats.

We also sited an old hut as a hide on the edge of the tarn. On early mornings in the spring and summer I spent a little time bird-watching before going on to work, watching dab chicks (little grebes) at the edge of the bull-rushes. A variety of ducks, geese, swans and waterfowl came through each year. Unfortunately the advent of mink reduced their numbers. Though we used box-traps to catch the mink, the traps were often thrown in the tarn by ill-informed walkers. If they found a mink in the trap, they would feel sorry for it and let it go. They seemed to be ignorant of the damage these alien, amphibious killers can do to wild life. Mink have no natural predators here and they are destructive.

COLOUR ILLUSTRATIONS

Figure 1.3. The head of Kentmere valley from Brockstones in summer by Jack Loan

LH's Windermere Grammar School
cap – Wetherlam House

Figure 1.4. Annie Mawson with her
Celtic harp

Figure
2.6a.
Christine
Denmead,
illustrator

Figure 1.19a. Harold Auty's sketches of Roland Robinson in Gilbert and Sullivan operas at Windermere Grammar School – see page 44

Figure 2.6. Willie, a happy and satisfied client. Illustration by Christine Denmead

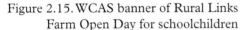

Figure 2.15. WCAS banner of Rural Links Farm Open Day for schoolchildren

Figure 2.16. WCAS Chief Executive, Christine Knipe, in centre with team, left to right: Patricia Bell, Susan Thomas, Veronica Wilson and Barbara Huddleston

Figure 3.12. Sandra and the children with our golden retriever, Amber

Figure 3.23. Studio family portrait circa 1972: Ingrid, Peter on my knee, Martin with Nicholas behind, Penny on Sandra's knee and Jacqueline – see page 145

Figure 3.21. Bill, Chairman of Round Table and Sandra, Chairwoman of Ladies Circle 1978-79.

Figure 3.20. Climbers on Calf Howe Crag in Kentmere

Figure 4.24. 1985 Ingrid, Mossop and baby, Sarah, with:
Front row, left to right: Penny and Jackie kneeling. Second row: LH's mother, Evelyn Hayton, and Sandra's grandmother, Mrs Tedcastle. Back row: Martin, Sandra, Sandra's mother, Pat Tedcastle, Peter, and Sandra's father, Ronald Tedcastle.

Figure 3.26. Picture of Portnahaven with arrow pointing to the cottage

Left: Figure 3.26a. Martin and Sandra at Saligo Bay on Islay

Figure 3.26b. Sandra and Peter outside the cottage at Portnahaven, Islay

Figure 3.26c. Sandra at Saligo Bay on Islay – see page 162

Figure 4.1. Low Bridge and Pumple Syke, Kentmere – a pictorial fusion of old and new by Stephen Darbishire. See page 177 for the description and identity of family and friends included in the picture

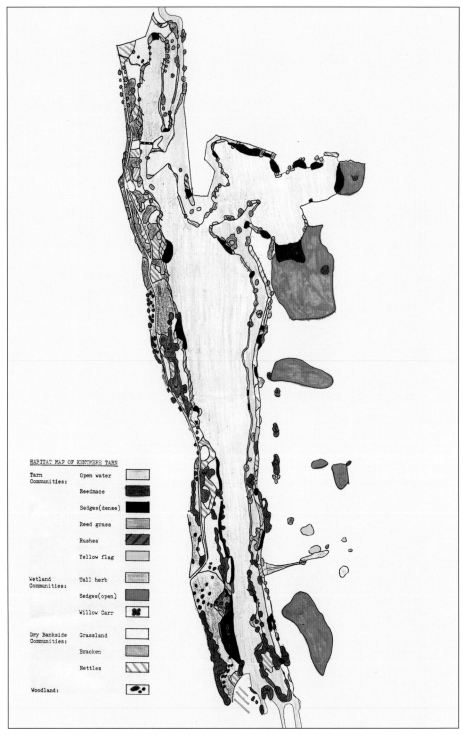

Figure 4.17. Key Plan to Ecological Report in Part 3 of Appendix

Originally they escaped from mink farms. There are no gamekeepers employed in Kentmere to maintain a balance, so mink and too many magpies can do damage to fledglings and their nests.

GOATS

The telephone rang at the office
I really should have known
For never a sweeter, creamier voice
Had I heard upon the phone.

I said for you, my own dear wife
I'd love a goat for ever
Go buy the thing and home it bring
No goat our love can sever!

Picasso had his periods
And I believe that one was blue.
The era of the goats with us
Was of a deeper hue.

Have you seen a goat?
Do you know a goat?
Have you seen its wistful eye?
Cunning, crafty, artful,
Intelligent and spry.

The goat is a browsing creature
It isn't like a cow
Nor wholly emulates a sheep
It is a freak somehow!

It only eats the best of food
Fresh morsels from the hedges
It climbs the rocks and at you mocks
As it skips along the ledges.

I refused to milk the crafty goat
She favoured not my touch
She kicked and held her milk back,
So I didn't like her much.

This same old goat called Sherry
Would cuddle up to Sand
Chew her hair, caress her
And nibble from her hand.

I really felt quite jealous
That this creature had "rapport"
She grew to love this winsome goat
While I felt rather sore!

Our meals delayed by milking
When the goats got cake and hay
Our children waited and their Dad
Whatever we might say!

One day the goat its tail did wag
At sixty times a minute
It padded round the cubicle
Possessed: the Devil in it!

So Sand who studied every move
Was sure there was a reason
And after giving it much thought
Pronounced: "The goat's in season!"

You may deprecate an arranged blind date
Or a meeting planned for you
But a goat that's on heat is glad to meet
A Billy you've taken it to!

Five months and a week, the same as a sheep
Emerged the kids a pair
When we'd sat up all night
Lest the birth was not right
She kidded when we were not there!

Then the number of goats so multiplied
There were sixteen in the herd
Demand for milk it snowballed
As customers spread the word.

Goat's milk is good for eczema
It eases constipation
But I was worried lest the knowledge spread
Throughout the entire nation!

© *LH 11.08.1980*

★   ★   ★

JONAH MOON

On a January evening going home in the car

"Look! Look up! Look up there Daddy
Up there in the Eastern sky
There's a blue black floating sperm whale
And it's eating the Moon!" was the cry.

Yes the Moon was in awful danger
In the jaws of a dark giant whale
Before our eyes the orb was shrinking
Its brilliant light snuffed out and pale.

But the whale didn't seem in a hurry
Strato-cumulus lay long on the line
As it slowly blacked out the moonlight
Like a black hole measureless in time.

Daddy, Daddy, where are you?
The whale has eaten the moon!
It's dark, so spooky dark, Daddy!
Can we get home very soon?

HOBBY FARMING IN KENTMERE
Ploughing & Threshing

In the early 1970s my wife Sandra and I built a two-storey bank barn at Pumple Syke, Kentmere. We did the blockwork and stone facing ourselves at nights and weekends. When a large stone-built house at Windermere was demolished to make way for the Abbeyfield Home, we bought the stone from the demolition contractor. I used to take my large flat trailer to the site on the way to work. The contractor loaded it while I was at work and I took it home, when possible, at lunchtime. Sandra and I unloaded it and I took it back to be loaded again in the afternoon. That way we got two loads each day until we had sufficient to face the front wall of the barn. It was hard work but we enjoyed it.

The downstairs made a garage for the car and the tractor as well as a shippen for Sandra's goats. Upstairs we housed hay and straw. We were into hobby farming and self-sufficiency for our growing family. We had Saanen goats and a small flock of Rough Fell sheep. I often wonder now how we crammed so much into the day!

I had managed to buy some land in Kentmere and I had bought a grey Ferguson tractor together with a plough, a grubber and a stitcher. I was collecting the old grey Ferguson system implements at farm sales. Harry Ferguson, the designer and manufacturer of his tractors and implements, was a genius. He developed the hydraulic sytem at the back of the tractor for lifting the implements. His system helped to mechanise the family farm after the Second World War.

Figure 3.29. LH's father, Joseph Hayton, with Sally, the farm horse, circa 1940

Prior to our attempts at cultivation the last ploughing in Kentmere was in wartime. I recall my Father telling me of the visit by the man from the War Agricultural Committee. Grandfather was "ordered" to plough a particular field which he knew was "bony" (rocky with little soil cover). He said he would plough the fields that would grow what they wanted but not that field because he said, "What! It would bruk oor ald Sally's back!" (Figure 3.28)

Grandad, who died in 1941, loved working with his horses and my father did not buy our Fordson tractor until about 1943. He was the first farmer to buy a tractor in Kentmere but others soon followed suit when they saw what a tractor could do.

Sandra and I decided to plough a three acre meadow. We planted potatoes, turnips and carrots in part but most of the field was sown with oats.

I remember this homely advice from the late John Pickthall, a well-known jolly farmer and raconteur. I asked him about preparing the soil for sowing corn. (Oats in our case.)

"Well," he said. "Thou ploughs thy land and harrows it until there is a fine powdery tilth on t'top. T'soil needs to be warmen up."

"Aye" I said. "But when is best to sow corn? Hoo can I tell?"

"Well, thou waits fer a warmish spring day. Then thou gaas inta field.

Thou louses doon thy gallasses and puts yan thumb inta soil an yan thumb up thi backside ... en when temperature is equal ... thou sows corn!" said John.

So we grew a field of oat corn and had a good crop. When it came to harvest time, I made a precarious seat mounted behind the Ferguson mower and a rack on the back of the knife-bed. That allowed Sandra to operate the reaping-rack with her foot so as to gauge the amount of cut corn needed to make a sheaf. We bound up the sheaves with straw in the traditional way and stood them in stooks of six or eight sheaves in the field to dry. Then we stored them in our barn ready for threshing.

The big problem was finding a threshing machine but I discovered a small barn-thresher miles away at Dacre near Penrith: but how to get it home? I measured the base and gave the dimensions to Tom Bland, the excellent Windermere blacksmith. Tom was a native of Kentmere and a good friend of my late brother, Jack. Tom made me a frame and axle (like a trailer chassis) which I took and bolted onto the thresher. It worked well for transport home and for use also on the farm.

The following is a verse I wrote at the time against myself which records part of my learning curve and our first threshing experience since I was a boy in wartime.

To interpret see glossary at end of verse.

T' THRESHING
Hobby farming style

We bowt a thresher last back-end
We thowt we'd thresh oor corn
It's a gay lang time sen it was med
Afoore t'year I was born.

T'wood was soond en sae was t'drum
Straw-walkers moved en o' -
En so we set it up ta thresh
We thowt we'd hev a go.

I'd tried a flail en clouted mi lug
Mi he-ed it ached fer lang
So t'thresher I was pleased ta see
En t'sheeves ta git amang.

First I med a pulley
Ta tak oor tractor belt
Oor barns to keep away fre it
Were varra firmly telt.

Well it wasn't turble easy
Gitten o' lined up
Belt wod lowp en twist a deal
En t'thresher then kekt up.

Howivver efter I had ligged
Kessen on mi back
Wedged it up wi lumps of yak
En levelled it wi t'jack,

Belt was straight en runnen true
We thowt we'd hev a go
I said to t'Wife, "Noo chuck yan in,"
'Cos t'drum was whinen so.

Sheeves went in fre t'barn aboon
Dust flew far and near
But nowt com oot of anywar
I thought it rather queer.

Whativver happened to oor corn?
Whativver sae ta t'streea?
I shooted up t'wife aboon
"War hes ta put it dear?"

Straw-walkers bounced en t'pulley whined
Belts waved theer in t'wind
But nut a trace of straw or corn
Could either o us find.

I scratt't mi heed en thowt a bit
I gev mi friend a caw
I telt him it appeared ta me
That thresher'd itten straw!

Nay nay, noo lad, thou is a dope
Thy belt's on t'wrang way roond
Straw-walkers chuck it oot at t'front
En dess it up on t'groond.

Nay twist in t'belt, they're garn t'wrang way
They'll choke thi thresher drum
T'corn will stick in t'deeter tray
En nowt fre t'shoots will come.

So back I went en twisted belt
Cleaned oot mi thresher trays
And then we gat oor threshing done
As they did in bygone days!

© LH 17.2.79

Glossary:

Caw = call
Clouted = hit
Deet = to dress or make clean; hence: to winnow corn
Deeter tray = winnowing tray which shakes the grain from the husk within the thresher
Dess = to pile up in layers (Icel)
Kekt or keckt = tipped up
Kessen = lying flat on one's back
Ligged = lain
Lowp = jump
Lug = ear
Streea = straw
Straw-walkers = mechanism in the front of the thresher that throws the straw on to the ground
Yak = oak

★   ★   ★

ODE TO SANDRA ON SALIGO BAY ISLAY

In the moonlight

Lady moon her soft light shining
Through the wisps of cloud on high
Spreads her moonbeams on the water
Over sand dunes where we lie.

Across the arc of silver seashore
Clean sand glistens in the light
Before my eyes a scene of beauty
Resplendent on this perfect night.

Great rollers gallop to the shoreline
Crested by their silver mane
Rise in splendour, phosphorescent
Break, then fall away to roll again.

Beyond the bay a jagged headland
Inky black in silhouette
Prescribes by rock the ocean's limit
Eternal granite solid set.

The sweep of sky a dome above us
Studded stars in bright array
Timeless patterns gems suspended
All along the Milky Way.

Not a sound except your breathing
Save distant lapping of the tide
You my love, asleep and dreaming
Serene and happy by my side.

Lady moon's soft light caressing
Through the ringlets of your hair
Touches lips, highlights your beauty
You, my angel, lying there.

LH Islay 20.08.1980

LANGSLEDDALE HUNT SUPPER
WI RON BELL
"A Merry Neet"

When Sandra and I were hobby farming, our friend Ron Bell, an experienced shepherd, who assisted us with our sheep, invited us to our first real Merry Neet. Ron had a good singing voice and was often asked to be a sort of chairman/MC of the proceedings.

It was customary to make a note during the hotpot supper of the people prepared to sing, play an instrument or tell a tale. Ron organised the entertainment so there was a variety of performances. Everyone was given encouragement and respect, whatever the quality of the performance. It was part of the social fabric of country life. This verse was written to recite at the next Merry Neet we attended with Ron and Margaret Bell.

★   ★   ★

Noo yan neet up Sleddale
As I can tell
Tull a taty-pot supper
We went wi Ron Bell.

Noo t'missus en me
We're a lile bit shy
We don't sing a note
So you'll understand why.

We were beeath rader tense
Mappen a lile bit flayt
'Cos it was o' new tull us
This Merry Neet date!

Why they stuffed us wi taty-pot
Carrots and peas
While doon under t'table
We were shak-ken a t'knees.

Mi belly was fair brossen
En mi britches were tight
I'd tae hod back mi wind
Wid all o mi might!

When t'taty-pot finished
On com t'apple pie
We couldn't resist it
So we gev it a try.

Well o' t'folk med us welcome
Fre far and fre near
En we ate t'apple pie
Weshed doon wi best beer.

When t'last sindins were cleaned
En t'supper had gone
We gat oor directions
Fre oor bearded Ron.

As there wasn't a closet
At Sleddale school
Ye mun gang back of woa
Ta louse out ye tool.

Noo there's yan thing certain
At sick a pill-dill
You'll not cause pollution
If you wittle downhill.

Thur's nae need for loos
Ner a fine WC
If it's up t'top of Sleddale
Thoo's gone oot on t'spree.

Well, when we'd o' med watter
En o' gitten back
Charged up oor pipes
En hed a bit crack

Evening was grand
We were gitten on weel
For a taty-pot supper
I was just gitten t'feel.

Then o'er o' t'hubbub
I hard this loud yell
"It's time to get started!"
'Twas the shout of Ron Bell.

Well, there was singen, reciten
En folk telling tales
While all o' t'while
We were suppen good ale.

There was revelry, laughter
Animated the talk
Interspersed bi a sang
Some verse or a joke.

The warmth of oor laughter
And the strains of yer sang
We'll treasure in oor memories
Oor whole life lang.

So taneet when I hard it
That familiar yell
I'se here yance again
Wi t'famous Ron Bell!

Glossary:

Beeath = both
Bi = by
Brossen = full to bursting
Closet = toilet (usually outside)
Flayt = frightened or nervous
Gitten = getting
Happen = perhaps
Hard = heard

Hubbub = loud discourse
Lang = long
Mun gang = must go
Oor = our
Pill-dill = a happy gathering
Rader = rather
Sang = song
Sick = such

Sindens = last morsels
Taneet = tonight
Taty-pot supper = Meat, potatoes, carrots, peas, black pudding, etc
Turble laa water = not very well or under the weather

Weel = well
Yan = one
Yance = once
Yer = your

★   ★   ★

This is a joke which we heard at a Merry Neet and I embellished a little and put into verse.

GIRL BUNNY

Glossary:

A'foor = before
Allus = always
Burra = burrow
Doo-er = door
Gurt = large
Hard = heard

If you would = if you understand
Leeved = lived
Lonnin = green lane or path
Rayder = rather
Reet = right
Thowt = thought

★   ★   ★

(Part one in country bunny voice)

I'll tell you a tale
About a girl bunny
Which I thowt when I hard it
Was rayder funny.

Girl bunny leeved
In a burra in t'wood
Beside a nice lonnin
If you would.

Noo lover boy bunny
A gurt rabbit buck
Went up t'doo-er
Ta try his luck.

He knocked on t'doo-er
She shouted "Who's there?"
"It's lover boy bunny
Wi time ta spare!"

"Come in, come in!"
She shouted with glee
For this happened quite often
Der yer see?

Well just across t'path
Sat a fine buck hare
Who watching this practice
Was driven reet spare.

He'd seen that each morning
Just aboot nine
This gurt butch bunny
Arrived allus on time.

So on t'following morning
At just a'foor nine
T'buck hare knocked on t'doo-er
En his whiskers did shine!

(Part two in posh bunny voice)

Girl bunny then shouted
"Who is there?"
And the usual reply
Came from the hare.

"Come in, come in!"
Girl bunny cried
It's warm and it's cosy
Here inside.

So in went the hare
And closed the door
Till along came boy bunny
Just hoping to score.

Boy bunny as usual
Thought he would knock
But on hearing the reply
He got quite a shock!

For girl bunny replied
"I've no time for you
I've got an appointment
I'm having a hare-do!!!"

★   ★   ★

LH. c. 1980

These words I wrote for Peter McArthur of Portnahaven who sang them to an old Gaelic refrain. He used to entertain us with his lovely tenor voice at the ceilidhs and in his home. Peter sang Scottish and Celtic songs, sometimes with gusto and at other times to haunting melodies with Gaelic words, which had to be translated for us. Peter and his mother, Naari, always made us welcome, like mariners home from the sea.

Later Robbie Ellis recorded and sang this beautifully on my CD: "Tales of a Lakeland Lad".

COME HOME MY LOVE TO ME

SONG

Recalling a tragedy (as told to me) off the rocks of Portnahaven
when a pretty young girl was drowned.
I wrote the words for Peter McArthur who sang it to
a haunting Gaelic Lament in Maureen's Bar in Portnahaven .

Chorus:
Drawn am I to the Rhinns of Islay
Fascinated by the sea
Spirit of my loved one calling
Come home, my love, to me.

★   ★   ★

On the wild and rugged headland
Where the rocks defy the sea
There my own sweet loved one perished
She was swept away from me.

I could only watch in anguish
Helpless I, a hapless boy
Taken by the hungry ocean
There I lost my pride and joy.

As she danced beside the water
Tempting waves on slippery rock
Back and forward like a plover
The mighty ocean she did mock.

Now she's gone, I'm left forever
Restless I like restless sea
But my heart remembers ever
Sparkling eyes that shone on me.

Chorus:

Drawn am I to the Rhinns of Islay
Fascinated by the sea
Spirit of my loved one calling
Come home, my love, to me.

LH 1975

Figure 3.30. Bowmore harbour with the round church – so the devil can't hide in the corners

NICHOLAS PAUL HAYTON

Nicholas, my stepson, was a little boy over 2 years old when Sandra and I married on 21st March 1964. He was a lovely child and treated in all respects as my son. Nicholas grew up in Kentmere and, like myself and his cousins, he was interested in motorcycles. He attended Staveley Primary School and The Lakes School, Windermere.

For some time he had ridden motorbikes round our fields and had taken part in mock motorcycle trials with his cousins on our land and at Brow Top Farm. I had bought a small sailing boat for the family and Nicholas and I were having sailing lessons on Lake Windermere with Chris Peters, a friend and one of Nick's teachers at the Lakes School.

Nick was a competent and careful rider and we had confidence in his ability. When he was old enough to have a licence and had saved up towards a road motorbike, we helped him to buy a small c.c. machine. Tragically, on the 21st March 1978, he was killed in an accident just south of Longhouses in Kentmere.

He was not travelling fast as the wagon driver later agreed, but was very unlucky to meet the large wagon, which was filling the road, right beside a stone gateway wall end. He was only 16 years old. We had many words of comfort and support from friends and family. The teaching staff and children at the Lakes School were very supportive and helpful at a very sad time, for which Sandra and our family will always be grateful. "Say not in grief that he no longer is with us but in thankfulness that he was."

The memory of that fateful day
Came flooding back to me
As on the bathroom cabinet
Nick's photograph I did see.

Though wisps of snow were in the air
Nicholas reasoned he should go
If only I'd been firm with him
This grief we might not know.

The axe of fate upon him fell
A fine boy full of fun
His crumpled body by the wall
He was our eldest son.

Though years have passed to ease the wound
The scar is always there
Sandra carries still his photograph
Her heart will always care.

Spring day the anniversary
Of the day that we were wed
Is by fateful accident
The same day I found Nick dead.

So each year that spring comes round
As long as time may run
We remember still Nick's happy life
For he was our eldest son.

Written in August 1980 on Islay

ISLAY

Dreams, Drams, Birds, Sea and Silver Sands

ISLAY CALLING

SONG

I climbed in my motor early one morning
The sun it was rising above the blue sea
I boarded the ferry and sailed for the Island
That has such sweet memories for all friends and me.

Headed west bound for Islay and sailed south of Jura
Up through the sound to the Port Askaig quay
I saw that fine Island that lay sheened in sunlight
An Island of beauty, so lovely to see.

I've wandered the rocks around Portnahaven,
I've sat on the quayside and pondered awhile
I've sat among seabirds, watched the flight of the fulmar
And laughed with your people, seen their friendly smile.

But never, oh never, have I ever, ever
Experienced such peace or friendship so true
Your welcome, your whisky, the joy of a ceilidh
Just the happy experience of being with you.

I'm so tired of the rat race, I'm sick of the system
I'm going back to Islay, that gem in the sea
For your life is the real life, a life that's worth living
Our lives are God-given: we must spend them free!

Robbie Ellis has put this song to music.
You can hear it on my CD, "Tales of a Lakeland Lad".

4
___

THE ROLLERCOASTER DECADE OF THE 1980s

A PICTORIAL FUSION OF OLD AND NEW
By Stephen Darbishire R.B.A.

By 1980 Jackie, Ingrid and Martin were at the Lakes School, soon to be followed by Peter and Penny. The loss of Nicholas in 1978 changed our lives, as my verse to his memory written on Islay in 1980 recalls, but life had to go on. Sandra, who was Chairwoman of the Ladies Circle at the time, had completed her year admirably and outwardly she bore the loss well. Everyone was very supportive and kind to us.

Sandra still had goats to milk and a busy life with the children. We had bought Kentmere Tarn and the land behind the lake to make a nature reserve in 1976. I had the tarn and my sheep to look after as well as work and law society obligations. I was also a governor of the Lakes School and a trustee of the Armitt Trust in Ambleside. My years in Round Table were coming to an end but I was given an honorary year in 1981.

In April 1979 we commissioned a large painting from the celebrated

Figure 4.1. Low Bridge and Pumple Syke, Kentmere - a pictorial fusion of old and new (See colour section.)

local artist, Stephen Darbishire, to hang in the lounge at Pumple Syke. It is over six feet long by three feet high. It evolved and was painted over a period of about a year as our ideas developed.

We wanted the picture to depict some of our family's various interests, together with local history and traditional activities in Kentmere. Thomas Blezzard, a farm-worker poet, whose verse *"Kent'mer Rayaces and Tup Fair"* appears in the dialect section of this book, described the scene in our field, Hallgarth Meadow, next to Low Bridge where the old Low Bridge Inn, now demolished, was situated.

Using artist's licence we included the inn in the painting in the approximate position as shown in an old photograph. The inn lost its liquor licence in 1888 following the refusal to renew by the Kendal Justices. The case Sharpe v. Wakefield was fought all the way to the House of Lords but the Court refused to reverse the decision of the Magistrates.

Figure 4.2. Our children enjoying the haymaking in Hallgarth Meadow

The official reason was that it was too far from police supervision. At the time the valley was divided between the temperance faction and those who enjoyed the local ale. The *Westmorland Gazette* reported the case in colourful detail.

Having purchased Kentmere Tarn in 1976, we incorporated the edge of the tarn in the painting and we included scenes from the Queen's Silver Jubilee celebrations which took place in 1977. It was traditional at such events to have country sports, pillow fights and a tug-of-war across the River Kent. Kentmere, being a border tenure valley, was originally divided into four quarters. Folk from Wray Quarter and Crag Quarter pulled against those from Hallowbank Quarter and Green Quarter!

In the painting appear our family with friends and neighbours from Kentmere. Everyone enjoyed the Jubilee sports. My son, Martin, has confirmed the identity of friends and relatives in the picture as follows:

in the foreground to the left of the painting appear my wife, Sandra, and I together with our six children, Nicholas, Jacqueline, Ingrid, Martin, Peter and Penny. My college friend, Reg Ashworth, is emerging from a swim in the tarn. Jackie and Ingrid are on the edge of the tarn with Amber, the dog. Bob Orrell, the author of "*Saddle Tramp in the Lake District*", who camped with us for a fortnight to rest his ponies, is shown with his fell ponies and our daughters, Jackie and Ingrid, to the mid-left of the picture. Alan Rhodes and Andrew Taylor are fishing.

In Pumple Syke garden are LH and Sandra with our little red Lotus and Amber, our golden retriever. LH is also pictured riding the Penny Farthing bicycle towards Low Bridge House. Sandra's brother, Pip, his wife, Joyce, and Sandra's brother, Neil, are standing by the wall. Sandra's parents, Ron and Pat Tedcastle, with our neighbours, Mr and Mrs Bialy, are outside their house. LH's parents, Joseph and Evelyn Hayton, are standing with Herman Wilkinson, an antiquarian bookseller friend from Windermere, by the porch of the old Low Bridge Inn. LH and his friend, Sam Murphy, are sitting on the bridge.

Our friend, Gordon Fox, and his son, Matthew, are shown on the Fordson tractor with my brother, Gerard, looking on. Iain Johnston, Colin Tyson, Alec Edmondson and Malcolm Tyson are leaning against the Range Rover. LH is on a red Norton Commando motorbike.

Seated beside the bridge are our friends, Gilbert Bainbridge, Richard Holloway and Alan Rhodes, who also bought a cottage on Islay. Sandra and friends are engaged in a pillow fight and her brother, Stuart, is rolling the barrel with his feet. Stephen Eccles, David Williams and our sons, Peter and Martin, are watching the pillow fight.

Holding the rope in the tug-of-war are LH and our friends, Roger Gardner, Bill Bewley, Stuart Tedcastle, Tony Sansom, Peter Matthews, Stephen Eccles from Wray Cottage, and John Sergeant.

On the right hand side of the picture, pulling the rope are, inter alia: Andrew Taylor, Peter Briggs, Michael Winkley, Graham Tedcastle and our son, Nicholas.

Stephen Darbishire entered into the fun of creating this picture, combining traditional aspects of the scene described by Thomas Blezzard with our records of the Silver Jubilee. Stephen Darbishire himself is in the picture, seated in the long grass in the foreground! As I no longer have a large lounge to display it, I have given the painting to my son, Martin, as a family heirloom. Martin now lives and works in London, so it is a reminder of his childhood home in Kentmere.

THE GALES OF CHANGE IN THE 1980s

With the advent of Margaret Thatcher, the gales of change which her governments used to curb the trade unions, did not stop there. They went on to commercialise the professions by creating competition and a market culture. They allowed banks and building societies to sell houses and, in effect, to control the financial market as well as provide all manner of services they had not previously had experience of providing. The new legislation allowed what had been safe mutual building societies to become banks, encouraging us all by giving incentive shares in the new companies. We all know the outcome now and have seen millions of pounds wasted by these companies. But in the 1980s the "steam roller" was unstoppable.

"A Lakeland Lawyer's Nightmare Song" (see after) with which I concluded my address to the National Vice-President of the Law Society, on his visit in 1987 to the Annual Dinner of the North West Association, indicates the worries and frustration we felt at the time.

The 1980s were at the same time exciting but also exacting. The radical changes which took place benefitted some companies and almost bankrupted others. On occasions during that period, when to save a situation was imperative, Mike Winkley and I worked all through the night to prepare documents in readiness for negotiation in order to save a business for clients.

Figure 4.3. Ron Bell clipping sheep

As a result of the threatened changes, my work representing the Association of North Western Law Societies also increased in volume, with meetings in London and in the northwest region, gleaning information and making representation, but the steam roller steamed on.

At the same time my hobby farming activity grew with the purchase of more land. I found that doing practical work on the land with my sheep was a good antidote to the stress and pressure of my office work. At one time I dreamt of making my living as a full-time farmer in the hope of sustaining my marriage, as we were always happy working together at home, but things did not work out like that. In both our interests and those of the family, I will not be dwelling on the cause and effect.

Happily our friend, Ron Bell, was able to help with shepherding at nights and weekends. Ron and I attended the Saturday sheep and tup sales at Sedbergh and Hawes markets. The arrangement was that Ron had his own sheep which ran with ours on our land, and we could both enjoy our hobby and help one another. He had mainly Swaledales and we kept Rough Fell sheep. Our crossing sheep were put to the Teaswater tup. The cross produced Masham lambs. The Rough Fell sheep is my favourite breed. It is a noble breed with a pleasant quiet nature. There are top class breeders in Westmorland whose beautiful animals are on display each year at the Westmorland County Show.

As a boy I had walked my father's sheep up the steep intakes to the Nook allotment. When we owned the Longhouses lots and part of the Green Quarter pastures which extended almost to Skeggleswater, I used to go the mile or so to high pasture by quad bike and then do some walking round the stock.

Figure 4.4. Some of our Rough Fell and Masham sheep

My growing up on a farm and having a go at farming myself was experience that stood me in good stead for understanding and dealing with the problems of farmers when they came to the office.

During this period our children were growing through their teens, with all that entails, and helping us in the fields sometimes. We also enjoyed working around the tarn, bird watching and learning about the plants and the behaviour of the creatures which lived in and around the Tarn. We did not allow shooting there. We had a good working co-operation agreement with the Staveley Anglers and we encouraged those interested in birds and nature to keep records of what they saw.

Figure 4.5. LH with quad bike on Green Quarter fell

Figure 4.6. Staveley Anglers re-stocking the eastern bay of the tarn

We took advice from the Lake District National Park Authority and tried to work with them. A copy of Philip Taylor's botany report appears in the appendix and is a record of the position in 1982. It could be useful in the future for tracking any changes over the years to come.

Along with my notes on Kentmere Tarn included in this section, Paul Robinson has kindly done a report of the species of bird which he has seen on and around the Tarn since 1978. Sadly my own bird sighting records have been mislaid in my various house moves.

A LAKELAND LAWYER'S NIGHTMARE SONG

with acknowledgments to W.S. Gilbert

When I'm lying awake
With a dismal headache
After wrestling all day for a client
And I think how little I've made
On poor Legal Aid
I get angry and deeply defiant.

I tumble and toss
And the bedclothes are lost
I dream I'm addressing Lord Hailsham
It's a terrible night
And I get a bad fright
With takeovers, woolsacks and maelstroms.

And suddenly when
I am breathing again
I am kneeling in supplication
Before the woolsack
But it's to the Lord Chancellor's back
I won't accept our profession is sinking.

His wig seems so long
And his perfume is strong
And the Law Lords
Seem all to be blinking.

He is propounding a scheme
To take problems that seem
Too simple for lawyers to play with
Away from his pay
And henceforth each day
Let Citizens' Advice be sufficient.

My head seems to burst
Overwhelmed with the thirst
To bash the meddlers and tinkers
I smash at the sack
And the Lord Chancellor's back
He turns – but now he's a female!

I am looking full face
At a powerful case
She's a schemer, a powerful hatcher
To prostitute all
With her monetarist call
Alas, it is Margaret Thatcher!

I stand my full height
Draw up for the fight
Her eyes on this lawyer do glower
She is bluff, she is rough
She is terribly tough
And she has the ultimate power!

So courage I found
And I stood my ground
I shouted
You're destroying professional ethic
You prostitute all
By your monetarist call
And the outcome will be quite pathetic!

You've made some good moves
Got us out of our grooves
Awakened our get up and go
But what of the brokers
And all the fast talkers
Who protects young Jilly and Joe?

And just when it seems
That I'm winning – she screams
By God – she is now a steamroller!

The pressure builds up
The gauges erupt
Steam belches from out of her boiler
In the billowing clouds
Forms a gathering crowd
Of MPs who obsequiously spoil her.

Like toy soldiers in black
They stand back to back
By the way she has now got an army!
And I am standing there
Half asleep and half bare
To fight on these odds would be barmy!

My pleas for support
From the public abort
They are brainwashed to think we deserve it
They've got "listening banks"
Barrack lawyers in ranks
And every kind of insurance.

They've got consumer protection
Revolts, insurrections
Fair trading and F.I.M.B.R.A. as well.

These confusing schemes
Are drafted in reams
Of gobbledegook, schedule and table
Which somehow conspire
To mount higher and higher
The orders through which they enable.

As no lawyer can charge
Any bill small or large
To interpret the tiers of tripe
So public departments
Expand their compartments
With a quasi-lawyer type.

I am writhing and screaming
I'm sweating and dreaming
I'm smothered in papers and dross
The estate agents are eaten
Emasculated and beaten
By Prudential and snorting Black Horse!

The professional field
Is having to yield
To commercial pressure and profit
Our caseload is greater
Solicitors work even later
While others are scraping the cream off it.

So I'm almost awaking
My body is shaking
The steamroller has rolled over me
I'm flattened – dejected
Not loved – or respected
No company wants to buy me.

In a last ditch desperation
I offer the nation
A prospectus of shares at a penny
But we are not privatised
Nor yet are we nationalised
And the market won't countenance any.

Then I rise from the mud
As a solicitor should
The dawn's in the north eastern sky
Like the Angel Gabriel
From out of the north
Here comes the Vice-President nigh.

★   ★   ★

Our tribulations are over
I'm lying in clover
The long night is past
It's daylight at last
The nightmare was long
Ditto ditto my song
And thank goodness they're both of them over!

LH 16th March 1987

TRAVEL – STAVELEY CROSSINGS AND BEYOND

Until the 5th May 1979 neither Sandra nor I had left the country but it was agreed that I should do a "May Trip" with Malcolm Tyson (MT) on his shoe and boot buying tour, which he used to do each year in May.

Background: The Tyson family footwear business has been going for over one hundred years. In 1979 Malcolm and his brother, Colin, had shops in Ambleside and Bowness. They had also developed a large mail order business. All the shoes and boots supplied to them were checked for quality on arrival from the manufacturer and if faulty were returned immediately. If rejects reached 5%, the manufacturer was warned, and if there was no improvement, the lines were discontinued. When the quality of British manufacturing became more unreliable, MT decided to do a survey of continental shoes and to look for a good manufacturer of mountain boots. It was as a result of this that they started to import stock from Switzerland, France, Germany and Italy.

Earlier in life MT had driven and been a navigator on Monte Carlo rallies. He had a detailed knowledge of continental travel and had also taken his family. That is why he took us over the alpine passes in Switzerland, Austria, France and Italy over the years on our Tyson Tours.

MT said that we Kentmere folk rarely travelled beyond Staveley Crossings! On my first May trip in 1979 our friends, Bill Bewley and John Sergeant, and I accompanied Malcolm in his perfectly polished BMW. On later tours MT and I were accompanied by Reg Ashworth and Alec Edmondson.

Sandra drove me to Staveley. Before we went any further, Malcolm jovially explained "The Tyson Rules of Travel":
1. Cleanliness: The car must be clean inside and out to begin the journey and on each day of our travels.
2. Passport surrender: Passports must be surrendered to Malcolm at Staveley to prevent delay and frustration at Customs points.
3. Job allocation: Each of us was allocated a job. Bill was responsible for internal and external cleanliness. N.B. MT had already given Bill lessons in preparing cars for concours competitions – which MT invariably won. John and Malcolm were the principal drivers on our first trip. Malcolm was also responsible for all the travel

arrangements, checking the fuel and oil and the engine maintenance. LH, surprisingly, was made the navigator – so that I would learn to read a road map and remember where we had been!

4. Navigator: Nobody was allowed to argue with the navigator at a road junction. The direction given by the navigator would be followed, even if it was wrong, and could only be challenged when a suitable pull-in was available. This proved to be an excellent rule. It gave me the opportunity to plan a diversion when time permitted!

5. It is better to travel at 5mph in the right direction than at 50mph in the wrong! One therefore read the map in good time and was prepared to give timely directions.

6. Windows: The windscreen and all windows were to be kept clean at all times. "No enjoyment in touring, if we can't see out!" said MT.

7. Eating: No eating food in the car – "It was not a travelling café!" said MT.

8. Twelve noon: Lunch was to be taken at noon each day – in this way we would avoid queues and be back on the road while others were eating – less traffic, better progress.

9. Six o'clock rule. As we did not pre-book accommodation, we booked in early and had the opportunity for a bath and relaxation before the evening meal.

10. We must not make a rush out of a pleasure. MT had a more robust expression for this, which I will spare you.

11. Parking: Always park at the end of a car park if possible, so that you reduce potential parking damage from third parties by 50% because only one side of the car is exposed.

12. Never park next to a damaged or uncared-for car. If its owner cannot look after his own vehicle, it is unlikely he will care much for yours!

13. On later trips a further rule was added. I had been reading Alistair Cooke's "America" and missed some of the scenery. Reading material should relate to Europe!

14. It is best to do one job properly than make a mess of two.

The Tyson Tours' rules might seem over-prescriptive but they proved very helpful and caused much laughter amongst ourselves. The routes varied each year. We visited the Mephisto factory in Sarrebourg, the Sioux factory in Bensheim, and principally the Raichle factory in

Kreuzlingen in Switzerland. MT had his favourite eating places and knew where the best cakes and ice creams could be found!

Because MT was one of their best customers, they put out the Union Jack for MT together with the Swiss and the canton flags. We basked in Malcolm's glory but our trips were not just to factories. We stayed in the Bernese Oberland, travelled down the Route Napoleon through the French Alps and in other years down through Italy. MT had a favourite family hotel in St Bartolomeo on the Ligurian Coast of Italy. Then we would go back via Monte Carlo and return home through France. Each year MT organised a surprise but perhaps the most memorable was the "Donkey Rides", as he teased us. This turned out to be a helicopter ride in a French helicopter that

Figure 4.7. Testing the Scales of Justice in Switzerland – This proves MT is heavier than me!

had a blue Citröen Diane body and a big fuel tank strapped on above the boot. We flew in this round the peak of the Eiger, over the Jungfrau and around the Lauterbrunnen Valley. It was a glorious experience.

Our 1979 trip was memorable for many reasons but an episode near the village of Echallon on the French-Swiss border brought home to us the legacy of war. In the mountains we came upon a plaque covered with flowers. It recorded the shooting by the Nazis of 100 local people and the deportation of others. As we parked the BMW, an old lady, dressed in black, walked over to us and spat on the car. She cursed us, thinking we were German. When we pointed to the GB on the number plate and spoke English, she smiled and apologised.

When we drove into Echallon, there was another plaque beside a burnt-out ruin. When we stopped to look, a school mistress came to us and explained that during the war the Gestapo had set fire to the house because there was a strong French Resistance movement in the area. Again people had been shot and others deported.

We were then joined by Marcel Donde, the Catholic priest, who himself had been in the Resistance. He insisted that he should get in the car with us. He guided us along a winding track through the forest to a clearing. At the time they had recently buried a "Major Heslop" and erected a cross in his memory. The Major had been in charge of the British paratroopers who parachuted into this same clearing. They, together with the Resistance men of the area, had succeeded in driving the Nazis out. Marcel, a very jolly man, then invited us to his home where he insisted we should sample his wine. By this time we were well behind our schedule and it would have been unwise to drive. His purpose became clear.

That day turned out to be the anniversary of the Liberation of France. There was a celebration with the Mayor that evening and he wanted us to be his guests of honour. When the Mayor in his regalia came down the steps of the Mairie into the village square, there was a large crowd in celebratory mood. The brass band played La Marseillaise and celebratory music. We shook hands with the Mayor and dignitaries and had a lovely evening. We were given wonderful hospitality and each of us was presented with a Liberation badge. This proved beneficial when we reached Monte Carlo: the only hotel accommodation we could find was a suite above our pocket. However, when the proprietor saw the Liberation badges he halved the price! We had a lovely view of the Mediterranean Sea.

The Tyson Tours in the following years were always enjoyable and enlightening. The change recharged our batteries and broadened the mind. I have much for which to thank Malcolm, both in respect of the enjoyment we had on the Tyson Tours and for setting some benchmarks in life. Try as I might I have never quite been able to reach them!

First Tyson Tour, Switzerland, 1979

Malcolm and his wife, Elsie, as well as his brother, Colin, and his wife, Margaret, are all clear thinkers and achieve objectives while others are still pondering the issues.

Thus we learned to travel. Sandra and I had a lovely holiday with MT and his daughter, Helen, in Grindelwald and later we took the family to Spain and Portugal. My work with the Poll Charolais Cattle Society took us both to Canada. The MT travel rules always proved helpful in our travels.

KENTMERE TARN
Some historical snippets

The scene on the front of this book is of Kentmere Tarn, looking north towards the church from the edge of the water. Jack Loan from Windermere, a professional photographer, client and friend, took the picture about 1985 during the time Sandra and I owned the tarn. What we see of the tarn today is man-made but originally it was a small lake with an interesting history. The present stretch of water was created by the removal of diatomaceous earth between 1929 and 1977.

Between 1800 and 1900 the great revolution in agriculture was taking place. Agricultural shows were promoted to encourage competition and prizes were given for the best animals. By the Inclosure Acts, some common land was enclosed and allocated between farmers with grazing rights. This was done to enable the breeding of better stock and for land improvement. There was a need to feed the rising population in Britain as the Industrial Revolution continued to develop. Land was drained to improve pasture and Kentmere was no exception.

A number of attempts were made to drain the original tarn/lake to improve the farm land in the valley bottom by lowering the water table. There was conjecture in my granny's lifetime as to when it was drained, but she always said it was finally drained in 1876 when she was a little girl living at Sawmill Cottage. Her father, Richard Mattinson, was the gamekeeper on the Kentmere Hall Estate for the Wilson family of Rigmaden Park near Kirkby Lonsdale, who owned the estate.

In 1929 diatomaceous earth (*a heat resistant substance consisting of the silica skeleton or valve remains of diatoms; a cubic inch of diatomaceous earth may contain forty to sixty million individuals*) was discovered in the bed of the old lake by Mr J.T. Browne and his partner, Philip Ireland, mining engineers. Mr Browne is reported to have said, " *The uses of this remarkable product include the manufacture of fire-bricks which are nearly three times lighter than ordinary fire-bricks and will save nearly 50% of fuel costs in some furnaces; lining sound, heat, cold and electricity-proof building and the making of fine concrete. It is also used in cotton piece finishing, as a filter for wines, in polishing and abrasive powder and in the manufacture of matches.*" J.T. Browne's son, John, was a good friend of my late brother, Jack, and me. In 1943 the Cape Asbestos Company Limited took over and mechanised the workings, at first excavating the diatomaceous earth by bucket and drag-line and later by floating crane and barges.

THE KENTMERE DIATOMITE DEPOSIT AND FACTORY

Figure 4.9. The pylon and drag-line at the point of extraction

Figure 4.8. Kentmere diatomite deposit and factory

At the time of my purchase of the Tarn in 1976, I obtained photocopies of old photographs showing the Kentmere diatomite deposit and factory circa the 1950s and a picture of the rotary kiln and the aerial ropeway used to transport the diatomite from the point of extraction to the factory. The pictures are poor but they are reproduced here. It is possible to see how the systems of extraction worked.

Circa 1954/55, a scientist, Dr Donald Walker, stayed with us at Brow Top Farm. As a teenager I helped and carried for him when he did a systematic survey of the depth of the valley basin for the Cape Asbestos Company which owned the factory. This included, in particular, the area of the old lake bed. He took core samples of the diatomaceous earth which had formed over many years, and we noted the depths of the material from which he later prepared a plan for his report showing the contours of the old lake basin. I have a copy of the survey plan which came with my papers when I bought the land in 1976, but it is too big to display here.

Dr Walker's paper is referred to in *"Diatoms of the Kentmere Diatomite*

Figure 4.10. Aerial cableway and rotary kiln

Deposits" by Dr John Clegg and Dr E.Y. Haworth, published in the Microscopy Journal, July-December 1985. I knew Dr Elizabeth Haworth at the time and provided her with local historical material, as a result of which she gave me a copy of their paper on Kentmere Tarn. This explains and illustrates the origin of diatoms and the formation of the original lake basin. A copy of the narrative text is included in the appendix.

Dr Haworth has also done extensive work on other tarns in central Lakeland with her colleagues at the Freshwater Biological Research Station on Windermere and with the Brathay Exploration Group, published in *"Tarns of The Central Lake District"* (2003).

In 1970 Mrs Connie Logan (née Wilson) was living and farming at Kentmere Hall Farm with her husband, Angus, and the children. They decided to sell Kentmere Hall Farm but to retain ownership of the area of land leased to the Cape Asbestos Company. She gave me instructions in 1970 to act for her in the proposed sale and asked me to check her title to the estate prior to sale, as it had been in her family for generations.

Figure 4.11. Later extraction system – floating crane, barge and tug on Kentmere Tarn

Her previous advisers had been unable to find all the original documents of transfer into her family when her ancestors had bought it from the Le Flemings of Rydal Hall. It had devolved through the family to her uncle, Christopher Gilbert Wilson, who was well-known to my father.

Chris Wilson was an earlier life tenant of Kentmere Hall Estate and was a bachelor. He lodged with my family at Brow Top Farm and his farm manager and family lived in the Hall, which was and still is the farmhouse. My grandmother, then called Mary Elizabeth Hayton by marriage, did bed and breakfast at Brow Top and took in a lodger from time to time. Diversification in farming is not new! She used to say, "Chris Wilson came to stay for a fortnight and stayed for seven years!" My father acted as his chauffer and companion from time to time on business trips from Kentmere and he knew the Kentmere Hall Farm and the Wilson family well.

I found the title deeds and documents, which I received from her previous solicitors, dated back to 1337 and they are of historical interest. The fishing and sporting rights on the River Kent and the Tarn, known in the past as Kentmere Broadwater, were included in the title to the estate. In 1971, with Mrs Logan's consent, I deposited the deeds on a temporary basis for recording in the Kendal Archives. A document analysis and timeline were prepared and are still available to the public for research at the Archives. These documents reveal ownership of the estate by the well-known Gilpin family. Bernard Gilpin, (1517-83), a distinguished clergyman, known as the "Apostle of the North", was born in Kentmere Hall. He was a strong supporter of Royal Supremacy in the English Church and defended himself against accusations of heresy. Though not Gilpin by name, there are descendants of the Gilpin family still living locally.

Following the Civil War and the Commonwealth under Cromwell (1649-1660) the Gilpin family lost the estate. The title documents show devolution through the Phillipsons and via the Le Flemings of Rydal Hall to the Wilson family of Rigmaden Park near Kirkby Lonsdale.

In order to prepare the sale in 1971, we needed to delineate the boundaries. My father, Joseph Hayton, had reliable knowledge of Kentmere Hall and he was able to do a statutory declaration, which exhibited an ordnance survey plan showing the boundaries of the estate. This was needed to identify the estate because very old deeds often described land by reference to occupation by other adjoining landowners at the time of the transfer. Few landowners would spend money to have a conveyance plan done. Where a farm does not change hands for a long time, these old descriptions can be of little help if someone disputes a boundary.

The beneficial ownership in the title had devolved in four legal shares from the Le Flemings and two of the moiety deeds were missing. I spent two days searching for the documents in the cellars of a London firm of solicitors who had dealt with the Wilson family estates for many years. After some searching, I found the links I was looking for in an old tin box and was able to complete the title to the beneficial interest.

There has been conjecture over the years as to when the original tarn was drained but in the Westmorland Gazette, published on 21st October 1876, it is reported as follows: *"An important step in the draining of Kentmere Tarn, which has been in progress for some years at the cost of Mr Wilson of Rigmaden, was taken last week when the embankment was finally cut through. The muddy condition of the Kent last week was due to this fact."*

The report confirms my grandmother's evidence to me. My grandmother, Mary Elizabeth Hayton, told me that two or possibly three attempts to drain the tarn were made and that two contracting firms had gone bankrupt in the attempt. The rock was extremely hard but Isaac Coward, a drainage contractor, succeeded in draining the tarn after sending rock samples and drills to London to have the drills hardened for the purpose. He was engaged by Mr Wilson of Rigmaden Estate, and he and his workmen lodged with my grandmother's parents in the big bedroom at Sawmill Cottage and at Millriggs Farm, while they were working on draining the tarn.

There is also a report in the same edition of convictions for poaching fish in Kentmere, when the police had been otherwise engaged at the Kendal Gala. Probably the drainage of the tarn was making it easier to catch the fish left in the diminishing water of the tarn!

Further evidence of the date of drainage appears in an advertisement for excavators, rock getters and contractors, which appeared in the Westmorland Gazette on 17th November 1871.

This was followed in 1876 by the advertisement

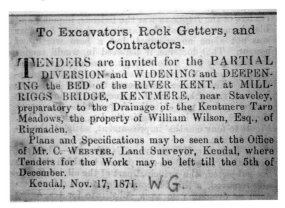

To Excavators, Rock Getters, and Contractors.

TENDERS are invited for the PARTIAL DIVERSION and WIDENING and DEEPENING the BED of the RIVER KENT, at MILLRIGGS BRIDGE, KENTMERE, near Staveley, preparatory to the Drainage of the Kentmere Tarn Meadows, the property of William Wilson, Esq., of Rigmaden.

Plans and Specifications may be seen at the Office of Mr. C. WEBSTER, Land Surveyor, Kendal, where Tenders for the Work may be left till the 5th of December.

Kendal, Nov. 17, 1871. W G.

Figure 4.12. Advertisement for tenders

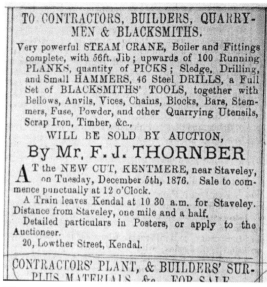

TO CONTRACTORS, BUILDERS, QUARRY-MEN & BLACKSMITHS.

Very powerful STEAM CRANE, Boiler and Fittings complete, with 56ft. Jib; upwards of 100 Running PLANKS, quantity of PICKS; Sledge, Drilling, and Small HAMMERS, 46 Steel DRILLS, a Full Set of BLACKSMITHS' TOOLS, together with Bellows, Anvils, Vices, Chains, Blocks, Bars, Stemmers, Fuse, Powder, and other Quarrying Utensils, Scrap Iron, Timber, &c.,

WILL BE SOLD BY AUCTION,

By Mr. F. J. THORNBER

AT the NEW CUT, KENTMERE, near Staveley, on Tuesday, December 5th, 1876. Sale to commence punctually at 12 o'Clock.

A Train leaves Kendal at 10 30 a.m. for Staveley. Distance from Staveley, one mile and a half.

Detailed particulars in Posters, or apply to the Auctioneer.

20, Lowther Street, Kendal.

CONTRACTORS' PLANT, & BUILDERS' SURPLUS MATERIALS &c. FOR SALE

Figure 4.13. Sale of the contractor's equipment

on the 5th December for the sale of heavy plant and equipment. The use of a steam crane with a 56 foot jib and rock drills is indicative of the heavy work involved in cutting the channel low enough to drain the lake. If you look over Waterford Bridge near the factory today, you will see where the river bed has been cut through the rock. The diversion channel is also evident through the wood to the east of the river.

It has always puzzled me that the Kentmere Corn Rent map of 1836 does not show Tarn Close as being a tarn because:

a) My grandmother told me that her father, the game keeper at Kentmere Hall, used to fish in a boat on the tarn in the 1870s.

b) The tarn, as already stated and evidenced by the reports in the Westmorland Gazette, must have existed because it was not finally drained until 1876.

c) The boundaries of the field 171 shown on the Corn Rent map of 1836 equate almost exactly to the edges of the tarn shown on the estate plan of 1806 and it is referred to as Tarn Close.

My observations relating to this and the plans referred to are set out in part two of Kentmere Tarn Appendix.

In 1942 an iron Viking spearhead was found in Kentmere Tarn by the Cape Asbestos Company during digging for diatomite in the old lake-bed. It was suggested that the spearhead might have been a relic of the Viking raids in Westmorland. A Viking spear was also found near Nan Bield Pass.

In May 1955 Leslie Ridding, working for the Cape Asbestos Company excavating diatomite, found a small boat three feet down preserved in the earth of the lake bed. Leslie, while operating the drag line, saw it in time and it was lifted on 7th September 1955 by the Cape Asbestos Company. The boat had a dug-out keel and five strakes (planks extending the length of the boat). Radio carbon dating gave the year as circa 1320 plus or minus 130 years. The boat is now in the British Maritime Museum at Greenwich. Later the factory site was occupied as a research station for British Industrial Sand and also for the making of filters.

Figure 4.14. Leslie Ridding working on the barge

I shall now return to the sale of Kentmere Hall Farm. By the 5th July 1971 I had completed my investigation and perfected Mrs Connie Logan's title. Mrs Logan sold the farm by public auction in Kendal Town Hall to the Blackburn family. Connie retained ownership of the site of Kentmere Tarn and the rough land to the west of the river, which was then ground-leased to the Cape Asbestos Co. Ltd. The fishing on the tarn was let to the Staveley Angling Association at the time of the auction. The Logans then moved to a farm in the Scottish borders but I continued to deal with their affairs in England.

In 1976 I was approached by a surveyor representing the British Industrial Sand Company Ltd. The company was then the owner of the factory and of the ground-lease of the land on which their factory was built. They wanted to swap the land which they owned on the east side of the river for the leased land on which the factory stood. Mrs Logan was not interested in swapping her land for theirs because she lived in Scotland and she asked me if I would buy the Company's land to facilitate the sale. Independent valuations were done and eventually we decided to go ahead.

On 6th August 1976 by a deed of exchange between British Industrial Sand (BIS) and Mrs Logan, BIS bought the factory site in exchange for the land to the east of the river. My wife, Sandra, and I bought the remainder of the tarn/lake bed which belonged to Mrs Logan. We also bought the former BIS land from Mrs Logan on the same day at market value to facilitate the exchange. As was the custom and as the buyer of the last part of the estate, I received the old deeds of Kentmere Hall and the papers relevant to it, which I intend to deposit in the Kendal Archives in due course.

Our 1976 purchase allowed Sandra and me to extend our hobby

farming activity. The land on the west side of the river behind the tarn was vacant, which allowed us to have our own nature reserve and take the goats to graze there from time to time. We made a bird-hide to watch the water fowl and other wild birds, which we noted at the time. Our children enjoyed exploring and bird-watching but we did not allow any swimming in the tarn because of the uneven banks, soft bottom and the varying depths.

I have always got up early about 5.00 a.m. and if the goats were to be taken for grazing, Sandra milked them ready for me to take them to the land behind the tarn on my way to the office. If time permitted, I would watch the dab chicks and waterfowl on the tarn for a little while from the hide. It was "heaven with the gate shut"!

Unfortunately, with my house-moves since leaving Kentmere, I have lost my own bird-sighting records but Paul Robinson has kindly allowed me to include his records of his bird sightings. See his report and sightings since 1978 to date.

We improved the access for the Staveley anglers to the western edge of the tarn. We also placed a small footbridge across the river, which facilitated access all around the tarn. My friend, Andrew Taylor, was the secretary of the Staveley Angling Association and we worked together to improve the track and the fishing. We placed a net across the mouth of the eastern bay which allowed the Angling Association to have rainbow trout in there. This helped the sale of fishing permits and our co-operation arrangements worked well.

There were wild brown trout in the western bay and in the top pool. Alec Redhead, a teacher from the Lakes School, caught a record brown trout in the top pool which weighed five pounds and four ounces. When I recently checked the weight of the fish with Andrew Taylor,

Figure 4.15. Andrew Taylor with daughter, Alice, on the west side of Kentmere Tarn

Figure 4.16. Sydney Dixon setting a mink trap – See page 154 section 3

he said, with typical fisherman's hyperbole, that the lake level dropped five inches when Alec lifted his catch out of the tarn!

Andrew used to enjoy Sandra's redcurrant and raspberry pies, which she made when he and the treasurer brought the Association's rent cheque each year. Because of her tasty pies, they preferred to bring the rent cheque to Pumple Syke in person rather than post it!

The land on the east side of the River Kent was originally part of Millriggs Farm. When we bought the land in 1976, it was subject to an agricultural protected tenancy with succession rights in favour of our friend, Colin Iceton. His father had farmed at Millriggs when I was a lad. I took my favourite cow, Nancy, to his bull, as recorded in my verse "Garn a Bullin".

In 1976 Colin and Mary Iceton lived at Round Hill, Kirkstone near Ambleside. About 1978 Colin asked me if I would buy out his tenancy on the land at Millriggs so he could buy more land at Kirkstone. I agreed to do so.

Tragically, some years later Colin himself was killed in a farming accident when working behind his tractor. I attended the inquest for the family. Unfortunately he had left the engine running while he was working between the tractor and the hay-bob machine attached to the back of the tractor. The hydraulic mechanism lifted the machine and killed him. It was the sad loss of a very nice man.

Over the years I attended a number of inquests concerning accidents at work. They were sad occasions when I represented the widow or the family. My role was not only to represent the widow or family at the inquest but to console them, as best I could, by gently helping them forward and taking the steps necessary to protect their interests at the time. We were not hide-bound by time records and the straitjacket of modern monetarism. Like many professions, solicitors were not so restricted by modern regulations and had more time for giving help in person.

In 1982 I had discussions with the Lake District Planning Board about tarn management and we took advice from their upland management team. In particular it was agreed that we should have an ecological assessment done and this was carried out by the Board's botanist, Mr Philip Taylor, in July 1982. Our copy of the report includes a botanical survey and key plan which is worth recording here.

For anyone interested a copy of the report is set out verbatim with the list of species around the lake in the appendix.

The key plan shows the locations of the species around a map of the tarn as it then was. *Figure 4.17. Key Plan to Ecological Report in Part 3 of Appendix.*

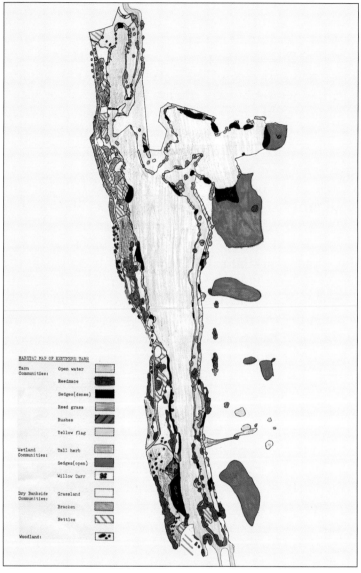

Figure 4.17. Key plan to ecological assessment – see full page in colour section

Unfortunately fate and the exigencies at the time required that I sell the main tarn and eastern bay in 1993. Later, in 2005 I sold the top pool to the present owner of Kentmere Hall and Hartrigg Farm, Mr James Sharpe.

★   ★   ★

I was requested by the Hotel and Caterers Association in 1984 to address them as guest speaker at their Annual Dinner which was being held at the Holbeck Ghyll Hotel, then owned by David and Mary Bunker. I concluded my talk with the following toast.

TOAST TO THE HOTEL AND CATERERS' ASSOCIATION

It is hard to be an hotelier
And catering is worse
But to entertain hoteliers
Is hell itself in verse.

You work from early morning
In a kitchen steaming hot
To produce a fattening breakfast
For your carefree holiday lot.

You cut their luncheon sandwiches
They're off walking for the day
However cheesed off you may feel
You must cheer them on their way.

Some friendly folk come year by year
Like relatives they've become
And expect those little extras:
A night cap, hot milk with rum.

While nouveau riche in flashy car
Blonde concubine in tow
Has come to stay the weekend
Wild oats he intends to sow.

On high stools in the cocktail bar
Attired in the latest vogue
What affectation he takes on
To conceal the scheming rogue.

"Book it to my room, good man
We'll have a ball tonight
This malt must be Glenfiddich
The Pink Lady tastes just right!"

When morning comes there is no sign
Of scheming rogue and concubine
They drank your wine and ate their fill
Used your bed but paid no bill.

Alas the Porsche pushed silently away
Number changed by break of day
Sped off with your best warming pan,
Small antiques and copper can.

For other guests you still must smile
Egon Ronay here a while
Does he pay I often wonder
To criticise and cast asunder?

Now we live in the age of "Which"
Consumer guides have made their niche
Critics now for critics' sake
From their guides a fortune make.

On the Planning Board I often ponder
Direction signs they ban down yonder
Snakes and ladders their policy games
Finding hotels down country lanes.

Grants you get for bedrooms more
Tourist conditions by the score
What will you do when you're all five star?
Give a free night and a brand new car?

★   ★   ★

Back to the guests who fill your beds
Back to the drinkers who dizzy their heads
These are the folk who pay your bills
Coming to visit our Lakeland hills.

Back to the day-books now on the computer
The cash and the cheques from the tired commuter
Checking the till and counting the takings
Convincing the staff that "takings" aren't "makings".

When the accounts are done for the year gone by
The tax man will wonder: "Why oh why
Is the profit so modest there's no tax to pay?"
But you spend your whole winter in St Tropez!

★　★　★

Oh it's hell to be an hotelier
When the season's in full swing
But your success is our success
It's the business the tourists bring.

So we'll drink to the Hoteliers and Caterers
We'll now entertain you reet
With songs and tales and music
On this your Merry Neet!

I give you the toast: "The Hotel and Caterers' Association"

The dinner was followed by a form of "Westmorland Merry Neet" with music, songs, verses and stories. I was asked to be the Master of Ceremonies and to tell some tales. Tony Kelly, silversmith and humourist, and John Shaw from Provincial Insurance provided music and laughter, with Ron Bell from Staveley, a real shepherd and singing countryman, who sang Lakeland hunting and country songs

LH 01.02.1984

KENTMERE WI

If you think that all power
Emanates from the sun
And its warmth is the source of life
Contemplate for a moment
What power she wields
The woman you have as a wife.

First she demands of your being
Procreation itself
Enchants you with hypnotic dreams
And while in this stupor
She tells you you're super
As she works on her womanly schemes.

Nature and women a conspiracy make
In a timeless recurring theme
Mesmerised by the righteous
We men play our part
But the illusions are not what they seem!

We men like tired old tups put out to grass
Or "the last of the summer wine"
That's when our ladies start to live it up
And how their eyes do shine!

Convinced she has given the best of her life
To her children and her man
She's bent on self-expression
And fulfilment if she can.

Now this latest inclination
Sends many ladies high
So often culminating
In them joining the WI.

The Federation National
Is seventy counties strong
With one hundred and eight Institutes
In Cumbria broad and long.

Four thousand amazons in this district alone
A force for good 'tis true
But what happened to sex equality?
Did they let some exception through?

If you think all power emanates from the sun
"It doesn't!" you'll hear men cry
It's not even from London or Parliament Square
It's from Kentmere WI!

LH 12.06.1986

★   ★   ★

Figure 4.18. Photo by Geoffrey Berry from the eastern approach to the head of Kentmere valley with Rainsborrow Crag, Ill Bell and Froswick

BIRDS SEEN AROUND
KENTMERE TARN 1977 to 2011
By PAUL ROBINSON

LH: Paul Robinson is a countryman native to the area, who has taken a keen interest in the birds that visit Kentmere Tarn and the Kentmere Hall Plantation over the last 33 years. His eldest brother, Christopher Robinson, was in my class at Windermere Grammar School and I first met Paul's elder brother, Terry, also of Burneside, when Terry visited my Tarn at Kentmere to watch the birds there and record them each year. He also visited our cottage in Portnahaven on the Isle of Islay, which island is an excellent sanctuary for many species of bird. Terry has since gone to live on the Greek island of Lesbos, which is noted for the sight of birds migrating. Paul developed an interest in birds following a visit to Islay with his brothers, Terry and Peter, in 1977.

Following this visit to Islay, Paul developed a new enthusiasm for bird watching and the study of birds. He has recorded his bird sightings at Kentmere Tarn and in Kentmere Hall Plantation and has kindly provided the list of his sightings which appears in the appendix. Happily, the new owner of Kentmere Tarn and Plantation has continued the work which we initiated and I am grateful to Paul who now takes up the story.

★   ★   ★

PAUL'S REPORT:

I began work as a blacksmith at Cropper's Paper Mill in Burneside in 1963 and my brother Terry worked there too. Terry always wanted me to get interested in birds but my hobby was train-spotting. It was not until November 1977, when I went for a weekend with Terry and my other brother, Peter, to Len's cottage on Islay, that I first started to take notice of birds.

Before then I thought there were sparrows, gulls, crows and ducks, but none else! My life changed on the boat to Islay when I watched shags and cormorants flying over the sea. After we arrived at Port Askaig on Islay it took us all day to go the 16 miles or so to Portnahaven because we were stopping every few minutes to watch the different species of birds on the island. It was amazing! I had my binoculars from my train-spotting days and while on Islay that weekend I saw more than forty species of birds that I had never heard of before.

My visit to Islay started me thinking. After a heavy night on New Year's Eve, Terry shouted out to me the next morning, "There's a peregrine going over!" So I started a list of birds and the Peregrine on New Year's Day, 1978, was the first bird on my list.

It is 33 years since then and I have seen 432 species of birds from all the places I have visited and I am lucky if I see a new one per year now. I am trained to ring birds. People may wonder why we ring birds, but if we can study their movements, we can help to prevent the shooting of birds on their migration routes and improve our knowledge.

My first recollection of bird watching up Kentmere was when as a newcomer to the hobby, my brother, Terry, took me up to Kentmere Hall Plantation to show me his nest boxes. This was the spring of 1978 and even now, 33 years on, I still get the same feeling of peace and tranquillity as I did then.

In the early years, when I was keen to see as many new species as possible, I went up to Kentmere at least once a month. I often used to walk all the way round the Mere because Len had a footbridge across the River Kent on to the sand bank at the time. I recorded many more birds than I do nowadays, when I settle for just walking up the track and around the wood rather than returning across the marsh.

One of my fond recollections of the early years was going up there one evening with my brother and his trainer (Terry was training to be a bird ringer) to ring the Pied Flycatcher and Tawny Owl chicks in the nest boxes. The Pied Flycatchers were easy enough. However, when we came to the Tawny Owls, the chicks had left the box and were scattered around the area of the box. We managed to catch two of them, which were duly ringed and put back on the ground near the box where the parent birds could find them.

The younger Owlet accepted this, but its sibling, which was older and larger, did not. Much to the surprise of my brother, his trainer and I, it took to the air on half-grown wings and somehow fluttered right down the wood and landed in the reeds at the edge of the Mere. One look was enough to tell us that if the bird released its grip on the reeds, it would fall into the water and drown. I wasn't having that happen, so trouser legs were rolled up and in I went after it. That was when I found out how high the reeds grew, because by the time I reached the bird, the water was above my waist! The Owlet was ok and thanked me for rescuing it by digging its claws into my hands!

Many years later in November 1997, I too decided to become a bird ringer and was duly taken once again by my brother Terry (now a trainer himself) to ring birds in the shrubbery behind the Kentmere works.

In 2006 Terry and his wife Susan decided that they would go to live on the Greek island of Lesbos. Needless to say I inherited the nest boxes, which over the years had become a bit run down. Of the 50 or so that once were there only about 35 remained, so I set to replacing the broken ones and filling in a few gaps until I had 47 serviceable ones for 2007.

I was then contacted by a resident of Kentmere who wanted to know if I was the chap responsible for putting up boxes in Kentmere Hall Plantation. "Oh dear, am I in bother?" I said. "On the contrary," was the reply I received. "The owner of the wood would like you to put up some more!"

This brings me to the present time when I have some 108 nest boxes which keep me pretty busy from April to July every year.

This picture was taken at Kentmere by Len's nephew, Edwin Hayton, who is an outdoor tutor at Dallam Summer School and Bendrigg Lodge. Edwin brought the children, who were on a "Wild Zone Week of Adventure", to look at the woodland environment. The children helped me to assemble an owl box and fix it on the tree.

Figure 4.19. Children helping Paul Robinson to assemble an owl box. Also see colour section

The list of species of birds which I have seen around the Mere and in the Kentmere Hall Plantation over the last 33 years is not meant to be a complete list because there could be other birds in passage which I did not see. The following list comprises my sightings of birds on my visits to the area on a fairly regular basis.

Little Grebe — Seen most years mainly in winter but has bred on the duck pond.
Great Crested Grebe — Seen 4 times only
Cormorant — Only seen in winter when they seem to fly up the rivers looking

for food sources.

Grey Heron — Seen nearly every visit

Mute Swan — There is a pair that is more or less resident on the mere, but is rarely successful at breeding.

Whooper Swan — Seen in only six years, there was a pair on the mere in the spring of 2011.

Greylag Goose — Sometimes seen on the fields near Kentmere Hall Farm.

Canada Goose — Only seen on eight occasions but at no specific time of the year.

Teal — They occasionally turn up in the winter. I once saw 22 of them sat on the ice waiting for a thaw.

Mallard — Common

Pochard — I used to see 1 or 2 most winters but sadly not in the last 6 or 7 years.

Tufted Duck — It used to be the most common duck on the mere but not in recent years.

Goldeneye — Can be seen all winter from October to April.

Red-breasted Merganser — This beautiful sawbill could be seen regularly from 1978-1986 then it disappeared,

however there has been a pair on the mere in 2010 & 2011

Goosander — I still manage to see the odd 1 or 2 but they are no way as common as they used to be.

Smew — I have seen only one. A drake in 2003.

Red Kite — Seen on 2 occasions in 2009 & 2011 & then only briefly.

Hen Harrier — Seen only once, in the winter of 1992

Sparrowhawk — Still fairly common

Buzzard — Seen virtually every visit. They breed in Kentmere Hall Plantation.

Kestrel — I don't see these as often as I used to.

Peregrine — Seen on only nine occasions, which is surprising when they breed so near to the site.

Pheasant — Common

Water Rail — Seen once only in the winter of 1996

Moorhen — Turns up occasionally, but may have been overlooked as they prefer the edges of the tarn.

Coot — Very common up until 1998 but not seen since.

Lapwing — A once familiar sight but not nowadays, the last one I saw was in 1987

Snipe — Seen once only in 1986 but as I don't walk through the marsh I suppose it is not surprising.

Woodcock — One of the delights of Spring is to watch these birds roding over the wood.

Curlew — There are still the odd ones about but they are nowhere near as common as they used to be.

Redshank — Seen on two occasions 10 years apart, 1980 & 1990

Common Sandpiper — I used to see this bird every Spring, but I have seen it only once in the last 18 years, in 2005

Wood Sandpiper — 1 sighting only in May 1987

Black-headed Gull — Seen most years but only on the odd occasion.

Common Gull — Seen most years as they roam around the countryside looking for food.

Herring Gull — Seen passing over on numerous occasions.

Lesser Black-backed Gull — Seen 4 times usually in a mixed flock of Gulls

Great Black-backed Gull — Seen only twice in 1981 & 1988

Stock Dove — Seen only once in 2005

Collared Dove — Seen only on 3 occasions around the tarn but see them regularly around the Church.

Woodpigeon — Common

Cuckoo — I hear this virtually every time I go up Kentmere in the Spring but rarely see it.

Barn Owl — I have seen this wonderful bird on only 3 occasions, which is not surprising as I am rarely there at dawn or dusk.

Tawny Owl — Present all year round & has bred in boxes provided for it.

Short-eared Owl — Seen once only in September 1986

Swift — I don't know whether they breed in the village or not, but I do see them flying over from time to time.

Kingfisher — It is always nice when one of these magnificent birds flashes past as you look down on the mere, but it has only happened on 5 occasions

Green Woodpecker — I hear this bird more times than I see it but it is ever present

Great Spotted Woodpecker — A familiar sight almost every time I visit the wood.

Skylark — I have not seen or heard one since 1981

Sand Martin — I only seem to see the odd birds on their way north in the Spring.

Swallow — Common throughout the Summer.

House Martin — I think they breed at the Pottery, I only see them occasionally

Tree Pipit — In the late 1970's they seemed to be everywhere, but alas now only 3 or 4 pairs are present.

Meadow Pipit — I don't see as much of them as I would expect to for a bird that is seen in good numbers further up the valley.

Yellow Wagtail — When I first went up Kentmere in the spring of 1978 this bird was a common sight sitting on the fences, But as with the rest of the country it is now very scarce.

Pied Wagtail — I see them every year but only on the odd occasion, mainly by the roadside.

Grey Wagtail — I only seem to see them about every third year although they are probably present in all years.

Dipper — Only seen in 9 out of 33 years

Wren — Common

Dunnock — A common bird but because of it's skulking nature it is heard more than seen.

Robin — Common

Redstart — 1 or 2 pairs breed in the wood

Black Redstart — Seen once only in November 1997

Whinchat — Another bird that was once seen annualy but has not been seen since 1991

Wheatear — Usually seen as they pass through on their Spring migration, but not every year.

Blackbird — Common

Fieldfare — Seen mainly on the fields when they arrive in the Autumn.

Song Thrush — Heard more than seen

Redwing — Same as Fieldfare one day dozens the next none.

Mistle Thrush — Seen nearly every year, they bred in the wood in 2011

Grasshopper Warbler — There was a pair in the early 1990's then they seemed to die out, however I am told that there has been a pair present in more recent times.

Sedge Warbler — I see no reason why it should not be breeding on the marsh, but I have not seen or heard one since 1998

Blackcap — Heard more than seen but present every year.

Garden Warbler — Heard more than seen but present every year.

Chiffchaff — Seen only twice but I heard at least 2 singing males in 2011 (probably because I now wear hearing aids)

Willow Warbler — Common throughout the Summer.

Wood Warbler — A pair were present from 1989 to 1996 but not since

Goldcrest — This is a fairly common bird in the wood, however it has taken quite a knock in the last two hard winters.

Spotted Flycatcher — Another declining species, but I usually manage to spot one each year.

Pied Flycatcher — Star of the show, although it has declined at other sites throughout the country but there are still around 27 pairs at this site.

Long-tailed Tit — Quite a delight to see about a dozen or so of these enigmatic little birds amongst a tit flock.

Marsh Tit — I have only seen this bird once, in the Winter of 1982

Coal Tit — Seen every year usually high up in the odd conifer tree.

Blue Tit — Common

Great Tit — Common

Nuthatch — They moved into Cumbria in the 1980's, now they are a common sight in woodland.

Treecreeper — Common & doing well, seen every year.

Jay — Heard long before you see it, this is a good site to see this bird.

Magpie — Common

Jackdaw — Common

Rook — Common

Carrion Crow — Common

Raven — Often heard gronking as it flies over.

Starling — Not as common as it used to be, I only see it on the odd visit nowadays.

House Sparrow — Only seen on rare occasions around Millriggs farm.

Chaffinch — Common

Brambling — Seen once only in 1984

Greenfinch — Surprisingly I have only seen this bird on 4 occasions.

Siskin — And this one on 3

Goldfinch — Fairly common but not seen every year.

Linnet — Seen only in 5 out of 34 years

Redpoll — And this one in only 7

Bullfinch — Seen more often than the other finches except Chaffinch.

Hawfinch — Seen once only in 1983

Yellowhammer — And this one in 1996

Reed Bunting — Fairly common but was mostly seen around the bird feeders near the offices.

THE COUNTRYSIDE AND ITS PEOPLE

In 1989 I was invited by the Cumbria Rural Enterprise Agency to address their conference at Shap Wells Hotel to be held on Monday 27th November 1989. As a solicitor practising in Windermere, Kendal and Ambleside since 1964 and a local person born and brought up in South Lakeland, I was asked to speak from the point of view of a local.

Reading my address again 22 years later, it is interesting to note that some issues have since been addressed while others still remain a problem. Housing policies for locals remain unsatisfactory. The draconian decision to impose a 10 mph limit on Windermere was highly divisive and unfair to many people.

On reflection, I think it is fair to say that the effect of planning policies which were followed in the years since 1947 and during my career has amounted to a form of social engineering. The effect of this and economics has been to move many young country people from the country into the towns, thereby reducing the number of children in country schools, which in turn has led to school and post office and consquential changes in the rural communities.

Thus poorly structured planning law and policy guidance from Whitehall put pressure on house prices. Small farms which became unprofitable were split up and the houses sold. Rarely could a local person buy them or use the redundant buildings for a workshop. Proving need was difficult when the artisan and his family were by then resident away from their roots.

Two main planning policies contributed to this:

1. The planners generally refused consent for any change of use to create small workshops in villages. Instead they concentrated most businesses on large industrial estates on the edges of our towns. When years later the effect was recognised, it was too late. Some small units were built for rent in the villages, but the demand had gone by then because most locals had left and artisans usually wanted to own their own unit as security for obtaining working capital to run their businesses. The restraints also inflated prices.

2. The lack of any "Planning Use Class" for holiday homes or a policy to maintain a balance between holiday use and residential use meant that young people had to look for homes and a workplace outside their parish. Had there been a planning use class for holiday homes with a base limit of up to say 30% in any parish community, there would have been facility and encouragement for young people to stay in the communities. The traditions and character of the parishes would have been richer in so many ways, not only for the locals, but for the holidaymakers and those retiring here. We welcomed people coming to live here because they brought new ideas, capital and work, but the system was out of balance.

Where there was a "special reason" or no demand locally for homes in a parish, the percentage allowed for holiday use could have been increased. In my experience all legal frameworks should have an in-built mechanism for appeal and special consideration, where the facts and common sense show good cause. The planning appeal system did not alleviate the problem because the inspector was bound by the same parameters.

Many times I have heard the point made that it was the locals who sold these houses. Yes, they did. Would not everyone want the best price, when he or she has to buy in the same market? My firm and I made a living from the lively market, but the effect of these two policies saw many of my school friends, when they married, having to buy houses in

Kendal and even further south. Then they commuted back to work in Windermere and the villages. Such planning did not help to save fossil fuel or prevent global warming! Their children were lost to the rural areas with all the effects we have seen on village schools, shops and post offices, as well as the customs and usages in Lakeland.

It is true that clumsy housing policies have now been cobbled up to overcome the inadequacy of the basic planning law, but two generations of young folk have already gone from the area.

Many new developments have an allocation of cheap houses for locals but most of these are too small for a family when children arrive. There are so many restrictions for anyone who wishes to make progress.

The policy of selling council houses was a breath of fresh air but it had a serious flaw with sad consequences. The sales helped to expand home ownership and encouraged the improvement of living standards. The big flaw in the scheme was that the sale proceeds were not ring-fenced and made available to build a new stock of council houses to rent. As a result there were even fewer units of social housing and starter homes available in our towns and villages

The controversial decision to impose a 10 mph limit on Windermere was not only unbalanced but draconian. The "Commercial Lake Users" – the businesses making a living from the lake - who provided good jobs for many, had already put forward a scheme for training and licensing lake users to avoid inexperienced and irresponsible people launching a speedboat or jet skis.

In 1939 Alderman H. Leigh Groves gave the Windermere Urban District Council £9,000 to buy the bed of Lake Windermere from the Earl of Lonsdale. However, as a result of the Local Government Act it became vested in South Lakeland District Council (S.L.D.C.).

The S.L.D.C. Lake Wardens and officers of the board had been working with us on a sensible scheme of regulation to improve standards on the lake. Yet it was ignored in the enquiry that followed. The Lake Wardens, who knew most about the problems on the lake, were not allowed to give evidence. Only the planning board's warden did so. Despite assurances that Windermere would remain the lake for recreation when other lakes were restricted, this assurance was ignored when the 10 mph decision was imposed.

The result of the imposition of the 10 mph limit was that people with power boats moved away, the lake revenue dropped and the S.L.D.C. increased the mooring and pier charges, which in turn discouraged the high-spending visitors who sustained the businesses. No doubt the economy is adjusting over time but the pain that followed the 10 mph decision could have been avoided.

If the training and licence scheme had been allowed to operate for a trial period, I am sure that with the normal supervision by our very competent wardens, it would have eliminated any irresponsible behaviour. It would also have created work for those who would run the scheme. I did have some knowledge of occasional offending behaviour on the lake over the years because I had worked with the police and Lake Wardens when I prosecuted cases for them before the Windermere Magistrates in the 1960/70s. The wardens did a good job in promoting safety on the lake, and with the proposed training and licensing system the jet ski problem could have been resolved.

The imposition of the speed limit was highly divisive, creating heated discussion and polarising opinion. Many responsible people, who enjoyed their simple pleasures with their boats, are now denied that facility because of a draconian reaction against the stupidity of a few fools on jet skis who created an outcry at the time!

Much of our modern law appears to arise from knee-jerk reactions. As a result the majority of us find our freedoms restricted because of the stupidity of a few. Sadly, I fear this brings the law and those who impose it into disrepute.

I have dealt with cases where the rigidity of planning policies has caused hardship and despondency, which not only adversely affected individual families but also the welfare of this district. I always found it frustrating that a planning applicant was discouraged from any discussion with members of the board or the development control committee on a site visit. How can they get a real feel of the issues?

While I am grateful to the planners and the Friends of the Lake District for preserving the visual amenity of this beautiful area, I am sure that, had they given more consideration to the economic wellbeing of our communities, we would have been stronger and better able to face the problems which confront us today.

I have always cherished the idea of having a cable car to the summit of a fell in Lakeland to allow access for less able walkers who wish to enjoy the glorious panoramic views across the hills and valleys in this beautiful part of England. When I travelled in Switzerland, Austria and Norway such facilities were readily available and they did not mar the scenery where care was taken to site them sympathetically. Scotland has chairlifts in the Nevis range and in the Cairngorms. Wales has the railway up Snowdon. We can enjoy wonderful views from the mountain railway on the Isle of Man as we climb to the summit of Snaefell.

A carefully planned facility such as this would attract more retired people to Lakeland and provide work. If we used the same resourcefulness we see in the tourist areas abroad, tuned to suit this area, then any extra car parking could be sited underground or in screened areas such as already exist on National Trust land and near the Lakeside landing stage.

Against this we must weigh all the good that the planners do in avoiding excesses and irresponsible development. Finding the right balance is not easy! Who would want to be a planner?

In fairness I respect and have worked with many planning officers and members of the planning authorities who are good folk. They work hard and have the wellbeing of the community at heart. Often they are restricted by central government planning directives and policy guidance as well as the "radical policies" of any new administration.

Figure 4.20. Photo by Geoffrey Berry of the approach to Kentmere Quarries – and looking towards High Street – Bryant's Gill, site of the Viking longhouse is off the picture up to the left. See Section 8.

5

TEETH, TESTICLES & TATTOOS
1984 to 1990

Why this title? How and why did a Windermere solicitor become involved in running a pedigree cattle society part time from his office for more than five years? The work involved travel and interesting new adventures in the world and politics of agriculture. Farmers and pedigree breeders are themselves a fascinating and amusing breed of men and women and I have been amazed by the standards of breeding, care and presentation which they work to achieve. The definitions below are useful in appreciating the work involved in this case.

Figure 5.1. The Poll Charolais Cattle Society Logo

SOME DEFINITIONS
Polled
An animal with absence of natural horn growth – an animal may be either smooth polled or scurred.
a) Scurred: a polled animal with rudimentary horn growth that will not develop into a normal horn. The rudimentary horn growth may or may not become firmly attached to the skull at an older age.
b) Smooth polled: a polled animal that has no scurs or horn growth and does not develop scurs later in life.

Homozygous
An animal that has two genes that are different for a trait, such as one gene for polled and two genes for horns.

Double Polled Pedigree
Both parents of the individuals are polled. A double polled pedigree does not ensure that the animal is homozygous but increases the chances that it may be.

POLL CHAROLAIS CATTLE SOCIETY GB LTD.

Almost forty years after my first experience in Kentmere of "Garn a' Bullin", one day in July 1984 I was summoned by John Geldard, a farmer friend and client (now a leader and entrepreneur in the Agricultural Industry) to attend a meeting in his farm kitchen, then at High Wray. It was a meeting of four pedigree cattle breeders. It was all hush-hush and he would tell me nothing on the phone about the purpose of my visit. John said I had been brought up on a farm and knew the back end from the front of a cow and that would do!

It turned out that they had formed a syndicate to import a Canadian Poll Charolais bull called Val End Commander and the British Charolais Cattle Society had, for political reasons more than any legal or logical reason, refused to register the bull or its progeny. The bull had a full Canadian pedigree and the Canadian Charolais Society was a full member of the International Federation of Charolais run by the French Charolais Society based in Nevers in the Loire Valley. Thus the four breeders I was to represent could not sell Val End Commander's progeny in a pedigree sale without having the cattle registered in a recognised pedigree society.

My brief was to form a new pedigree cattle society company for the Poll cattle and have it registered with the Ministry of Agriculture. I also had to get recognition under EEC directives in time for the Perth bull sales in Scotland in October of that year. The Perth Bull Auction was then the largest pedigree sales centre in Europe. I had to learn how to set up a pedigree register and later a grade register – a tall order in the timescale for a novice!

Nevertheless, the deadline was met and the Poll Charolais Cattle Society GB Ltd. (PCCS) was formed. We took the first Poll Charolais bulls to MacDonald Fraser's Perth Bull Sale in October 1985. They sold well but did not startle anyone. The buyers became members of our Society and so began five years of increasing membership and registrations.

Because of a legal challenge by the British Charolais Cattle Society it was decided that I should be the official Secretary of the Society, keep the Society's pedigree register in my office and do the registrations of the Poll Charolais cattle from our members until the legal issues were resolved.

The threat by lawyers acting for the horned society of a "passing off action" against our new society caused me to study the origins of the

French breed of Charolais. Likewise I studied how the Charolais breed came to be in Canada and America. Interesting questions arose.

What was the definition of a "Charolais"? The French and British herd books of Charolais cattle listed almost 100% horned animals. To live in groups in modern buildings meant these animals needed to be dehorned to avoid them damaging each other. The French and British Societies wanted to control the Charolais herd-books. They did not want a rival society. Nor did they want the import of poll cattle from Canada. Pedigree animal politics can be interesting!

A poll animal is one which is born with no horns and no horns grow. The Poll Charolais bull, known as "Val End Commander", was imported from Canada by Messrs Ken Evans, Gus Davies and John Geldard. It was homozygous: that is to say it had two poll genes dominant. A homozygous poll bull will produce a poll calf even when mated with a horned cow. This avoids dehorning the calves and prevents slowing growth of the animal at dehorning time. The Canadian Poll cattle were taller and slimmer and did not have the large double muscles on the hind quarters to the same extent as the French and British cattle. There had been problems with calving because of the large double muscles on the hind quarters. This was particularly so where European bulls had been used on dairy cattle. This was less of a problem with our Polls.

Val End Commander, when crossed onto pedigree horned animals, produced poll calves including young poll bulls. That did not mean that his progeny when crossed a second time with a horned cow would always produce a poll calf. However, some of his sons also proved to be homozygous.

There is an International Federation of Charolais Societies run by the French. The headquarters of this and the French herd-book are in Nevers, France. The Canadian and American Societies were members of the World Federation along with many other countries around the world. The annual meeting was held in a different country each year.

Figure 5.2. Val End Commander with his wives and family

As it happened, that year (1985) the Federation meeting was to be held in Houston, Texas, at the Livestock and Rodeo Show. The Canadian Society's secretary suggested we should go to Houston because I wanted to see the constitution of the Federation and find out how "Charolais" was defined.

I also wanted to know how the Canadian herd-book could qualify for membership of the Federation when the British Charolais Cattle Society, backed by the French Society, could refuse to register the progeny of the Canadian registered Val End Commander bull. I spoke to Joyce, the Secretary of the Canadian Society register, and she arranged with the American hosts for John Geldard and me to attend as their guests and observers.

There we could learn more as to what constituted a "Charolais". We paid for our flight and hotel accommodation but we were given international guest status and treated like lords. We joined the week-long cattle shows and sales along with the Rodeo celebrations. Then followed a week touring Texas, which included the NASA space station and the Alamo and being hosted by Texan farmers in grand style. Astonishingly, all this lovely experience arose because of the controversy over the "Poll" gene!

My law-partner, Mike Winkley, arranged to accompany us at his own expense, as he had always wanted to visit the USA. Mike and I were delighted when we met Buzz Aldrin, the second man to walk on the moon! We had a long and interesting talk with him, which Mike often recalled in his entertaining after-dinner speeches.

The fact that our tin–pot Society could muster two lawyers to attend the World Federation meeting in Texas seemed to completely demoralise the British Charolais Cattle Society (BCCS) representatives. In fact after an initial frostiness we got on well with the official British delegation.

We caused them some puzzlement when we pointed out that not all Charolais came from Charolles. Unlike the famous champagne case, which the BCCS cited, where only genuine champagne is made in the Champagne area of France, Charolais cattle were bred all over the world and registered to standards which the BCCS had accepted across the world.

In Houston we posed them this question: how could they deny our Canadian bloodlines in the U.K. when they were accepting the Canadian and American registers as members of the International Federation of Charolais?

It followed that they could not legally deny the pedigree of Val End Commander. To deny him his pedigree did not make sense. Their "passing-off" case collapsed. They probably came to the view that the legal costs of a certain loser would be enormous for them. Politically they still declined to open a separate Poll register in the BCCS.

When we got home we received a letter to say that the BCCS was discontinuing the passing-off action and would henceforth treat our Society as friendly rivals. Our strategy had worked. As my old teacher at Kentmere School used to say: *"There are more ways of killing a pig than choking it with butter."*

Though the legal issues were resolved fairly quickly after our visit to the World Federation meeting in Texas, we continued to do the cattle registrations at Windermere for over 5 years. I learned a lot about pedigree cattle breeders and the exacting standards they impose upon themselves in striving for perfection. Government interference and bureaucracy is the greatest threat to the industry.

As a result I had to check the pedigrees of cattle entered at the Perth sales, and later at Carlisle, as well as at farm herd reduction sales. This work took me out of the office and away from home because I had to visit farms around the country with the Chairman, checking that animals were fit to grade up to pedigree status when new members joined. The Society grew quickly before "foot and mouth" arrived.

Why the title *"Teeth, Testicles and Tattoos"?* With our Society's vet, Tony Sansom of Windermere, we had to check the animals' teeth, testicles and tattoos before they went on parade and into the auction ring for sale:

a) Tony checked that teeth were not over or under-shot.

Figure 5.3. Vet, Tony Sansom, and my daughter, Ingrid, checking bulls – Frank Park with his back to the camera

b) Testicles had to be well formed and correct.

c) I had to see that our PCCS registered numbers were correctly tattooed in the ears of the members' cattle.

I had to deal with any issues which arose and sit with the auctioneer to answer any questions which might arise concerning the pedigrees. It was an odd assignment for a country solicitor!

The breeding and presentation of pedigree cattle is an art. I learned to admire and respect the farmers and breeders who took a pride in

their animals, both poll breeders and horned breeders alike. Their care and dedication to their animals has to be seen to be appreciated: not only the time and work involved but also the devotion to their animals which produces amazing results.

Figure 5.4. Perth Bull Sales with Auctioneer, Jack Young, selling a Poll Charolais bull – LH beside him

For some years my work for the Society took me round the U.K to shows, open days and pedigree sales, also to Calgary and the Winter Fair in Regina, Canada. On the continent I visited state farms in Hungary before the "Iron Curtain" came down. I visited farms in Belgium and France. We sold Poll Charolais semen on the Canadian stand at the Royal Show and at other events around the country.

The farmers seemed to prefer buying the semen from the ladies. Over the five years that I was Secretary, the registrations in our herd book were done by my well organised staff: Christine Sutton, my farming daughter, Ingrid

Figure 5.6. Chris Sutton in debate with PCCS Council Member, Bill Broach

Jopson, and my late wife, Joy. All three of them were attractive and had a great sense of humour. At the Royal Show, the Royal Welsh Show and other shows which we attended there was much leg-pulling and hilarity, but they sold the semen and the Society register grew year by year!

At the Regina Canadian Winter Fair in 1986 I saw the largest and tallest black Angus bull that I have ever seen. It was even bigger than a Charolais. Such cattle were bred up with long legs to keep above the scrub and cacti in order to calve in the open and get away from predators on the prairies.

While running the PCCS I sometimes reflected that "much water had gone down the River Kent" since that spring morning when I had first "garn a' bullin" with Nancy, my favourite cow!

Figure 5.7. PCCS Council at Quarry Garth, Windermere
Front row, left to right: LH, Chairman, Tom Brewis, Avril Evans, Vice-Chair, John Geldard and Christine Sutton
Back row: Peter Hutchinson, Ralph Needham, Robert Needham and Bill Broach

THE UK RISING STAR
(Canadian Western Agribition 1986 in Regina, Saskatchewan, Canada)

In the winter of 1986 I accompanied the Vice Chairman, John Geldard, with my law partner Tony James* and members of the Poll Charolais Cattle Society GB Ltd (PCCS) to the Winter Cattle Show and Sales known as the Canadian Western Agribition. Tony and I went to visit his brother Hugh in Pittsburgh on the way to Canada. Tony was training to be a Judge and he received an invitation to visit the Saskatchewan State Parliament and Justice Department while we were there.

Our Society's programme included examination of animals for sale, searching for suitable blood lines, embryos and semen for import. We also visited herds on farms in winter temperatures of 30 degrees below! In the evenings we attended small functions put on by the different cattle breed societies.

During one such happy function it was announced that the speaker for the main conference dinner the next night (with 450 people attending) had given backword and there was no speaker for the dinner. To my astonishment Vice Chairman John Geldard stood up and said he had just the man to address them, pointing at me! He said I could entertain them and also tell them our story of the "Poll Charolais Rising Star" in Britain. I was landed with it and as it was topical in the Farming Journals at that time and there had been amusing episodes along the way, I was given a very warm welcome and a happy applause. I ended my talk with this verse which I wrote on the morning of the Dinner. It turned out to be a memorable occasion.

> When last night they sang of cattle
> And extolled the Angus breed
> Vice Chairman giant Geldard
> To his scribe he then decreed.

---

*Tony James was one of my partners in Hayton Winkley who was well respected, could be most amusing and competitive. Later he trained as a Deputy then was appointed a District Judge and so retired from the firm.

"Go to thy room young Hayton
And write of Charolais
Of Canadian blood in Britain
And Polls that are on the way.

"Tell them we need cattle
To augment our English breed
Clean in belly – fleshy rumps
Lean meat for housewives' needs.

"Tell the world at Agribition
Our breed is on the way
Membership is growing
With the rise of the Poll Charolais."

We embrace the cream of Canada
The cream of Britain too
As we combine the best of both
Then we'll sell them back to you.

While agriculture through the world
Uncertainly looks wan
The leaders of the industry
Courageously must plan.

New markets and new progeny
The best weight across the scales
You MUST identify priorities
To maximise your sales.

Let not your spirits falter
Nor panic in the fright
Food is still important
We've to get the balance right.

Our Charolais delivers
The best meat the market buys
While Poll's an added bonus
For the discerning and the wise.

Broad base of bloodlines
We must have
We buy our base from you
But mark you well
For we will sell
Much better back to you!

★ ★ ★

I ended with a Toast to the Agribition.

Next day we had a television interview with Saskatchewan TV
for their farming programme but this time it was my turn to point to
Vice Chairman John!

★ ★ ★

EXTRACTS FROM MY POLL CHAROLAIS DIARY 1984 TO 1990

POLL CHAROLAIS TIMELINE AND NOTES

Polling pre-1984:
1968 – Robert Needham of Gayton-le Wold, Lincolnshire, had begun a polling programme with twenty of his best pedigree Lincoln Red Polls by crossing and being served by Charolais Bulls. By 1983 Gayton Tally Ho and Gayton Topper were accepted into the British Charolais Cattle Society (BCCS) Herd Book. Robert joined the PCCS in 1985 and became a council member as did another experienced poll breeder from Louth, Ralph Needham (no relation to Robert).

1979 – John and Rachel Geldard founded their Wraycastle herd of Charolais and their polling programme commenced in 1983.

1980 – Ken Evans and Gus Davies found a Poll Charolais bull named Val End Commander in Canada with a full Canadian Charolais Society pedigree, but the BCCS refused to register the bull in the BCCS register despite the fact that the Canadian Society was a full member of the International Federation of Charolais. The World Federation was run by the French Charolais Society in Nevers, Charolles, in France. Val End Commander was a homozygous Poll Charolais bull and he sired progeny which again the BCCS refused to register.

1983 – Val End Commander was displayed on the Canadian stand at the Royal Show at Stoneleigh.

November 1983 – Tom Brewis, a well-respected pedigree breeder from the Scottish borders, bought Pen-y-Parc Progress and a heifer at auction.

1984: New Society formed: Poll Charolais Cattle Society GB Ltd.

July 1984 – LH was invited to a meeting by John and Rachel Geldard at High Wray Farm, near Hawkshead. Present were John Geldard, Avril Evans (Raglan, South Wales), Tom Brewis (Lempitlaw in the Borders) and Gus Davies (Marden, Hereford). LH was acquainted with the facts and was informed that the BCCS were refusing to register Val End Commander or his progeny in their breed register. This was so, even though he had a full written pedigree in the Canadian Charolais Pedigree Society (CCPS). The CCPS was a full member of the International Federation of Pedigree Charolais Societies.

It seemed clear to us that opposition to register was more political than factual. Neither the French nor British Societies appeared to want North American and Canadian bloodlines in Europe! LH was instructed to form a new pedigree society with a company limited by guarantee and obtain the necessary approvals.

11th September 1984 – LH incorporated the Poll Charolais Cattle Society GB Ltd. The BCCS threatened legal action in a long letter from their solicitors against the founding members of the PCCS. As a result PCCS appointed me as Company Secretary and Breed Secretary, which meant that I had to open a new Herd Book to record the ownership and details of all their animals eligible for registration. I had also examine the basis of the legal threat very carefully, do my legal and factual research and see if there was anything to fear in the threat of action.

1984 – Because of the legal threat from the BCCS, inter alia, we needed to know the wording of the definition of "Charolais" in the constitution of the World Federation. The Canadian Society suggested that they should ask the American Society to invite us as international guests to the World Federation Conference, which by chance was being held in Houston, Texas, in February 1985. This they did. The Canadians thought we would see the North American animals and get the feel of the matter. Thus John Geldard, Michael Winkley and I went to Houston, mainly at our own personal expense because there were only four members of the Society then and it was also a holiday for us. I had a contribution to the air fare from the Society. It was a delightful and very memorable experience.

September 1984 – LH drafted the Society's Rules as well as the grade register rules for the Herd Book. We also prepared the PCCS registration system.

October 1984 – Perth Bull Sales – LH attended his first sale at MacDonald Fraser's Auction in Perth. The first Poll Charolais Society bulls were sold – Average price £2625.

Figure 5.8. LH at PCCS sale in Secretary of PCCS mode

18th to 26th February 1985 – 20th WORLD CHAROLAIS CONFERENCE – at the Shamrock Hilton Hotel, Houston, Texas Continental breakfast – Ragsdale Ranch Party included a visit to the ranch of William Arlitt in San Antonio, who was the President of the American Charolais Association.

19th February 1985 – Technical meeting held all day at the S.H. Hotel.

20th February – General Assembly and Technical Meeting and Wine & Cheese Party in the Embassy Room.

21st February – Transfer to the Charolais Show – Ladies Luncheon & Fashion Show for ladies – none for us men!

22nd February – The Sale of Sales – amazing! Cattle were sold by auction in the enormous dining room of the Shamrock Hilton Hotel. They were brought up a ramp from the enormous garage area below, where all the cattle had been on display in carpeted stalls with attendants to catch plops! There were tellers around the room with hearty bidding. The sale started towards the end of dinner, when everyone was in a positive and jolly frame of mind. I had never seen anything like it.

23rd to 26th February – Programme of visits – the NASA Space Centre, a Fiesta on the river and tour of the Convention Centre. We visited the site of the Alamo. Enjoyed a magnificent evening with a mock market and posse chase. There was a very realistic gun battle with cowboys and a posse, which burst on us so suddenly, it seemed real.

Our NASA visit included a talk on the Moon Landing. John, Michael and I had an interesting discussion with Buzz Aldrin who was the second man to put a foot on the moon. We were all "chuffed to have the opportunity to talk to Buzz Aldrin but Mike Winkley was "over the moon"! Buzz was with Neil Armstrong, the Commander of Apollo II, when they landed on the moon at 10.56 a.m. on the 21st July 1969.

The third astronaut, Michael Collins, remained in the spaceship.

15th July 1985 – Open Day at Pen-y-Parc Farm, Raglan, Gwent, the home of Mrs Avril Evans, for the Poll Charolais Cattle Society. This was the home of Val End Commander and the largest herd of Poll Charolais Cattle including Canadian blood lines. Guests were conveyed round the fields seated on bale on trailers to view the cattle. It was a glorious day.

24th September 1985 – Our EEC application to register was accepted and the PCCS received official recognition under Directive 77/504 of the European Economic Community. Directive: Pure-Bred Breeding Cattle.

Figure 5.9. A Poll Charolais Pedigree Pen-y-Park dam- Butte Lee Tiny Karen

2nd to 14th July 1986 – World Federation Conference in Canada – Holiday and business with Poll Charolais to Canada – Sandra and I went with Frank and Maureen Park and Bill and Isabel Broach – 4 nights in Vancouver –Toured Expo 86- wonderful inovations- sailed to Vancouver Island – through the Rockies by train, 2 nights in Banff to Lake Louise, 4 nights in Calgary –We attended the International Charolais Conference at Calgary which was followed by the Calgary Stampede.

Figure 5.10. At the Calgary Stampede: Isabell Broach, Maureen Park, Sandra, and Frank Park standing

2nd July – Arrived in Vancouver.

3rd July - Visit to World Fair "Expo 86" – celebrating man's achievements in transport and communication.

30th June – 3rd July 1986 – Royal Show with Poll Charolais at Stoneleigh. Chris Sutton and John Geldard promoted the breed on the Canadian stand and sold semen.

1st August 1986 – Open Day at High Wray Farm, Wray, Ambleside for the Poll Charolais Cattle Society. Programme included a resume by Tom Brewis, then chairman of the PCCS, and an address by Rowley Fraser of MacDonald Fraser, livestock auctioneers of Perth, Scotland – changes in the livestock market plus inspection of the Wraycastle herd.

February 1987 – Tom Brewis handed over chairmanship of the PCCS to John Geldard at the AGM, and John remained Chairman until the societies merged in 1990. Tom Brewis was unanimously appointed President of the Society with acclaim. Tom Brewis was a very well-respected farmer and pedigree cattle breeder with long experience. He had also been the President of the Angus Society so he had a great deal of experience as well as sound common sense. The Society was well served with Tom and his wife, Pam.

6th July 1987 – POLL CHAROLAIS – Royal Show with daughter, Ingrid Jopson, and Chris Sutton

6th July 1987 – 27th International Convention (UK 1987) – BCCS Jubilee Celebration, 8pm. Guests.

8th July 1987 – POLL CHAROLAIS TOUR of polled herds with international guests – the first stop was at Avril Evans' farm at Raglan in view of Raglan Castle. This intrigued the guests. We climbed on trailers to tour the farm and they were delighted to see Canadian imports among the British Charolais.

Figure 5.11. Canadian and American tour visitors at High Wray with John Geldard

Same evening arranged a Medieval Banquet for them at Clearwell Castle, Forest of Dean, Gloucestershire, and moved on next day to John and Rachel Geldard's farm at High Wray, Hawkshead (a National Trust farm formerly belonging to Beatrix Potter).

We had an informal banquet at the Wordsworth Hotel in the evening where we stayed overnight – I rode my Penny Farthing for them and did some verses. We visited Alan Goodland and Robin Garland, then on to Frank Park's farm at Bannerigg, Windermere, to see the progeny of imported semen from "Spain's Show Me". Lunch at the pub.

26th September 1987 – Avril Evans' reduction sale at Pen-y-Parc Farm, Raglan.

7th-10th December 1987 – POLL CHAROLAIS – Attended Smithfield Show with Peter Hutchinson and members.

February 1988 – Drafted and prepared Society's news bulletin – the first publication of the "Poll Press" – much admired. Work on grade register and visited farms with John Geldard as in previous years and until 1990.

17th February 1988 – Poll Charolais Council Meeting at the Langdale Chase Hotel on Lake Windermere.

23rd May to 7th June 1988 – BUSINESS/HOLIDAY – POLL CHAROLAIS – International Federation Meeting in HUNGARY – Frank Park (Senior) decided to go at the last minute with me. Sandra took me to Staveley, where John Geldard met Ingrid and me. We travelled to meeting with Jeremy Hunt of Farmer's Weekly then via Glyn and Brian Jones' farm at Abergavenny –also saw their commercial herd - lunch in Brecon and on to Raglan where Avril Evans took us on a tour round her pedigree herd of Poll Charolais. Then to Pangbourne and stayed overnight.

Tuesday 24th May – Went on to Rushmore Hill Farms – tour of farms – John and Ingrid left for home at 4.30pm while Frank and I went to Gravesend – stayed at Tollgate Moat house Hotel and joined Canadians and Americans, who were to travel with us, for dinner.

25th May – Took coach via ferry to Dunkirk. Called at Delft and stayed overnight in Amsterdam.

26th May – We did canal boat tour round Amsterdam, then to a clog factory. We went on to Arnhem, Koblenz and Boppard on the Rhine – stayed overnight.

27th May – We went sightseeing in Boppard then down the Rhine on the ferry to Bingen, where coach picked us up. Then 6 hour coach trip to Lucerne (arrived 7.30 p.m. and stayed at Flora Hotel).

Saturday 28th May – Early morning walk – left for Interlaken at 9.30am then round Lake Thun and back to Lucerne.

29th May –This was a Long haul – 6am start – travelled out of Switzerland via Alberg Tunnel through Austria – Lunch near Innsbruck – arrived late at Hungarian border – Frank had to get a visa – I was stopped by a large army officer from going with him to the headquarters – Arrived at our hotel at 2.05 a.m., tired out.
Hungary still under Communist rule.

30th May – Congress opened at 1pm with a video on cattle breeding in Hungary followed by delegate country's papers – then to dinner with the Lord Mayor – Food dreadful!

We toured farms where staff seemed uninterested and crops poor except in their own gardens. We saw a wonderful display of horsemanship followed by a trundle around in a cart drawn by two large white oxen. A New Zealand farmer on secondment to improve sheep breeding in Hungary painted a sad picture of the communist farming operation at the time. As we arrived at the headquarters of a state farm we were greeted by a brass band and American style drum majorettes who marched up to the coaches and then escorted us to the farm headquarters and community hall. It all seemed sad having seen children without shoes or adequate clothing on the outskirts of the town – water available to them only at stand taps. It was all very different from the U.K. Since then we have seen great changes in the communist world which started in the "Roller Coaster 80s".

3rd-6th July 1988 – POLL CHAROLAIS at the Royal Show. Promoted the Society and sold poll semen. Sold first semen to a French farmer!

15th July – POLL CHAROLAIS – Open Day at Avril Evans' Pen-y-Parc Farm, Raglan Gwent.

15th July 1988 – Poll Charolais OPEN DAY at Robert E. Needham's Manor Farm, Gayton-le Wold, Louth, Lincolnshire.

18 to 21st July 1988 – POLL CHAROLAIS at the Royal Welsh Show

26th November to 2nd December 1988 – Canadian Western AGRIBITION at REGINA, Saskatchewan. Flew with Tony James to Toronto two days earlier and diverted to Pittsburgh – stayed with Tony's brother, Hugh, for Thanksgiving – most enjoyable – then on to Regina – where we met up with John Geldard – a very enjoyable trip and well organised event – we were right royally entertained and met the

Minister of Agriculture – Tony James was shown over Parliament by an MP while we were on PCCS business. Tony and I were introduced to the "Get Cracking Club" blindfold: a rather odd invitation for international guests!

Agribition Dinner – The night before the dinner it was announced at the Angus ceilidh that the guest speaker had given

Figure 5.12. Member, John Sutton, & I at Canadian Western Agribition Stand, 1988

back word. John Geldard unilaterally proposed that I should stand in to address the 450 delegates, which to my amazement was taken up.

It was a challenge at the time but we had a story to tell, so it was an enjoyable evening of laughter and fun.

7-8th December – Royal Smithfield Show – with Poll Charolais stand – commercial animals.

6th to 9th February 1989 – PERTH Bull Sales – POLLS sold on 7th & 8th February.

24th April 1989 – Poll Charolais COUNCIL Meeting at the Langdale Chase Hotel – arrangements for "Beef 89" in May – Joy and Ingrid in attendance.

10th May 1989 – "BEEF '89"at Stoneleigh – LH with John, Ingrid and Joy. This was a special exhibition of Pedigree beef breeds where the breeds were competing for attention.

To promote two of the virtues of the Poll Charolais we commissioned some cartoons from the late Christine Birchall to display on our stand.

1. **The Poll factor** – No need to de-horn the animal – and so no loss of weight gain and no stress to the animal.

Figure 5.13. Poll Charolais don't have horns. See series in colour section.

2. **Easy Calving** – This series of cartoons was to highlight easy calving.

Figure 5.14. Poll Charolais do it splendidly themselves.
See full calving series in colour section.

Figure 5.16. PCCS signing Transfer of the Poll Charolais register, 1st January 1990: LH and Chairman, John Geldard, with Joy and my daughter, Ingrid

3rd to 6th July 1989 - Royal Show with Poll Charolais – called at Warwick Castle with Frank Park.

24th/25th July 1989 - POLL CHAROLAIS – Royal Welsh Show. We had an excellent display of our poll cattle.

14th July 1989 – PCCS Council Meeting at the Langdale Chase Hotel.

24th October 1989 – POLL CHAROLAIS – Extraordinary Meeting at the Station Hotel, Perth. Resolution– that the Herd Book be transferred into Book 2 of the BCCS Herd Book + Grade Register and 2 members of the PCCS Council were co-opted onto the BCCS Council. The PCCS to negotiate an Agreement in writing.

JOHN GELDARD:
YOUR COUNTRY NEEDS YOU
(And many more like you)

On your Sixtieth Birthday – 20th April 2011

"**Going Forward**" your favourite expression
Making progress every day
You buy Pullets by the thousand
All ready at the point of lay.

You are Chairman of National Bodies
Fellow of "The Agriculture Society Royal"
Always pursuing the highest of standards
With amazing application and toil.

You walk and talk with our future King
You counsel those high up in power
Your opinion is sought by the media and press
You "**Go forward**" on **mobile** hour by hour!

Rising each morning so early
The wild birds haven't got out of bed
To look all your stock and go farming
With new Ideas and Sparks in your head.

Packing the shelves at the nearest Asda
Negotiating with Top Brass in Leeds
Where no-one can hoodwink John Geldard
"Because he's got all the facts that he needs"!

Gathering producers together
Marketing all they can make
The best local food grown around here
Through Plumgarths Hub you can take.

To market the produce from Foulshaw
And help other farmers on the way
You have opened new Vistas and Contacts
Across most parts of the UK.

You have topped the Great Shows with Cattle and Sheep
Judged stock throughout most of our Nation
Attended more meetings than any man
You've worn a path to Oxenholme station!

I first met you as a Tenant Farmer
You were a Tenant of the National Trust
But for you and Rachel your Burning Ambition
Was to buy your own farm: **'twas a must**!

You first bought a property at Coniston
To establish a foundation freehold
"Going forward" you bought pedigree cattle
Took measured risks: progressive and bold.

Ahead of your peers you saw opportunities
To acquire best bloodlines and hone skills
Again **"Going forward"** you both worked long days
To build up capital and service your bills.

From Young Farmers Club-days to your heady days
Of winning Championships at National Shows
You forged lasting friendships and gleaned a lot
You've inspired others by example. How many? Who knows?

To Richard, Charles and Victoria
You have passed on your knowledge and skill
But above all you have given them the **freedom**
To make their own decisions as they will.

You still may advise and press a few points
Yet deep in your hearts you know
That they too are Geldards "**Going forward**"
Because Rachel & John: I see your admiring glow!

I could write of the travels and puzzles we've solved
Relate amusing tales by the score
The friendship sincere and stable we've all enjoyed
These last 30 years and more.

So now you are **60,** three score years have gone by
You have so much of which to be proud
You have the advantage you're two feet taller than most!
So what of the future: what do you see over the crowd?

You have ploughed and sown, you have reaped and mown
You are so far-seeing and knowing
But now you need time to relax and have fun
Because you've seven fine grandchildren growing!

So – Family Farmer John "Going Forward":
In recognition of your work the promotion of family farms nationally and towards a better understanding of farmers, in celebration of all you and the family have achieved at Foulshaw and Plumgarths. Now let us celebrate your Sixtieth Birthday: THE TOAST IS HAPPY 60th BIRTHDAY JOHN AND MANY MORE TO COME.

Also I rejoice in my long and happy friendship and business relationship with you. Jean and I present you with this tankard which we hope you will enjoy and fill to the brim!!!

© *Len & Jean Hayton*

6

A NEW BEGINNING

AND TIME JUST TO BE

When in reality our marriage had come to an end, Sandra and I both had difficulty in coming to terms with the fact and it caused great strain for both of us and our family. We both know the reasons for the breakdown of our relationship and it is best to accept that we both bear the burden of that knowledge fifty-fifty.

For my part, in addition to a busy schedule of professional work, the 1980s had become a roller coaster with the effects of political change worrying the profession. This in turn involved a change of direction in the firm and an increase of my involvement in the Association of North Western Law Societies. Our family was maturing and our hobby farm had grown into a business and something had to give.

With the events that happened and after unsuccessful attempts at reconciliation by all parties, I found myself in hospital with heart failure for two weeks in February 1991 and six months away from full-time work; though due to the diligence of my secretary/PA, Jean Cowling, and our staff, I was able to continue and supervise most of my work from home.

My work for the Westmorland County Agricultural Society following acquisition of the new Lane Farm site was kept moving, as well as the commercial work at Windermere for which I was responsible. I managed to steer this work and progress with the help of my partners at Windermere. Andrew Bromley and Keith Wood and I have always conferred with each other on the larger undertakings and we have enjoyed an excellent working relationship. This happy and productive relationship proved its worth at the time. Michael Winkley at Kendal took over my work on the Windermere Lake 10 mph limit inquiry, so the office work did not suffer. The partners and staff, both at Kendal and Windermere, were supportive and helpful throughout the period.

Ron Bell, my sons-in-law and members of my family helped with the farming activities and with the auction of farm equipment as well as the sales of sheep and cattle. Despite our mid-life crisis, friendships and goodwill saw us through, for which I am eternally grateful.

With the love and sincerity of Joy, the support of my niece, Heather, and the members of my family, I recovered my strength. When the right balance of medication was found, coupled with regular sleep, exercise and cycling, I gradually recovered my strength. As soon as I could, I went cycling three to five miles before breakfast each morning and expanded the distance as time went on.

I was then able over the next few years to sell my land at Kentmere and to agree terms with Sandra, whereby Pumple Syke was partitioned to allow her to remain in Kentmere, as that was her wish. All this took time and I was grateful to my daughters and sons-in-law for the practical help they gave in partitioning Pumple Syke at the time.

Divorce is a sad and stressful process and despite the healing of time and real attempts to reconcile, it has caused lasting damage in some branches of my family. The recession as well the political rollercoaster ride through the 1980s and early '90s were rapids in life, which sometimes proved difficult to navigate. Yet we came through and on reflection there were also some benefits to the family and others.

Happily, when our landholdings were sold in the early 1990s, Jacqueline and her husband were able to acquire Grandy Barn, Hall Garth and the land around their home to make their own small farm. My nephew, George, was able to buy land to add to the family farm at Brow Top, which made it more viable in today's world. Other farmers also acquired land to add to their holdings at the auction and by private treaty, which doubtless improved their scope in farming.

Figure 6.1. Sunday lunch at the Angel Inn at Hetton near Grassington with Heather and Roger

After being discharged from hospital in 1991, I stayed with the Gardners at Natland Mill Beck Farm for some months. Heather and Roger were very generous, understanding and hospitable. They allowed me time to recover after my heart failure. From time to time we enjoyed a Sunday lunch out in the Lakes or the Yorkshire Dales.

In 1991 Joy and I purchased Eskdale, No. 3, Helme Lodge, in Kendal. This was a lovely ground floor apartment with a spacious lounge and a glass cupola in the roof. The lounge had been the billiard room of Helme Lodge, a Georgian house built in 1827 and designed by George Webster. The Gardners' farm surrounds the estate and we could watch their animals grazing in the fields.

The apartment was ideally situated to access the cycle track along the canal. So my early morning cycle rides allowed me to get stronger and to explore many of the interesting places in and around Kendal. In our new home I had peace, loving support and time to think.

My niece, Annabel Williams, a gifted photographer, daughter of Gillian

Figure 6.2. Joy on our front terrace at Helme Lodge with our neighbours, Geoff and Bernadette Milton, and Geoff's mother

and my late brother, Jack, kindly gave us the pictures that she had taken around Helme Lodge. (See Fig. 6.3, 6.4 and 6.5 colour section)

Our home looked south under the branches of a split-leaf beech tree (sadly since felled) across an extensive lawn to open fields and the old orchard. We were often entertained by busy garden birds and we occasionally saw birds of prey. Rabbits would frisk across the extensive lawn from the Gardners' adjacent farmland.

At last I was able to relax and have time just to be. The words of the Welsh poet, W. H. Davies, came to mind: "*What is this life if, full of care, we have no time to stand and stare?*"

One beautiful morning I was looking out across the lawn and what I saw prompted me to write "Dew Bath on a May Morning".

Figure 6.6. Dew Bath on a May morning.

DEW BATH ON A MAY MORNING

An early May morning was breaking
Through mists in a dappled dawn sky
And shafts of golden sunlight
Cast rides through the meadows close by.

I seated alone on the terrace
Could hear from the garden ground
The rapture of Nature awakening
In the clear morning air all around.

The brush of the mighty Sun-God
On split-leaves of our large beech tree
Spot-lighted excited movements
On the palm of a branch near me.

Three little birds were dancing there
And bouncing playfully
Alert to all around them
Yet revelling merrily.

Then down to the dew-drenched lawn grass
They bathed in the morning dew
Beating their wings like a flurry of flails
While through the sunbeams droplets flew.

Never were diamonds more sparkling
Than those dewdrops in the sun
Never the heart more jocund
By such a joyful display of fun.

But in that glorious moment
While carefree in a world of their own
Came a helicopter–gunship magpie
Soundless and flying alone.

Attack can come without warning
In predation and Nature's law
Revulsion and hatred no solace
Mother Nature levels the score.

But like a bright flight of Red Arrows
They rocketed skywards asunder
Leaving one mesmerised magpie
And me? ...Well ... just lost in wonder!

May 1994. (Helme Lodge, Kendal)

★ ★ ★

TALKS AND CHAIRING GARDENERS' QUESTION TIME

When I got more of my strength back, in the early 1990s I received a number of invitations to recite some of my dialect verse and to talk about growing up in Kentmere. Much of this material is already covered in the earlier parts of this book. Joy and I had some lovely evenings as guests of a wide variety of organisations, particularly in the autumn and around Christmas.

However, I was amazed and not a little apprehensive when Peter Howarth, our resident Lakeland guru on all things horticultural, asked me to chair some of his evenings based on the B.B.C.'s radio programme, "Gardeners' Question Time".

The problem was that I had been used to growing things like turnips, potatoes, kale and corn with an old grey Ferguson tractor, using the wonderful machinery of the "Harry Ferguson system". I did not have green fingers or any qualification suitable for the task.

Nevertheless, Peter was sure that I could introduce the panel, allocate the questions and help to make the evening enjoyable. So in April 1993 Joy and I went to Ambleside and I had my first experience as Chairman of a Gardeners' Question Time.

The panel was very knowledgeable and delightful. Panel members were: Peter Howarth himself, who had wide experience in horticulture, having spent eight years at the Royal Horticultural Society at Wisley and then with the Ministry of Agriculture as the national adviser for the whole of Britain on fruit and vegetables and greenhouse crops – in addition he had years of experience in his own horticultural business; Dr David Kinsman, scientist and director of the Freshwater Biological Association, with his own smallholding, who had a great sense of humour; Michael Hutchinson, the head gardener at Sizergh Castle; and Dennis Robley, head gardener for Glaxo at Ulverston. In the presence of such an erudite panel I felt a real country bumpkin and still do.

We had a lively audience and a super evening. There followed a number of similar evenings over the next six years, raising funds for associations and charities, all memorable for their spontaneity, sharing of specialist knowledge and the laughter we all generated in the process. This prompted me to resume writing my verses and musings.

★   ★   ★

Joy was always a loving, loyal and wonderful companion and wife to me. She nursed me through the time I was in hospital with heart failure and afterwards. We loved each other deeply and she was highly protective of me in all respects. For a short period of time when this verse was written, she was experiencing a woman's hormonal changes, which could sometimes give rise to mood swings, all of which were out of character. Small issues could be viewed rather out of proportion. I would remember Roger Gardner's "mutual hug theory" and they were soon overcome. The following poem really amused her and her lovely face beamed with smiles.

ODE TO MY LIONESS: TO JOY

Unwavering your love
Unbending your will
Like a lioness in fury
Coming in for the kill

Green eyes sharp as arrows
Transfix me in stare
I'm paralysed by your anger
Your tirade about care.

About how I am hapless
Irresponsibly bad
How I couldn't be worse
I'm a careless old cad!

I'm selfish, unthinking
Not caring for you
I'm stupid and dense
I'm a twit through and through.

But does attending a meeting
That's crucial to us both
Justify a bombardment
More fit for a sloth?

I know I was naughty
And stayed far too long
But Joy, oh what language
Excessively strong!

Your address about honour
In pure English was grand
Your dramatic performance
The best in the land.

But forgiveness and mercy
Were far from your mind
Gone was my Joy-girl
So lovely and kind.

I tried to placate you
Be calm for a while
In the hope you might soften
Dissolve with a smile.

But implacable in anger
Inspiring in pose
You brooked no ceasefire
Till I'd swallowed the dose.

I know you mean well
And you were sorely tried
But the tirade was excessive
And I'd nowhere to hide.

So take it on the chin Len
She's right, sure I know
Joy's honest in love
And it has to be so.

You're a gem Joy!
I love you and I'll take it now and then
But please don't despatch me
Your poor brow-beaten Old Len!

I too have my anger
My limit, my steel
I'm just different and tactless
You must think how I feel!

You inspire me and protect me
Your love is divine
It rides on my shoulder
Gives me strength all the time.

So just as a token
Of thanks for your care
You'll find a small parcel
Concealed over there.

I know you can't wait
It will be oh so frustrating
The search for the treasure
You'll be anticipating!

This gift, a sincere thank you
For your love and your care
On the times when I'm thoughtless
And drive my lass spare.

I just ask you my lioness
When next time I ERR
That you count up to ten
Before tearing my FUR!

LH 20. 10. 1992

★　★　★

TONY & JEN SANSOM'S SILVER WEDDING

When Tony Sansom first came to Windermere to practise as a Veterinary Surgeon, he and his wife, Jennifer, came to me as a local solicitor and instructed me to bid at the auction for Black Moss Farm at Windermere. It was the beginning of a very happy friendship, which has lasted ever since. I knew that my mother's parents had been tenant farmers at Black Moss in the 1920s, and so it was doubly interesting to walk the fields with them before the auction. They have made Black Moss their home and lived there happily ever since.

Jen is full of energy and ideas. For some years she ran the "Women's League of Health and Beauty Courses" which Sandra attended. Tony was the "Vitnery" for the Poll Charolais Cattle Society to which I have referred earlier. Together Jen and Tony experimented in all manner of interesting ways of augmenting their family income. They have a lovely small flock of pedigree Rough Fell sheep as well as a beautiful oil painting of the sheep by Patrick Cleary. Jen runs a successful cattery and she has designed and marketed special feeding bowls for puppies. They are an enterprising pair.

Figure 6.7. Tony and Jen Sandsom, May 1997

Tony is one of the "Chums" who used to accompany me on our Islay weekends with Bill Bewley and Peter Matthews. I also remember that on three occasions we climbed to the top of Ill Bell in Kentmere and slept on the mountain top in order to see the sun rise on Midsummer's Day!

Joy and I were invited to celebrate Tony and Jen's Silver Wedding and I prepared this ode and toast for them.

ODE TO YOUR FIRST MEETING

How sweet the love which kindled
A lasting lifetime's flame
When Jen to Tony's surgery
With her pregnant Pug she came.

She, a lissom lovely girl,
Gazelle-like, young and neat
Trained in health and beauty
And nimble on her feet!

He was Welsh – don't blame him
Because he'd lived in many lands
She shared his love of animals
Saw his skill with tender hands.

Jen watched him bend to tend her Pug
His rump was most appealing
A warm affection flushed her cheeks
Her pulse and head were reeling!

He chatted as he felt the Pug
Explaining her condition
But troubled by a change in him
Some energy transmission.

The nearness of this lovely girl
This vibrant, sparkling beauty
Caused quivers of his manliness
Conflicting with his duty!

I only know the moment
When their love affair began
I know Jen to be a lady
And "Tone" an honourable man.

I shall not reveal their courtship
Through long, languid, summer days
When our Vet revealed his secrets
Of love and all its ways.

I know that Jen is qualified
In the health and beauty league
And she has trained her Tony
Not to tire from any fatigue.

They have borne a lovely family
All healthy, young and fair
Who now are here amongst us
Brought up with love and care.

Jen & Tony

Your friends have many memories
Which we all can share with you
But it would take days to do them justice
We could recite the whole night through!

In the transplant of embryos
To advance the Poll Charolais
Or in the breeding of your finches
You have both shown us the way.

You provide holidays for humans
And time out for their pet cats
With accommodation provided
In your luxury feline flats!

There are animals and humans
All over the place
Who are happy and grateful
You accepted their case.

But there's one little dog
We can't forget in our greeting
Your own pet pregnant Pug
The raison d'etre
Of your very first meeting!

CONGRATULATIONS, GOOD HEALTH AND HAPPINESS
Good wishes from Len and Joy on your Silver Wedding Day
17th October 1995

THE HELME LODGE INDEPENDENCE DAY

1996

Joy and I purchased an apartment, Eskdale, 3 Helm Lodge, Kendal, in 1991 and lived there for almost seven years. We were blessed with good neighbours who became good friends. It was a very different way of life from living in Kentmere.

Helme Lodge, the original mansion home of the Crewdson banking family of Kendal, was designed by George Webster and was originally built in 1823. The developers were McAlpines. There were freehold properties which had been erected in the grounds, and the main house and the mews had been very tastefully converted into apartments.

We had wonderful communal facilities in the basement of the main mansion, including a large billiard room, a gym, a sauna and solarium and a Jacuzzi, all ideal for my recovery. At the beginning I worked from home, with the professional assistance of Jean Cowling, Joy and our staff, until I was fit to resume full time work at Windermere.

The gardens, grounds and the freehold of the apartments, when we bought our apartment, belonged to McAlpines. All the maintenance was done by a company from away. This proved to be unsatisfactory and our Residents' meeting decided to ask me to negotiate terms to buy the freehold of the whole site. The ownership of the freehold ground had changed hands by then and we were concerned for the future. There was still finishing work to be done by the developers, and the maintenance company was not employing the best painters and craftsmen.

We therefore began negotiations in 1995 to buy the freehold of the grounds and to have the sinking fund transferred to us, so that the work could be done by contractors

Figure 6.8. Aerial picture plan of Helme Lodge

of our own choice. We wanted to ensure ownership did not get into the hands of a profit-making maintenance company in which we, the resident owners, would have little influence to control the expenditure. There were examples in the press of developments like ours being used by opportunists to squeeze excessive profits from expensive maintenance policies. There was also a risk that a freeholder might seek extra development on our estate. We wanted to avoid any such exploitation.

We formed a new company called Helme Lodge Homes and Gardens Ltd to receive the transfer of the freehold estate. All the home owners, except one, contributed to the purchase cost. Each contributing home owner then had one share in our new company and equal voting rights. Thus the Helme Lodge estate now belongs to the owning residents themselves and they control their destiny, which is much better than was the case.

Will Duffield, one of the residents, who was very practical and meticulous in his work, as well as highly humorous, was appointed as our maintenance manager. He made some improvements in line with all our wishes. He monitored our facilities and helped put the whole estate in very good condition indeed. He also mowed the lawns and did the painting and maintenance work. Edna Porter and her team of residents helped with the gardening for the common good.

In March 1996 when we had sealed the deal, I penned the residents an early morning verse which follows.

EARLY MORNING PROCLAMATION
Sunday, March 31st 1996

If you listen very carefully
And stay silent in the dell
Or lie down among the crocuses
You may just hear the whisper swell.

For the crocuses and the daffodils
Are dancing in the breeze
And the field mouse is awakened
By the chattering in the trees.

The news has spread like wildfire
There is even gossip in the grass
Our Helme Lodge estate is vibrant
By our achievement come to pass.

But I sense withdrawal symptoms
'Mongst our Helme Lodge chatterboxes
'Cos I've missed two early mornings
Dropping notes in letterboxes!

★　　★　　★

So here is the information
Which I make by proclamation
On orders of Vice-Chairman, worthy John.

With his noble knight Geoff Leaver
Our consultant business beaver
To the sanctum of the lawyer they had gone.

And there by quill in contact
With the Helme Lodge purchase contract
They signed the deal for all of us to share.

So now let's pull together
Through fine and stormy weather
For Helme Lodge at last is in our care!

31st March 1996

The home owners at Helme lodge conspired with Joy to hold a festive Independence Day in the main hall at Helme Lodge to celebrate the purchase of the freehold. I was not made aware of it until shortly before it happened. We all had a wonderful banquet in the hall with entertaining songs and stories. Will Duffield dressed up as a ventriloquist-type country yokel and appeared with his famous Duck. He composed an epic poem about the history of our negotiations, which was hilarious, but it would not be prudent to print it here!

Will, along with Norman Yates and others members with thespian tendencies, gave us a very enjoyable time.

Figure 4.25. Langdale Chase Hotel, LH with Malcolm Tyson and Bill Bewley at Bill and Jenny's wedding – serenading the bride – August 1989

Figure 4.26. © Windermere Lake Cruises

Figure 4.27. © Windermere Lake Cruises

Figure 4.28. Kentmere Tarn looking up the Kentmere valley

Figure 5.5. My daughter, Ingrid, Avril Evans and Chris Sutton selling semen on the Canadian stand at the Royal Show

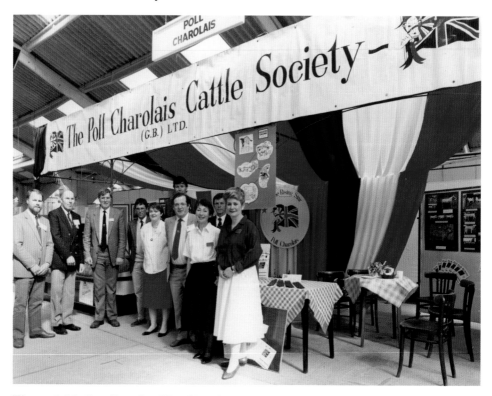

Figure 5.15. Our Stand at "Beef '89 Show" held on Royal Show field, Stoneleigh: Left to right: Brian Jones, Ralph Needham, Jim Goldie, Derek Calder, Ingrid, LH with John Geldard behind, Polly, Alan Goodland and Joy

Figure 5.13. Avoid the problems of de-horning

Figure 5.14. Poll Charolais do it spendidly by themselves

Figure 6.3. Annabel's picture of LH with MG and Annabel's daughter, Polly
Inset: Figure 6.4. Joy at Helme Lodge

Figure 6.5. LH off on his
morning bicycle ride

Figure 6.10. A Christopher
Cartoon presented to LH on
Helme Lodge Independence Day

Figure 6.6. "Dew Bath on a May Morning"

Figure 6.17. Joy's arrival at the Wedding with Reg Gifford in the Bentley

Figure 6.17a. Bentley bonnet adorned with flowers

Figure 6.20. LH and Joy with daughter Lindsey and son Graham with Geraldine

Figure 6.21. LH and daughters Penny and Ingrid

Figure 6.22. LH and Joy with Chums and wives: Left to right: Geoff and Bernadette Milton, Best Man Bill Bewley and his wife, Jenny, Reg and Pam Ashworth, Peter and Joan Matthews, Tony and Jen Sansom, Roger and Heather Gardner

Left: Figure 6.23. LH and Joy with left to right: Sam & Gil Murphy, Martyn and Pam Wrathall, and my brother, Gerard, and his wife, Carol

Below: Figure 6.24. LH and Joy with left to right: Christine and Peter Briggs, Andrew Bromley, Kate Ainsworth, Myra Huddleston and Jean Cowling

Figure 6.25. LH and Joy with her cousins, Jean and Margaret, and family:
Left to right: Gordon Elliot, Jean and Gordon Whitney, Russell and Margaret Elliot and Karen Elliot

Figure 6.26. Joy's cousin, Judith, with daughters, Gillian and Helen

Figure 7.2. View across the valley from the garden at Quarry Foot with stone forum and arch built by Jonathon Hayton and LH

Then to my surprise I was presented with a lovely glass bowl, engraved with an accurate picture of Helme Lodge and the words arranged as follows:

To Len
in appreciation
Helme Lodge Residents

In addition I was presented with a Christopher Cartoon which incorporated my hobby interests: the Penny Farthing, my 1954 TF MG, my old 1928 Marston Sunbeam and my

Figure 6.9. Will and Val Duffield at home

favourite books. Joy had clearly been in on the fun! (Figure 6.11 colour section)

As if the above was not enough, all the residents had contributed to the hire of two Harley Davidson motorbikes and riders to take Joy and me on their pillions for a half hour ride. It was amusing to see other residents also having a ride that day. It was a lovely sunny day of rejoicing, fellowship and good humour. We had lots of happy days at Helme Lodge leading up to our wedding and afterwards.

Figure 6.10. Presentation of engraved bowl
Left to right: Bernadette Milton, LH and Joy

Figure 6.11. Joy on Harley Davidson ride

Figure 6.12. Bernadette Milton, Joy and Ann Maidley

Figure 6.13. Joy with her favourite book, relaxing in the arbour which LH made for her

YOU WILL NOT GO LONELY

Poem to Joy on her going
into hospital for an operation.

Courage will not be lacking
Or the will to see it through
All our love like a laser beam
Will warm and strengthen you.

For you will not go lonely
Into your painless dream
Your noble spirit I'll protect
When the surgeon works his fleam.

And after his work is over
When rest is what you'll need
There'll be lots and lots of lovely books
To read and read and read!

And you will not be lonely
When you float from your dreams to earth
Whatever may be the outcome
We are chums in love and mirth.

Through all our tribulations
Through all the joy and pain
You have been my strength and guardian
Over and over again.

And you will not come lonely
Back to your home spick and span
But to the love of the one whom you've cared for
Since our life together began.

My modest manly efforts
Within the domestic role
Will doubtless cause some amusement
Even when I've given my all!

For though you know I'm wonderful
And my personality is great
I fully expect some fireworks
If fate sometimes makes me late!

So my Jollity you will not be lonely
Take strength from our love today
Let your courage and spirit be nourished by mine
For a star-like emerald points the way!

Nobbut-Me! LH April 1996

★   ★   ★

"RENOIRS" – WINDERMERE

I have always enjoyed good food. My partner, Keith Wood, was often amused because, when I returned from holiday, it was not the places that I recalled first, but the cuisine I had enjoyed en route!

I was brought up at Brow Top in a family that believed in eating fresh food, mainly produced straight from the farm. We had a good early breakfast, then "10 o'clocks", a good lunch at 12/12.30 p.m., followed by 3 o'clock drinks and 6 o'clock porridge at night.

We had a mixed farm, so greens and root crops were grown. We had soft fruits in the garden and orchard, which Mother and Granny used in season and "bottled" for winter. We kept two pigs to eat the waste food and for home consumption. We had hens, ducks, geese and turkeys, which we dressed and sent to our bed-and-breakfast guests at Christmas.

As a result I have always believed that if my work for other folk could not produce sufficient to afford a tasty meal at lunchtime in a local café or bistro, then the job was not worthwhile. It was also useful for keeping in touch with local affairs.

In my early practising years in Windermere I ate at Mrs King's "Post and Gate Café" with some of the business men of Windermere: characters like Neil Smith, father of Robert and David Smith of Rayrigg Motors, Eddie Simpson of Musgraves, Herman Wilkinson, known as Wilkie, an antiquarian book seller, John Snaith, a jeweller in Bowness, and other business men and commercial travellers. I suppose in "new speak" it would be called net-working today! It was helpful to me in making new friends, building the practice and understanding how the business world ticked. In those days solicitors were not allowed to advertise, so one's track record and personal recommendations were important. Advertising was "touting" in the profession then, and how much better our profession was regarded.

I recall that on one occasion Neil, Wilkie and I found time for an outing on the steam train from Settle to Carlisle before taking the very last return journey by train to Keswick when the line was finally closed. The "Post and Gate" closed a few years after Mrs King retired, but happily Colin and Pauline Sandy converted part of Woolley's garage into what we know as "Renoirs" today.

Colin and Pauline's concept of Renoirs Coffee Shop and Bistro was inspired and the layout and décor is attractive, timeless and enduring.

It is still as they designed it. The food and coffee was always good and so it became my lunchtime haunt two or three days per week.

The food was always reliable, tasty and delightful, but in July 1996 David and Gillian Howarth, the present owners, excelled themselves with a smoked ham, leek and mushroom pie. Such was the quintessence of taste that I was moved to write an ode on my napkin which I gave them. It later appeared in the local newspaper, The Lakeland Echo.

4   THE LAKELAND ECHO   July 11, 1996

The cream of coffee shops

ONE of the success stories of Windermere in recent times has been the Renoirs Coffee Shop in Main Road, owned by David and Gillian Howarth, which has established an enviable reputation over a wide area.

A coffee shop was first developed on the site five years ago by Mr and Mrs Colin Sandy, who at the time owned Woolleys garage next door. A French theme was brought in to compliment the Peugeot-Citroen dealership at the garage.

Later the coffee shop was named Renoirs, although this was something of a misnomer as the vivid blue and yellow theme was, in fact, the colour scheme of Monet's home.

Few establishments have so quickly established a loyal following as has Renoirs — and few establishments will have had customers penning odes to one of its dishes. But that is what one has done at Renoirs, where Mr Len Hayton was so impressed that he penned the following, 'on the spot,' so to speak, entitled: 'Renoirs — Ode to the Smoked Ham, Leek and Mushroom Pie.'

I'm a regular customer
come in most weekdays
I enjoy all your cuisine
delightfully cooked; in so
many ways.

Your cottage pie is delectable
and your quiche is just great
but today you've excelled
with the best up to date.

This smoked ham and leek
with mushrooms in bake
I am savouring the pleasure
each mouthful I take.

So I'm worried for the future
if this gets around
such quintescence of taste
no spare seats will be found!

Historical note: Pierre Auguste Renoir (1841 — 1919). Born at Limoges. Became one of the leading painters of the French Impressionist movement.

LEFT: The attractive exterior of Renoirs Coffee Shop, Main Road, Windermere.

BELOW: David and Gillian Howarth, proprietors of Renoirs Coffee Shop, Main Road, Windermere.

Figure 6.14. Renoirs of Windermere

RENOIRS-OF-WINDERMERE

ODE TO YOUR SMOKED HAM, LEEK AND MUSHROOM PIE!

Written at the time on a paper napkin

I'm a regular customer
Come in on most weekdays
I enjoy all your cuisine
Delightfully cooked, in so many ways.

Your cottage pie is delectable
And your quiche is just great
But today you've excelled
With the best taste up to date.

This smoked ham and leek
With the mushrooms in bake
I am savouring the pleasure
With each mouthful that I take.

So I'm worried for the future
If this fact gets all around
Such quintessence of taste
No spare seats will be found!

July 1996

★   ★   ★

Having run a successful agency for the Bradford & Bingley Building Society (BBBS) in Windermere since 1964, I was from time to time over the years invited to join a group of other agents for a celebration of our progress.

On this occasion Joy and I were invited and given £10 each for a flutter at the Bradford & Bingley Handicap at the York Ebor Races. Our Area Manager recommended that we should give it to the Agent from Rochdale, who enjoyed a reputation for success at horse racing.

This is a verse I wrote after the race for the Agents' Dinner that evening.

Rhyme to "Rochdale Nick"
(To be recited with an American cowboy's drawl)

York Races

You may have heard of Nell the Eskimo
Or even Dead-eye Dick
But they pale to insignificance
When you meet bank-rolling Rochdale Nick.

Well, we were guests of the "Brad and Bing"
And Nick wore his coat tails low
And when it came to beating the bookies
There ain't nuthen he don't know.

McKenzie John, head-of-region-man
He issued a money decree
"We'll hitch our wagon to Rochdale Nick
For he's cooler than you and me."

Then we peeled our tenners from off the wad
And we staked them to "Rochdale's" roll
Clearly this was the man of destiny
Not bound for distress or the dole.

We each had our flutters and won a few dimes
But naught compared to Nick
I figured it was the "Doc Holliday" coat
And cool stare that did the trick.

With winnings in hand, the last race on the board
Then he threw the gauntlet down
"Do you want to wager the **whole** of this poke?"
But the lawyer began to frown.

They say there's none so wise as these lawyer guys
But for our caution Nick did not care
Our dithers and doubts were cast aside
By the power of his gambler's stare.

In his long frock coat he strode out to the course
With his Eva upon his arm
What a gal was she as she grinned at me
With the warmth of a woman's charm!

Nick placed ALL of the bet
On the best odds anyone could get
And returned with a knowing smile
He was calm, he was cool and unflustered
For Rochdale Nick had style!

We novice gamblers gripped the rail
As we cheered the horse to win
Like escaped young nuns from a convent
Discovering the roots of sin.

Well "Ruznama" devoured the furlongs
And won by the length of its nose
For "Money Management" Rochdale Nick
Spontaneous cheering arose.

And we all rolled our eyes in glad surprise
Lawyer Len had a sheepish grin
Then we joined in the fun as Eva begun
To count our winnings in!!!

© *LH 22.08.1996*

THE FARMER'S SON CAME RIDING
Ode to Roger and Heather Gardner on their Silver Wedding Anniversary

Ladies and Gentlemen,
Members of the Gardner and Hayton families,
Relatives, Friends and Guests

In the last 24 hours – nudge – someone should say something – propose a toast. You'll happen be saying something? That's how farmers usually start!

Then I thought: well where do I begin? There are so many wonderful things you can say about Roger and Heather, Julia and James, John and Eva and the family.

Then I started thinking about Roger's cow philosophy or his Bovine Theory of Relativity! Like Einstein, Roger does a lot of thinking – when he comes in from milking and sits on the floor by the Aga! That is Roger's place for thinking, planning and philosophising. He has a

paternal ancestor, who was a very good teacher and taught my mother. So I warm to Roger's theory of relativity.

Roger tells me that there is no difference between the behaviour of cattle in a herd and the behaviour of humans. They have natural leaders, aggressive ones, headstrong ones, quiet ones and sexy ones! Only cattle are more honest about love-making and less complicated – Roger is quite straightforward about such things!

Now when Roger visited Kentmere over 25 years ago, I have a feeling that his theory of relativity was in its embryo stages. When he

Figure 6.15. Roger and Heather in playful embrace at Ullswater

clapped eyes on Heather in her hot pants and with her long hair, he clearly saw her 'as best young heifer around!' He did not waste a lot of time.

In all good farming circles, farmers look at pedigree. Heather and Roger are the progeny of a long line of farmers and brainy folk on both sides. Their daughter, Julia, and son, James, are intelligent and gifted. Clearly Roger has applied his relativity theory in full measure with Heather! He also has a 'hug theory' – always hug rather than argue!

John and Eva Gardner both have good conformation, are full of good sense and wit, and both are lively characters. John has to take his boots off when he goes in the house and he is not allowed in until he has done all his work – and certainly not with any oil or cow-shit on his overalls! (*John has many uses for his cap, which are listed in the book elsewhere.*) Eva sets high standards. She is very clean and house-proud and she has great skills in flower arranging and teaching others.

So when Roger's old motorbike broke down at Kentmere when he came courting Heather, and Gerard said, "Bring it into the living room where we can see it, lad," Roger was amazed. You see Gerard, as you all know, is a genius with engines and all things mechanical. The challenge of curing an ailing engine, even on a cold, dark night, would always immediately take precedence over all other considerations – and still does! So into the living room went Roger's motorbike.

Well, Roger thought it was wonderful. Alice, Heather's mother, used to protest mildly and sometimes wildly, but she basically indulged Gerard in his Hayton idiosyncrasies – it runs in the family! I am not sure if any of Roger's bulls have the same conformation as Gerard, but he and Alice produced their daughter, Heather, and three handsome sons, Edwin, George and Jonathon. Sadly, Alice cannot be with us because she died when her grandson, James, was just a baby.

Heather was always a tower of strength to her father and her brothers, for they were all still young when Alice died. Heather rose to the challenge. I am pleased to see so many of Alice's family (the Bingley family) here tonight. A lot of warmth, good humour and application genes come from the Bingley side. The stories we could tell about Tony – such as the one in the goose barrel!

But enough about pedigrees. Let us pay tribute to Roger and Heather, Julia and James. When I say there is a couple who are truly united in mutual love, respect and trust – no one can demur.

When I say they have given love, understanding and encouragement to Julia and James and brought them up in an exemplary way – no one can demur.

When I say Heather and Roger remain as united and honest in their love as they were twenty-five years ago – no one can demur.

We are proud of you and you can be justly proud of your achievements. You stand as an example to us all.

Ladies and gentlemen – Do you remember that shy, teenage girl in hot pants – a contradiction in itself? Heather had to hang on the back of Roger's old 'Matchless' motorbike. She shone her father's torch up the road and into the woods, because she was always nervous of the dark - and the old bike had no lights! Roger used to panic when Heather shone the light away from the road because he could not see! They could not have known then how happy they would be, and how much they would become the hub of both the Gardner and the Hayton families.

Their support and help to us all in times of trouble have been beyond measure. Both Heather and Roger have a quality of patience, understanding and sheer reliability and application, which still remains a strength to all their family and friends.

This Silver Wedding is a milestone on what we all hope is a long journey of continued happiness for you both and for all your family and friends. We all love you – and we must tell you, Roger – your Bovine Relativity Theory works!

★　★　★

THE FARMER'S SON CAME RIDING

The stars were bright in the firmament, as he rode the Ratherheath way
The road was a ribbon of moonlight and none would say him "Nay"!
The farmer's son came riding, riding, Honda-borne he came
And the call of the wild was beckoning that none of us can tame.

I could hear the whine of the engine as I stood in the evening cold
And the farmer's son came riding, riding, purposeful and bold
Deterred not by frost nor fingers numb but spurred by lover's zeal
His heart aflame with love's delight was all that he could feel!

He was homing to my brother's daughter under the starlit dome
Sweeping through the hills and corners like a pigeon racing home.
And the farmer's son came riding, riding, along the valley floor
Gerard's daughter cocked her ear as the sound came through the door.

There in the Brow Top kitchen doing her nightly chores
Was the girl of his dreams, listening, listening, hearing her brothers'
snores
For Heather was the boys' big sister, the apple of her father's eye
Cheerful and always reliable, but her womanhood was nigh.

Above in the bedroom, now wide awake, having heard the Honda's
roar
The brothers tiptoed, tiptoed, and closed the bedroom door:
Edwin, George and Jonathon like young throstles in a nest
Leaned out of Brow Top window clad only in their vests.

For the farmer's son was Roger – and "Rodge" was coming now
And Dad he was a-milking, milking, milking every cow.
"Roger is coming to see Heather! Here he comes now!
And Dad he's still a-milking, milking every cow!"

And the farmer's son came riding, riding, up to the farmhouse door
And Heather, shy like Granny, excited, was washing the kitchen floor
Restraining her longing by doing things, but lost to the thrill in her
breast
The farmer's son came knocking, knocking; and all of us know the
rest!

The Toast is for Good Health and Long and Happy Lives Together!

TO ROGER AND HEATHER

LH 12.02.1997

A SPARROWHAWK'S DINNER

Like intermittent puffs of pipe smoke
Wisped away on summer breeze
So it is my eye is taken
By distant movement under orchard trees.

I lazy, lounging in the evening
Under Georgian façade
Where roses climb cast-iron veranda
A fountain plays in the old courtyard.

My evening slumber is soon discarded
Bird binoculars I take in hand
Sunbeams strike the floating feathers
As I focus on the orchard land.

A sparrow hawk has caught his dinner,
Alert and watching all the while
Plucking feathers from a ring-dove
His cold eyes scan radar-like, but never smile.

The hawk dissects the ring-dove swiftly
Mantles his prey with wings outspread
The dove's mate mourns across the orchard
Trembles and flutters in fear and dread.

★   ★   ★

Later I viewed his dining table
His plate a feather circle on the ground
No meat or skin was wasted
Only scraps of skull and claw I found.

Sad, yet nature breeds more ring-doves.
Of sparrow hawks we see but few.
When my time comes – come sparrow hawk
For I doubt if the ring-dove ever knew!

LH 5· 8. 1997

TO A WORLDLY LADY!

★   ★   ★

In the bath she is warm and caressing
She kisses and fondles your toes
Enveloping, embracing your being
In a way that only she knows.

In anger she's wild and exciting
Untamed, unbridled and free
A rainbow in double refraction
Or iridescent on the waves of the sea.

She appears in the soft glow of morning
Through curtains of gentle rain
In the form of a mermaid twinkling
Patterned on the window pane.

For she is the power, the Mother of Life itself
And Life is her only daughter
You may ask me who this phenomenon is:
I reply: *It is only Water!*

★   ★   ★

Figure 6.15b. Ref. The Farmer's Son Came Riding. My niece, Heather Gardner with her brothers Edwin, George and Jonathan at George's wedding to Sarah.

A GRASMERE WEDDING

The day dawned beautiful on the 30th of May 1997. Joy, my bride, and my niece, Heather Gardner, on the invitation of our friends, Reg and Elizabeth Gifford, owners of Michael's Nook Country House Hotel in Grasmere, had stayed there on the eve of our wedding.

Roger and I had meantime stayed overnight at the Wordsworth Hotel in Grasmere, also owned by the Giffords. I had done the legal work for Reg and Elizabeth when they acquired the ruined hotel and redeveloped it some years before. It was here where our nuptials were to take place. I shall always remember my early morning shower in the feature giant Victorian shower bath. It was like standing under a water fall – the volume of water was so great!

Thus cleansed by the shower, inspired by an early morning walk along the river with Roger and a

Figure 6.16. My niece, Lucinda Hayton, preparing the Bride

good breakfast with the sun streaming through the windows, I reflected on the previous six years of "apprenticeship". My divorce petition had not been made absolute until March of that year. Now I looked forward to securing and celebrating my future with Joy.

Figure 6.17. Joy's arrival at the Wedding with Reg Gifford in the Bentley

Bill Bewley was my Best Man. His moments of panic, when he discovered our wedding rings had been removed from overnight custody in the safe, were overcome when I explained I had collected them and they were in my pocket.

Reg decorated his Bentley,

borrowed a chauffeur's cap and conveyed Joy to the Wordsworth, and after the wedding he took the two of us for a spin round Grasmere before returning to our guests for the "Wedding breakfast".

At the wedding reception my Best Man Bill, backed by Tony Sansom and Peter Matthews, pulled my leg mercilessly and Joy joined in the humour in my defence as usual just as she also had a warm, witty way of putting me straight too!

Our wedding pictures were taken by my niece, Annabel Williams, and given to us as a wedding present. As the pictures here and in the colour section show, we had a lovely day amongst family and friends. See colour pictures 6.20 to 6.29.

We had a lovely weekend honeymoon at Michael's Nook, courtesy of Reg and Elizabeth, and in the August we holidayed in London, did the sights, dined with my son, Martin, and his partner, Richard, and enjoyed a Gondoliers night at the Proms in the Royal Albert Hall.

Shortly after our wedding we had an open house and garden party at Helme Lodge for our friends and neighbours. Geoff and Bernadette Milton were, as always, generous in their hospitality and opened their terrace and home for the party.

Will Duffield and his wife, Val, together with Norman and Margot Yates, and Steve and Sue Johnson, all kept us entertained as usual. Paul and Ann Maidley and their friends, Tom and Pam Newton, joined in. Paul had a go at riding my Penny Farthing on the lawn, as did John Gardner. Paul did not find it as easy as scoring goals for Leeds United!

Figure 6.18. Just married!

Figure 6.19. A comment from the Bride

It was a lovely summer day with lots of laughter and fun.

Figure 6.27. Paul Maidley tries my Penny Farthing for size

Figure 6.28. Keith Young, Geoff Leaver and John Gardner on the Penny Farthing

Figure 6.29. Joy and LH celebrating under the tree at Helme Lodge

7

LEVENS AND OUR "JOLLITY" YEARS

GO WITH THE TIDE OF GOOD FORTUNE

★ ★ ★

Some mornings one wakes up with a zest for life and there seems to be a tide of energy and inspiration which makes the heart sing. Joy was always an inspiration and was well named, and I called her "Jollity" because she brought fun and jollity into both our lives.

Figure 7.1. Annabel's picture of Joy and granddaughter Emily on Geraldine's shoulders

Joy and I moved to Quarry Foot, Levens, in October 1997 and were busy with extending the bungalow. Joy's son, Graham, and his wife, Geraldine, already lived in the village and welcomed us here. It was lovely for us to see their two children, Emily and Robert, growing up.

Fred Martin's Aunt Agnes (shown in figure 2.2) is also my aunt, so Fred and I are related. Fred and his wife, Ruth, as well as Chuck and Averil Mason made us welcome and introduced us to the community of Levens.

I had worked with Fred when the Showground at Kendal was sold. Fred and Ruth are retired farmers now living in the village, but they formerly farmed at Lords Plain in the Lyth Valley, where their son, David, and his wife, Louise, now farm. Fred is an ex-Chairman and President of the Westmorland County Agricultural Society. The Martins and the Masons all play an active role in the Society and also in the community. They have a delightful sense of humour, so life was not dull when we came to Levens!

We felt a new zest for life. They invited us to family functions, village events and the Christmas parties at the Heaves Hotel and Levens Hall.

John Geldard encouraged me to attend the Oxford Farming Conference each year in January with the representatives from the Society. With the building of our house extension at Quarry Foot and the exciting work load at the office we felt a new vigour. As John Geldard would say: "We were going forward."

★   ★   ★

GO WITH THE TIDE OF GOOD FORTUNE

An Ode to a Cheerful Approach to Life

Be gone cold corpse of pessimism
Weak winter of weaker sun
Free the tide of good fortune
Which flows through your soul
And let your spirit run.

Open your face to the sunlight
Like a harbinger of spring
Let the tide of good fortune
Which flows through your soul
Make all your body sing.

Raise your eyes to the far horizon
Seek the beckoning pathway between
As the tide of good fortune
Which flows through your soul
Makes all of your journey serene.

Smile as you meet fellow travellers
For smiles are the sunshine of life
Then the tide of good fortune
Which flows through your soul
Helps others to free them from strife.

Rejoice in your Maker around you
Let good cheer range wide and free
For the tide of good fortune
Which flows through your soul
Raises awareness in all that you see.

Think on the mysteries within you
But don't ponder too long on the way
For the tide of good fortune
That flows through your soul
Flows on to another day!

LH 8.9.1998

When Joy and I moved here, we were not conscious at first of my mother's family connection with Levens. We just liked the village and the location. Then I discovered that across the valley I could see "Canny Dale", a small farm where my mother, Evelyn Mary Jackson, was born. I also discovered that my maternal grandmother, Jane Prickett, was born in Beathwaite Green, which is the original name for part of what is now Levens village. My mother used to say that one of her ancestors, John Prickett, was a builder and worked as a mason when Levens Church was built. I have since found evidence that there were two generations of our Prickett family who were builders, and a John Prickett was a builder in Beathwaite Green at the time. Somehow we felt very much at home, still in "Westmorland", where my ancestors have lived since before 1650.

I was feeling like a "Real Live Native" of Lakeland as the American lady had said years before. *See Musings and Amusings.* We soon felt as "heafed or hefted" to Levens as sheep that are brought up on a common and return to their native roots!

My nephew, Jonathon Hayton, and his building partner, Sam Nelson, were our building contractors, assisted by Jonathon's brother, Edwin. Jonathon does not cut corners; his building work, skill and attention to detail, is of the highest order. He served a real apprenticeship as a young man. The three of them made us a lovely home. We designed the terrace and paths at Quarry Foot so that a wheel chair or buggy could drive up onto the front balcony, if ever the need arose. We sketched our requirements for the extension, and the plans were ably prepared by Gary Jeffrey of Jeffrey and Rigg, building surveyors of Windermere. Mel Jeffrey and Colin Rigg were my school friends at Windermere Grammar School and had drawn plans for me at Kentmere over the years.

There were lovely views across the valley to Whitbarrow Scar. At the bottom of our garden ran the open water catchment dike which attracted swans, water hens, coot, ducks and herons. I recall when

Emily, Joy's granddaughter, was about seven, she and I made a list of over 40 different species of birds which we had seen in and from the garden, in the copse behind and in the fields in front of the house. It was a haven for birds.

Sometimes when we were working in the garden, and once when friends were leaving our house, we saw a large male fox sitting on a rock, in the steep copse behind Quarry Foot. It used to sun itself, watching us from above. It was a beautiful animal and probably lived in one of the natural small caves in the limestone rock face which rose steeply between our road and Low Gate.

We enjoyed our lives at Quarry Foot. We made a second garage for the MG and the Sunbeam motorcycle, and a hobby workshop under the new extension. It was accessed through the main garage into the back garden, but it involved a lot of manoeuvring to get the old car in there.

Joy enjoyed sewing. She made or altered dresses for family and friends and for the ladies at Cancer Care, where she helped part-time after retirement. We both assisted my nephew, Jon, when, after the main extension was completed, he came to do building jobs for us. When we added a porch at Quarry Foot, we did the labouring for him. Joy was not just a pretty face; she was practical and positive and she could turn her hand to most things.

Figure 7.4 and 7.5. Joy and LH wheeling barrows with my nephew, Jon, mixing concrete in the background

JOSSY AND THE KAKAPO

I had been watching the *"Life of Birds"* programme on BBC TV presented by Sir David Attenborough in his delightful and informative style.

The documentary had included the unusual habits of the almost extinct Kakapo, a flightless, green parrot-type bird which lives in New Zealand. I found the programme fascinating. The male Kakapo climbs high up in the mountains and hollows out a love-nest in the ground. Then he inflates himself to make loud, booming mating-calls. Meanwhile his mate, having walked up a tree, gathers leaves for the nest within the tree canopy before answering his booming call and joining him. I imagined an old farming couple having a conversation after seeing the programme.

Jessie and Jossy were a Lakeland farming couple, who discoursed in dialect. They had both enjoyed the programme about the Kakapo but Jessie was equally fascinated by Sir David's description of the Albatross with wings up to eleven feet wide, which requires a very long runway to take off into the wind! As for Jossy: well, he admired the Peregrine Falcon which can dive on its prey at up to 200 miles per hour. He wanted to emulate a Peregrine!

Glossary:

Aboon = above

Chasser = a chasser was a defective male sheep much given to pursuing and annoying females; a man with a similar propensity towards women was so named

Cloods = clouds

Croods = crowds

Dross = grossness, unwholesomeness

Du = do

Fer sham o thisel = shame on you

Flee = fly

Hubbyshoo = a commotion, a state of confusion.

I'se = I'm, I am.

Langer = longer

Mear = more

Noo = now

Nowt = nothing

Sae = so

Varra = very

JOSSY AND THE KAKAPO
Jessie teases Jossy

Jossy:
"Aye Jessie mi Lass, I du feel sae elated
Whenivver I watch a bird."

Jessie:
"Fer sham o thisel at thy age
Woman chasser! It's nowt but absurd!"

Jossy:
"Nay Lass, I'se talken aboot flee-en
Like a bird flees high aboon t'cloods
Aboon traffic jams en o' t'grid-lock
Away fre t'hubbyshoo en croods.

"If I was a Peregrine Falcon
I would dive at a turr-a-ble speed!
Oh Jessie, I'd bring thee a pigeon
En o' t'fresh meat thou could need."

Jessie:
"Nay Jossy! I've been watchen Sir David
Thou'd be mear like an Albatross
But thou'd need a far langer runway
Ter tek off wid thy belly en dross!

But nay! I'se sure thou's a Kakapo
Puffed up with love-boom distinct
And gay feckless as a lover
But noo flightless and varra near extinct!"

LH 8.11.1998

PETER GREY MATTHEWS ESQUIRE

A long-winded birthday leg-pull and greeting from your Chums

FIRST some explanatory notes:
   a)   An invitation from Joan and Peter to celebrate Peter's birthday
        for a lovely sunny lunchtime at Miller Howe Hotel beside
        Lake Windermere and
   b)   Concerning the multifaceted character of our Chum Peter:-

1.   Peter has a propensity for labelling his chums with nicknames:
(i)   William John Bewley is variously dubbed by PGM as *Muscular,*
       Butch, Grub, Pugnacious or *The Artisan*, because Bill is manly,
       purposeful, intelligent and capable. Mrs Jennifer Bewley is known
       as *Jen* or *Jenny*.
(ii)   Anthony John Sansom is called *The Vitnery, Toad, Toady* or *The*
       Welsh Vet because he is the most intelligent of the three. It was
       Tony who explained how LH suffered from splanchnic pooling
       after eating too much – there is a rush of blood from the head to
       the large intestine, which causes drowsiness. (Jean, my new wife, a
       retired nurse specialist, calls it the "dumping syndrome"!)
(iii) Mrs Sansom is not called Mrs Toad in deference to her, but rather
       by her maiden name, *Miss Wolstenholme*, because Chanticleer is
       very genteel with ladies!
(iv)   Because I am so simple, I am just known as *Our Boy* or *Uncle Len*
       and for Joy read *Jollity*, as was my favourite name for Joy – adopted
       also by the Chums and their wives.

1.   In response we, Peter's Chums, have dubbed Peter as:
(i)   *Chanticleer* – because of his likeness to a majestic Rhode Island
       Red cockerel when appearing on his auctioneer's rostrum. In truth
       and fairness, Peter was an exceptionally good and professional
       auctioneer and surveyor. A good cockerel is also by nature generous
       towards his hens, as any poulterer among you will know! Or:
(ii)   *Foggy* – he has the mannerisms and characteristics of Foggy
       Dewhurst in "The Last of the Summer Wine", especially when
       discussing his "war wound" – his rather odd finger! Or:
(iii) *Pete, Petricoff or Pet for short …*

Figure 7.6. The four Chums pictured in 2010, left to right:
Bill Bewley, Tony Sansom, Peter Matthews and LH

CHANTICLEER – How to recognise "Chanticleer" – His Appearance & Characteristics :-

- Tall
- Willowy
- Females find him attractive in an avuncular way!
- Males find him tiresomely proud of this latter attraction – or are purely jealous of his good looks!
- Long, strong legs reminiscent of an ostrich or other large flightless bird, slightly bowed
- Walks very fast over mountains to prevent lesser, broken-winded, more rotund mortals like me from keeping up!
- Bright eyes which usually smile warmly, except when thoughts of expenditure cloud their serenity
- Eyelids still retain a hint of the membrane of his extinct ancestor – the pterodactyl.
- He likes his chums to admire his war stories and hold their breath, while he embroiders long accounts of how his finger end was lost in a battle. This is so despite the fact that we all know his account is not logged in any of the annals of British military campaigns!
- Drops hints of his days as an entertainer during the famine so that his chums will call upon him to sing his favourite song, "My Meatless Day".
- A past master in his true vocation as an auctioneer, extracting bids on behalf of the sellers from would-be buyers, none of whom ever

intended to stretch their resources to the extent cajoled and enticed by Matthews of the F.R.I.C.S.

- Makes thrift an art form. Chums have noticed a growing tendency for Chanticleer to rub his hands while counting his fortune, growing more stooped with coin counting in candlelight, while allowing Joan and himself to freeze as the central heating is switched off for long periods.
- While keeping slim and lissom themselves, when we chums are their guests, Joan produces the most excellent cuisine. Pierre, like a good Chanticleer, furnishes us with the best of wine with all the art and practice of a flamboyant sommelier.

On a serious note lest anyone is misled by this leg-pull, we do hold Peter in high regard, as he is well known for his integrity and professionalism in our community and beyond. We dare not extol his virtues too much. Indeed, it would be unwise for us to overpraise him because the bird characteristics, which I have described in him, could manifest themselves in puffing out his feathers or even worse: like the ostrich he could bury his head in Joan's lap and present us with his less gracious parts.

At this celebration lunch and on this auspicious day we fear such a display would be wholly inappropriate, especially at Miller Howe…. which is normally out of the reach of those of us who live south of Staveley Crossings. So on the occasion of Old Peter's Birthday – don't know which birthday – *Petrikoff is very secretive you know, especially about his age and his money!* – I have penned a sort of leg-pull nonsense verse as follows:

ODE TO CHANTICLEER, THE TOAD, YOUNG BUTCH AND ME

I suppose our friendships grew in Table
Working for the common good
Young men with energy a-plenty
Spending youth as young men should
We raised money for local causes
We rolled up our sleeves you see
We laughed in fun and fellowship
Old Pete, Young Vitnery, Muscular and Me!

Then to Portnahaven's harbour wall
Where I bought my hovel fair
Though the roof might leak and walls be damp
We found peace and freedom there
Free to talk and free to walk
Time to muse and ponder
Free to wander in the wind beside the timeless sea
Chanticleer, Young Toad, Pugnacious Grub and Me!

In that roofless toilet on the shore
One can gaze to the stars above
As the moonlight glistens on the lapping waves
Blissful seals on the rocks make love
And Hector Torrie an old seafaring man
Shouts, "Len-art, er ye commen for a dram?"
So in Heartbreak Hotel on the edge of the sea
There's Petricoff, The Vitnery, Young Butch and Me.

Before Judge Richard rose to the Bench
And left us plebs far below
He loved the banter, the verse and the wit
And he cooked us a wonderful show
In the Hector Torrie which he built in his yard
We often went fishing to sea
And we drank a wee dram and quite often sang
Old Pete, Young Grub, Welsh Vet and Me.

Since those balmy (or barmy) halcyon days
Life has altered us all for certain
Those mid-life crises for three of us
We'll leave them behind the curtain
But common to all the four of us
We're glad our wise wives can see
That lads will be lads and we need to play
Old Foggy, Young Toad, our Muscular and Me.

So we'll have to forgive young Muscular Grub
Who cannot be here today
Though we'll tell him what we've thought of him
But not what we really say
The Southern Hundred beckons Butch
And so we are down to three
That leaves just Foggy Mattthews,
Our Ladies, the Vitnery and Me.

And lest Peter should feel slighted
With the focus now on Butch
We'll have to eulogise good Chanticleer
Though we dare not say too much
We'll not mention all his millions
Nor him counting them with glee
We'd rather recall him buying a haggis or dram
For Young Toad, the Artisan, Himself and Me.

Thus Toad and I are honoured,
That Joan has invited us today
With Miss Wolstenholme and Jollity
We join with our Wives to say
That Peter is our champion, our mentor and our sage
But should we celebrate our birthdays
When we get to such an age?
Oh yes! We're pleased we've made it. Yes, yes, I see
Such birthdays come to all of us

Old Chant, Old Vitnery, Young Muscular and Me.

★   ★   ★

Happy Birthday Peter and many of them!
A TOAST to the almost retired – young and fit – handsome – wealthy
– hill walking – Joan cossetted – lucky – friendly – successful man of
charm and property

We give you a toast – It is all we can afford!

LH 8th July 1999

REQUIEM FOR A HAPPY PAIR
OF BANK VOLES

Whilst watching Sir David Attenborough's programme on the *"Life of Birds"*, I was fascinated to learn how a vole finds its way home through the long grass and how the kestrel locates its prey.

Vegetarian Bank Vole, when first leaving his hole
Does not travel by map or a compass.
There's a forest of grass through which Voley must pass
Without making a sound or a rumpus.

Voley nibbles and gnaws fresh grass in his paws
As he opens a path through the thicket
He sniffs at the air, looking here and there
For vole predators ... they don't play cricket!

So he marks all his track to find his way back
By squirting his u-rine in dots
And he sets out his border of vole-law and order
Which he claims as his property lots.

The squirts which he leaves, he hopes and believes
Will find him a mate on the way
Though it means nought to me, to Miss Vole, do you see,
She sniffs of the nuptials one day!

Both smell their way back along vole-smelly track
Where they frolic in conjugal bliss!
But high up above, while they make "v-underful" love,
There's an "Awac" locked onto their piss!

Unknown to the voles, both innocent souls
Ultra-violet reflects from their u-rine
The Kestrel has ways of seeing **ultra vi-o-let** rays
As if they are bathed in sunshine!

So "*au moment critique*" when the Voles have gone weak
The Kestrel dives down on its prey.
That fatal food chain has claimed life again
But? There are many more voles on the way!

LH November 1998

THIS *"THING"* WE ALL NEED

Whatever one's station
Whatever one's creed
We all visit daily
This "Thing" that we need.

Long before the Stone Age
When the wild woods would do
The spirit of nature
Was worshipped all through.

No disinfectant was needed
No pipes nor a flush
The tribe kept a look-out
For wild beasts in the bush.

When kings went to battle
It wasn't the royal throne
That they valued as much
As a receptacle two tone.

It was fashioned in oak
And gilded in gold
It was velvet and soft
In the brave days of old.

In youth in my valley
It was way up the yard
From a warm bed each morning
The journey was hard.

A large hole for Father
Was too big do you see?
So a second he made smaller
Especially for me!

We sat there together
And looked down the dale
While newspaper cuttings
Hung down from a nail.

Though this function we don't mention
There are euphemisms galore!
Where graffiti and carvings
Are all over the door.

Each home has its palace
Tiled right up the wall
With soft scents and tissues
And pot plants so tall.

But of all the fine palaces
And décor I've seen
There's none to compare
With one place I have been.

Where the sky was my ceiling
And the moon shone above
There I sat in the ruin
And heard seals making love.

The hinges were rusty
Where hung the old door
While waves were heard lapping
Nearby on the shore.

Sweeping the night sky
Was the lighthouse beam
Spotlighting my haven
With its far fleeting gleam.

Though the walls were all covered
With moss and green slime
And the sand blown all over
Was mingled with grime

The sea air was so bracing
I felt peaceful and free
My spirit soared like a fulmar
Sweeping over the sea.

And there on that Island
Where the moon lit the shore
As I sat looking out
Through the old ruined door

I reflected:
Whatever one's station
Whatever one's creed
It's the one place we're all equal
On this "**Thing**" we all need.

LH 20.7.1999

Please see figure 3.25 – Portnahaven, and figure 3.26 – map of Islay, to get the lovely feeling of remoteness. The "Thing We All Need" which inspired this verse was situated down on the seashore at Portnahaven on Islay. It had walls and a door but the roof had blown away in the gales. At night the only illumination was from the moon or the intermittent beam of the lighthouse on the little island of Orsay. Before we installed a toilet in our cottage, we had to use this basic facility! I shall always recall it being uniquely in tune with the natural world around me, as I listened to the cries of the seabirds and the waves lapping on the shore.

As I discovered on my Viking Trail in section 8, the Norse men stayed on Islay too. They also had a "Thing" – it was a meeting place or parliament – as in the case of the Tynwald on the Isle of Man. For my part, the "thing we all need" is a place for thought and contemplation. For those of you good enough to purchase this book, the "thing we all need" is a good place for "browsing"!

★   ★   ★

IT MUST BE IN THE GENES

Three uncanny likenesses with 160 years between.

Some years ago, while doing alterations at our Kendal office, which was then at 14/16 Finkle Street, we had to move a number of old deed boxes and tin trunks out of the attic. Some had my ancestors' names painted on them.

It was agreed that, rather than throw them out, I should have the old boxes of papers to help me with my family research. I checked through them and discovered that they contained a fascinating cross-section of papers from the nineteenth century. They included records which related to the Reverend Gerard Hayton and my other ancestors from around Grayrigg, Whinfell and Orton in the old County of Westmorland, now part of Cumbria. Rather than destroy centuries-old papers, many other documents were deposited with the County Council Archives service at Kendal.

A probate which caught my attention was that of the Will of the Reverend Gerard Hayton. He was born in 1809 at a little farm at the bottom of "Huck's Brow" on what we know as the A6, in the dip about three hundred yards past the sharp bend where the old Leyland Clock stood. This was the main route to Scotland before the present motorway was built.

His parents, Joseph Hayton and Agnes (née Huck), also ran an inn there. Gerard was the vicar of Kentmere from 1846 to 1880.

In his box I found copies of letters written by him on behalf of his parishioners. It was clear that he had acted as clerk and scribe for them.

One letter was written on behalf of the tenant of a farm in Kentmere to his landlord. It explained why, in legal terms and in the circumstances then pertaining, the tenant would not comply with the notice to quit. There were laws protecting agricultural tenants' rights even then.

The first likeness I noticed was that the Parson's letter was couched in the same tone and he used the same expressions as I would write today on behalf of a client in those circumstances! I was reading my own prose! He seemed to be doing good legal work for his parishioner, as often was the case with country parsons in those days.

The second uncanny likeness which struck me was in relation to the form of the Parson's signature.

It has been a tradition in our family, until the present generation, for the eldest son to be named Gerard and Joseph alternatively. Thus my eldest brother Gerard's son is Joseph Edwin and our father was Joseph. Our grandfather was Gerard and so on, back to and beyond the birth of Parson Gerard's father, Joseph, in 1775. See "*Poken Aboot Amang Papers*".

My late brother, Gerard Hayton, who had never ever seen his ancestor's signature, signed his name with a particular style of G and H. The style of the G and the H in my brother's signature was almost an exact replica of his ancestor's style. The Reverend Gerard Hayton had signed the letter to the landlord on behalf of the above tenant over 160 years ago!

But that is not all. The third uncanny likeness arose following an occasion, not long after moving to Levens, when Joy and I attended a musical evening for charity, held at Levens Hall. Another guest, Mrs Diana Matthews, a descendant of the Pattinson building family of Windermere, leaned across to me and enquired if I had an ancestor who had been a parson at Kentmere. I confirmed the fact. She then informed me that an ancestor of hers had taken, in satisfaction of a debt, a large quantity of glass negatives by a Lakeland photographer who had come on hard times. The glass slides had been stored with her family ever since. At the time of our conversation she was having the slides catalogued and amongst them was a slide marked "Reverend G. Hayton".

I did not know that a photograph of the Parson existed, as he died in 1880. I was excited by the prospect of seeing his appearance and I readily agreed to pay £20 to her favourite charity for the use of it.

I took the negative, faint but intriguing as it was, to a friend who is a professional photographer, Jack Loan of Windermere, a perfectionist in his work. He had his own dark room and all the necessary equipment. I watched the process as he worked on the old glass negative.

In the tray of developer, gradually visible through the quivering liquid, I saw what appeared to be my eldest brother Gerard's face forming before my eyes. It was such a true likeness to my brother that the sight of the face, smiling out of the liquid, was quite unnerving! I have the photograph to this day.

The picture showed the Parson in the raiment of a vicar with a long black coat and waistcoat, wearing his gold watch chain. My own father, Joseph, had inherited the watch chain and he used to wear it when he was smartly dressed up. The Parson's face and his build bore a most striking resemblance to my brother, Gerard.

It must be in the genes!!!

In a sequel to my discovery of the Reverend Gerard's photograph, Jean and I were invited to the wedding of our friends, Jean Cowling and Steve Lear, on the 10th September 2011. Sitting with our mutual friends, Ken and Ann Clarke, we were discussing Ken's interest in early photography in Lakeland. I discovered that Ken had studied in depth the Brunskill family, who were early photographers based in Sedbergh and Bowness-on-Windermere. Ken knew of the collection of photographic plates from which my ancestor's picture had come. Ken had done detailed research and published a

Figure 7.7. The Reverend Gerard Hayton, Vicar of Kentmere 1846 to 1880. Picture from glass negative by R and JW Brunskill

comprehensive paper on the Brunskill family, a copy of which he gave me.

From Ken's findings, it is clear that the plate we had used to develop the photograph of the Reverend Gerard came from the collection which Mrs Diana Matthews had arranged to be catalogued. The slides are now lodged with the Armitt Trust in Ambleside. The Reverend Gerard was aged 71 when he died in November 1880. His image suggests he would be in his mid-sixties when the photograph was taken.

Ken's research shows that Richard and John William Brunskill had opened their Bowness Studio in 1873 at Sunbeams House, which was built by G.H. Pattinson, the ancestor of Diana Matthews. This suggests to me that the photograph of the Parson was probably taken by the brothers, R and J.W. Brunskill. It is further evidenced by the fact that Ken confirms that the glass portrait negatives of the years 1858 to 1906 were received by the Pattinson builders as a part debt payment owing on the Brunskill premises. This explains how Diana Matthews was in a position to lend me the negative plate of the Reverend Gerard's photograph. The Pattinson family's Penny Farthing cycle, which appears in the Figure 7.8 with Diana's husband, David, is of the same era as the portrait of the Reverend Gerard Hayton. The Penny Farthing was owned and no doubt also ridden by the builder Pattinson – another co-incidence!

I am sure it would never have occurred to the Parson that one day, over a hundred years later, his photograph would be in the hands of his own great, great grandson! I still have his grandfather clock and barometer which were passed down to me when my father died.

Figure 7.8. David Matthews, Reg Gifford and LH, with Geoff Jones serving champagne at the Windermere Festival

DO YOU REMEMBER?

Can you complete the British currency in common parlance pre-decimalisation? The correct amounts should add up to the total. Answers are in the appendix.

£   s.   d

1. A stone
2. A bicycle
3. A male singer
4. Part of the leg of a monkey
5. A man's name
6. A kind of pig
7. The sun, moon and Mars
8. A leather worker
9. 50% of ladies' pants
10. A royal headdress
11. To hit repeatedly
12. An unwell sea creature

Total £32   17   8 ½

MICHAEL WINKLEY'S 60th BIRTHDAY TRIBUTE

My partner, Michael Winkley, decided to retire from the firm as a partner in 2000 when he reached 60 but remain for a while as consultant at Kendal. Our Kendal partners, Peter, John and Naomi decided at that time that they wanted to steer their own ship and so we agreed on a demerger to take place the following spring. Thus my 35 years practising in partnership with Michael came to an end.

Figure 7.9. LH as Best Man to Mike at his Wedding to Kate

Kate, Michael's family and friends organised an evening at Kendal Golf Club to celebrate Michael's 60th birthday to which Joy and I were invited. Kate asked us to do a verse to Mike.

The tribute which follows I have reproduced in full because it records an evening which was special for many of Michael's friends, family, business colleagues, golfing pals, as well as for Kate, Joy and me. With the loss of Michael in 2010, the memory of Mike's happiness that evening is the more poignant. It also gives a flavour of the man who was my friend for 52 years and my law partner for 35 years.

60th BIRTHDAY TRIBUTE
Saturday 2nd December 2000
at Kendal Golf Club

Ladies and Gentlemen: Mrs Winkley – Nora, Kate, Rosemary, Heather and Alex, Friends, Colleagues and Guests:

I declare that this is a **Without Prejudice Meeting** which means you cannot use what I say in evidence!

Everything is **Subject to contract**: which means you cannot bind me to it!

I give **No Indemnities, Warranties or Guarantees**:
which means I won't be responsible for what Joy or I may say
about Michael!

It is on a **Volenti non fit injuria** basis:
which means Mike & Kate asked us here so they are
deemed to have given consent to whatever we might say!

CONFESSION:
But it is **without prejudice also,** because I have a confession to
make to you all, the good people of Kendal and South Lakeland:

I carry a heavy responsibility, because I invited Mike to
Kentmere in 1958

I invited him to join me in partnership in our Kendal office
in October 1965

SO WE CELEBRATE TONIGHT not only his 60th Birthday but
also our 35 years in partnership

Ladies and Gentlemen:

THOUGH I carry this heavy responsibility, for it is my fault that MSW
came to Kendal, I know that he has **always been the best and most
reliable Law Partner I could possibly have had.**

He is a true professional – He always puts **the interest of his Client
first** – sometimes to the annoyance of his partners, his family and even
his golf pals. He is the epitome of a good family Solicitor as solicitors
should be.

He **is reliable and loyal,** he works like an ox and he has **resources
of energy** which frankly amaze me. Mike has done **a great deal of
good work in the town**. He has also provided lots of laughter, fun
and goodwill amongst all his friends and acquaintances. I made an
excellent move when I took him into partnership 35 years ago –

Aside – I could fill many verses with anecdotes of Mike's visits to
Kentmere and our fun going to Blackpool in my old car but it would
take all night. Michael used to love coming to Kentmere then. He loved
to drive the tractors on our farm and he would turn hay then scale it –
back and forth across the meadows. He was "cab happy" as we called

it. His capacity for physical work and his energy seemed infinite.

When we were digging the hole for the septic tank for my parents' retirement bungalow in Kentmere in 1959, it was getting a bit deep for me to throw the earth out. Mike was taller (6 feet 4 inches), so he dug and dug all day until his head was level with the surface. A neighbouring farmer had watched this and enquired of my brother, "Who's gurt Irish navvy thou's gitten diggen that hoo-al? By God, he can dig!"

My father always said you could recognise a real friend by whether he would get his jacket off and help you when you were working. Mike did that and has proved to be a fine and reliable friend!

BUT IT HAS NOT ALL BEEN ROSES AND SUNSHINE!

Joy and I will now pull **his** leg a little.

LEN:
Having practised with Michael Winkley
For more than four decades
I know his little secrets
I have witnessed his tirades!

I have practised and I've practised
To emulate Mike's skill
In getting all his own sweet way
With his unbending iron will.

And what his Client needs or wants
Is Mike's only aim and creed
God help us all around him
Because the Client has prior need!

"Don't ring me now, I'm busy
Don't talk to me today
A fax, a note, a memo
Will all get in my way."

"Don't ring me on a Sunday
That is the 'family day'
And God forbid, I'll wage ten quid
He's golfing Saturday!

JOY:
But lovely Len, my husband plump
You still respect him so
He drives you hairless now and then
And you jolly well let him know!

He can be a tactless, thoughtless stubborn mule
The ultimate 'Chauvinist Male'
But his smile, his hug, his integrity
And his loyalty never fail.

He can bluster and strut and steam as he will
You sometimes do just the same
You are both as stubborn as any men
But you always play the game.

LEN:
Well he's quite a good old skin really
When he fills in his own tax claim
He insists I'm a dependent relative
That's my only claim to fame!

Skilful in drafting documents
He is always sure they're right
You change them at your peril
Unless you want an endless fight

He ploughs the straightest furrow
Through rock and mire and fen
And twenty-four hours later
He rings up 'our Len':

"You might be right, it's possible
But I don't think I was wrong
It's just your lateral thinking
Which I was thinking all along!"

I tried my hand at speaking
And he thought he'd have a try
He outshone me with his wit and jokes
So I gave legal politics a try.

He followed me as President
Of Westmorland and the North West
And even there his energy
Has proved he is the best.

So he'll have you know I'm a country lad
Supported by Mike Winkley
My comfort is I younger look
While he's getting old and wrinkly!

JOY:
But Mike has always helped you
Since you met in student days
And you've been chums together
In so many happy ways.

Long before he came to Kendal
He drove tractors on the farm
Up Kentmere he was cab-happy
But he never came to harm.

He scaled muck around the meadows
Made hay in summer too
And all the time was thinking
If he could put up with you!

LEN:
AYE! Ya knaa he was six foot tall
When he was nobbut a lad
En we were diggen fer a septic tank
En he said to oor Dad:

"You short-arsed Kentmer fellas
You'll need a man in theer!"
So he lowped doon in t'hoo-al hissel
I thowt it rather queer!

Well oor nebber cem past laughen
When he sid o' t'soil shooten oot
He said, "Whaa's that gurt Irishman?
He'll be a navvy ne'er doot!"

JOY:
Well he might be "That Gurt Irishman"
But you recognised his skill
And you and he like beavers
Have worked with iron will.

When Clients' needs required it
You have both worked through the night
And many folk can thank you
For doing what's straight and right.

But now you both are sixty
Life hours are worth much more
Kate and I have ideas for retirement
When you close that office door.

Wherever your successors may steer
However many more years you may do
You two will always be "Brothers"
For each other you'll see it through.

So let's rejoice on Mike's sixtieth birthday
Tell us how it all began
When Mike saw his **first nude lady**
Didn't he hand her a fan?
Tell them about it.

LEN:
Mike, Reg Ashworth and I met at Blackpool Tech in 1958 to study for
the Law Society's Intermediate Exam.

Our Law Faculty was situated on the same floor of the building as the
Art College. We used to see the life models going to the life drawing
classes and we were all rather curious to have a look at what went on!
Mike in particular! This brings me to the poem I wrote for the office

Christmas Party one year.

In the days before office parties were spoiled by noisy discos, we used to hold ours at the Blue Bell at Heversham, when it was in its prime. We dined on the best of John Chew's cuisine with the best hospitality one could wish for. Mike and I used to tell stories. That is where he began as a

Figure 7.12. Mike, Reg Ashworth and I on our 50th anniversary visit to Blackpool Law College, 15th September 2008

raconteur. To begin with it was his custom to recite Stanley Holloway's "Albert & the Lion".

Staff took bets on how many verses he would remember! So for tonight I decided to do a sort of Stanley Holloway monologue for Mike and tell you about a prank we got up to, when we were students at Blackpool Tech.

MICHAEL AND THE MODEL

With apologies to Stanley Holloway!

There's a grand seaside place called Morecambe
That's renowned for Eric Morecambe and fun
It was there that the large Michael Winkley
Grew up and his law studies begun.

Now this is an un-authorised version
But authentic! – That mean's it is true
So we'll take the lid off young Winkley
And examine his sixty years through.

Well he was born a big baby to Nora
Of his masculine gender Alf Winkley was proud
And Michael grew up, well, fairly handsome
Because he stands quite high in a crowd!

And there's another seaside place – it's called Blackpool
Which is renowned for bonny girls and fun
It was there that I first met big Michael
At the law course where our studies begun.

Well, I was shy, en nobbut a country lad
Not used to the ways of the world
But Michael was handsome and confident
As our days at college unfurled.

Our lecture rooms adjoined the Art College
The artists' models were simply divine
And our masculine sap was moved by this
That urge of the male sublime!

When life drawing was in progress a notice said
"No entry. Knock and wait."
So Mike moved the notice to another door
As our lecturer was arriving late!

We explained to our kindly lecturer
You see he was gullible and slow
We told him the artists had more light in our room
But he wasn't bothered to know.

So straight way the brave little fellow
Not showing one morsel of fear
Took the door by its polished brass handle
And strode purposely reet in theer!

Big Mike and all of us following
Pushed in through the open door
A lovely blonde model in her birthday suit
Lay languid on the polished floor.

Our lecturer was most as-ton-ished
He turned in confusion and ire
While I noticed the blonde was a true blonde
Before she pulled on her kim-ono attire!

Well Michael was very gentlemanly
He felt he must comfort the blonde
Because Nora had taught Mike about manners
He could not just run off or abscond!

He pulled off a masterly confusion
We all left held in high esteem
And the lecturer too was bemused by Mike
For his persuasion drew off the steam.

It was then that I thought that's the fellow
This Mike is an unusual man
And I'm a bit odd and eccentric
That's how our friendship began!

★   ★   ★

A happy Toast to Mike's 60th Birthday and 35 years in Partnership followed

Len & Joy Hayton 2.12.2000

"POKEN ABOOT AMANG PAPERS"

They say *"the road to Hell is paved with good intentions."* Over the years I have occasionally found time to start tracing my ancestors, but I have not completed the branches of my family tree, so it cannot appear here. By the year 2000 I had traced the male line back to John Hayton, who had married Margaret Longstaff in 1702. I went looking for wills in the Archives at Carlisle. After looking at papers all afternoon, I wrote "Poken Aboot amang Papers" the following morning.

PROLOGUE
Three Hundred Years of Haytons

"Ald John" begat Joseph in 1702, **Joseph** begat Joseph in 1739, **Joseph** begat Joseph in 1775, **Joseph** begat Gerard in 1809 (Reverend Gerard), **Reverend Gerard** begat Joseph in 1847, **Joseph** begat

Gerard in 1870, **Gerard** begat Joseph in 1895 and **Joseph begat my brother Gerard in 1929, my brother Jack in 1931 and Leonard – that's me – in 1940.**

A Visit ta Archives ta Find Ald John Hayton's Fadder!

I was wanten ta knaa wha'd faddered **ald John**
Fer it seemed o' oor records en papers hed gone
En whar were his parents, his sibbins, his wife?
Whar (where) did he leeve (live) en wat soo-art of life?

So off up ta Carrel (Carlisle) I med mi arn way
I was poken amang papers for t'main of a day
T'Archivist lant up wid a turble ald Will
O John Hayton and Family: did they leeve at t'Gill?

T'Gill was a farmstead under Orton Fell
If' t'farmhouse could talk, what tales it might tell!
Mappen wad knaa what happened ta ald John
Fer he nobbut married his Maggie in seventeen-o-one!

Maggie bore lile Joseph in seventeen-o-two
Thomas a bit later, wid a third commen through!
Then John on his deathbed left his Will-makken late
Because he deed three days later: that was 1708!

So on t'28th of October o that seam eer
John left o' his belongings ta them he held dear.
T'Will said: "Sick in his body but soond in his heead"
But three days later, he was liggen deead!

John left all his heirlooms ta his eldest lad, Joe
And there's a second lad Thomas, the Will let's us know.
"To his loving wife Margaret and the child in her womb"
He left annual rents when he went to his tomb.

As John was a tailor at a gay fancy time
He wod likely mek folderals and fashions sae fine
That t'gentryfolk buyers wod pay him gay weel
En he'd mak a fair profit fre ivvery deal!

To his best friends and brothers he left hats, coats and rings
O' his clay-uths en his brutches en his fine personal things
But what happened ta Margaret? I'se gay moidered ta knaa
What of t'barn she was carry-en? Did it fend? Did it graa?

Well John left forty pund if t'barn was a lass
But a lad wod git fifty – if that com ta pass!
So dootless relieved when t'barn was a lad
She caw'd him lile John, mebbe efter his Dad.

Well I hope that t'ald sayen proved reet in the end
That *"A woman will thrive whar a man cannot fend"*
But alas in t'ald records just twelve eer on
Maggie hed deed leeven Joe, Thomas en lile John.

Joseph survived because mi line he begat
En t' prologue records t'whole o that
But I was gitten di-verted fre ald John's fadder
I needed ta find t'next step up t'ladder.

Well in t'sixteen hundreds thur's Haytons galore
O' leeven roond Orton, but behint which doo-er?
Thur was an ald Thomas wha leeved at t'Gill
He hed a son John, but I'se wonderen still …

Poken aboot amang papers three hundred eer ald
Can git turble misleaden when t'evidence is cald
En yer heead gits o'er–heated as puzzlement graas
Fer corroboration is elusive as I'se sure thou knaas!

So I'se still wanten ta knaa wha faddered ald John⋆
I gat up a blind alley en mi time hed gone
If I could nobbut find ald John's bayens (bones) up Orton way,
I'd call in them experts on D.N.A.!!!

LH 26.09.2000

Notes. i) We have now established that John's father was named
Lancelot and came from Asby – the next parish to Orton. We have also
visited a place called Hayton Holme in the said parish, but we do not
know if he lived there at the time of the Civil War. ii) For dialect words
please see General Glossary.

ODE to JOY, A REAL WOMAN
on your 60th Birthday

For Joy's sixtieth birthday on 17th January 2003, Chris Sutton and Jean Cowling helped me to arrange a party for her on the 18th January at the Lyth Valley Hotel. It is a favourite venue because George Doodson, the proprietor, provides excellent cuisine which is consistently so. Her children, Graham and Lindsey, were surprise guests, because I had gently persuaded her that it was not appropriate to ask them. They had suggested to me they would make the cake, so Joy was surprised and absolutely delighted when they came.

It was a relaxed and amusing evening. Bill , Tony and Peter had written a ditty for Joy, which they performed to acclaim, but their wives, Jen, Joan and Jenny, also did a marvellous performance of a comic version of "Phenomenal Women" by Maya Angelou which seemed very fitting indeed and was enjoyed by all. Tony James did a lovely tribute for Joy, and Mike Winkley entertained us with his mimicry, jokes and stories – laughter galore. Averil Mason did a lovely monologue about Jollity and Joy made an excellent off-the-cuff thank you to everyone, both sincere and comprehensive.

As usual I had my leg pulled lot in all the speeches. There was mock sympathy expressed for Jollity having to put up with me, but I had written an "Ode to Joy A Real Woman" which I gave towards the end of the evening.

★   ★   ★

Woman to a man is a puzzlement
Not capable of definition
Yet Man begotten, beguiled and bemused
Is sculpted, fashioned, moulded and used

An innocent pawn; devoid of suspicion.

Woman is not a female man
A different species altogether
As brave as a lioness protecting her pride
And proud as a peacock with a man by her side

But as changeable as the weather!

Woman to man is a puzzlement
She has dominion over him
A femme fragile as porcelain; a damsel delicate as a petal
Can inspire him to greatness or fire up his fettle

Simply by exposing a limb!

Woman is not a female man
She is far and away more clever
Proud Man the hunter, Man the leader
She makes Man her lover and Man her feeder

Then with love and care rewards his endeavour.

★   ★   ★

These things I have learned in the last twelve years
Since our mid-life crises I've recovered my spurs
Joy, you love the evenings while I love the morn
You get up at six, but I wake at dawn.

So I rise as the birds sing at a quarter past five
When all systems are go and I feel most alive
But I've learned at my peril, I must not wake you
So I work on my computer or read in the loo!

You've taught me to be tidy and take off each shoe
Lest the leaves or the muck are carted all through
I hang up my clothes now, which you iron with zeal
Of the benefits and burdens I'm getting the feel.

I'm a qualified shopper, I've got the highest award
As you sample each garment, I've learned not to be bored
I comment on style, on colour and tone
To avoid "I shouldn't have bought it" the usual moan!

Now I'm so accomplished in feminine fashion and style
If you buy when I'm absent, I have only to smile
My frown now a saving, you rarely buy without me
My only budget sanction's a frown, do you see?

But my Lioness you're loving and caring as well
Any threat to my wellbeing you would banish to hell
"Have you had your tablets? Have you got your spray?"
Is your primary concern at both ends of the day.

What matters the price of a hairdo or perm
When my Jollity is with me to extend my life's term?
You are young, you are fit, you are fun, you are free
Your love is sincere for both our families and me.

You're a tease and a tomboy, a devil may care
Concerned for appearance and styling your hair
But practical, sensible: Yes, you've got it all
Beside you with pride "your little fat Man" walks tall!

★   ★   ★

But still Joy to me: you're a puzzlement
You show no signs of wear
Your sixty years don't show at all
You are still so young and fair.

I am sure you're not a female man
Of that I am most certain
But that evidence is my evidence
Which remains behind the curtain!

I give you the toast: my Wife, my Joy
The centre of life to "Our Boy"
Good health, long life and happiness too
Together in love we'll see it through.

Happy Birthday to my lovely "Joy, Jollity or Joyous"

LH 17.1.2003

★   ★   ★

To a Phenomenon

You must be the most self – deprecating
Person who ever walked this earth.
You invite your friends to gather around you
And let them make you the butt of their mirth.
You take it all with extreme good humour
And beguile us with your delightful rhymes:
You never flinch from the bold confession
Nor falter in the difficult times.

How do you find the courage?
Is it the honey on the porridge?

You win the respect of all who know you
And the love of a charming and gracious wife.
Together you host a wonderful party
To mark a milestone in her life.
We celebrate with the greatest pleasure
Knowing there is real happiness there,
And both of you are the inspiration
For a JOYOUS evening that all can share.

What is the secret of the marriage?
Could it be honey on the porridge?

You wake at dawn in creative mood;
Joy wakes at six to prepare the food.
You steer your clients through the legal maze
Joy helps her Docs in so many ways
And still you have time for our highs and lows,
Our hopes and fears and our laughs and woes.

And so we unite to pay you homage……
And hurrah for the honey on the porridge.

Elizabeth G.

who also has honey on porridge

Written following Joy's birthday party on 18th January 2003

Picture of Elizabeth Gifford's poem

A PRAYER FOR TODAY

LAKELAND DIALECT SERVICE, 13th May 2004

Glossary:

Anudder = another
Blaa-en = blowing
Browt = brought
Dew = do
Dowk = an old carrion crow
Fadders = fathers
Feyten = fighting
Fre = from
Gaa = go
Garn = go and
Ivver = ever
Gay = rather, quite
Gussmer = Grasmere
Hubbyshoo = a commotion or state of confusion.
Hebben = heaven
Hee-ad = head
In turble laa watter = downhearted, miserable
Knaa = know
Lang sen = a long time ago
Larnen = learning

Maapment = daftness, silliness
Mayer = more
Nebber = neighbour
Neet = night
Nivver = never
Nobbut = only
O = of
O' = all
Oor = our
Owt = anything
Tagither = together
Thowt = thought
Udders = others
Watter = water
Weel = well
Wha = who
Wod = would
Yan = one
Yansel = oneself

READ BY LEN AND JOY HAYTON in RYDAL CHURCH, near AMBLESIDE
Introduction

Jessie and Jossy are an elderly, retired, farming couple living in a Lakeland valley.

E Montibus Virtutem (We get our strength from the hills) was the motto of the Old Windermere Grammar School where Jossy had his secondary school education

Jessie and Jossy both believe in Jesus' teachings which they learned in church and at their local primary school. The main rule was:-

"Love thy nebber as thysel and dew unto udders as thou wod be done by."

Aye, Jessie and Jossy still derive comfort en stability fre that early larnen en fre t'hills en dales en t'beauty o Lakeland. But Jossy "gits turble down in t'dumps" or "in turble laa watter" as he would say "o'er o' them hubbyshoo wars en feyten in t'Middle East".

Jossy says: "Them hard-line terrorists en Sharon er yan as bad as t'udder!"

Jossy is sure forgiveness is much better than revenge.

Jossy admires Archbishop Tutu from South Africa. Archbishop Tutu chaired the Truth, Reconciliation and Forgiveness Commission, which was instrumental in avoiding civil war. It brought people together as friends who had been enemies before.

JOSSY (Len)

"O' that hubbyshoo en feyten in t'Middle East! Yon fella Sharon wants ducken o'er hee-ad in oor slurry tank ta cool his hee-ad! Retribution en revenge hev nobbut med things warse en encouraged mayer bloodshed. Bomben en blaa-en up yan anudder – What! It's o' maapment en daft."

JOSSY

When I was lile and nobbut a lad
We prayed last thing at neet
Knelt beside oor beds wi did
En bent oor hee-ads on t'sheet.

We talked ta Gentle Jesus
Love yan's nebber like yansel
En o' wod be weel in Hebben
En naybody wod gang t'Hell.

We slept gay soond wi Jesus
Fer it was common sense we thowt
Because o' this revenge en feyten
It nivver comes ta owt.

When we were born 'twas Hitler
Wha med a turble hubbyshoo
But courage en pullen tagither
Browt civilisation through.

Yet fer o' oor fadders' efforts
Ta unite Nations o' in peace
Genocide, wars and conflict
Seem nivver ivver ta cease.

JESSIE (Joy)

Thou is an ald miserable dowk lad
Thou's in turble laa watter taday
Just thee git thisel oot on thi bike lad
En gang biken up Gussmer way! (Grasmere)

Ald Wordsworth mused aboot daffodils
En wandered in Dora's field
Garn git some fresh air in them mountains
En gaa fer a walk o'er Nan Bield.

Fergit o' them bombs en commotions
Thou teks it o' o'er much t'heart
Good o'ercomes o' sick evil
Thy hero Tutu's med a grand start.

JOSSY

Aye Archbishop Tutu's mi fella
He explains Jesus ta me and ta you
On the cross Jesus said, "Forgive them
For they knaa not what they do."

Even t'Vikings wha invaded oor country
En ravaged oor district lang sen
Hev larn't aboot peaceful co-existence
En t'civilisation o men.

JESSIE & JOSSY together

As we pray midst the mountains of Lakeland
On the rock of our faith we are sure
That truth and forgiveness will heal them
And through love and compassion endure.

Len & Joy Hayton, April 2004

COUNTY SHOW ADVERTS 2004 to 2006

These adverts were broadcast at different times during the day on Lakeland Radio over a fourteen day period coming up to the Show, and I had some amusing reactions to them! They originally started in 2004 and have been used in various versions since.

Greetings, Ladies and Gentlemen. Welcome to County Show time!

This year I'm honoured to be your President of the Show. Joy and I welcome you and hope you'll all come to the Show.

★   ★   ★

Version 1: When oor stock is fit fer market
And the harvest gathered in
When oor food's safe fer winter
And there's fuel in oor bin.

Then cast off o' yer troubles
Be free fre o' yer care
Polish yer be-ats en gird up yer gallasses
En let's o' gang ta t' County Show Fair!

So hark, hark, hark forrad,
Hark forrad, come, come away!
T' fourteenth of September
Is oor County Show Day!

So write in yer diaries
T' fourteenth is the date
Before you're diverted
Lest your plans are too late.

Noo we welcome oor visitors
Wha come fre far en near
To sample oor good takkins
Mak merry en good cheer.

Thur's o' maks o animals, bring yer young folks ta see
T' best breeds in t' country as thur can be
Thur's o' maks o yows en o' maks of cows
Horses en goats, pigs, poultry and sows.

Thur's gallopen horses, Women's Institute courses
Thur's o' maks garn on en plenty ta see
If thou's keen on fresh me-at en t' best country fare
Well t' food hall's a must: we'll be see-en you there!

What, we've acres of Trade Stands wi goodies galore
To buy at t' Show means sae much more!
Ye'll find o' them trantlements, ye've sought far en wide
Though tractors en implements fre t' wife thou can't hide!

But don't worry cos t' wife en t' children en o'
Can find what they want at oor grand country show
En we've fancy boddies commen: celebrities I mun say
But I can't tell yer noo: you mun come on the Day!

Version 2: Hark! Hark! Hark forrad! Hark forrad, let's away
On t' fourteenth o September it's County Show Day!
* But it isn't just farming, thur's country pursuits
Business en commerce, pleated skirts en fine suits!

Ancient but modern I.T. courses we run
For all ages at all stages: we mak learning fun!
Oor Society is active throughout t' four seasons
A community dynamo fer many, many reasons.

Oor Rural Links Team holds Farm Open Days
When schoolchildren en students see best farming ways
Like oor founding pioneers two centuries ago
We promote best farming practice on oor farms and on t' Show.

But oor Show is t' flagship, oor "raison d'être"
There's plenty ta do en ta see etcetera, etcetera
Fer o'er two hundred year folk hev com tul oor Show
Sick grand traditions we mon't let em go.

So remember, remember t' fourteenth of September
The Westmorland County Show
Relax, watch t' wrestling en o' t' ring events,
O' t' displays en crafts roond t' showfield in t' tents.

En young folks, please remember oor traditions lang sen
When coy country lasses would wink at thur men
Thur'll be bonny lasses on horses; aye, lasses o' roond
Wi young hansom fellows on t' County Show Groond!

★   ★   ★

So we're o' looken forrad ta see-en you at t' Show
It's turble good value as maist o yer will know.
En hev a good day oot!

Yer knaa t'ald folk used ta say:
"A good laugh en a good crack wi yer friends is worth o' yer physic!"

August 2006

WESTMORLAND COUNTY SHOW 2006

Joy and I were delighted when the Society elected me as Vice-President in 2005, followed by President in 2006. We had the pleasure of shadowing the 2005 President, George Procter, and his wife, Hazel, on a lovely sunny Show Day.

Background – My work for the Westmorland County Agriculture Society began in 1989 with the task of co-ordinating the sale of the old Kendal site, then through the saga of finding a new site, with

Figure 7.13 County Show 2005: Joy with President George Procter and his wife, Hazel, Jennifer Read, Jonathon Mason and Fred Martin

the eventual move to Lane Farm at Crooklands, near Kendal. This brought Joy and me into contact with a wider circle of the farming community of South Lakeland. We found all the farming families and business people who are members and/or support the Society to be the salt of the earth, reliable, friendly and a delight to know.

The legal issues I had worked on included charity matters and redrawing the constitution with the late Chris Lambert, Roger Read, and the present Chief Executive of the Society, Christine Knipe. I have seen the tremendous work done by the Management Committee and the Showfield Director, Stephen Procter, in establishing the show in its new location. Since then Christine and her team have continued to carry out the Society's evolution policy and made the show blossom.

With the establishment of the Country Fest at the end of May and the study courses the Society provides, there is an all year round service to the members and to our community. The work throughout the year, which goes into the preparation for the annual Westmorland County Show, has to be seen to be appreciated.

The vitality, drive and expertise of our Show Director, Stephen Procter, and his dynamic team of volunteers, in putting the Show together and dealing with the practical problems on the Show Day, need to be seen to be truly understood.

Though the move from Kendal was controversial at the time, as Roger Bingham in his history of the Society, "From Fell & Field", has related, it has brought substantial benefits as described in Section 2 of this book.

Joy and I had enjoyed the bi-centenary celebrations, 1799 to 1999, which included a service on the show-field conducted by the Right Reverend Bishop Harland, Bishop of Carlisle as well as a banquet in a splendid marquee on the 22nd August, 1999. Our President in that important year was Dorothy Lambert, whose husband Chris had been the Society's secretary for twenty six years. Dorothy and her family had worked hard with Chris and given their full support to the Society throughout. Dorothy welcomed Lord Plumb, who was the excellent guest speaker. It was a large gathering of members and friends of the Society, which occupied sixty four tables in the marquee. For the record, I have included in the appendix i) a list of Secretaries 1799 to date; ii) a list of Chairmen 1895 to date; iii) a list of Presidents 1799 to date.

THE COUNTY SHOW 2006

Joy

I wish I could say that the Show Day of 2006 dawned as bright and sunny as it had in 2005, but alas the rain was almost continuous until about 5 p.m.

Christine and her team had encouraged Joy to bring back the old custom of the President's lady wearing a hat. So Joy had bought a lovely hat from Janet Bobbet's exquisite hat shop in the Shambles in Kendal. Joy's smart hat seemed to symbolise the determination of everyone not to be dismayed by the weather.

Although it rained most of the day, what I can say is that the spirit of "get up and go" and "let's rise and shine in adversity" distinguished the whole day. There were large crowds of people enjoying themselves, even though dripping wet. The spirit of good old England was fit and well! We had much laughter and fun, muddy boots and wellingtons and many umbrellas, but nobody seemed at all miserable. There was a good turnout of visitors supporting the Show and the judging proceeded as smoothly as usual. The Show Director, Stephen Procter, and Chief Executive, Christine Knipe, and their teams kept everyone happy and focussed.

On the President's tour we were transported and escorted between marquees and displays on the President's "buggy", ably driven by past President, Fred Martin. Fred is so well versed in the day's procedures that our day "ran like clockwork".

At the Grand Parade in the afternoon, when all the trophy winners collected the cups and shields for the excellence of their animals and farming, they were drenched – but smiling warmly from ear to ear. To speed the process both Joy and I presented the trophies. Joy's hat was still in place under a large umbrella – good humour flowed and the rain was forgotten. There were excellent animals of all breeds and it was a pleasure to see their owners enjoying their success. There were also trophies for excellence in farming practice and for the best managed farm. So it was evident that the principles and objectives of the Society when formed over two centuries ago were still pursued with the same vigour, competition and determination!

Figure 7.15. Champion Rough Fell sheep with owner and breeder Roger Sedgwick of G.M. Sedgwick and Son

Among the sheep the Rough Fell breed were always my favourite, probably because I was brought up with them, and also because they are less excitable than the Swaledale.

My father's cousin, Anthony Dixon from Kit Crag, Selside, James Dixon's father, used to tease my father about our keeping Rough Fell sheep. In jest he would call our sheep "porcupines" because of their strong wool. He was a top breeder of Dales bred. Such friendly leg-pull still exists between breeders, but there is a strong bond of competitive camaraderie between farmers. The witty exchanges and the imagery portrayed in a few words are a continuing joy to me!

★   ★   ★

OXFORD FARMING CONFERENCE AND OXTAIL DINNER

John Geldard, John Pickthall and John Burra persuaded me to attend the Oxford Farming Conference about 15 years ago and I attended most years until 2008, sometimes with Joy. The Conference is an international function which attracts leading farmers and advisers to the industry. Papers have been given over the years by our UK Agriculture Ministers, as well as those from countries in Europe, USA, Australia, Canada and New Zealand. The programme includes presentations from scientists on food, global warming, crop improvement and animal husbandry, as well as the career successes of individual farmers with pioneering ideas.

The Chris Lambert bursary, in honour of his unstinting work for the Westmorland County Agricultural Society, enables us each year to send two farming students or young farmers, picked on recommendation from the Young Farmers' Clubs, to the conference, which is held in early January. These young farmers usually get their eyes opened and come back feeling they have a future. They get fired up by the example of successful farming entrepreneurs who have addressed the conference and been thoroughly questioned. Some farmers see difficulties as opportunities – and no one is more resourceful than a farmer!

On the last evening at Oxford some of the directors of the Conference and delegates, who prefer to travel the next day, attend the Oxtail Dinner which is held in Worcester College.

Richard Halhead, who is Chairman of "the Oxtail", asked me to write "An Address to the Oxtail" to be performed before the Oxtail Soup is consumed! The procedure and the address are as follows:

THE OXTAIL CLUB

CHAIRMAN Richard:

Latin:
GAUDEAMUS CUM GAUDENTIBUS FUNDITORES ET CONVIVIUM BOVILLUM
(*Interpretation* – Let us rejoice with those who celebrate the founding of our Oxtail Dinner.)

Chairman recalls historical notes – See Appendix

TOAST to the Founding Fathers – beginning in Lakeland Dialect:

Ya winter's neet lang sen they forecast snaa, en t'wind was blaa-en
strang
Some delegates at Oxford thowt thur journeys were o'er lang
Fre Scotland en North Counties, fre Kent en Devon anaa
They conflabbed o' t'gither: "It's nut safe fer us ta ga."

"We'll stop the night in College": Worcester was the choice
"We'll have an Oxtail Dinner," they intoned together in one voice
And so it was that long journeyed folk have often come together
And now we stay for Auld Lang Syne in any sort of weather.

I give you the Toast – The Founding Fathers

AND NOW PLEASE . . . BRING IN THE OXTAIL

The oxtail is then presented before the Chairman.

As it reaches the Chairman, LH or his successor,
still standing intones:

So of this succulent meat
Now let us eat
And quaff our wines a-plenty
Give birth to mirth
Pass round the port
Among us the Cognoscenti.
(The Connoisseurs)

The Chairman calls upon LH or successor..

ADDRESS TO THE OXTAIL

Oh noble tail the hindmost part
Did in thy time waft many a fart
From ox's entrails.

And many's the time with whip-like switch
Thou eased a smarting bovine itch
From blue arsed flea.

Oh pure meat mascot of this Oxtail Night
Swat meddling politician and parasite
From our persecution.

Inspire and teach them common sense
The way to banish badger and bovine pestilence
From our land.

That never more thy kind be put to fire
No holocaust nor theories dire
From ignorance.

If we must import the third world meat
Let fair rules apply and ban the cheat
From competition.

Now noble fare what better taste?
No morsel shall we ever waste
From thy last sacrifice.

Now noble John .... with platter aloft
March round this ancient under-croft
With tasty tail piece.

Richard/Chairman receive this trusty fare
Sourced and tagged and produced with care
From British farmstead.

And let us with lusty humour it devour
Take time for tales to pass the hour
Free from tribulation.

And toast the Oxtail on last Oxford night
The conference puts all things to right
From long experience!

LH or Successor – Toasts the Oxtail.

LOSING JOY

My verses and odes to Joy provide a glimpse of the happy relationship we enjoyed during our 17 years together at Helme Lodge and Levens. My last verse to Joy is personal, but it may be helpful to others facing bereavement. We all know we travel that way one day, but while we have happy memories and hope, we have strength to survive and see the sun shine again.

Though both Joy and I were still working until Joy retired in 2003, we managed to have some enjoyable holidays, mostly with Bay Farm Tours of Morecambe. We stayed at Lake Garda in Italy and visited the surrounding area and Venice. In succeeding years we went to Austria, Switzerland and Norway. The advantages of the Bay Farm Tours were that we could relax and travel with farming folk and visit the highlights of the country, accompanied by a well-informed guide, usually the very helpful Bernadette Tomlinson. We visited a few farms on the way to learn about agricultural methods and met the local people and saw their way of life; so we got a real feel of the country. We had lots of fun and good repartee amongst the farmers!

After we completed the alterations at Quarry Foot we purchased a good second hand two berth caravan. During the summer we sited it at Melmerby, east of Penrith, and toured the villages and places of interest at weekends. We also sited it at Pow Foot on the south-west coast of Scotland near Annan. We had holidays on Caravan Club sites in Scotland and near York. Those were relaxed and

Figure 7.20. Joy and LH 'thumbing for a bus' at the Calf of Man!

happy days. We enjoyed visiting the Isle of Man and staying with Bill and Jen at Port Erin. I took my 1928 Sunbeam in 2003 and 2004 to do the Manx Rally with Bill. See *Two Wheels and Four Wheels.*

We had a holiday with Malcolm and Elsie Tyson in Vence near Nice and visited Monte Carlo and toured in the Maritime Alps and on the Cote d'Azur.

Joy and I also enjoyed city breaks and attending musical shows and concerts, when time and funds permitted. We had a memorable weekend visit with Tony and Jen Sansom to Glyndebourne to see Mozart's Don Giovanni.

We visited my son, Martin with his civil partner, Richard, in London from time to time. They are both very capable and have made a lovely home together. We enjoyed hearing about their enterprising, adventure holidays. They do sponsored treks abroad for charity and have enjoyed walking in Canada, the Yosemite National Park in

Figure 7.22. Richard and Martin in British Columbia, Canada

California and in the Himalayas as well as in the Lake District. Joy was Martin's Godmother and they always kept in touch.

Joy and I led a full and happy life together. We enjoyed visits to Ibiza with Bill and Jenny Bewley and to Spain with Peter and Joan Matthews. In October 2005 Jenny Bewley organised a surprise party for Bill in Venice for his 60th birthday and suggested that the Chums should fly separately, so that Bill would suspect nothing. For two days we had to avoid each other with Jen informing us of their whereabouts by text messages from her mobile phone!

When Ingrid and Moss were planning to emigrate with their family to South Dakota, U.S.A., we went with them in 2004 to assist in locating a site on which to build a new dairy farm. We also visited the Black Hills of Dakota with Ingrid and Moss. We saw Mount Rushmore and then we visited the Crazy Horse North American Indian Memorial. Since 1946, following the request of Chief Standing Bear in 1939, Korczak Ziolkowski and his family have been sculpting the figure of the famous Sioux warrior, Crazy Horse and his horse. The scale model is shown in Figure 7.27 in white with the sculpted mountain behind.

Figure 7.27. Crazy Horse scale model in front of the 563 feet high sculpted mountain

After Joy left our firm in 1990 she worked at Station House Surgery at Kendal for a few years. There she made new friends: Sue Ratajski, the Practice nurse, Margaret Playfoot, Sarah Bell and Helen Stainton, all of whom remained good pals, even after Joy moved to become Practice Manager at St Mary's Surgery in Windermere for Dr Pagan Burns and partners. The friends met for an early evening meal every three months and visited us from time to time on a "Jacob's Join" basis.

★   ★   ★

When I started this book I resolved to celebrate the happy times in life and to share my verses and musings in a happy frame of mind without writing an autobiography. However, it is difficult not to include some events and experiences in life to explain the background and settings which gave rise to the writing.

2007 saw the loss of my brother, Gerard, to pancreatic cancer in July and Joy being diagnosed with the same condition on the 11th July. The disease was so far advanced that it was incurable. We were in the process of taking our time to move houses in Levens, when we got the news of Joy's diagnosis. We decided to move at once, and with help from my son-in law, Gordon Strickland, and his brother, Philip, we advanced our moving date and moved into Sunny Bank the same week.

On hearing our dreadful news, our Chums and their wives, our friends and relatives all came to help and supported us in so many ways. Ruth and Fred Martin came to our aid with quiet, practical help and advice. Ingrid and Moss made arrangements for their 750 milking cows to be cared for while they were away, and they flew back from the U.S.A. to visit and comfort Joy and me. It was not easy for them and they came again in December.

Joy resolved not to have treatment because it was clear by then that there was no cure. She decided that she wanted to enjoy our last months together as much as she could. She was very positive and clear and was more concerned for my future than her own. Joy asked to see our Vicar, the Reverend Ruth Crossley, who proved to be a great comfort and friend to both Joy and me. *It seemed as if a new serenity glowed inside us and sustained us in the last months of Joy's life.* It was an experience which brought into real focus the relevance of Christian values and the true worth of good friends and neighbours. The swell of goodwill and the love of all our friends, which sustained us, are an abiding strength to my faith in humanity.

Figure 7.30. Joy with Ingrid, Kayleigh and Michael on the terrace at Sunny Bank

Joy asked Ruth Martin to make enquiries for someone to help in the house two days per week .By good fortune Ruth contacted Janice Wilson who is and was a tower of strength through the sad times and after. Janice still helps us with the house work and ironing twice per week.

Sue, Margaret, Helen and Sarah also visited regularly, and I have a happy recollection of them doing a jig with Joy on our terrace in the October of that year. It was the last time she was able to dance. They also kindly brought me meals after Joy died to keep my strength and spirits up.

Figure 7.31. Joy dancing the 'cancan' with left to right Margaret, Helen, Sarah and young Harry, and Sue

When my niece Annabel heard the news of Joy's diagnosis, she suggested that she should do a photo-shoot as a gift for us, before Joy became too ill. When I asked Hal and Susie Bagot, the owners of Levens Hall, if we could take some pictures near the Hall, they kindly gave us access to the gardens too. The Hall is usually closed to visitors at the weekend; so we could take our time. The sun shone and we had freedom to enjoy and record some treasured moments with Joy's family there. Some of the pictures taken that day appear in the colour section. They speak for themselves.

Figure 7.32. LH and Joy at Levens Hall

To all our good friends and kind neighbours, the Doctors, Nurses, Macmillan and Marie Curie Nurses and support staff, all the lovely people who helped Joy and me in those months up to Christmas 2007, I wish to express my sincere and grateful thanks.

Nevertheless when Joy passed peacefully away at home on the 23rd December with Graham, Lindsey and I beside her, all of us comforted by the presence and loving care of the Macmillan Nurses, I felt profoundly numb. An extract from the verse I wrote in the early morning of her funeral day follows. I have no doubt most people in the same circumstances have similar emotions.

This is an extract from a sad farewell on 4th January 2008, placed in Joy's coffin with beautiful letters from my son, Martin, and my granddaughter, Kayleigh.

I CANNOT SAY FAREWELL FOR YOUR SPIRIT IS STILL WITH ME
My words are inadequate but encapsulate my sense of loss this morning

You are my heart's delight
Your spirit lives on in my inspiration
Through all the myriad parts of my being
Flows my Jollity's thrilling sensation.

You came to me when I was lost
You loved me to all our cost
A true love, unconditional and pure
Sound as oak, as strong and sure.

In adversity we stood our ground
In true companionship new courage found
You fought for me, not for glory or for wealth
But to restore my will, my faith and my health.

I cannot believe you've left me
For your spirit is in my heart
I can feel you still inspiring,
Telling me be strong, my new life has to start.

I hope you can see – all the good wishes
And how our friends have loved you so
The respect, the warmth, the outpouring
From all the folks we know.

I've done all the things you've asked me
Yet the pallor of your clay
Grieves my heart beyond measure
As I approach this your funeral day.

Graham, Geraldine, Lindsey and Marc
Have all proved so helpful in giving the spark
To the order of service and things we must do
To honour your memory and see the day through.

Mossop and Ingrid your admirers they are
Tell me in the night sky there is now a new star
It shines down on them, as it does now on me
It's the spirit of my Jollity, all our families can see.

My "Jollity Star" will no doubt twinkle and shine
And beckon me one day to your new home divine;
Meantime on your CD and in pictures galore
Your voice and your beauty I still can adore.

I love you beyond measure, my tears fall free
For your love, loyalty and courage: the life you gave me
I cannot believe your spirit has left
At once you are gone, yet I'm not bereft.

I can still hear you saying "Get off on your bike,
Take your pills and keep tidy, go for a hike."
While my "Jollity Star" still shines above
In my heart everlasting is a casket of our love.

*Thank you for opening your eyes and your lovely fleeting smile
before you went into your long sleep.*

All your agony was over and it seemed that you died content then. It will live in my mind forever. My agony is not yet over but your love and example will be my armour, my guide and protection. I will always love you, whatever may befall.

BEING POSITIVE

In the six months before Joy died, she kept telling me I had to be positive. "Buy a new motor cycle with an electric starter and get out and about." She told me that I should not contemplate living alone but at the time, of course, I was not interested in the advice and I just wanted to look after Joy. It was more than two years before I could think of meeting anyone. It is difficult to describe in words the searing ache inside or the deep, dark feeling of black emptiness which follows on the death of someone so close as being part of you.

Joy died on the 23rd of December 2007 and so the prospect of Christmas without Joy seemed hollow and empty. My friends, Mike and Kate Winkley, would not countenance my being on my own and I did not wish to dampen the spirits of my grandchildren at Christmas. Kate's sisters, Sue Robinson and Roz Everitt, and their husbands, Mike and Greg, are a wonderfully close family with Kate. The family had arranged to have a joint Christmas dinner at Shoestone at Garnet Bridge in Longsleddale, the home of Mike and Sue. I was invited to join them, along with Kate's son, Jonny, and Roz's sons, Luke and Daniel. It was a tremendously warm relief for me to be with them. I spent Boxing Day with all the family at Mike and Kate's home in Kendal.

I spent the rest of the festive season and the New Year visiting my family in Kentmere and Staveley, but I found I also needed time on my own to adjust to a new life. It was the first time in my life that I had been without a female companion, so recipe books became priority reading. I need not have worried because friends and family arrived almost daily with food parcels and wonderful, tasty things to fill the freezer. Nevertheless, I experimented with cooking and my experience on Islay with Richard and the Chums meant I could make a tasty cottage pie!

Then I saw a lovely red motorbike in the street which I recognised as being a Moto Guzzi. It had a low seat and a low centre of gravity to suit my short legs! I remembered Joy's advice: it had an electric start! I sold my Vincent Comet which used to backfire because I could not get the ignition to stay stable. I studied the model of Moto Guzzi, the road tests and specification on the internet. The nearest dealer was in Dalton-in-Furness, as it happened on the way to Furness General Hospital, where I had an appointment the following day.

Figure 7.35. Mike in the kitchen with Kate, Roz and Mike's daughter Alex.

When I entered the dealer's showroom there was a range of Moto Guzzis and, as if by design of fate, there was the very model which I had seen in the street, a Brava 750 c.c. in the same lovely red. Not only that, but the prices had been cut to just over cost, because the dealership was closing down. I felt that somehow Joy had guided me there. Later that day I had a test ride on a second-hand version of the same model and I decided to buy the new red one.

So in the spring of 2008 I began over 4000 miles of travelling the highways and byways of Lakeland and the Yorkshire Dales. I had occasional trips further afield to Scotland to see Martyn and Pam Wrathall and other friends. I felt content on the bike, as if Joy was with me even high on the passes in the remote and beautiful areas here in the North West.

I had a holiday with my daugher, Ingrid, and Moss and the family in South Dakota in 2009. I went for my granddaughter Kayleigh's graduation from High School, which was a very happy occasion. See colour section.

I continued to attend Levens Church most Sundays where I was warmly welcomed and felt a feeling of belonging. I have always had a strong belief in the teachings of Jesus but, like many in life, I was not a regular church-goer until recently. I have not always agreed with the way that some branches of the church interpret Christ's guidance. I am sceptical of hearsay evidence on which some biblical stories are based. It is the essence of Jesus' teachings that matters to me: love, understanding and forgiveness, which are the most important.

When Joy and I visited the Millenium Dome in London among other inspiring displays, we saw a reassuring presentation of worldwide religious and philosophical beliefs, emphasising the commonality of thought between them. How I wish everyone could rejoice in the things that unite us rather than divide.

At Levens Church we have thought-provoking guidance relevant to our daily lives and condition. The Reverend Ruth Crossley and Canon Tom Thompson, who is retired but occasionally takes the service, both have a beautifully balanced way of making the Christian faith live in our hearts and minds. Our lay readers, Mary Orr and Frances Makin, are in the same mould, backed by experience as well as biblical and historical research. Together the four make a wonderful team and are an inspiration.

I was still living alone when Bishop James Newcombe came on his pilgrimage around the South Lakeland villages. He was then the Bishop of Penrith. Robin and Mary Orr suggested that I might like to accompany them to an evening at the Heron Theatre at Beetham to hear Bishop James speak. I found him inspiring and I attended another meeting at Preston Patrick the same week which was on another topic, but equally positive. He does not sidestep the difficult questions and makes clear what he believes and why. I then took my niece, Heather Gardner, to hear the Bishop at a rock and jazz evening at Kirkby Lonsdale Church, where the Vicar has his own band. It was another "Meet the Bishop" evening for all ages. The church was full and Bishop James entered into the spirit of the evening. He was dressed in a simple, monk-type raiment and he talked to us rather than lectured.

His theme, which has lived with me since that evening, was that we should "make Jesus our friend" and let him walk with us in our lives. I am not a religious zealot or one who would try to press religion on anyone. We all have our own state of mind in such matters. All I can say is that the sincerity of Levens Church community and Bishop James' advice helped me to walk from sorrow and sadness back to life.

I truly believe that the warm feeling of serenity which replaced my sadness has by some divine gentleness brought my lovely Jean into the autumn of my life. She is a lovely person and kindness itself. In persuading and helping me to write this book, Jean now knows more about me than I recall myself, but she rejoices in having found me. "There's nowt sae queer as folk!" my old Granny used to say.

8

LAKELAND DIALECT AND VIKINGS

THE DIALECT OF LAKELAND
IN MY LIFETIME

I come to the subject of Dialect in Lakeland, not as a professional historian or specialist linguist in the origins of our language, but as a country lad who grew up with the old dialect words and sayings of my parents and grandparents. Nevertheless, I have enjoyed many interesting hours reading and collecting books on the dialects of Westmorland, Cumberland and Furness. As mentioned in "My Viking Trail", I have visited sites with Viking or Northmen connections in Norway, Ireland, The Isle of Man, Islay, Whithorn, York and other sites in Cumbria and the North West.

In the 1970s the late J. C. Robinson, then Chairman of the Lakeland Dialect Society (LDS), invited me to join the Society. Ironically, as a former headmaster of Staveley Church of England Primary School, he had spent his professional life teaching country children to speak the King's and Queen's English, but in his spare time he revelled in speaking good Lakeland dialect. He also wrote some of the hymns which we sing in dialect at our biennial Dialect Church Services.

The Society's aims are to preserve and promote the use of our old Lakeland words. We don't want them on road signs or to impose them on anyone. We just want folk to enjoy the rich nuances and expressions used by our "fore-elders" as well as to understand the influence of the Angles and Norse on our language and place names in Lakeland.

The annual subscription at the time of writing is £6. Anyone interested is welcome to join. We publish an LDS Journal each year. The Society holds meetings at different venues around Cumbria with lectures and discussions as well as new writers' contributions. We have had readings of the old Grasmere Dialect Plays (Keith Coates of Rydal has researched these) and had recitations of well-loved traditional verses written in good dialect of the last two centuries.

Our President, Ted Relph, Chairman, Tommy Coulthard and our

Secretary, Jean Scott-Smith are all good dialect speakers and are very active in promoting the use of dialect, as are the officers and members of the committee, who appear in the picture (Figure. 8.1, colour section).

To help prevent the use of our old words dying out altogether, the Society promotes a competition each year between the Young Farmers' Clubs of Cumbria. We would like more young people and folk of all ages to join the Society to preserve, learn and enjoy the old words and expressions. It is fun to "hev a good crack tagither!"

With the abolition of fox hunting, the number of 'Merry Neets' held has declined. A traditional Merry Neet usually involved those attending contributing songs, amusing stories and recitations; some would be in dialect, some not. If in support of a hunt, then hunting songs were included. A hotpot supper or the like was served part-way through the proceedings. Usually a chairperson or master of ceremonies ordered the proceedings and gathered the names of those who would participate in the entertainment. I describe a Merry Neet in *"Langsleddale Hunt Supper wi Ron Bell"*.

Though many of the best native dialect speakers in the Society have passed on, the Society has made recordings of their speech and anecdotes for posterity. There are tapes and CDs in our archives which are updated and copied as recording methods have developed over the years. We also have many of the early studies of dialect in book and

Figure 8.2. Robbie Ellis in his recording studio at home

pamphlet form in our archives. We have published our annual LDS Journal each year since 1939.

Robbie Ellis of Penrith, seen here in his home recording studio, is busy updating our Society's recordings even now as I write. He has also recorded my reading most of my dialect verses which appear in this book.

The everyday use of the old words of Lakeland began to decline with the changes in society after 1918. Many of the old customs and usages died during the First World War, but my parents and grandparents and many other families like them were still speaking dialect in the 1940s when I came on the scene. However, I did notice the difference in speech between my eldest brother, Gerard, ten years older than me, who remained on the farm and had more contact with our grandfather and heard his dialect speech. I was only one-year-old when Grandfather died and I discovered later that Gerard had a much wider inherited vocabulary of old dialect words than I did. However, my grandmother, Mary Elizabeth Hayton, did pass on to me the words and sayings which I have listed later in the book.

My brother Jack was nine years older than me. He was managing clerk in T. O. & J. K. Jackson Solicitors' practice at 14/16 Finkle Street in Kendal. By the time I commenced my articles with J. K. Jackson of that firm, Jack was speaking plain English. He had done his national service in the Army Legal Services in Egypt, so the dialect had been largely knocked out of him.

Nevertheless, we could understand the old dialect-speaking clients of the firm when they came to the Monday livestock auction and they called on us for some reason. We could still converse in their language. I have found this ability very useful during my career and a lovely way of putting country folk at ease.

I recall meeting "Uncle" Anthony Dixon from Kit Crag, my father's cousin, in Finkle Street the very first week of my articles. I started at the bottom as office boy, delivering the hand-letters round Kendal. He said, "Noo then Leonard, I hear tell thoo's gone in fer law but thi Grandmother wanted thee to be a parson! What, thoo's gone ta t'Devil!" He was a grand chap, a great farmer and full of fun. He asked me, "Hes ta hed any o them barn fatheren cases yet?" I said, "Well no, what er barn fatheren cases?" He replied, "Thoo mun ex yoor Jackie, he'll tell thee."

When I had delivered the post and returned to the office, I posed the question to Jack. He smiled and said nothing but handed me a large legal tome about three inches thick called "Lushington's Affiliation and Bastardy". It was all about making fathers stand up to their responsibilities long before this branch of practice was greatly simplified by the advent of DNA testing.

With the requirement in schools for us to speak what I will call plain English and the influence of radio and television, the daily use of local dialect has been in steady decline during my lifetime, but of late there seems to be a revival of interest. People appear to have realised at last that the dialect of Cumbria, with all its nuances, is a rich part of our heritage and as important to preserve as the artefacts and antiquities of Lakeland.

Over many years I have been invited to speak at dinners and

functions. I have recited some of my dialect verses and talked about my work and my childhood. Some dialect verses appear in other parts of this book and there is also a general glossary of dialect words in the appendix section.

Latterly, to help keep the old words and sayings alive and to create some debate about dialect, I made a random list of 'Dialect Words', where possible with their origins, for my audience to write down their meanings. Everyone, off-comers and locals alike, were enthusiastic to take part. Usually the audience did this in pairs. Then I would use some of the listed words during my talk, which kept everybody alert and helped them to find clues to the answers. We had much fun and laughter as we did so. I tried to make the words alive and interesting and I provided a small prize for the three top scores. The locals often won because of their background knowledge, but not always, because there are many enlightened folk who have made their homes in Lakeland and value the preservation and use of the old words and sayings. Some people got impressive scores, which is heartening indeed. See if you can answer the following questionnaire.

*   *   *

HOW MANY OF THESE WORDS AND SAYINGS DO YOU KNOW?

Here are some of the words my granny and parents used when I was a lad.
Please write what you think the word means on the dotted line.
Note: some words have more than one meaning.
ON = Old Norse; OE = Old English; AS = Anglo-Saxon; Icel = Icelandic Old Norse; WS = West Saxon; Dan = Danish; Fr = French; Celt = Celtic; Gael = Gaelic

WORD & ORIGIN of word where known   ANSWERS

1 BRANT   ON *brattr* . . . .
2 BRAT   OE *bratt*. . . . .
3 BOGLE or BOGGLE   Celt *bwgwl* . . . .
4 BYRE   ON *byr* . . . .

5 CAM   ON *kambr* . . . .

6 CLARTY   ON *leir* . . . .

7 CLAGGY   Dan *kloeg* . . . .

8 COPPY-STEAL or COPPY-STOOL   AS *copp* . . . .

9 T'HEV A GOOD CRACK   OE . . . .

10 CRAVICK'T WS . . . .

11 CREEL   ON *krili* . . . .

12 CUSH CUSH   Icel *kussa*   Calling what? . . . .

13 GIS GIS   ON *gris* Calling what? . . . .

14 DUB   ON /Icel *djupr* . . . .

15 DOWLY   ON /Icel *dauligr* . . . .

16 EFTER   ON *eftir* . . . .

17 EASINGS   Icel *efesan* . . . .

18 ELDIN   ON /Icel from *elda* . . . .

19 FASH or FASHMENT   Fr *fâcher* . . . .

20 FELL   ON/Icel *fjall* . . . .

21 TO FEND   Icel *fe'na* . . . .

22 GILL or GHYLL   ON/Icel *gil* . . . .

23 HAY-BAY or HUBBYSHOO . . . .

24 HEAF or HEFTED   ON *hefda* . . . .

25 LAIKING ABOOT   ON *leika* . . . .

26 LANG or LANG SEN   Icel *langur* . . . .

27 LAIT   ON *leyta* . . . .

28 LONNIN   ON leyna . . . .

29 LOWSE – LOWSE OOT   *ON laus* . . . .

30 PIGGIN   Gael *pigeon* (not a bird) . . . .

31 RANNEL BAWK   Icel . . . .

32 REEAN, REIN OR RANE   ON *rein* . . . .

33 REEK or REAK   ON / Icel   *reykr* . . . .

34 ROWAN TREE   ON / Icel   *reynir* . . . .

35 SARRA . . . .

36 SCALE or SCALES   ON Icel   *skali* . . . .

37 SHIPPON or SHIPPEN   AS *scypen* . . . .

38 SILE   Icel *sili* . . . .

39 SKOGGERSLOPS ON   *skochr* . . . .

40 SLAPE   ON / Icel   *sleipr* . . . .

41 SLECK   ON   *sluekya* . . . .

42 SMIT   AS / Dan s*mitta* . . . .

43 SNECK & SNECK POSSIT   Manx *sneg* . . . .

44 SPRINGEN   OE *sprengan* . . . .

45 STANG   ON / ICEL *staung* . . . . On evenings
of Christmas Day and New Year's Day revellers would mount those
they met astride a . . . . and carry them to a pub and
compel them to stand drinks all round. Note also RIDING T'STANG:
When a man or woman of the village committed adultery they would
be carried from house to house on a . . . . in disgrace.

46 STEG   ON *steggr* . . . .

47 SWELTERED   Icel svoeldr . . . .

48 SUMP or SUMPH   Dan s*ump* . . . .

49 THYVEL   AS *thyfel*   ON *thyvell* . . . .

50 TARN   ON *tjörn* . . . .

51 THRANG   ON *thraungr* . . . .

52 THWAITE   ON/Icel *thveit* . . . .

53 YAK / YACK / YEK   Icel *eik* . . . .

54 YAK BOB DAY . . . .

55 YAT or YEAT   AS *geat* . . . .

What is the meaning of these sayings?

56 *It's a case of lile clogs makken bigens run!*
57 *A lee is hauf way roon t'world afore t'truth gits it clogs on*
58 *I'se gay watter shaken*
59 *What he's that tight that he can nayder stand, sit ner hod be t'guss!*
60 *He's gitten t'wrang pig be t'lug!*

Total number of correct answers: . . . .

See appendix for list of answers.

HOO LANG IS "LANG SEN" IN LAKELAND?

Hoo lang is Lang Sen in Lakeland?
Mappen on this we sud ponder
Oor forelders strutch back two thoosen eer
Aye en a lot mair be-gattins back yonder.

Nobbut forty generations hev gan past
That macks up yan thoosen eer
While at eighty back t'Celts were thrang
En nobbut sixty sen t'Romans left here.

T'Anglians lant efta t'Romans went yam
En t'Norse com sean efta that
Noo I rayder like t'Scandinavian folk
Thur words en thur expressions en chat.

T'Normans nivver mannished ta tame us
Oor dales nut in t'Domesday Book
Oor forelders who valued thur freedom
Would hev a fierce en formidable look.

In t'genes en blood of ald Lakeland folk
Thur's Celt en Anglian en Norse
The'v left thur mark on oor place-names
En in oor characters o course.

Thur's "pen" fre t'Celts en "ton" is an Anglian yam
T'Norse browt "thwaite" en "beck" en "ghyll"
En if yan maanders aboot through Lakeland
Yan can see o' sick-like origins still.

So "Lang Sen" is lost in t'mists o time
"Lang Sen" is long ago
It just soonds reet when yan says "Lang Sen"
En yan pictures scenes lang ago.

But hoo many be-gattins sen Genesis
Or since evolution began?
Lang Sen strutches oot tull infinity
Yan's maazled by t'history of man!

Maazled noo by oor world in turmoil
Hes man larn't nowt wi suicide bombers galore?
Desperate passions across an unsettled globe
Still bedivilled by t'cacophony o war!

Yet hoo lang is Lang Sen in Lakeland?
Oor brant fells en bonny dales still remain
Oor forelders fowt fer peace on t'borders
Through fire en brimstone en rain.

When t'hubbyshoo en fratchen is o'er
When commonsense taks hod yance agen
We'll still hev a good crack here in Lakeland
En ponder: hoo lang is Lang Sen?

© *LH July 2005*

Glossary

A crack = a good talk or conversation.
Begat = beget
Begattings = generations
Beck = a river or stream
Brant = steep
Eer = year
Fowt = fought
Fratchen = disputing and disagreeing
Gill or Ghyll = ravine
Hubbyshoo = a commotion or affray
Lang sen = long ago
Lant = landed or arrived

Larnt = learned
Maanders = meanders
Maazled = amazed or puzzled
Mappen = perhaps
Nobbut = only
Strutches = stretches
Sud = should
Thoosen = thousand
Thrang = busy
Thur = their
Thwaite = clearing
Yam = home

"IT'S NOBBUT ME!"
"It's Only Me!"

This lovely poem by John Richardson in his book *"Cummerland Talk"*, published in 1886, is one of my favourite old dialect verses to recite. It is in Cumberland dialect, which differs a little from Westmorland in pronunciation and spelling, but is a delight to read. The words in the poem are spelled just as Richardson wrote them in his book, but in Kentmere in Westmorland we would tend to say "knaa" instead of "know" and "whaa" instead of "who". The poem is so well known throughout Cumbria that I believe it has been recited in the vernacular dialects of many of our Cumbrian villages and hamlets.

Please read it aloud a few times so that you can enjoy the sound of good old Lakeland speech for yourself.

It recalls the old way of courting in the valleys. Often parents would retire to bed and allow their daughter to wait downstairs for her sweetheart to call. If he was a welcome visitor, she would leave the door latch open. The latch was called the "sneck". To lock the door all one did was to put a wedge above the sneck.

If the would-be suitor was unwelcome, she would "sneck possit him": put the wedge in the sneck, so as to keep him out.

In this poem the young man was obviously welcome!

"IT'S NOBBUT ME!"

A tale of courting in the old days
by John Richardson, 1817-1886

Ya winter neet, I mind it weel
Oor lads hed been t' fell
An' bein' tir't, went seun ta bed,
An' I sat be mysel'.
I hard a jike on t' window pane,
An' deftly went to see ;
An' when I ax't, "Who's jiken theer?"
Says t' chap: "It's nobbut me!"

"Who's *me*?" says I, "What want ye here?
Oor fwok er aw i' bed." -
"I dunnet want your fwok at aw
It's *thee* I want," he sed.
"What cant'e want wi' me?" says I ;
"An' who, the deuce, can't be?
Just tell me who it is, an' than" -
Says he, "It's nobbut me."

"I want a sweetheart an' I thowt
Thou mebbe wad an' aw ;
I've been a bit dean t' deal to-neet,
An' thowt 'at I wad caw ;
What, cant'e like me, dus t'e think?
I think I wad like thee" -
"I dunnet know who't is," says I,
Says he, "It's nobbut me."

We pestit on a canny while,
I thowt his voice I kent ;
An' then I steal quite whisht away,
An' oot at t' dooer I went.
I creap, an' gat him be cwoat laps,
'Twas dark, he cuddent see ;
He startit roond, an' said, "Who's that?"
Says I, "IT'S NOBBUT ME."

An' menny a time he com agean,
An' menny a time I went,
An' sed, "Who's that 'at's jiken theer?"
When gaily weel I kent :
An' mainly what t' seam answer com,
Fre back o t' laylick tree ;
He sed, "I think thoo knows who't is,
Thoo knows it's nobbut me."

It's twenty year an' mair sen than,
En ups an' doons we've hed ;
An' six fine barnes hev blest us beath,
Sen Jim an' me war wed.
An' menny a time I've known him steal,
When I'd yan on my knee,
Ta mak me start, an' then wad laugh –
"Ha! ha! IT'S NOBBUT ME."

THOMAS BLEZZARD'S ORIGINAL WESTMORLAND SONGS

In 1868 Thomas Blezzard, a farm labourer and ploughman of Ings near Staveley, published his "Original Westmorland Songs", which were printed by Titus Wilson of Highgate, Kendal, which said firm is the predecessor of my printer, Titus Wilson, today.

The title and contents pages of Blezzard's book pictured here give some clues as to life in South Lakeland during the mid-1800s. In his preface Blezzard stated that for the last 35 years prior to the publication of this book, he had not let any individual see his "*humble musings on paper*", which he said he had composed while "*plodding after the plough*". Nevertheless, the list of his friends and subscribers, which is printed in the book, exceeds 460 names from the local area, so his songs must have been popular. The dialect in these songs and verses gives a clear indication of the words in general parlance at the time as well as paints a picture of the happenings described.

The following song, "*Kentmer Teap Fair en' Rayaces, Lang Sen*", provides an historical bird's eye view of the goings-on in Kentmere at that time. The reference to having "*taverns toow*" is interesting. There was an inn at La-Brigg (Low Bridge) and "*The Jerry et th' Reak How*" (Rook Howe). A jerry was a beer house. The Low Bridge Inn was where the Teap (Tup) Fair and the Day Sports were held.

The Low Bridge Inn was closed in 1887 and made history when the appeal Sharpe v. Wakefield went to the House of Lords and failed. The official reason for the loss of the licence was: "*it was too far from police supervision*". There was a temperance lobby at the time. Contemporary reports in the Westmorland Gazette of the case state stated that there had been an inn there for 300 years and revealed some colourful episodes as described in the evidence given in Court.

"Letters from the Lakes" in 1820 described a stay at Low Bridge Inn: "*The floor was spread with tubs, pans, chairs, tables, piggins, dishes, tins and other equipage of a farmer's kitchen…there was no fireplace, but a paved area of about two square yards raised six inches from the floor and attached to the end wall formed the hearth where the fire burned. It was a peat fire and peat was piled all around drying beside the fire.*"

Blezzard's song refers to the wrestling and sports which followed the Tup Sale (sale of rams). He goes on to say, "*Than the in-door glee began*" and describes very lively dancing and merriment that continued all through the night until daybreak.

The song is reproduced here with the same spellings as appear in his book. It needs to be read aloud two or three times to get the real measure of the words and their meaning.

KENTMER TEAP FAIR EN' RAYACES, LANG SEN
Tune = "When first in London I arriv'd"

Kentmer iz tha playce fer glee,
Kentmer Rayaces! – Kentmere Rayaces! –
This is my theme en' sang sal be.
Theayr I us't ta jig ;
E' eighteen en' thirty-three,
Fray tha Ings, Jack Tate en' me,
Up owr Raismer, ful a' glee,
Went trippin teth' La-Brigg.

REPETITION:
O – O ! – Kentmer, Kentmer ! – O wat glee!
O wat Rayaces ! – O wat Rayaces!
Fam'd e' sang, fer land en' lang,
Kentmer still sal be!
(C.R.) Fam'd e' sang, etc.

Formerlee this stir wez held
On a thorsda, - on a thorsda;
It o'udders sooa exceld –
It fer miles wez kent ;
"Twas a saying far en' near –
"Kentmer Rayaces en' th' Teap Fair,
E' October ivrey year,
Et' thorsda eftert' tent,"
(R.) *O – O ! – Kentmer, etc.*

At the time which I relate,
Lads en' lasses, – lads en' lasses, –
Fill't tha roaad fray Stayvla-gayt,
Ulthet fowk tuct' lead;

Lots en' lots fill't ivrey roout,
Fray t'Hill Bell ta Sleddal fooat,
En'fray Trootbeck, roond aboot
Byth' Ings en' Stayvla Heaad.
(R.) *O – O ! – Kentmer, etc.*

Sean there wez a buslin fair –
Teaps kept cummin, – Teaps kept cummin ;
Fowk west there fray far en' near,
Nippy clean en' trig ;
Varra few wez left et hayam, –
Frayt' Greenwarter en' t' Brockstayan,
T' Preest en' t' Clerk, en' ivrey yan,
'Ed mizzled t' th' La Brigg.
(R.) *O – O ! – Kentmer, etc.*

Just et twooa ta Trail began –
Than wat crakin! – than wat crakin!
Auld Jim Hutchysen's hoond wan –
'Twas'nt beh a deel,
Beht Jim sed, he'd "lay a poond,
Neht a man – tekt' countre roond –
Cud produce ez good a hoond,
En' bang 'em aw sa weel!"
(R.) *O – O ! – Kentmer, etc.*

Than wez shown a Kemp-woo hat –
'Twas ta ren for – 'twas ta ren for, –
Auld John Cowperthet sed 'et
It wez werth a heat,
Than he tuc't en' tryd it on,
Than he stript, en' off he sprang,
Than weh cheers o' Kentmer rang!
But auld John cuddent dea't.
(R.) *O – O ! – Kentmer, etc.*

Than began "Tug Skill and Might" –
O wat Reslin ! – O wat Reslin ! –
Gersgarth Jim gev Gilpin t' toit,
Than Joawn Rigg sed "fair,"

Than Tom Gilpin up he rose,
En' began a plantin blows,
En' a pummin Joawn his noaws,
En', bless us! hoo he swayre !
(R.) *O – O ! – Kentmer, etc.*

Than the in-door glee began –
O' went rarely – O' went rarely;
Warst on't was, Jim Hutcheysen
Med o' th' wimmen sham;
First he brag'd aboot 'iz dogs,
Than aboot 'iz Herdwic hogs,
Than aboot 'iz private jobs,
Than spew'd en' toddel'd hayam.
(R.) *O – O ! – Kentmer, etc.*

'En ith' loft – O wat a seet!
Bonny lasses – bonny lasses!
Reel'd en' jig'd, en' aw that neet
Moments merr'ly flew ;
En' et th' Jerry th' Reak-How,
There wez dancing aw neet through;
Kentmer wasent ez it's noo,
They than 'ed Taverns toow.
(R.) *O – O! – Kentmer, etc.*

Thus tha neet went merr'ly on
Till't was dayleet – till't was dayleet;
Ripe for ivry kind a' fun,
Nowt a' to com rang:
Merrymuckheapt on tha fleear,
Hauf a skooar wez spralin there;
Wee'd nayah wish to hev a shayer
En' sayah wi off en' sang.
(R.) *O – O! – Kentmer, etc.*

BRANTHET NEUK BOGGLE

It is fortunate that in the 19th century there was a surge of interest in the dialect of the then counties of Cumberland, Westmorland and Furness – now known together as Cumbria. The spoken word varied between the old counties and even between valleys. The words recorded in these writings of old are part of the heritage of Lakeland.

The "Branthet Neuk Boggle" (1868), which I include here by Alexander Craig Gibson, is a good example of old Cumberland dialect. It paints a picture in the colourful words of the time around a rather scary ghost story which is nevertheless amusing. Try reading it a few times to get the lilt. The translation is mine and any faults in it are mine! It is not a literal translation but it expresses the sense of the poem.

Who knows, you may be tempted to look for old books of dialect verse and stories, and enjoy using a few of the colourful words and expressions in your daily life.

BRANTHET NEUK BOGGLE (A TEAL FOR A WINTER NEET)
by Alexander Craig Gibson, FSA (1868)

'At Marron Beck's a bonnie beck,
what mazelin wad deny?
An' what comparies wi' Branthet
Neuk 'at Marron Beck ga's by?
Wid hooses white, an' worchets green,
an' Marron runnin' clear,
Eigh! Branthet Neuk's a heartsome
spot i' t' sunny time o' year!

But loave! It is a dowly pleace when
winter neets growe lang;
For t' lwoan ligs dark atween its
banks, – a flaysome rwoard to gang
When t' wind rwoars wild in t' trees
abeun, an' Marron rwoars below, –
An' Branthet Neuk's a hantit spot, as
I've some reet to know

THE BRANTHWAITE NOOK GHOST (A TALE FOR A WINTER NIGHT)
translated by Len Hayton (2011)

That Marron stream is a bonny
stream, no fool could deny
And what compares with Branthwaite
Nook as the Marron stream goes by?
With houses white and orchards green
And Marron running clear
Yes, Branthwaite Nook is a heart-
raising place in the sunny time of year!

But look! It is a dull and lonesome
place when winter nights grow long;
For the lane lies dark between its
bank, a frightening road to go
When the wind roars wild in the trees
above, and the Marron roars below, –
And Branthwaite Nook is a haunted
spot, as I've some right to know

They say a heidless woman woaks at
sartin neets o' t' year,
An' greans an' yewls at sec a rate as
freetens fwoke to hear;
I wadn't mind sec teals, but yance I
gat a freet me-sel'
I' Branthet Neuk, an' hoo it was, just
lissen an' I'll tell

Ya neet, lang sen, at Cursmass time,
wid Cursmas mak' o' wedder,
A lock on us at Branthet met, to hev a
glass togidder;
We crack't an' jwok't, an' drank an'
smeuk't, while hoaf o' t' neet went by,
For Isbel Simon' drink was gud, an'
we war rayder dry!

'Twas lownd an' leat – past yan
o'clock – wid nut a spark o' moon;
An' like a clood o' cardit woo', thick
snow keep't sinkin doon,
When reet up t' Neuk three Jwohn's
an' me went wadin' heam through t'
snow –
Jwohn Suntan, an' Jwohn Bell o' t'
Rayes, an' Jwohn o' Craypless Ho'

We'd gitten hoaf o' t' way up t' lwoan,
– nar Edard Beeby' yat,
An' theear we stopp't, for marcy me!
A parlish freet we gat:
Lood greans we heard – lang hollow
beels, 'at shak't ooor varra beans,
"For God-seak, lads, mak on" says
yan, "them's t' heidless woman's
greans!"

"Buy nay," says I, "if wantin' t' hed,
she raises sec a rout,
I'd like to see what way she taks to
fetch sec haybays oot;

They say a headless woman walks at
certain times of the year,
And groans and yowls at such a rate
which frightens folk to hear
I wouldn't mind such tales, but once I
got a fright myself
In Branthwaite Nook, and how it was,
just listen and I'll tell

One night, long ago, at Christmas
time, it was Christmas type of weather,
A lot of us at Branthwaite met, to have
a glass together;
We laughed and joked, and drank and
smoked, while half the night went by,
For Isobel Simon's drink was good,
and we were rather dry!

It was still and late, past one o'clock,
with not a spark of moon;
And like a cloud of carded wool, thick
snow kept sinking down,
When right up the Nook three Johns
and me went wading home through
the snow – John Suntan, and John
Bell of Rayes, and John of Craypless
Howe

We'd got half-way up the lane – near
Edward Beeby's gate
And there we stopped, for mercy me!
A parlous fright we got;
Loud groans we heard – long hollow
bawls, that shook our very bones,
"For God's sake, lads, get on" says
one,
"they're the headless woman's
groans!"

"But no," says I, "if without a head,
she raises such a noise,
I'd like to see how she manages to
make such an uproar;

They say yan stops a woman's noise
    when yan taks off her heid,
But this, by gock was mak yan sweer
    they're noise whick or deid."

It's Burns 'at says Jwohn Barleycworn
    can mak yan bold as brass;
An' Isbel' drink mead me quite keen
    this greanin' thing to feace.
We shootit Edard Beeby up an' mead
    'im git a leet –
He grummel't sair to be disturb't at
    sec a time o' neet,

But brong yan oot; – an', led bee t'
    lugs, we follow't efter t' soond,
While clwose to t' swine-hull dooar we
    com, an' stopp't, an gedder't roond.
"By gockers, lads!" Jwohn Suntan
    said, "it's no'but Edard' swine"
"Nay, nay", says Edard, "mine's I'
    soat – it's nea pig o' mine!"

"Well, I'll ga in, an' see," says I. O' t'
    rest steud leukin' on
As in I creep't wid t' leet, an' fund
    greit lang Joe Nicholson
Hoaf cover't up wid mucky strea, –
    soond asleep, – and snworin',
As if o' t' Bulls o' Dean war theear,
    an' ivery bull was rwoarin'

We trail't him oot, an' prop't him up
    agean t' olad swine-hull wo' –
An' dazet wid coald he glower't aboot,
    an' dadder't like to fo' –
We help't 'im in, an' hap't 'im weel, on
    t' squab aback o' t' dooar;
He said his wife had barr't 'im oot, as
    oft she'd deun afooar

They say one stops a woman's noise
    when one takes off her head
But this, by gosh, would make you
    swear they're noisy alive or dead."

It's Burns who says John Barleycorn
    (alcohol) can make you bold as brass;
And Isabel's drink made me quite
    keen this groaning thing to face.
We woke Edward Beeby up and made
    him get a light –
He grumbled sore to be disturbed at
    such a time of night

But he brought a light out; – and,
    led by our ears, we followed after the
    sound,
While close to the pig house door
    we came, and stopped and gathered
    round.
"By gosh, lads!" John Suntan said
    "It's only Edwards's pig"
"No, no," says Edward, "mine's in salt
    – it's no pig of mine!"

"Well, I'll go in and see," says I. All
    the rest stood looking on
As in I crept with the light, and found
    great long Joe Nicholson
Half covered up with mucky straw, –
    sound asleep, – and snoring,
As if all the Bulls of Dean were there,
    and every bull was roaring

We dragged him out, and propped him
    up against the old pig-house wall –
And dazed with cold he glowered
    around, and doddered as if to fall –
We helped him in, and wrapped him
    well, on the slab behind the door;
He said his wife had barred him out,
    as often she'd done before

Says Jwohn o' t' Rayes, "if iv'ry neet
  he maks sa gurt a din,
It's rayder queer a wife like his sud
  iver let 'im in;
It's varra weel we hard 'im though, he
  med ha' dee't o' coald!
Come, let's git heam!" – an' laughin'
  loud, we lonter't oot o' t' foald

Jwohn Sunant's rwoad left oors gay
  seum, an' sooa dud Jwohn Bell's,
An' Jwohn o' Craypless Ho' an' me
  went poapin on oorsells,
An' no'but slow, for t' snow was thick,
  an' mead it bad to woak,
Sooa mid-leg deep we striddel't on,
  but offen steud to toak

Jwohn hed a faymish crack in 'im, –
  his fadder hed afooar 'im, –
At teals an' sangs, an' sec like fun, not
  many cud cum ower 'im;
An' thear an' than, dud Jwohn set on,
  at t' furst gud rist we teuk,
To tell me hoo ther com to be a ghost
  I' Branthet Neuk

Says Jwohn, says he, "I" Branthet
  Neuk, as varra weel thoo knows,
'Tween t' beck an' Edard Beeby'
  hoose ther stands some broken wo's;
Lang sen, when they hed roofs on
  them, yance, leatish on I' t' yar,
Some tinkler fwoke gat leave fray t'
  lword, an' com to winter theear

"Two oald fwoke, wid a scrowe o'
  barns, an' ya son, just a man, –
A handy chap to shap' a speun, or
  cloot a pot or pan, –
An' this chap had a bonnie wife, 'at
  dudn't leuk like t'rest,

Says John of Rayes, "if every night he
  makes so loud a noise,
Its rather queer a wife like his should
  ever let him in;
It's very well we heard him though, for
  he might have died of cold!
Come, let's get home!" – and laughing
  loud, we loitered out of the yard

John Suntan's road left ours very
  soon, and so did John Bell's,
And John of Craypless Howe and me
  went walking in the dark ourselves,
And only slow, for the snow was thick,
  And made it bad to walk,
So mid-leg deep we strode on, but
  often stood to talk

John had a famous story in him – his
  father also had before him –
At tales and songs, and all such fun,
  not many could surpass him;
And there and then, did John start at
  the first good rest we took,
To tell me how there came to be a
  ghost in Branthwaite Nook

Says John, says he, "In Branthwaite
  Nook, as very well you know,
Between the stream and Edward
  Beeby's house there stand some
  ruined walls; Long ago, when they
  had roofs on them, once late on in the
  year,
Some tinker folk got permission from
  the lord, to come and winter there

"Two old folk, with a lot of children,
  and one son, just a man, –
A handy chap to shape a spoon, or
  mould a pot or pan, –
And this chap had a bonny wife, that
  didn't look like the rest,

But fair, clean-skinn't, an' leady-like,
    an' ol'as nicely drest

"An' hoo she com to be wid them was
    niver reetly known,
But nebbers so' she wasn't used as if
    she'd been ther oan;
For t' oald fwoke soas't her neet an'
    day, – her man – a durty tike! –
Wad bray her wid a besom-stick, a
    thyvel, or sec like;

Tull yance a nebber teuk her in, when
    t' tinklers flang her oot,
An' she let fo' a wurd or two 'at brong
    a change aboot;
She telt o' sum geese an' sheep, an'
    whoar they hed them hidden;
Of mutton up on t' sleepin' loft, an'
    skins anonder t' midden

"It wasn't many wurds she said, – but
    wurds she said anew
To bring t' oald tinkler an' her man
    tull what was weel ther due;
For lang I' Carel jail they laid, an'
    when t' assize com on,
T' Judge let t' oald waistrel lowece
    agean, but hang't his whopeful son

"An' back frae Carel t' tinkler com, to
    Branthet reet awa,
An' 'ticet t' poor lass frae t' nebber's
    hoose, whoar she'd been fain to stay;
He promish't fair to treat her weel, an'
    dud while t' seckint neet,
An' than, (reet pleas't was Branthet
    fwok), he mead a moonleet fleeght

But fair, clean-skinned and ladylike,
    and always nicely dressed

"And how she came to be with them
    was never rightly known,
But neighbours saw she wasn't treated
    as if she'd been their own;
For the old folk sauced her night and
    day, – her man – a dirty fellow! –
Would hit her with a birch stick, a
    porridge stick, or such like;

Until once a neighbour took her in,
    when the tinkers threw her out,
And she disclosed some words that
    brought a change about;
She told of some geese and sheep, and
    where they had them hidden;
Of mutton up in the sleeping loft, and
    skins underneath the manure heap

"It wasn't many words she said – but
    words she said anew
To bring the old tinker and her man
    to what was their just due;
For long in Carlisle jail they laid, and
    when the Assize Court was held,
The Judge let the old wastrel loose
    again, but hanged his woeful son

"And back from Carlisle the tinker
    came, to Branthwaite right away,
And enticed the poor girl from the
    neighbour's house, where she'd been
    glad to stay;
He promised fair to treat her well, and
    did until the second night,
And then, (right pleased were
    Branthwaite folk), he made a
    moonlight flight

"An' days went by, an' neabody went
  nar to t' tinkler's dooar,
At last some barns peep't in an' so'
  some huller't bleud on t' flooar
An' than t' hoose dooar was druven
  in, an' sec a seet was theer,
'At sum 'at so' 't went reid wid reage,
  an' sum went white wid fear

"Squeez't up intull a durty neuk, an'
  bleudy, stark, an' deid,
They fund that nice young lass's corp,
  bit niver fund her heid;
T' oald tinler hoond hed hagg't it off
  afooar he mead a fleeght on 't,
An' tean it wid him, fwoke suppwos't,
  to gud his-sel' wid t' seet on 't

"An' nin o' t' clain at efter that I' t'
  country side was seen;
But iver sen a hantit spot hes that
  Neuk-lonnin' been,
For t' murder't woman woaks aboot,
  an' greans, for o' she's deid,
As lood as what we hard to-neet, –
  they say she laits her heid!"

"Whey, weel deun, Jwohn!" to Jwohn
  says I, "an' thenks ta for they teal,
It's mead me hoaf forgit hoo t' snow
  maks o' my teas geal;
Th'u's just at heam, – gud neet, my
  lad, but first hear this fray me, –
If iv'ry teal 'at's telt be true, thy
  stwory's nea lee!"

"And days went by, and nobody went
  near to the tinker's door,
At last some children peeped in and
  saw some owl's blood upon the floor
And then the house door was driven
  in and such a sight was there,
That some who saw it went red with
  rage, and some went white with fear

"Squeezed up into a dirty nook, and
  bloody, stark and dead
They found that nice young lass's
  corpse, but never found her head;
The old tinker hound had cut it off,
  before he made his flight,
And taken with him, folk supposed, to
  goad himself with the sight of it

"And none of the clan were seen in
  the countryside again;
But ever since a haunted spot has that
  Nook lane been,
For the murdered woman walks about,
  and groans, even though she's dead,
As loud as what we heard tonight –
  they say she searches for her head!"

"Why, well done, John!" to John said
  I, "and thank you for your tale,
It's made me half forget how the snow
  makes all my toes ache;
You're nearly home, – good night, my
  friend, but first hear this from me, –
If every story that's told is true, your
  story is no lie!"

Ref: "The Folk-Speech of Cumberland and some Districts Adjacent" by Alexander Craig Gibson, FSA

SOME WESTMORLAND SAYINGS IN KENTMERE WHEN I WAS A BOY

What follow are recollections of old sayings which we used in the family when I was a boy. No doubt there were influences from the districts in Westmorland where the family originated. Following my family tree, it is clear that the male line of my family have all lived in Westmorland, latterly in Kentmere, but before that in the parishes of Grayrigg, Orton, Shap and Asby. Great Asby is not far from Appleby, our old county town.

The history of Appleby, and the area surrounding, it is fascinating. Sir Martin Holgate, in his wonderful history, *"The Story of Appleby in Westmorland"* writes: *"Few towns have been caught up in so much history. Beginning as a cluster of Danish settlers over a thousand years ago, it alternated between Scottish and English Kingdoms and became the seat of a powerful Norman barony."* He calculates that over the period between 945 and 1174 A.D., Appleby fluctuated between England and Scotland six times. So it was in England for 87 of those years and in Scotland for 142 years.

So with the successive settlements of Celts, Anglo Saxons, Norse and Danes, and with the influence of the Scots, we in Lakeland are truly a "polyglot lot"; the dialect and the place names of our area reflect that. My own study of place names and of the Vikings in Lakeland confirms this.

On my maternal side, my grandmother, Jane Prickett, was born in Beathwaite Green, part of what is Levens village, where I now live. My mother was born at Canny Dale in the Lyth Valley, and her parents farmed at Howe Lodge and Esp Ford. My mother's father, John Jackson, came from a family of charcoal burners and woodlanders in the Furness area; so the dialect of south Lakeland mingles with that of north Westmorland – only to be driven out of me at school!

Nevertheless old sayings creep into our conversations even today, as often they are succinct and to the point.

ANIMALS and BIRDS

Cragfast e.g. T'ald yow's gitten cragfast – Said of a sheep or foxhound which has got stuck on the ledge of a crag.

Garn git that ald yow er hoond doon that's gitten cragfast – Go and rescue that old sheep or hound that has got stuck in the crag face.

Flacker – Wings flapping in consternation e.g. **There was a gay darn'd flacker en craack in t'hen hus when Renart gat amang t'hens** – There was a lot of flapping and hens squawking when the fox got in the henhouse.

Kessen – Yon ald yow's liggen kessen on its back – That old sheep is lying on its back and unable to get up.

CRITICAL OBSERVATIONS

He's gitten varra lile off – He has no initiative and no drive.

Come day gang day, God send Sunday – Easy-going, careless of time passing.

A come day gang day body – An easy-going person.

A Jack of o' trades en maister ev nin – Knows a little about a lot and not much about anything; a non-specialist!

T'hedge isn't dry war t'hippings hung – The hedge is not dry where the nappies were hung out to dry – meaning he/she is young, inexperienced.

Wet ahin t'lugs – Wet behind the ears, young and inexperienced.

Thoo's o' nicked in t'heed – You are wrong in the head.

Thou's nowt atween t'lugs – You have nothing between the ears, you are ignorant.

Thoo's oot of nowt, gitten be nowt, so hoo the hell can tha be owt? – An insult to someone in a heated argument: a worthless person!

Trailen aboot as if deed lice war droppen off him – Dawdling about, so idle and slovenly that even lice find him inhospitable.

Thur was sick a turble hubbyshoo when they fell oot – An argument, disturbance or commotion.

Varra lile off e.g. He's gitten varra lile off – He has no initiative, no drive.

He's nobbut en ald scoggerslops – A slovenly fellow with no self-respect: scoggers were worn round the ankles and shins like leggings and tended to get dirty in the mud and soon looked slovenly.

Raken roards – What! She's nivver still; she's allus raken roards – Always going somewhere, never stopping to get on with her work.

She's nowt in er tins – She is inhospitable; she has no cakes or biscuits in her house to welcome you.

He's gitten t'wrang pig be t'lug – To make an error or wrong assumption.

He'll gaa through and through t'wood an' still git a creaked (crooked) **stick** – Said of a man looking for a wife who, having tried a lot of ladies, still ends up being disappointed!

She'll leuk at t'mooan till she fa's in t'midden – She will look at the moon until she falls in the muck store or slurry tank: said of a girl who searches for a man above her station.

Thi socks er med of uneasy woo – Your socks are made of worrying wool: said of a restless person who won't stay still.

It's a case of lile clogs makken gurt yans run – He's got his girl pregnant and run away to another place or emigrated.

EATING and DRINKING

Brossen – I'se var near brossen – I'm so full I'm nearly bursting.

Dodderam shakkem – jelly – **I wod like some dodderam shakkem wid a drop o cream ta finish t'efterneen tea.**

What! I'se as drunk as a fiddler or **as drunk as a potter.**

What, he's that drunk that he can nowder stan, sit ner hod be t'guss – He can neither stand, sit nor hold on to the grass!

EXPLETIVES

Drat it!

Dord, dam en blast!

Fer sham o thisel! – Shame on you!

GREETINGS, EXCHANGES, ORDERS and INSTRUCTIONS

How do, hoo's t'garn on? – Hello, how are you?

Nut ut o' badly, ta – I'm not at all bad, thanks.

Aye, why nowt but weel – All's well: this was often said at the end of a conversation in the street on market day when folks met.

Git garn or **Gaa yonder en look sharp back!** – Get a move on!

Noo leuk sharp! Louse doon thi gallasses as thou gaas en fassen up as thoo cums away! – Get a move on! Unfasten your braces as you go and don't waste time when going to the toilet!

Shut t'yat – Close the gate.

Thoo'll hev ta sowk a hinder pap – You will have to be last in the queue or last in the line of inheritance: doubtless based on the runt piglet trying to get the last teat!

Nay, I want nowt wid thee: thoo's sneck posset – The girl has put the wedge above the sneck to prevent her suitor gaining access to the kitchen after her parents have gone to bed.

Thoo's a bonny soart o lass, bigum – You are a lovely girl.

Be off wi thi marpment! – Away with your silliness and nonsense!

It's nobbut me – Its only me!

Put t'wood in t'hooal – Close the door.

HEALTH and BODILY FUNCTIONS

I was that turble cravacked, I could hardly git yaa leg past tudder – I was so bent and stiff of my back I could hardly walk.

She's turble heavy wi barn – She's pregnant.

He's that blarn up he wod blaa closet dooer off – He's got flatulence!

I'se starved ta t'bane – I am frozen to the bone, feeling very cold.

What sick tune is ta in? – Enquiry as to a person's health or well being.

I'se in gay good blaa – I'm in good health or good humour.

I'se nobbut middlin – I'm not very well.

I'se on t'mend – I'm getting better.

She's nobbut prop't – She is only propped up, very frail.

I'se nut reddy ta pop mi clogs yet – I'm not ready to die yet!

It fair maks me hisk – It really makes me gasp. Said when drawing breath with difficulty or through closed teeth, because of pain or cold or a fright.

I'se gay watter shaken, I'll hev ta gang t'closet (or **t'petty** or **t'thunner box** or **t'lile hoose**) – I'm bursting to urinate, I'll have to go to the toilet.

A short-nebbed (short-beaked) **sparra would touch it** – In urgent need to excrete!

HUNGER and THIRST

Mi belly is clapped ta mi back – I'm very hungry!

I'se dry bagged – I am thirsty.

I'se turble dry – I am very thirsty.

What, I'se as dry as a sand bed or **as a limekiln** – I am very thirsty: where limestone was kibbled to spread on acid soil, the lime was very dry and dusty.

As dry as dust – thirsty.

SIMILES and METAPHORS

As black as Hell Bess as if she was burn't tul a cinder – Very black and dirty.

He's as deep as a draw well –Intelligent but keeps his own counsel.

Garn like a blew arsed flee efter a butcher's cart – Going quickly or in haste like a bluebottle fly following the butcher's van.

Garn like a blea lowe – Going like a blue flame: perhaps reminiscent of a burning fuse when blasting rock in a quarry.

As kittle as a mousetrap – Finely balanced, easily set off or ticklish.

As lish as a lile March hare – As nimble or active as a little March hare.

As blind as a mowdywarp or mowdy – As blind as a mole.

Garn that slaa that dee en lice were droppen off him – Going so slowly that day that lice were dropping off him: idling or dawdling, wasting time.

Thrang as a bumly – Busy as a bumble bee.

Thrang as ald Throp wife – Busy and industrious as Mrs Throp; I have no idea who she was, but she was universally known as a hard-worker.

Is thur a monkey on t'riggen? – Is there a mortgage on the property?

Anybody leuken oot o t'chimley? – Does someone have a mortgage or charge on the property? These two queries would sometimes arise when a person was slow in paying his debts or hard up.

He's gitten o' t'watter on t'wheel – He is working his utmost or he is heavily committed – possibly derived from the water miller using the full flow of the mill race to mill the corn. Or it can mean he has borrowed a lot and is finding it hard to service.

As wake as wow – Weak, feeble or limp, having no energy.

SOOTHSAYINGS

A good crack's worth o' thi physic – A good conversation is the best medicine.

A lang churn maks bad butter – Said of a job which goes on too long.

Nivver say nowt but laff – Don't comment, just laugh.

Aye why nowt but weel – All's well: this was the expression used by my parents at the end of a conversation with relatives and acquaintances whom we might meet in the street on market day. As a small boy I recall being eager to get to a shop, and I used to wait for this saying as a sign of departure.

A bawling coo sean fergits – A wailing cow (person) who makes the most noise is soon over his/her sorrow.

A woman will thrive war a man cannot fend – A woman will survive with less sustenance and stand more pain than a man.

Least said seanest mendit – Least said, soonest put right.

Merry neets mak sorry mornins – Merry nights make sorry mornings. If we were out late after midnight, you could be sure our parents would shout this upstairs to wake us up half an hour earlier than usual in the morning! Cows needed milking on time in the morning, no matter what time you went to bed.

Teckins er nut meckins – Takings or turnover are not profit.

It caps langcrown – It's very puzzling, inexplicable. My grandmother used this expression often and I could never find out its origin. Has anyone any knowledge of this? Could it refer to King Longshanks perhaps?

It taks an ald dog fer a hard road – When life becomes difficult, experience counts.

A lee is hoaf way roond t'world afoor t'truth gits its clogs on – A lie spreads so quickly that the truth cannot catch up.

It's nut what yer ex, it's what y'ull tack – It's not the price you ask, it's what you will take or finally accept as the agreed price.

Mi pockets er full o em thanks – A sarcastic reply when someone might be given thanks but might be expecting a tip!

STATE OF MIND

I'se in turble laa watter – I'm miserable, depressed, dejected: possibly originating from the miller who was down-hearted because there was not enough water in the beck to drive the water wheel.

Doon in t'dumps – Miserable, depressed.

Thoo leuks as miserable as an ald dee-ad dowk craa – You look as miserable as an old, dead carrion crow!

WEATHER

Wind was blaa'en that cald, it was blaa'en t'nebs off oor geese – It was so cold, it was blowing the geese's beaks off.

It's rayder clashy soart o wedder – It is rather blustery weather.

It's a gay nipper up t'orchard – It is cold enough to frost the fruit blossom on the Lyth damson trees.

It's a raw hasky morning – It is a hard, frosty, glistening morning.

It's fit to starve a geavlock – A gavelock is a cold steel crowbar or lever which is ice-cold to handle in winter!

Rud sky ut neet is a shipperd's deleet – Red sky at night is a shepherd's delight.

Rud sky in t'mornin is a shipperd's warnen – Red sky in a morning is a shepherd's warning.

MY VIKING TRAIL TO DISCOVER
What evidence exists to show the Vikings were here in Cumbria and when they came?

This is not intended to be a definitive history of Vikings in the north-west of England but rather an account of my wanderings and readings looking for traces of "The Men from the North" and their connections and influence on our district and dialect. Looking for the evidence of Viking settlement in the North West has been a fascinating experience, as well as providing a positive means of coping with bereavement after Joy died

Mine is a lay-person's approach to local history and the study of the origins of our dialect. It has provided reasons to travel, to observe and to make enquiries in some lovely places. When my late wife Joy and I visited her cousin Jean and husband, Gordon Whitney, in Gosforth, I was fascinated by the Gosforth Cross, over 14 feet in height with pagan and Christian symbols carved upon it. Why is that so? The cross has stood there in the churchyard for over 1000 years!

I have had a recurring interest in the "Northmen" or Vikings from time to time as the exigencies of life allowed. This is then a summary of what I have learned so far. My Viking trail began in Kentmere Primary School in the 1940s with the exaggerated portrayal of Viking

Figure 8.3. Gosforth Cross with LH

exploits in children's books and with the discovery of a Viking spear in Kentmere Tarn in 1942. A second spear was later found on Nan Bield

Pass between Kentmere and Mardale. These spears are now in the Kendal Museum.

Along my trail I have found useful references in books written by professional researchers and experts on their subject. The books are listed in the bibliography of this book and referred to in the text. For those wishing to study this subject in greater detail they are essential reading.

In 1955, what is believed to be a Viking-type boat (carbon-dated *circa* 1300) was unearthed by Leslie Ridding when the Cape Asbestos Company was extracting diatomite from the old Kentmere lake bed. It is now in the Maritime Museum at Greenwich.

B. J. N. Edwards in his book, *"Vikings in North West England – The Artefacts"*, not only gives a comprehensive description and illustration of the spears found in Kentmere but also detailed information about burials, weapons, jewellery, coin hoards and sculptures found in Cumbria and the North West.

Then between 1981 and 1985, while I was still living in Kentmere, Steve Dickinson and his team discovered the remains of a Viking longhouse at Bryant's Gill in the Kentmere valley on the hillside beyond Hartrigg. The ten metre building with a central paved area produced a single radiocarbon date of the 8th or 9th century. The team unearthed eight lathe-turned spindle-whorls and twenty wet-stones together with iron artefacts, slag and worked stone believed to be from the Viking period. All these finds in Kentmere provide tangible evidence of a Viking presence in Lakeland. (Figure 8.4, colour section).

"Viking" has become the common name used for the Norwegians and Danes who invaded our shores long ago. These Vikings could not all have been fierce fighters and "pirates from the sea" but were settlers and farmers, who intermarried with the native population. The Vikings appear to have farmed on the higher ground in Lakeland. Those who came from Norway must have felt very much at home among the Lakeland hills and would have found our climate much milder than their Scandinavian homeland. They had a long-term effect on our dialect and our family names and place names, as did the Angles and Celts who came before them.

The following extract from my verse *"Hoo Lang is 'Lang Sen' in Lakeland?"* summarises the polyglot origins of our Cumbrian ancestors.

★   ★   ★

Figure 8.5. Spindle whorls and whetstones from Bryants Gill, Kentmere, 8th or 9th century

T'Anglians lant efta t'Romans went yam
En t'Norse com sean efta that
Noo I rayder like t'Scandinavian folk
Thur words en thur expressions en chat.

T'Normans nivver mannished ta tame us
Oor dales nut in t'Domesday Book
Oor forelders who valued thur freedom
Wud hev a fierce en formidable look.

In t'genes en blood of ald Lakeland folk
Thur's Celt en Anglian en Norse
The'v left thur mark on oor place-names
En in oor characters o course.

Thur's "pen" fre t'Celts en "ton" is an Anglian yam
T'Norse browt "thwaite" en "beck" en "ghyll"
En if yan maanders aboot through Lakeland
Yan can see o' sick-like origins still.

★   ★   ★

Setting the scene and some pointers:-

1. The Viking Era. It is generally accepted that the rise of Scandinavian influence on Britain began with the Viking raid on Portland Wessex in 789 AD and the raid on the Monastery at Lindisfarne in 793 AD. These raids were followed by raids on Iona in 795, 802, 806 and 807 AD. The Viking Era of authority in England ended with the English King Harold's defeat of the Norwegian King Harald Hard Ruler and the routing of his army at the battle of Stamford Bridge in 1066. Viking influence in the Isle of Man and the Western Isles of Scotland continued into the 13th century.
2. The battle of Stamford Bridge was followed three weeks later by the Norman Invasion of Britain and the defeat of King Harold himself at the Battle of Hastings.
3. "William the Conquerer" of Normandy was himself descended from Vikings. By 840 AD Paris was under constant Viking attack followed by the eight months' siege of Paris in 885 AD by Sigfrid. Then in 911 AD Normandy was granted by treaty from Charles the Simple to the Viking Chieftain Rollo. Rollo was baptised in 912 AD and the Vikings established themselves in Normandy and remained there. They built castles and buildings in stone and the Norman architectural techniques were brought to England after 1066. The Tower of London is an early example.
4. Vikings were not just "pirates from the sea"; they were farmers,

Figure 8.6. Viking longship

seafarers, settlers, workers of metal and traders. They had a considerable influence on developments and trade in Europe for over three hundred years.

5. Between 600 and 700 AD we know that tillage and farming practice as well as iron production had improved in Scandinavia.

6. Shipbuilding methods also improved with better design and clinker-built boats using riven timber and rivets. The design and construction of their boats then allowed them to beach almost anywhere and to sail along coasts and up rivers as and when they chose.

7. There were essentially three types of superior sea-faring boats which were designed to give easy access on to beaches and into rivers:

    i) The Viking warship or longship was designed for speed.
    ii) The merchant ship was built broader in the beam for cargo capacity.
    iii) Smaller coastal fishing boats and ferry boats.

8. Initially they were pagans, fierce fighters, but left little written evidence of their era, preferring to hand down their adventures in stories later included in the Icelandic sagas. We have to rely, therefore, on archaeological evidence and the writings of others, often written later, and often written by those who themselves had been attacked and plundered.

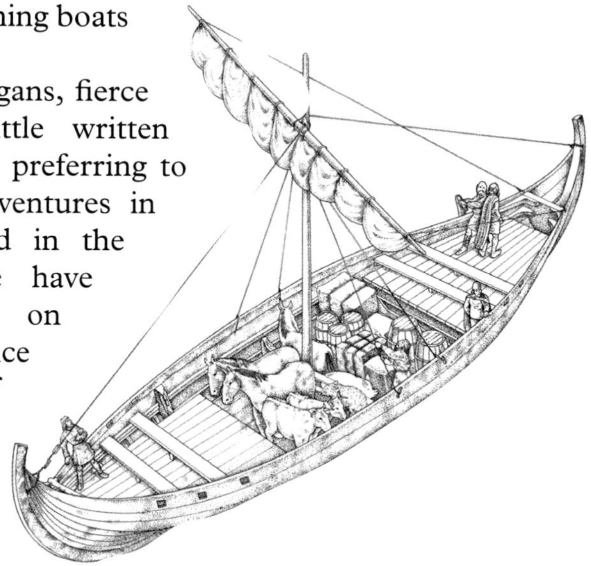

Figure 8.7. Viking merchant ship showing cargo.
© J.G-C & F.L. Ltd.

9. It is thought that the Norse influence on Lakeland started about 900 AD. Although state intervention from Norway ceased after the Battle of Stamford Bridge in 1066, Norse influence and trade seem to have lasted well into the 13th century. The King of Man was still under Norse control until 1266. We still have many Norse place names in Cumbria to this day. Valleys such as Wasdale and Langdale have

names of Norse origin, as do mountains such as Scafell and Harter Fell.

10. We know the Vikings arrived in the River Liffey in Ireland with sixty ships in 837 AD and established the first Norse fortified settlements near Dublin in 841 AD. Evidence suggests that they settled, intermarried and were Christianised in Ireland but retained some of their pagan culture, before coming to Cumbria as refugees when they were expelled from Dublin in 902 AD. The Gosforth Cross in West Cumberland symbolises this, because it bears pagan as well as Christian symbols and carvings. See later references and picture of the Gosforth Cross.

11. There were also Viking settlements in Ireland at Larne, on Rathlin Island and as far south as Wexford, Waterford, Cork and Limerick, as well as on Anglesey.

12. The Isle of Man has a Tynwald (parliament hill) which has survived to this day for more than 1000 years. New legislation on the Isle of Man has to be confirmed by the people in July of each year at the Tynwald. A system which allows individuals to petition parliament has its origins in Norse Law before the end of the 10th century. The word "law" itself is of Norse origin (*log*).

13. There was a "Thing" or parliament on the Wirral and W. G. Collingwood, (1854-1932), the great artist, author and antiquary, identified a "Thingmound" in Little Langdale in Cumbria in the 1890s. Matthew Townend in his book, "*The Vikings and Victorian Lakeland: The Norse Medievalism of W. G. Collingwood and his Contemporaries*", published by the Cumberland and Westmorland Antiquarian and Archaeological Society, provides an in-depth study of the influence of the Vikings in Cumbria.

14. The large Cuerdale hoard of coins and silver found on Friday, 5th May 1840, by men repairing the bank of the River Ribble south of Preston, included silver ingots from Ireland and coins minted in York which date circa 900 to 910 AD.

Who were the Vikings and where were they from?

1. Although not exclusively so, the Scandinavian Vikings may be divided into three groups: the Norse who came from what is now south-west Norway, the Danes from what is now Denmark and its vicinity, and the Swedish Vikings who occupied the eastern side of Scandinavia up to Finland. Their areas of influence are well laid

out on James Graham-Campbell's maps on pages 22, 27 and 88 of his book, "*The Viking World*". (Figure 8.8, colour section.)

2. The Norse or Norsemen were mostly from the area which is now Norway. They colonised parts of the Shetlands, the Orkneys, the Faeroes, Caithness, the Western Isles, Islay, the Isle of Man and Iceland, and they settled in parts of Ireland. They also went to Greenland and Nova Scotia.

3. **The Norwegian Vikings** appear to have had greater influence on Lakeland than either the Danish or the Swedish Vikings. This is indicated to an extent by the place names in Lakeland. In Cumbria place names are predominately Norse. Those homesteads and place names which end in *thwaite, dale, fell, beck* and *kirk* are mainly in the west, while further east there is **Danish influence** on place names from the areas now known as Yorkshire and Northumberland. In the north-east of Cumbria there are many place names ending with the Danish *by (byr)*. All these place names were established over a period of 300 years. The ending *byr* was also used in Norway.

4. **The Swedish Vikings**, known as the "Rus" from the Finnish word for Swede, gave their name to Russia. They mainly went east and south from there, establishing Kiev in 862 AD, and travelled south to the Black Sea and Constantinople and further east to the Caspian Sea. They traded from there with middle-eastern countries. (Figure 8.9, colour section.)

5. **The Danish Vikings**: in 851 AD the Danish invaders took winter quarters in Thanet and the Great Danish Army attacked Britain in 862 AD.

6. **The Danes captured York** in 867 AD and established themselves in Britain, mainly to the east of the Pennines with their stronghold in York. The Jorvik exhibition in York recreates the Viking era in the city and is well worth a visit.

7. **King Alfred forced a treaty with the Danes** in 886 AD which settled the area of Danelaw to the north of a line from Chester to North London. The Danelaw area also included Yorkshire, east of the Pennines, and Northumbria.

Historians seem agreed that the Vikings who settled in Cumbria were mainly Norse-Irish Vikings, having settled in Ireland and become partly Christianised before coming here. If that is true, then the question arises: why did they not settle along the Cumbrian coast at the same time as other Norsemen settled in Ireland? Though it appears there were earlier attacks from circa 750 AD in Ireland, and settlement in Ireland began to take place between 837 and 841 AD, yet we have no clear evidence of them coming to Cumbria until circa 910 AD. Was it because the Angles arrived first and repelled them? Or was it that the people of Strathclyde, which included Cumbria and was governed by the Scots, kept them out?

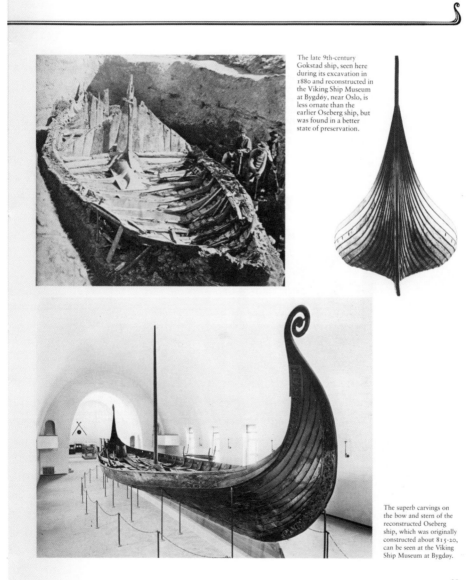

The late 9th-century Gokstad ship, seen here during its excavation in 1880 and reconstructed in the Viking Ship Museum at Bygdøy, near Oslo, is less ornate than the earlier Oseberg ship, but was found in a better state of preservation.

The superb carvings on the bow and stern of the reconstructed Oseberg ship, which was originally constructed about 815-20, can be seen at the Viking Ship Museum at Bygdøy.

39

Figure 8.10. Gokstad & Osberg Boats

This question has troubled me along my Viking trail and, like many before me, I have tried to find reliable evidence of early Norse occupation and influence in Cumbria.

My interest was revived with my visit to Norway in 2004. My 'Viking trail' took me to Norway with my wife Joy in June 2004. We went with Bay Farm Tours of Morecambe, who do a ten day tour of Norway each year, visiting Oslo and Voss, Hardangerfjord, the Flam railway, other fjords and Bergen, and including some farm visits.

We saw the splendid restored Gokstad and Oseberg ships in the Bygdøy Museum near Oslo. Both these ships had been found in burial mounds at Gokstad and Oseberg respectively on the west side of the Oslo fjord. They revealed much of historical interest. When these boats were unearthed, the contents in the burial chambers of these longships dramatically enhanced our understanding and knowledge of the Viking age and sparked interest in and outside Norway.

Robert Ferguson in his book, "The Hammer and the Cross", says that there were in fact three ships. The first ship to be excavated in 1867 at Rolsvøy was the Tune, which was built about 900 AD. Behind the mast were the remains of a man, a horse, spears and the remnants of a saddle.

The excavation of the Gokstad longship in 1900 aroused national and international interest. Examination of the burial chamber revealed a giant of a man buried with twelve horses, six dogs and a peacock. The mound also contained five beds, three small boats, a bronze pot with suspension chain, as well as many utensils. Recent post-mortem examination of the body from the Gokstad ship has revealed amazing details of his medical condition and how he died.

The Oseberg ship was discovered in 1904 and reconstruction was completed in 1926. Analysis shows it was built from trees felled in 820 AD. After treatment, it proved possible to use 90% of the original oak in the reconstruction of the keel. Robert Ferguson states that the contents of the Oseberg ship included two women and revealed the culture of the period in the range and quality of the items buried, which far outstripped the grave goods found in other burials. (Figure 8.11, colour section.)

Unfortunately, no such boat burials like these have been found in Cumbria to provide the wealth of evidence that might have revealed the culture of the Viking era in Lakeland. However, there is a boat grave at Balladoole on the Isle of Man, which is referred to later. The Norwegian boat burials and the boat grave at Balladoole provide a time marker and an insight into the Viking era.

Figure 7.3. Joy with a welcome home meal at Quarry Foot

Figure 7 14. County Show 2005: LH and Joy with Angus cow

Figure 7.10. Mike and Kate on their Wedding Day

Figure 7.11. Joy with Mike and Kate at Versailles

Figures 7.16. Westmorland County Show, 2006: President LH, Joy and Guests: Front row, left to right: Jen Sansom, Joan Matthews, Joy and LH, Olive Clarke, Alma and Alan Thompson. Middle row: Rachel Geldard, Keith and Christine Wood, Kate Winkley, Martyn Wrathall, Jenny Bewley, Pauline Sowray, Bill Bewley, Maria and John Blake. Back row: Tony Sansom, John Geldard, Mike Winkley, Chris Sowray and Peter Matthews – see page 311

Figure 7.17. LH and Joy on the showfield with my daughters, Jacqueline and Penny and their families: Front row, left to right: LH, Jacqueline with Millie, Rebecca, Kieran, David and Joy
Back row: Gordon, Mark, Penny and Michaela

Figure 7.18. In the Food Marquee with my daughter, Ingrid, and grandchildren, Nicholas and Michael Jopson

Figure 7.21. Joy, Malcolm and Elsie Tyson and LH sitting at the Café de Paris, Casino Square, Monte Carlo

Figure 7.26. Bill's 60th – relaxing in Venice, left to right: Tony Sansom, Pat Wilson, Joy, Jenny Bewley, Jen Sansom, LH, Bill and Alan Wilson – see page 317

Figures 7.23, 7.24 and 7.25. Martin and Richard kayaking and walking in the Lake District

Figure 7.28. Joy with the Jopsons at the Crazy Horse Memorial, 2004 – see page 317

Figure 7.29. The Jopsons at Bellmanground Farm, Windermere, before emigrating to the USA.
Left to right: Nick, Sarah, Michael, Ingrid, Mossop and Kayleigh

Figure 7.33. Joy with grandchildren Emily and Robert in Levens Hall gardens, July 2007 – see page 319

Figure 7.34. LH and Joy with Emily and Robert, Graham and Geraldine, Lindsey and Marc

Figure 7.36. LH with Moto Guzzi on Kirkstone Pass 2008

Figure 8.1. Lakeland Dialect Society Officers & Committee, 2011:
Front row, left to right: LH (Vice-President), Ted Relph (President), Louise Green (Editor), Jean Scott-Smith (Secretary) and Tommy Coultard (Chairman)
Back row: Keith Coates (Vice President), Bryan Dawson (Vice Chairman), Donald Angus, Robbie Ellis (Recording Editor) and John Holmes (Treasurer)
Absent: Keith Balmer, John Handley, John Hunter, Reverend Brian Pedder and Bruce Wilson

Figure 8.4. Norse influence: Kentmere Valley showing Rainsborrow, Ill Bell, and Froswick on left with Scale Knotts in middle distance, behind which lies Bryants Gill, site of Norse longhouse and Scales Farm in front: ON *skali* for shieling or shelter. Nan Bield Pass, where a Viking spear was found, lies east of High Street

Figure 8.8. Areas of Scandinavian settlement – Copyright: James Graham-Campbell and Francis Lincoln Ltd.

Figures 8.18, 8.19, 8.20, 8.21. Braaid site of foundations of Viking longhouse and Celtic roundhouse of First Millennium with Jean, Bill and Jenny Bewley

Figure 10.14. LH and Reg with our escorts: David Williams, John Wood and Andrew Taylor at Michael's Nook in Grasmere

Figure 10.15. LH and Reg Gifford riding past Rydal Water from Grasmere to Ambleside on a charity ride

After Oslo we sailed down the fjords and visited a number of interesting sites, including an ancient rope maker who created rope from tree bark, after it had been soaked in seawater for a year or so. The rope was amazingly strong and it seems likely that this type of rope would have been used on Viking longships.

We had two farm visits near Voss, which gave us a real feel of the country and an opportunity to meet and talk to the locals. When I was a lad at Brow Top, Kentmere, my father would say, "*Garn git some fire eldin fre t'hog hus*". Fire elding was kindling to light the fire. The "hog hus" was an old farm building up the yard where Father had a workshop and store for wood and bracken.

My most abiding memory of the Norwegian holiday relates to a well-weathered, wooden chalet on one of the old farms near Voss. It stood on stone pillars about three feet above the ground. Walking up the steps to its entrance, I saw carved above the door the words: "Eldin Hus". It was an ancient smoke house! The Old Norse word "hus" means house and "eldin" means fuel. Joseph Wright in his celebrated English Dialect Dictionary, 1905, states that in Cumberland and Westmorland, "*Fire eldin included peat, turf, ling, whins and wood for kindling a fire.*"

Those two words, "Eldin Hus", that I saw carved on the old wooden chalet, poignantly reminded me of Father's words and brought home to me real evidence of the Norse connection with Cumbria.

In the spring of 2009 I visited my friends Reg and Finn Ashworth in Donegal. There, in a lovely old museum village of Irish life by the sea, I bought a book called "*The Vikings: An Illustrated History*" by Ailbhe MacShamhrain.

This book gave me a glimpse of the Irish perspective of the Viking period. I read how the Orkneys and the Western Isles as well as the Isle of Man, became steps on the sea route and supply chain for the Norse adventurers to Ireland. I learned that the first Viking raids on Ireland occurred between 750 and 800 AD, pre-dating the attack on Lindisfarne of 793 AD. They established a large trading base on the River Liffey, near what is now Dublin, between 800 and 850 AD.

It is believed that there was a further great exodus of the Norse people from Norway, which occurred after 880 AD, when Harald Fairhair sought to unify the areas of Norway under his kingship. It appears that this caused a further tide of adventurers and refugees to emigrate from Norway.

In her book, "*The Northern Conquest*", Katherine Holman indicates that the Norwegian settlement of Lakeland occurred between 900 AD and 950 AD. There appears to be a consensus amongst historians that the Norse Vikings arrived in Cumbria about this time, mainly from Ireland. If that is so, then there had been some settlement over two or three generations in Ireland for at least 60 years before they settled here. It is thought they came as refugees from Ireland. This appears to be the reason why historians believe the Norse people were Christianised before coming to Cumbria.

So what kept them out of Cumbria for more than 60 years? Along my trail of tracing the Norse influence on Cumbria, I have tried to make sense of the period after the Romans left up to 900 AD. I have looked for some clues as to the state of affairs in Cumbria when the Vikings came and what kept them out so long.

It appears that there was a great upheaval caused by the withdrawal of the Roman army. West of the Pennines was the land of the Cymry which stretched northwards into Scotland (Strathclyde) and south to Wales. By 600 AD the power of the Cymry was in decline. At the Battle of Chester in 615 AD the Angles were successful against the Cymry and drove a wedge between the Cymry of Wales and the Cymry of Cumbria.

In chapter 4 of his fascinating book, *"A History of Man in the Lake District"*, published in 1967, Dr. William Rollinson tells us that from about 540 AD Anglian peoples, who came from the North German Plains, began settling along the Northumbrian Coast. By the end of the seventh century Anglian influence had increased and they had also moved into what is now Cumbria.

By 685 AD the Angles had settled around the Cumbrian dome of mountains. They were mainly lowland farmers and interested in the fertile, ploughable areas of land. Study of Anglian place names shows that the Angles settled around the fringes of Lakeland before the Vikings came.

Time does not permit a detailed study of the Anglian era here, but my thanks go to Noree, widow of Michael Davies-Shiel, who generously gave me access to Michael's notes on the Angles and Vikings in Lakeland. He had hand-out sketch-maps which he used with his talks and lectures. Noree has kindly given me permission to use these here. Michael taught me economic history and geography at Windermere Grammar School in the 1950s. He also carried out splendid research on the economic and social history of Lakeland throughout his career and through his long and happy retirement.

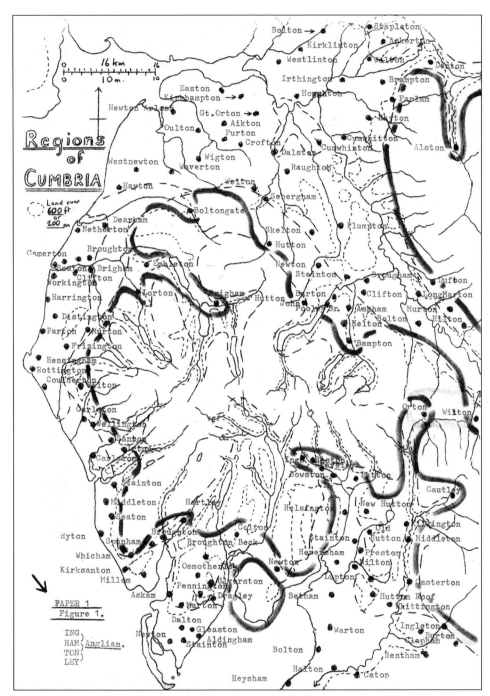

Figure 8.11. Michael Davies-Shiel Map of Anglian settlement in Cumbria with place names

Figure 8.11 illustrates the number of settlements with Anglian place names around the Cumbrian dome, many of which must pre-date the advent of the Norsemen.

Figure 8.12 *Norse settlement in the fell country* provides an illustration of valley settlement with a helpful key to W. G. Collingwood's work on the pattern of settlement in a dale using the Norse place names and interpretation.

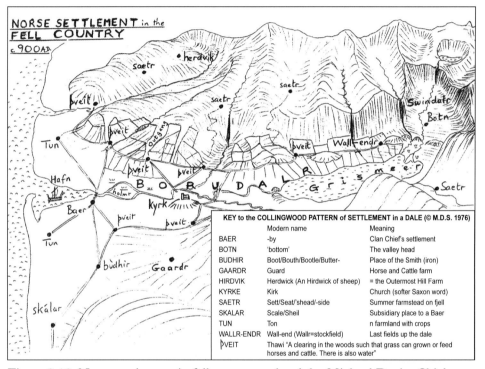

KEY to the COLLINGWOOD PATTERN of SETTLEMENT in a DALE (© M.D.S. 1976)

	Modern name	Meaning
BAER	-by	Clan Chief's settlement
BOTN	'bottom'	The valley head
BUDHIR	Boot/Bouth/Bootle/Butter-	Place of the Smith (iron)
GAARDR	Guard	Horse and Cattle farm
HIRDVIK	Herdwick (An Hirdwick of sheep)	= the Outermost Hill Farm
KYRKE	Kirk	Church (softer Saxon word)
SAETR	Sett/Seat/'shead/-side	Summer farmstead on fjell
SKALAR	Scale/Sheil	Subsidiary place to a Baer
TUN	Ton	n farmland with crops
WALLR-ENDR	Wall-end (Wallr=stockfield)	Last fields up the dale
ÞVEIT	Thawi "A clearing in the woods such that grass can grown or feed horses and cattle. There is also water"	

Figure 8.12. Norse settlement in fell country – sketch by Michael Davies-Shiel

His notes also illustrate his study of the movement of the successive waves of settlers in Cumbria and the movement of the boundary between Strathclyde and England before Scotland became one nation. The historical events in Strathclyde, Alba, Dalriada and Northumbria have all had an influence on Cumbria which would fill volumes. For the purpose of condensing and illustrating Cumbria's races and settlement patterns, Mike provides us with a good illustration of Norse, Anglian and Celt settlement in figure 8.14.

In figure 8.13 MD-S 3 Mike also assesses the likely position of the boundary of Strathclyde (governed from Dumbarton Rock), as his research shows it to be in 945 AD, when King Edmund of

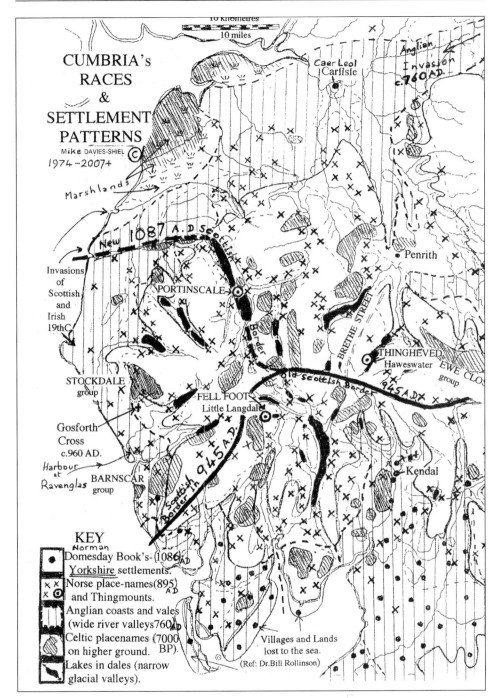

Figure 8.13.Cumbria's Races and Settlement Patterns with boundaries of Strathclyde in 945 and 1087 AD.   © Michael Davies-Shiel

Northumberland defeated King Duvenald (Dunmail) and handed Cumbria to Malcolm I of Scotland in return for military support.

I find that the boundary at 1087 AD in the MD-S 3 map reflects the earlier exchange of Lothian for Cumbria by King Canute, and then the seizure by Malcolm III, King of Scotland, of that part of Cumbria north of the River Derwent and the Eamont. Thus Cumbria was part of Scotland when the Domesday survey was done and it does not appear in the Domesday Book. When William II, Rufus, son of the Conquerer, came to Carlisle in 1092 AD, the Anglo-Saxon Chronicle tells us that he found Bishop Dolphinus in charge of Carlisle and ejected him.

The boundary with Strathclyde had earlier been pushed back by King Athelstan of Wessex in 927 AD to roughly the position shown at 945 AD in Figure 8.14. Athelstan successfully unified the kingdoms of England under his rule – he being the first King of all England. In 927 AD the King of Strathclyde and the King of the Scots and the earls of Northumberland recognised Athelstan's supremacy.

Later in 937 AD, when the King of Dublin with the support of the Kings of Strathclyde and the Scots tried to recover York, they were soundly beaten by Athelstan at the Battle of Brunanburh. No one seems sure where this battle took place as so far there is no archaeological evidence. Places mentioned in the conjectural debate as to the site of the battle are: Burnswark in Dumfriesshire, somewhere on the Wirral, Bromborough in Cheshire and near the Humber estuary.

We know that in 902 AD Viking rulers were expelled from Dublin after a massive defeat by the Irish. It is thought that some Norse-Irish families came to Cumbria and the Wirral at that time. Stephen Harding in "*Viking Mersey: Scandinavian Wirral, West Lancashire and Chester*" refers to documentary evidence of a wholesale exodus across the Irish Sea from Dublin in an ancient Irish annal, now known as the "*Three Fragments*".

There were further expulsions of Norsemen from Ireland and on Good Friday in 1014 AD, following the Battle of Clontarf, Brian Boru with his Hiberno-Norse army sacked Dublin but died in the process. More Norse-Irish then fled to the Isle of Man and also to Anglesey, the Wirral, and again to parts of north-west England.

The influence of the Vikings who settled in Cumbria continued long after 1066 in our customs and in our place names. Clearly there was still trade going on after the Norman Conquest. I saw evidence of this on my visits to the Isle of Man and to Furness Abbey. I found links between the last Norse King of Man and the Isles, Rognvaldr, with Cumbria in the 13th century. King Reginald (Rognvaldr), who is buried at Furness Abbey, having been killed in an internecine war with his brother in 1229, had, like his brother, granted licences to fish round the Isle of Man to Furness Abbey, Holme Cultram Abbey and also to St. Bees Abbey. Rognvald had dealings with the English King John, of Magna Carta fame.

In the summer of 2009 I visited the Isle of Man twice. I enjoyed some days watching the TT races on my first visit and the Manx Grand Prix on my second visit. I found time on each visit to travel here and there by bus and steam train in order to explore the Viking heritage.

Though the Isle of Man seemed to me to have fewer Norse place names than Cumbria, Sir David M. Wilson in his book, "*The Vikings in the Isle of Man*", shows the distribution of place names ending in "*by*". He cites this as "*a clear indication of Norse settlement*". There are also instances of "*dale*" and "*fell*": e.g. Foxdale and Lambsfell. Likewise in Cumbria we have fell (*fjall*), dale (*dalr*) and by (*byr*) in Scafell, Mardale and Appleby, but as explained later, the list of Norse place names in Cumbria is extensive.

The Tynwald Parliament (*Thingvellir*) on Tynwald Hill is a Norse-based institution. The Isle of Man together with the Isle of Islay and the Western Isles were once colonies of Norway and were ruled from there until the Treaty of Perth in 1266.

My visit to the Peel Museum on the Isle of Man and my study of Professor Wilson's book led me to search out and visit Viking sites on the island. The boat-grave at Chapel Hill, Balladoole, on the south of the island near Castletown, was particularly interesting. It is sited in a large enclosure where there is a 360 degree view of the sea and all the country around. So far no "boat-graves" have been found in Cumbria. The pattern of the stones in the shape of the boat buried within is shown clearly in my picture of the Balladoole grave. The contents of the grave are on display in the Manx Museum in Douglas.

I also visited the Norse gravestones at Maughold Church which are housed in a shelter at the edge of the graveyard. The church is lovely and contains some interesting relics.

There are many sites on the Isle of Man, but my purpose was to look for connections with Cumbria. Was there a "Thing" (*Thingvellir*), a meeting place or parliament in Cumbria?

It appears that W.G. Collinwood in the 1890s certainly thought that the tiered earthworks on a site in Little Langdale could be a "Thing".

Figure 8.14. Viking Burial Ship Burial – site notice on the Isle of Man

Figure 8.15. Balladoole Ship Burial Site near Castletown, Isle of Man

Dr. William Rollinson also refers to this in his "*A History of Man in the Lake District*".

My Viking trail was interrupted in 2010 by the events described in "The Magic of the Internet". Happily, my new wife Jean has shown enthusiasm for visiting places of interest which are connected with my Viking trail. Jean has embraced my interest in the Viking trail, inspired me and given wholehearted support in the production and editing of this book.

In August 2010 we were guests of our friends, Bill and Jen Bewley, in Port Erin on the Isle of Man, and were able to combine an interest in motor cycling with further Viking research.

I took Jean to see the boat burial site at Balladoole as well as Maughold Church with its Viking artefacts. In addition we visited the Viking settlement at the Braaid. This site consists of a pre-Norse round house and two other buildings which belong to the Viking Age, as verified on re-excavation in 1963. (Ref. Sir David M. Wilson – "*The Vikings in the Isle of Man*".) See Figures 8.17, 8.18, 8.19 and 8.20, colour section of this book.

Figure 8.16. Braaid on site display with sketch of Viking longhouse

We also went to the Manx Museum in Douglas to see the items found at Balladoole and the account of the rich Viking history of the Isle of Man.

After our wedding in July 2010 we spent the first few days of our honeymoon in a lovely cottage in Dumfriesshire, kindly lent to us by Jean's friend, Helen White. We visited our friends, Martyn and Pam Wrathall, who live nearby above Dunscore, and then sailed over to Northern Ireland. Our Viking trail took us to the small, but beautiful, Rathlin Island, off the north coast of County Antrim. There we spent a happy time watching the many puffins and other seabirds. We learned that Rathlin Monastery was attacked by Vikings in 795 AD and that the influence of the Vikings affected Rathlin until 1180. The monastery was still occupied by monks in 848 AD. Ours was a day visit and the island is worthy of a much longer stay.

On our return from holidaying in County Donegal with our friends, Reg and Finn Ashworth, in early August 2010, Jean and I stayed overnight in Port Patrick on the Ayrshire coast. Following our Viking trail we decided to visit Whithorn in Wigtonshire on the way home. Unfortunately, we had little time to explore but it is a fascinating place. In the 10th century Vikings came to Whithorn, the monastic community following the cult of Saint Ninian. In their book, "*Vikings in Scotland*", Professor James Graham-Campbell and Colleen E. Batey, write that archaeological research in Whithorn shows evidence of the manufacture of antler horn combs in Whithorn. It is thought that the Vikings developed a trade in the export of combs made of antler horn and such combs have been found all over the Viking world.

Jean and I learned of the annual Whithorn lectures and gleaned more evidence from the published lectures as to why the Vikings came later to Cumbria than to Ireland. We purchased a copy of the Fifth Whithorn Lecture, "*The Churches of North Britain in the Viking Age*" by David N. Dumville, Professor of Palaeography and Cultural History at the University of Cambridge. In this lecture he refers to the first third of the tenth century i.e. 900 to 935 AD. There he makes it clear that the most powerful political entity in Scotland at that time was the Kingdom of Alba, whose predecessors were the kings of the Picts and their neighbours, the kings of Strathclyde. He tells us that from the first appearance of Vikings in their territories, Alba and Strathclyde had resolutely opposed them.

This evidence of opposition to early Viking settlement by Strathclyde and Alba may well be the reason why the Vikings did not establish a foothold in Cumbria as early as they did in Ireland, because Cumbria was then part of Strathclyde.

The Fifth Whithorn Lecture by Professor Dumville and the Eighth Whithorn Lecture by Professor James Graham-Campbell give fascinating insights into the Viking era in Galloway and Southern Scotland, as well as casting further light on the Viking influence in Cumbria. David Dumville indicates that at some point between the Viking seizure of York in 866/7 AD and 927 AD, when King Athelstan seized York and made inroads into south-west Cumbria, Strathclyde's territory had expanded down through Cumbria as far as the River Derwent and eastwards as far as Rere Cross on Stainmore "on the crest of the Pennines". Athelstan made himself king of all England in the same year.

Nearer to home, given the activity of the Vikings around the coast of the Irish Sea and round the Isle of Man, it seems more than likely that they would venture into the River Kent estuary and the River Bela. There is evidence of their settlement in the place names of Old Norse origin such as Beathwaite Green (*thveit meaning clearing*) – now part of Levens village, Ackenthwaite (*Acca* or *Hakon-thveit*), Crosthwaite (*kross-thveit*), Heaves (*hlif* meaning "sheep pasture"), Lyth (*hlid* or *hlith* meaning "sloping hillside"*)*, Sedgwick (*Siggi-vik*), Ninezergh and Sizergh (*Sigred-erg* meaning "Sigred's summer pasture"), etc.

Professor Dumville refers to an abbot of Heversham, named Tilred, who apparently fled east over the Pennines and bought himself a living in Chester-le-Street and the abbacy of Norham-on-Tweed circa 911 and 914 AD. This is referred to in *"Historia de Sanco Cuthberto"*. Professor Dumville infers that Tilred was probably fleeing from Viking incursions during that time.

Stephen Read, the secretary and driving force of our Levens Local History Society, invited Jean and I to attend a day course on the 2nd April 2011 at Lancaster University, entitled: "Medieval Settlements in the North West". The more one delves into a subject the more there is to learn! It was that day when we found further reference to the debate about the expulsion of the Norse-Irish from Dublin in 902 AD. (Ref. James Graham-Campbell & Robert Philpott's *"The Huxley Viking Hoard: Scandinavian Settlement in the North West."*) It is argued that refugees from Dublin dispersed to the Hebrides and along the Cumbrian coast, because it would be an attractive destination away from political authority.

It is also postulated that between 905 and 910 AD a band of refugees from Dublin based themselves on the River Ribble and that they were connected with the massive hoard of silver and coins found during work on the river at Cuerdale, south of Preston, on the 15th May 1840. Much of the silver bullion in the hoard came from Ireland. B.J.N. Edwards in his book *"Vikings in North-West England – The Artefacts"*, discusses the origins of the coins and mentions five main groups of coins totalling between 7000 and 8000, of which nearly 5000 coins were Viking coins, mostly minted at York. The hoard also included coins minted in East Anglia and in France and fifty Arabic dirhems, showing how far trade with the Vikings extended.

My Viking trail has not just involved travel to see places of interest with Viking connection but also reading and browsing through many admirable books containing detailed research and study on Vikings and the Norse influence on Cumbria and its language over the last 150 years. I have already included reference to present day luminaries in this field as well as in my bibliography.

The information I gleaned on my Viking trail was helpful in preparing a talk to the Lakeland Dialect Society which our President, Ted Relph, and I gave on the 19th March 2011 at Mungrisdale. I dealt with some of the historical evidence of the Vikings in Lakeland and Cumbrian place names of Norse origin. Ted dealt with the etymology of our dialect and illustrated his talk with pictures from his visits to Norway, showing the similarity in words and culture.

Jean and I had spent a happy time in preparation for the Mungrisdale talk, visiting the Gosforth Cross and locating places with Norse prefixes or suffixes to their names. Like William Rollinson, Mike Davies- Shiel and others before us, we saw that the Norse place names were generally, but not always, on the higher ground and mostly in the Cumberland and west of Westmorland areas. Those place names with the suffix "by" (*byr*) were mostly in the east which suggests that Danish Vikings settled up the Eden valley from east of the Pennines. However, we cannot be specific because the word *byr* was also used in Norway and there was clearly some fusion between the Norse Vikings of Cumberland and Westmorland and the Danish Vikings from what is now north Yorkshire and Northumberland.

There are many other place names with Viking influence but we limited our study to *beck, thwaite, dale, scales* and *by* only. We are not sure that we have located all the place names in Cumbria with these prefixes and suffixes. In the following summary ON = Old Norse and Dan = Danish.

To summarise, we found place names as follows:
1. *Beck*, a stream or river – (ON *bekkr*) – 11 instances in Cumberland and 14 in Westmorland.
2. *Thwaite*, a clearing or enclosure which often became a farmstead – (ON *pveit*) – 54 in Cumberland, 10 in Westmorland and 17 in Furness.
3. *Dale*, a valley – (ON *dalr*) – 14 in Cumberland and 17 in Westmorland.
4. *Scales*, a shieling or hut – (ON *skali*) – 6 in Cumberland, 3 in Westmorland and 3 in Furness
5. *By*, a farmstead – (ON & Dan *byr*) – 50 in Cumberland, 21 in Westmorland and only 1 found in Furness.

As my readings have progressed, I realise how little I know and how much more there is to learn and how much the earth has yet to reveal. There are Viking graves hewn out of rock at Heysham, and crosses, hog backs and other sculptures on many sites in Lakeland yet to be visited. As I have discovered, the study of the Gosforth Cross is a whole subject of its own! There is much more to study and enjoy about the origins of dialect words used in Lakeland and those we use every day in our modern-day English language.

Early this summer (2011) Jean and I were browsing in a bookshop and by chance came upon a DVD called "VIKING" produced by ITV Border Television in 2005 and introduced by Eric Robson. This excellent series, of which we were previously unaware, gives a comprehensive and authoritative history of the Viking settlements in Cumbria and around the Irish Sea, which is termed as 'The Viking Lake'. The series includes discussion and commentary from a number of erudite professors, archaeologists and historians.

Referring to the Gosforth Cross, Professor Richard Bailey describes the competence of the sculpture as world class. Inter alia, he explains the depiction of the death of the Norse god Loki on one side of the cross and the crucifixion of Christ on the other. It is a fascinating analysis as he explores the relationship between the pagan beliefs and the Christian religion. He thinks that the Gosforth Cross is an innovative and theologically extraordinary monument which contrasts and draws parallels between the traditions of the patron's Scandinavian homeland and the Christian world over 1000 years ago.

New finds and discoveries are still being made and add to our information.

Only recently in the Westmorland Gazette of 7th July 2011 it was reported that a hoard of 92 silver coins and artefacts, dating from

895 to 960 AD, was found scattered in the ground on farmland near Dalton-in-Furness. Among the hoard were ingots and one near-complete silver bracelet, plus a pair of Arabic dirhem coins – silver currency which circulated in tenth century Europe. This find has yet to be carefully evaluated but here again we have tangible evidence of the Vikings who settled in Cumbria. It is an exciting discovery which will add to our knowledge.

The Norse people appear to have been Christianised fairly quickly, interbred and disappeared into the Cumbrian landscape as they were gradually assimilated into the local population. What is fascinating today is that in a recent televised study a significant percentage of men living in the Penrith area had Norse DNA on their Y chromosomes. The Y chromosome is transmitted from father to son only. It seems likely that the Viking invasions a thousand years ago contributed a significant fraction to the Cumbrian gene pool. The fusion of Scandinavian, British, Irish and Celtic traditions must have helped to create a vibrant and prosperous society, from which base the people of Cumbria must go forward. I have yet to learn if I have any Viking genes but my stocky build suggests more Anglian or Celt!

LH CHRONOLOGY: To understand the conditions before the Viking invasions, to make sense in time of the information I gleaned on my Viking trail and to put it in context, I began a timeline for easy reference, which shows events in three periods :-

(i)   During the period from 300 BC up to 789 AD, when the first recorded Viking raid on Britain occurred at Portland in Wessex and the first recorded raid in the north at Lindisfarne in 793 AD.

(ii)   The Viking era in Britain, usually quoted as 793 AD (the raid on Lindisfarne) to 1066 AD (the Battle of Stamford Bridge). The period clearly lasted longer in Scotland and the Western Isles up to the 1266 Treaty of Perth following the Battle of Largs in 1263.

(iii) The post-Viking era by which time the Vikings had been mainly Christianised and had integrated themselves into Cumbrian society.

The timeline cannot and does not encompass all there is to know about Vikings. Some dates and times remain controversial, so it is for my guidance only. Historians will do their own research.

The evidence clearly suggests that the Norsemen/Vikings settled in parts of Ireland first before they settled in Cumbria, but it seems unlikely to me that there were no incursions into Cumbria before 902 AD. The coasts of Cumbria and southern Scotland around "The Viking Lake" could easily be seen. The Norsemen were also traders. There were estuaries and old Roman roads across our area, accessible to them to both the east and the south. The lack of archaeological evidence in Cumbria before 900 AD and the warring kingships of Strathclyde through their occupation of Cumbria mean we have little reliable evidence on which to get a firm date of the first Norse settlement. On this "the jury is still out".

Clearly, we have many erudite professors and historians, (see bibliography), who have made a lifetime's study of the Scandinavian influence on Cumbria and they have enriched our knowledge in doing so. Who knows what our good earth of Cumbria may reveal in the future?

The Gosforth Cross is a landmark in time and place. The place names in Cumbria with Norse element in them reveal widespread settlement, trade, integration and influence for many years during and after the Viking era in Britain. Along my journey I have enjoyed filling in some of the blanks on the canvas of my Viking picture of Cumbria. What is clear is that the Scandinavians had a much greater influence on the development of Europe than I ever imagined.

That Norway, a former warrior nation, now promotes peace and civilised behaviour in our troubled world by action and example, most famously, perhaps, by the annual award of the Nobel Peace Prize, means we all have hope. Dum spiro spero!

So it is at this point, that I must leave our Viking trail. Could the Orkneys or Iceland be our next port of call I wonder?

9

MUSINGS AND AMUSINGS

The following is a miscellaneous collection of whimsical and reflective pieces which I have written from time to time, as the spirit has moved me.

FACES

The fact that there are millions of people on earth, all with different faces, is a continuing wonder and fascination for me. There are people who look similar and there are look-alike twins, but I fancy they make up a very small percentage. A face is expressive and as variable as the weather; it seems to mirror the soul. How can all the faces on Earth be so different?

★   ★   ★

There are faces alike but still different
There are millions of faces on Earth
So how does the Great Creator
Make us all individual at birth?

Contrast cold clay of the death mask
Which sets as your loved ones depart
With the affectionate smile of the living
Sustained by a loving heart.

Yet most of our living faces
Are as changeable as the sky
One moment bathed in sunshine;
The next: well, a cloud sails by!

On to this screen, this human canvas
Is projected from within
Maybe a soul open and honest
Or the stains of a hidden sin.

Contrast the fair face of pubescence
Innocent when in her prime
The blush, the rich embarrassment
When she attracts her mate first time.

No word or sound may be uttered
Yet the meaning between them is clear
The facial expression is more telling
And the warmth of exchange more sincere.

And so a new face is created
When the courting and nuptials are done
A new canvas conceived to be painted
Oh! The "creation" of faces is fun!

LH 5.04.1999
My 59th Birthday!

"REAL LIVE NATIVES"

I recall an occasion at Ambleside over twenty years ago. I was with my good friend, Bill Bewley, chatting and having a quiet drink in the bar of the Waterhead Hotel at the head of Lake Windermere. Unknown to us an American lady, rather overdressed and bejewelled but full of enthusiasm, had been listening to our conversation.

We were talking about Bill's business and work. In those days he used to pull my leg and say that he was "just a poor boatman" but behind all the leg pull he has always been a loyal and inspiring friend to me and my family and a sound businessman of Lakeland.

The American lady interrupted our conversation as through the window we watched the large lake steamer called the "Swan" docking at Waterhead Pier.

"Gee fellas, does the Queen Mary dock at this pier?"

We looked up in amazement. Windermere is a lake, the biggest in England, 11 miles long, but the American lady had clearly not considered the implications.

"Say, do you come from these parts?" We nodded in agreement and explained that our ancestors had lived in Westmorland for centuries.

Before we could say another word she shouted and waved her arms at her husband on the other side of the room.

"Hey, Wilbur-Fred, baby! Come here Wilbur! Here's some real live natives!"

Figure 9.1. The Teal, sister ship to the Swan, on Windermere

REAL LIVE NATIVES

Ya neet a lile bit sen
It was summer sort o wedder
A local pal and I went oot
Ta hev a sup tagither.

We talked en joked, we laughed en smoked
As time went murrily by
When a yankee woman powdered and permed
Cem exen us reasons why:

Did the Queen Mary dock at Waterhead?
Where was this Roman camp?
She wanted some of this Lakeland rock;
Was England always wet and damp?

Did we really live in Lakeland?
Were we really born and bred?
"Say honey baby, come and see
Here are some real live natives! Wilbur-Fred!'

Well Bill and I felt special then
And ever since that day
I've felt a real live empathy
With the red Indians down Wyoming way

I say to myself is this a reserve?
Are we country folk on display?
Or can we keep a balance,
Give pleasure, yet let them pay?

When a theatre's full they close the door
And no one parks in the aisle
If I barge into a performance
I'm not greeted with a smile.

Should the tourist pay an entrance fee★
Or visit our Lakeland free?
When I go to a town or a theatre
I buy a ticket; they charge me!

★An interesting thought prompted by the fact that when we entered Switzerland by road in 1979 we had to buy a *carnet* to put on the windscreen. It was a kind of toll for using the roads and tunnels which the Swiss had built and which were being used to shorten journeys by travellers from neighbouring countries through the Alps rather than go around them. It was clear that neighbouring users should contribute to the maintenance costs.

I have often thought our Government and planners could learn a great deal from the Swiss. They provide excellent facilities for tourists without spoiling the visual amenity. Visitors also get special travel passes and facilities to enhance their enjoyment in return.

We could use the tolls accumulated to improve our facilities for tourists – underground car parks – keep toilets open – a cable car – to support local trusts like the Armitt Library and grant-making trusts for apprenticeships !

BANK LOAN FOR SMITHFIELD
The London Cattle and Meat Market

Glossary

Borra = to borrow
Cem oot = came out
Er = are
Garn = going
Gay = rather, somewhat
Gitten = getting
Hev = have
I'se = I'm or I am
Lang sen = long ago

Lant back= came back or landed back
Lile = little
Smithfield = Smithfield Cattle Show and Market in London.
Sneck-lifter fee = entry fee or loan fee
Takken = taking
Telt = told
Thoo = thou
Turble grand folk = very pleasant folk

★   ★   ★

Lang sen when bank managers were turble grand folk
Geordie Smilethwaite went in fer a quiet lile loan talk.
Geordie was takken t'wife ta Smithfield Show
But wanted ta borra "two hundred pund" to go.

"I've three hundred lambs that er gitten gay smart
So thoo'll hev o' thi brass back when I tak em ta t'mart."
T'bank manager telt him his sneck-lifter fee
So Geordie cem oot "o'er t'moon" in his glee.

Next day Geordie lant back, wanted five hundred pund more.
Bank manager agreed but puzzled asked "What was it for?"
Well Geordie looked sheepish like a mischievous lile barn
"Thoo sees I'se still off ta Smithfield *but t'Wife isn't garn!*"

★   ★   ★

FREE, FREE, FREE

SOME REFLECTIONS ON OUR FREEDOM

But Hope Springs Eternal

What happened to Truth, Trust and Integrity?

Freedom without Responsibility
Yet we have more regulations and state control than ever

We are free, free, free!
Free to gamble, free to sin
Free to kick our rivals in.

We are free, free, free!
The teacher can't restrain us now
Disillusioned are the police somehow.

We are free, free, free!
Free to claim and free to blame
Now our basic instinct to complain

We are free, free, free!
Free to quote the patients' charter
Free to make oneself the martyr.

We are free, free, free!
We've thrown restraint and chains away
To invent the wheel another way.

Yet though we're free, free, free,
Now we are monitored on camera
By C.C.T.V.

Yet still we are free, free, free
To lose our skills far across the sea
And reap the whirlwind of idolatry.

MPs must be free, free, free
To do important work for you and me
They are the basis of our democracy.

Today the media seem free, free, free
To massage the truth on the slant they see
For the best return in print, the internet and on TV.

And is trial by media really free, free, free?
When we lose good MPs and our sense of fair play?
What price justice? The mob rules this way.

The pseudo bankers were free, free, free
Of ethical banking skills and nous
Even free to lend on a paper house!

The Revenue may be free, free, free
To tax banking and bonus excess
But the true ethics of traditional banking
Are much more likely to cure the mess.

The media must also be free, free, free
To be ethical and factual as it used to be
To tell us the TRUTH without slant or sensation
While upholding the interests of our worthy nation.

Meanwhile we citizens will have to pay, pay, pay
And rue the day
When TRUST, TRUTH and INTEGRITY
Were traded and squandered away
For candyfloss profit
To finance moral decay.

Yet there is still hope because we are free, free, free
To balance the role of money and its worth
As a means of exchange not a right of birth
Not an icon or master, a god or a goal
Because we are still free, free, free
To restore Trust, Truth and Integrity
To our nation's soul.

It is a paradox that while we have achieved freedom in so many ways, our freedoms have been and are being curtailed by knee-jerk answers to media pressure and by fiscal restraint. We are not short of new ideas but we keep missing opportunities to develop them. We seem to prefer short-term economics, so we buy cheap goods from the Far East, thus losing our skills and creating financial balance of payment problems and currency devaluation in the longer term.

In the last 60 years we have seen improvements to health, longevity, wealth and our standard of living. We have so much to be proud of but we must not dismantle the foundations on which our freedom is based. We have lived in a golden age – but what are the prospects for those who follow?

We have had umpteen Crime and Punishment Acts but none have done anything to eliminate the causes of crime and reduce the number of prisons (the colleges of crime). We have spent the money instead on politicising the judicial system through the back door, thereby undermining the independence of the judiciary – one of the pillars and safeguards of our true freedom.

Our money would be better spent matching offenders to craftsmen, skilled people and gifted youth leaders. We should reduce the prison population by paying suitably skilled people to mentor and teach offenders the skills which will give them a trade or calling and a true sense of worth and self-respect. Most offenders need to build relationships and we should recognise that most have abilities which can be built upon to make them worthy citizens.

Johann Wolfgang von Goethe, the German poet, dramatist and scholar, (1749-1832), wrote: "*Treat people as you would like them to be and they will become what they are capable of being.*" I remember the prison governor of Bela Prison near Milnthorpe in Cumbria coming to Round Table as a guest speaker. His main theme was "*Your behaviour reflects the behaviour of those with whom you wish to stand well.*" He gave examples of criminal behaviour where this applied and illustrated the way that young offenders could put crime behind them, when they were inspired by a person whom they could respect and work with.

Truth, responsibility and fair play, as well as the rules of natural justice, are often lost sight of in the media and in some government legislation. In the name of economics, by giving the police more and more discretion to impose penalties, the police are becoming more alienated from the community and we draw nearer to a police state. I suggest the more use of guns by the police, the more gun crime there will be.

Experienced MPs are essential to the nation's wellbeing. Our children's future depends on wise and experienced MPs controlling the excessive exercise of power by the executive government. The newspapers were right to expose the expenses' problem but it became a witch hunt. Knee-jerk legislation made in response to popular outcry normally proves to be poor law and brings the law into disrepute.

MPs have to serve in two places: their constituency and London. That costs money and, like judges, they need to have no reason to worry about money. Some bad apples have tainted the rest. When we pay footballers, pop stars and television pundits much more than people whose work is essential to preserving our nation and its values, something is out of balance. The salaries of MPs should be higher and their expenses properly accounted for.

I wonder how we can expect anyone of character and ability to leave a successful career and go into Parliament to benefit the nation with his or her experience. Successful, experienced candidates are needed, not just publicity experts, researchers and those with degrees in politics. We need the right mix.

Most supervisory legislation increases bureaucracy and creates a straightjacket. It drains the energy of the nation and takes the focus off dealing with the issues that really matter. Commercialisation and the outside regulation of the professional ethic has done much to destroy the value of self-regulation, because it tends to put profit first, whereas a true professional must put the client's problem first and focus on it.

We did not need umpteen volumes on employment law to train and promote good relations among our staff. I found in my working life that by rewarding and promoting respect for ability and good sense, there was a happy relationship between staff and a willingness to pass on their skills to younger members. This usually produced excellent results from colleagues and employees alike, and a constant demand for our services. When reasonable standards are set by example, the wonderfully tolerant and sensible citizens of our land use their common sense.

When over-restriction becomes repressive, it prevents progress and creates more hurdles to jump. It squashes the enthusiasm for new projects on which the nation's future depends. Parliament legislates to control the fools in society and at the same time restricts the freedom of everyone. It is time to re-assess knee-jerk legislation and restore the integrity of the press and the media.

If we ourselves could manufacture more of the plant required for green energy before fossil fuel runs out, it would be a start. It would also make us less dependent on oil from the Middle East, banking profits and the erratic, tidal flows of money around the world.

By failing to settle the terms of a sensible, federal constitution for Europe when it was under debate, we have missed the opportunity to prevent creeping, undemocratic regulation from the Brussels Commissioners. We are controlled by the fiscal allocation of funds to those employed to implement policies of sameness! But that is a large subject and not one I am qualified to address. Just a thought!

LH 28.12.09

A BILLIONAIRE'S BANK LOAN

(Rhyme based on a Mike Winkley story)

To a large Liverpool bank, a skyscraper in glass
Came a loan-seeking Ferrari owner, clearly upper class!
"Can you loan me five thousand, personal Bank Manager man
Take the Ferrari as security, if you can?

"I'll be back in three weeks the loan to repay
So calculate the interest up to three weeks today!"
The bank secured the Ferrari in its compound below
Did a credit check on the owner, but were puzzled to know:

★   ★   ★

An entrepreneur? A famous billionaire?
Why a five thousand pound loan
When he has millions to spare?

★   ★   ★

When the owner returned from his foreign safari
Repaid his loan, his interest and collected his Ferrari
The Bank Manager bemused by his professional pomposity
Was determined to satisfy his puzzled curiosity.

"Why borrow £5,000: you've loads of money to spare?"
"Well, I placed my lovely Ferrari in your tender care
You may think I'm a bounder, a spiv or a fool
But for thirty one quid
It's the securest parking in Liverpool!"

MSW/LH 2009

"BLOFAT" THE QUARRYMAN POACHER
And the Boggle at Sissy House

My parents used to tell stories about "Blofat". He was a colourful independent character who lived in a slate dresser's shack on the quarry-tip at the head of the valley, just south of Kentmere Reservoir. There were many stories of his escapades. My Granny said he was also a very generous and caring man with a sense of fun.

Quality green slate was produced at Steel Rigg and Jumb quarries at the head of the valley. See the view of Kentmere quarries on page 4. In the old days the quarry men stayed in the old quarry barracks during the week, but at weekends they walked about 5 miles to the pubs in Staveley (Low Bridge Inn in Kentmere having been closed in 1875).

"Sissy House", the local name for Low Millriggs, was a ruin of broken walls, and it was believed to be haunted. Certainly my hair stood on end, when as a boy I rode past on my bicycle. It was situated just north of Ulthwaite Barn and the site of Old Ulthwaite Mill – both since demolished. On their way down the valley to Staveley some of the quarrymen set fishing lines in the river and they would collect any fish caught on their lines on their way back.

Glossary:

Aboon = above
Boggle = ghost
Eshes = ash trees
Harnted = haunted
Hezzel = hazel bush
Har'd = heard
Lang = long
Lan't back = came back

Lonnin = lane or road
Sissy Hoose = Low Millriggs See map
Stayvla-Gayt = old name for Staveley*
(* See Blezzard's Westmorland Songs, published 1868)
Ullet = owl
War't = where the
"White side oot" = White lining out

Yan neet lang sen up Kentma
When t'quarries were rive-en slate
Blasters, rivers en dressers
Trudged down to Stayvla-Gayt.*

They cracked en joked, they sang and talked
As five miles of lonnin went by
For t'Eagle's beer was varra good
En they were rayder dry.

At Sissy Hoose, a harnted spot
War t'ullet nests in t'woes
T'quarrymen went quiet like
As t'hair on their backs it rose.

They scuttled by en took ta t'fields
War t'River Kent flows clear
To set their lines, collect some trout
As they lan't back for t'beer.

Noo Blofat was a lonesome man
Who followed in thur wake
A bearded, capable, crafty man
A poacher on the make.

The moon behint a bank of cloud
The night was dark en still
As Blofat dodged alang t'banks
Aboon auld Ulthwaite Mill.

War t'hezzel bush en eshes grow
He hard a foot trod crack
'Twas t'bailiff makken fast up t'beck
Like hell he med back track.

Then silent as a hunting cat
Patient he lay still
Beside t'harnted Sissy Hoose
Prostrate on rocky hill.

Under t'shadow of t'ruin
Cast by t'risen moon
He turned his jacket "white side oot"
His chance would com quite soon.

Blofat wailed en bayed ta t'moon aboon
An ullet hooted "Ta whit ta woo"
T'bailiff fled from t'fearsome Boggle
Then Blofat poached thur fish-lines through!

LH circa 1984

★   ★   ★

A RETIRED SCOTTISH DOCTOR CALLS

Noo Doctor MacPhysic was retired you ken
And this was a story that was told to our Len.
The doctor returned to his own bailiwick
Where he had practised and cured most of the sick.

An avuncular man most caring and kind
A lovely old doctor, the best you could find
He called on two old ladies cultured and prim
Who were excited and delighted to welcome him in.

"Will you have a wee dram or a nice cup of tea?
Perhaps your favourite cakes like they used to be?"
So off to the kitchen the two ladies went
While he looked round and enjoyed the sweet flowers' scent.

The sun shone brightly across their boudoir grand
A beautiful Steinway with music on the stand.
But there in the sun's rays a small packet did glow
Curiosity got the better: he had to know!

A condom in a packet he was amazed to see!
What need had the ladies? How could this be?
So when the ladies returned with the tea on a tray
He enquired about the packet to see what they'd say.

"You see Doctor MacPhysic, we found it out on our walk
We read all that it said and we had a good talk;
'Place on the organ was the clear direction
To get full protection from any infection.'"

Well Doctor, you see, we have no organ to play
So on our grand piano we placed it that day -

And do you know, Doctor, we haven't had a cold all winter!!!

★   ★   ★

FOX versus LAMB

(The Foxhunting Debate)

An early spring morning is breaking
Across the white waste of the sky
As sunbeams caress the fell tops
Lifting gossamer from pastures in-bye.

Twin lambs newborn are waking
And wobbling to their feet
Instinct urges colostrum
So they seek their mother's teat.

The ewe first licks their nostrils
So both her lambs can breathe
Consumes the membrane round them
Their new bodies to unsheathe.

A dog fox has been observing
From higher up the hill
Waiting deliberately waiting
To make advance and kill.

He has no need for breakfast
For his abdomen is full
Bloodletting is in his nature
And now he feels the pull.

There's no one here to help the ewe
She has neither fang nor claw
Her lambs are at their weakest
And the ewe can't bolt a door.

So she stands like brave Horatio
Stood on the bridge at Rome
Horns held high, she stamps her feet
To defend her heaf and home.

The fox moves round to mesmerise
Innocent noses nuzzle beneath
The ewe cluthers her progeny by her side
To protect them from its teeth.

By baiting the sheep till she charges the fox
The lambs are cast asunder
The fox now takes off with one of them
As she makes this timeless blunder.

The lamb's head now lies severed
With the body left to rot
Sometimes the head is buried
Is this a future fox delicacy? I know not.

★   ★   ★

I feel for the fox when hunted
Or when it is shot or maimed
I want to see beautiful foxes
But this killer will never be tamed.

The fox has no natural predator
Except in the form of Man
Thus the balance has been kept in a natural way
By hunting since time began.

Lamping with guns and poison
Snares, gassing, traps and pills
Are all abominable concepts
Far worse than the hunt and the spills.

The wisest and fittest fox from the hunt
Will normally escape away
To raise healthy cubs and maintain its line
Forever and a day

So leave us alone to our well-tried ways
Our country foxes are healthy and strong
If the fox was to vote, I conclude it would note
That the fanatics have all got it wrong.

LH 14.03.2006.

PARTY GIRL

New Year's Eve party, Bowness-on-Windermere
1960's style!

Jiving, rocking to the music
Dancers swayed and swung around
Crazed with passion for the motion
Hooked upon the beat and sound.

When all at once a striking beauty
Nubile nymph on young man's arm
Turning heads of all the dancers
Entered with magnetic charm.

Clinging shimmering silver lurex
Side-split skirt with glimpse of thigh
Overdressed but only slightly
Made poor father heave a sigh!

Skipping, jaunting, proud of sweetheart
Son smiles under father's gaze
Introduces him to girlfriend
"Pleased I'm sure," she shyly says.

Father seems somewhat uneasy
As his wife is standing by
Guests stop dancing, eyes upon him
All at once they wonder: why?

Eager son for signs of favour
Looks to one and then the other
Father dignified and stately says:
"My girl, I knew your mother!"

★　　★　　★

SMILEY BUNGLE AND THE SLURRY TANK

Smiley en Bessie Bungle farmed in t'Lake District. Smiley en Bessie hed saved up en installed a new slurry tank. It was one o them steel circle-types.

It was towards full en Smiley hed been up ta t'top of ladder ta tighten a bolt. While he was worken, he took his jacket off en hung it over t'top rim but it fell inta t'slurry.

Aboot 10 minutes later Bessie cem oot looking fer Smiley and he was naewhar ta be seen. Bessie hard some splutteren en swearen comen fre t'tank. So she climmed up t'ladder en looked o'er t'top o rim. Smiley was swimming aboot in t'slurry.

"Whativver is ta dewen?" shooted Bessie.

Smiley cried, "I've lost mi jacket. It fell in and I mun find it."

"What!" shooted Bessie, "It will be nay good now."

But Smiley insisted, **"Nay, I mun find it! I will hev ta find it – mi sandwiches er in t'pocket!!!"**

I'SE IN TURBLE LAA WATTER
(En t'wife's gitten fasht wi me)

When thou leaks oot of t'winda
En it does nowt but rain
Thi legs er o' hurpled wid arthritic pain
When thi hee-ad's full o bad news
En t'wife starts ta natter
I git doon in t'dumps
"I'se in turble laa watter".

If thou listens ta t'wireless
Happen thou'll hev a TV
There's Clinton lousen it oot
Wid a lass on his knee
Them Japanese banks thur o' garn bust
While fanatical Jihadists
Finance terrorist lust.

Wife:
Hush man! Them coves o' want feeden
Fash! What does it matter?
Thou'll nut git owt done
When thou's in turble laa watter.

Mi fields er o' flooded
It does nowt but rain
Mi back's turble cravacked
I can't harvest mi grain.
Russia's devalued en t'rouble's worth nowt
If they sell them nuclear weapons
We'll hev ta leak out!

Wife:
Aye man, o' thi worrits
Whativver does it matter?
Git thisel oot
O thi turble laa watter!

Them coves o' want feeden
Thur's lambs thou can spane
Thou'll just hev ta face it
O' t'mud en o' t'rain
It's nay good thee gurnen aboot t'B.S.E. ban
Cos it's allus bin sayem
Sen life began.

Thur's allus bin danger
And what does it matter?
Thou'll just hev ta clim oot
O thi turble laa watter!

© *LH 25.08.1998*

Glossary:

Allus = always
Coves = calves
Clim = climb
Cravacked = stiff-backed or stiff-jointed
Doon =down
En = and
Fash! = Bother!
Fasht = weary or fed up
Garn = going
Git = get
Gurnen = pulling a face, grumbling, being miserable
Hee-ad = head
Hetta = have to
Hev = have
Hurpled = lame, stiff, limping
Laa = low
Leak = look
Lousen = to loosen, untie
Mi = my

Nowt = nothing
Nut = not
O = of
O' = all
Oot = out
Owt = anything
Saem = same
Spane = to wean lambs from their mothers
Thi = thy
Thisel = thyself
Thur = there and they're
Turble = very
Turble laa watter = depressed or downhearted
Watter = water
Wi or wid = with
Winda = window
Worrits = worries

MY ISLAY MINCE

On one of our long weekend trips to Islay with Bill, Tony and Peter, it was my turn to cook the evening meal. My speciality was a sort of cottage pie. Thus the four of us called in at Mrs Gibson's, the butcher's and general store in Bowmore, the main town on Islay, for provisions. Mrs Gibson had a lovely, warm Hebridean accent.

While being barracked and teased by the Chums, much to Mrs Gibson's amusement, I asked for *one* piece of cheese, *five* carrots, *one* turnip, *six* potatoes, *two* onions, *six* shallots, *eight* rashers of bacon for breakfast, *one* packet of beef stock and *one* of chicken.

I then asked for some mince for the cottage pie. Mrs Gibson looked rather quizzically at me and smiled warmly. In a lovely melodic voice she said:

"And hoo many strands of mince will you be wanting?"

Figure 9.2 Chums and wives at 10 Shore Street, Portnahaven

HOMO SAPIENS?

Driving nature backwards
To the sterile wastes of hell
Men burn the earth still blindly
And destroy the living cell.

Do we think when we press onwards
How with ever mounting speed
We burn our life and energy
By materialistic greed?

More oil, more oil, we all proclaim
We must have more nuclear power
We build pipelines beneath the sea
And turn marine life sour.

In the name of economics
In pursuit of GNP
We lose the life we live for
If we don't stop and see

That nature needs a balance
And we our part must play
Lest animals, birds and flowers
We lose upon our way.

No grass to feed the cattle
No meat to eat or stew
No birds to eat the insects
And humans but a few.

LH 14.03.1974

RENEWABLE ENERGY

Reflections & regrets – some thoughts!

"Homo Sapiens" was written 37 years ago. I have always been interested in the generation of energy from water: hydropower and tidal power from the sea, as well as other natural sources of energy.

Apart from helping clients to pursue their projects in this area of work, I regret not having taken a more active role in promoting renewable energy long ago. Unlike Norway, the UK has not used sufficient of its revenues from North Sea gas and oil to build our own renewable energy resources.

Our past governments, it seems, have preferred to tie us to long-term agreements to bring oil and gas from the Middle East and elsewhere. We have spent a fortune on the infrastructure for doing so: funds which might have been better spent developing renewable energy capability and manufacturing here.

Fortunately, as oil prices rise and the countries producing oil have become unstable, we are at last becoming more focussed. We now have research and development going on at our universities and we have engineering skills in Kendal and at British Aerospace. Sadly most manufacturing of renewable energy systems at this time comes from Europe and abroad. Surely our skilled engineers, now being made redundant as war plane orders in this recession decrease, could turn their skills to making our own renewable energy equipment and plant?

Nevertheless there are exciting new developments for producing the energy we need and hopefully we will take a leading role. Wind turbines produce mixed responses from the public and clearly we don't want them all over the place. There are more interesting and reliable sources. Developments in solar power and ground source heating are producing good results.

Anaerobic digestion and biomass have a contribution to make, not only in energy production, but in reducing land-fill and turning waste into energy. Hydropower has been a source of energy for centuries but is underdeveloped. There is great scope for this in the Lake District, Scotland and Wales.

There is an experimental tidal-energy power plant on the island of Islay, not far from Portnahaven, which is unobtrusive. We have hundreds of islands and places around our shores where small tidal power producing units could be situated to feed the National Grid, but progress has been slow.

David Brockbank of Staveley has for some years been promoting his turbine and bridge proposal across Morecambe Bay to the Furness district. With turbines below the bridge activated by the tidal flow, it would not affect water levels in Morecambe Bay area or disturb the wildlife around the bay. A bridge across the bay would shorten the journey to and from Barrow-in-Furness and save fossil fuel.

If only we could develop our skills and our own manufacturing base to produce the turbines, we could develop opportunities to revitalise our home industries and provide apprenticeships and real work for our young people. For too long, investors have financed cheap manufacturing abroad for paper money. We have preferred to buy cheap goods from abroad rather than support our home industry and keep a balance. We are not short of ideas and great inventions, but our mind-set as a nation needs to change.

The farming industry is also experimenting in ways of covering energy costs and producing surplus energy for the National Grid, but will entrepreneurs and energy companies be allowed to get on with it? What will our planners say?

Food Security: There is an urgent need to develop an economical alternative to diesel oil in order to power farm tractors and food distribution wagons. We are now far too dependent on diesel oil to produce our food. Food security does not have sufficient attention. Oil is the fossil fuel which underpins the production of our food in the UK and also the importing of food by air and sea. We no longer have lots of small, self-sufficient farms with a large labour force to fall back on in a crisis, as was the case in the last war. Our navy is depleted and could not protect what is left of our merchant fleet. As most merchant shipping is now under foreign control in our global economy, our food supply from abroad is less secure.

It is also important that the districts of the U.K. support the production of food that is capable of being grown locally. By that means we can maintain the security of food supply locally. It may be economical now to produce monocrops of food elsewhere, but it leaves us exposed when food has to be transported, particularly if the oil supply is cut off or the price of oil rockets.

We must put more emphasis on the development of our manufacturing base in Lakeland. By doing so we shall be more secure and less exposed to the tidal flows of money when panic paralyses the markets and produces more and more pessimists. Such *Job's Comforters* undermine our confidence and promote what they predict. So let us banish the pessimists and get on with doing things. We need sustainable development and manufacturing appropriate to each community.

If we want good pensions on retirement we need to generate a greater proportion of the wealth required to do so from British industry and innovation. Our pension system in Britain was amongst the best in Europe until the main incentive to save in that way was removed. That in turn has affected the ability of retired consumers to invest and spend for the benefit of all. It is surely time to invest in a sound future for our children and grandchildren.

We have lived in "Cloud Cuckoo Land" too long. Our "candy floss" economy has melted. We can no longer afford to police the world except through the United Nations, properly financed by all the countries of the world, in proportion to their gross national output.

TOASTS AND HOSTS

Until "I called it a day", over the years I have been asked to propose toasts and address a variety of organisations at Christmas dinners and special functions. From time to time I was asked to write speeches for friends at weddings. I remember a delighted farmer, by way of thanks, coming to the door and handing Joy an enormous salmon fresh from his river. It made her jump when she opened the bag and its big fishy eyes stared at her!

BURNS NIGHT SUPPER SONG at the 41 Club
Originally composed for Kendal Caledonian Society Luncheon

A TOAST
Recalling Andy Stewart and Duncan Macrae at Hogmonay singing "Campbelltown Loch I wish you were whisky"

"Len-art ma lad"
(Me talking to myself and wishing I'd been born a Scot)

Chorus:
Och Len-art ma lad, I wish ye were Scottish
Len-art ma lad, och aye!
Och Len-art ma lad, I wish ye were Scottish
And I'll tell ye the why.

For I'd be born in a glen and they'd call me MacLen
Ma legs would be hairy and frisky
I'd enjoy a wee dram to set me off hame
And my blood would be warm with the whisky!

Chorus:

Och if I was a Scot, it's as sure as it's not
That I'd be a man of brains
I could be a hob-nob with the very top job
Where the "Iron Chancellor" reigns.

Chorus:

I could run at some pace, and grimace ma face
As I heave and toss the great caber
So with ma muscles in order I'd rove over the border
And harass my English neighbour.

Chorus:

Och Len-art MacLen you could go now and then
To grave out your peats in lots
Or peacefully float in a bonny wee boat
And empty your lobster pots.

Chorus:

I could go as of reet to a jolly Burns Neet
To the Haggis I'd write a wee ode
And return to ma sleeps full of whisky and neeps
Doon Tam'o Shanter's road.

Chorus:

I could pipe secret peat-water to a still that I oughter
Not use without Customs' consent
But in a wee but–en-ben this naughty MacLen
Could make nectar one hundred per cent!

Chorus:

I could tell a wee joke in this mack-o-talk
And sing with a highland lilt!
I could find a wee lassie: aye and make a wee passie
And show her what's under ma kilt!

Chorus:

Like the late Duncan Macrae I'd enjoy Hogmanay
If I could recite "The Wee Cock Sparra"
If I happened to roam far away from ma home
I would take ma strang bow and ma arra!

Chorus:

On this Bonny Burns Neet, och we'll no hev a fight
But we'll sing of Auld Lang Syne
We'll all join our hands with folks from far lands
And pray for World Peace in our time.

★   ★   ★

But I leave you with the thought
Ma ancestors sailed here in a Viking lang-boat
With the Norse-blood rich in thur veins
To dwell in Strathclyde which stretched doon here from the Clyde
After lang fights o'er the border, there is now law and order
And it's the Haggis and the Whisky that reigns!

Now let's toast you good Caledonians
May all of you be Aeonians:
That means everlasting, forever;
And no matter what: each be a good Scot
And don't lose your character – Never!

I give you the Toast

TO OUR SCOTS FRIENDS

THE BSE HOLOCAUST

I'm a cow
An innocent cow
Among thousands of cows like me.

I'm a docile cow
A friendly old cow
There are thousands of cows like me.

I'm a productive cow
A valuable cow
Milk flows from thousands of cows like me.

My ancestor cows
The war-time cows
Fed the nation from cows like me.

I'm a cow
An innocent cow
Condemned among thousands of cows like me.

★   ★   ★

I'm walking to death and destruction
To be burned and totally lost
There is meaning in life if they eat me
But now they waste all I cost.

Who are these humans to condemn me?
They rule by fear and by mob
Hysteria, a story, a sensation
Justice destroyed and truth they rob.

Where are the animal rights folk?
Do they stand guard at the furnace door?
Or are they silent in the mob
Like the holocaust gone before?

It's all may be, could be, rumour, might be
BSE is their fear and dread:
So innocent I go to slaughter
Sacrificed in a pagan ritual not yet dead.

I'm a cow ... an innocent cow ...

© *LH May 1996*

★   ★   ★

GREEDY MAN
Should have a Rhumen like a Cow!

Whativver did God mak Man fer?
Man wod be better designed as a coo.
I doot if we'd hev o' these earthquakes
Ner "oot o toon shoppen" we hev noo.

If we nobbut munched guss and wild floo-ers
Leav-en coo-claps ta nourish oor fields
We'd hev nay need fer plastic containers
En all t'rubbish that packaging yields.

North Sea gas we sowk oot fer heat-en
En pump billions o gallons o crude
Makken stinks as we burn hydrocarbons
Producen synthetic en tasteless food.

They say oor Earth spins roond en roond
With tsunamis and twisters, thur's summat amiss!
We've howked o'er much fuel fre out o t'grund
Mappen we've knocked Earth off its axis!

If it's wark we mun spar oor muscles!
Modern hydraulics may do it instee-ad
With the time that we gain, we can jog oot in t'rain
Then do weight-lifting and strut-chen with lee-ad.

Nay wonder oor earth crust craks open
Nay wonder some hooses foe doon
Nay wonder oor climates garn crazy
En thur's Soddam en Gommorah in toon!

T'lile birds we've lost in gurt numbers
Their grub chain affected by greed
As man wid his global economy
Shops round t'world fer much cheaper feed.

So if Man was a bovine species
He'd nivver hev fed brains to a coo
So the BSE holocaust burning
Woddent be happenen noo.

Oh I wish we'd been designed with a rhumen
Ta munch guss en clover somehoo
We woddent need falderments ner transport
En GOLD en BANK CRASHES.
Well! ... They mean nowt tull a coo!

Postscript:
Since musing upon the aforesaid
My thesis has been stabbed through the heart!
Cows are charged with gross global warming
Allegedly from the METHANE they FART !!!!

Figure 9.3. Robert Needham judging a Poll Charolais cow and calf

THE TASTE OF PICKLED DAMSONS

Evelyn Hayton's Recipe

The taste of pickled damsons
It tingles round my tongue;
We had a pilgrimage to the Lyth Valley
Each Spring when I was young.
My Mother had been raised there
Where the blossoms bloom and blow,
The hedges and orchards team with fruit
To be preserved for the winter's snow.

The taste of pickled damsons
Mother's recipe I'll share:
Prick damsons first to fill your jar,
When you have time to spare;
Then half a pint of vinegar
With a pound of sugar boil,
And you'll be well rewarded by
This age-old country toil.

I love the smell of damson plums
When you pour the liquid on
And leave it standing in the bowl
Till twice twelve hours have gone;
Then pour the liquor off the plums
And bring it to the boil,
Mix and leave for one more day
Lest the delicious taste you spoil.

And oh the aroma of cinnamon!
Add two pinches to the pot;
Just a few cloves put in the mix
And boil again the lot;
Preserve your pickle in sealed jars
And wait six weeks for use;
Serve with your stews and casseroles
This delectable damson juice!

© *LH 17.11.1998*

TOAST TO THE LAKELAND RHODODENDRON, CAMELLIA AND MAGNOLIA SOCIETY

The Society's Christmas Dinner, 2008

⋆   ⋆   ⋆

Robert Smith, Secretary of the Society, gave me details of the members' programme and their horticultural outings including visits to Monet's garden at Giverny in France and to gardens in Cornwall. With due deference to Gilbert and Sullivan's "Nightmare" song in Iolanthe, I wrote these verses for the Society and finished my "Tales of a Lakeland Lad" with the following toast.

A NOVICE GARDENER'S NIGHTMARE

I could not help thinking,
While dozing and blinking
What theme I might use tonight.
Horticulture and me are a mystery, you see
For I never can get it right.

However I toil, the muck and the soil
Don't suit the shrubs or the flowers
Though I read all my books
Nothing brightens their looks
Yet I tend them for hours and hours.

And that Botanist Swede⋆
Who perceived the need
To classify all plants in Latin
Perplexes my brain and causes such strain
That I try yoga seated on satin!

I sleep and I dream
About strawberries and cream
But the strawberry plants are all lost.
If it isn't the slugs or some mammoth-like bugs
It's a beautiful spring but late frost.

So I'm afraid that last night
My sleep was not right
A nightmare distorted my slumber!
I went down a hole, too tight and too small
But squeezed out in a greenhouse of lumber.

There were broken plant pots
And lots of what-nots
Cobwebs and weeds all asunder
The glass was part broken; I sensed guidance unspoken
And emerged in a garden of wonder!

The moon was so bright
Camellias opened at night
And I dreamt you were all there in the trees
You'd arrived on a bus without any fuss
And you walked on Monet's bridge in the breeze.

Now the scene green and pink
We're in Giverny, I think
Midst a colourful Monet Impression
It's a bright sunny morning and you are all yawning
With your best Pierre Magnol expression!

There are roses in posies
And roses on bushes
There are roses on arches and thrushes in bushes
There are poppies and copies; yes! rides of pink poppies
As far as the eye can see.

There are lilies on water
Blooming white as they ought to
The willows are bending, weeping all over me
But oft in our gladness, life is tinged with some sadness
And there's a serpent coiled up in the tree!

It was sneering and hissing,
My rib suddenly went missing!
In Monet's Eden, God created a fair damsel for me
But the serpent rejoined and got Eve in a grapple,
Proffered to her that symbolic apple
Alas, my lady fell tempted, you see.

So ever since then,
All Earth's women and men
Have had to grow food from the soil
But as agriculture advanced, leisure time was enhanced
And less time was needed in toil.

Thus Pierre Magnol found magnolia
Joseph Kamel, I'm told, found camellia
So you Botanists all
Likewise can pursue your pet goal
Growing exotics and varieties of camellia.

Then like swallows in flight
We flew through the night
We left Monet's philodendrons, we sought rhododendrons
I dreamt we were in heaven, somewhere south of Devon
Where camellias and magnolias in splendour grow.

We all woke the next morning,
Not grumpy or yawning
The blooms in the sun were aglow:
Black Lace, Inspiration, Lovelight, Anticipation
Japonica, White Nun and Cornish Snow!

Rhododendrons in rhyme
I'll leave to some other time
Lest my true ignorance I should show
Yet your kind invitation has given me inspiration
In areas of study and beauty I did not know.

Thank you Mine Host, now let us toast:

★   ★   ★

I give you the toast:

"The Lakeland Rhododendron, Camellia
and Magnolia Society

*Carl Linnaeus (1707-1778), Swedish doctor and botanist, often called the
'Father of Taxonomy', invented a system for naming, ranking and classifying
organisms, which is still in wide use today.*

© LH 20.1.09

10

TWO WHEELS AND FOUR WHEELS

I have always had a love and respect for wheels because of all the benefits which have flowed from the invention of the wheel. My father made wheelbarrows and carts for the farm, as well as to sell. I admired seeing him make the precise, angled joints between the wooden spokes and the nave. His uncle, Tom Hayton, had taught Father how to make a wheel. Tom was a wheelwright and coachbuilder at a time when horses were the motive power to move things on wheels.

Though the definition of a wheel on the internet is similar today, I prefer the one from my old "The Century Dictionary" 1900 edition in 16 volumes published by The Times. It has two large pages devoted to the definition of many types of wheel, but the first one on page 6889 (!) reads as follows:

"A circular frame or solid disc turning on an axis. Wheels, as applied to vehicles, usually consist of a nave, into which are inserted spokes or radii, connecting it with the periphery or circular ring.

Wheels are most important agents in machinery, being employed in a variety of forms and combinations for a great variety of purposes, as for transmitting motion, regulating velocity, converting one species of motion into another, reducing friction, equalising the effect of forces applied in an intermittent or irregular manner, etc."

This was written in the age of the horse at a time when the motor car, then called the "horseless carriage", was in its infancy.

My fascination with wheels as a boy got me into trouble – not serious trouble – more like Richmal Crompton's character, "Just William." First I "borrowed" the cast iron wheels from Father's old sheep rack: a moveable, hay-feeding rack for sheep. He was not pleased when I used them to make a bogie or a Geordie as it was also called. We had no plastic toys to ride on in those days. I pointed out that he had given me a saw, wood, nails and bolts to make myself a conveyance, so I needed wheels. He could not hide his amusement and I won that one!

However, the sheep rack wheels were solid cast iron and clumsy. The friction on the ground caused them to move too slowly and they tended to slide sideways on corners. Our lane was quite steep and the bogie was hard to pull back up the hill with its heavy wheels. What I needed were some lightweight pram wheels: this is when I got into trouble.

My first experience of negotiating a deal was at Kentmere Primary School when Bobby Brunskill, who then lived at Kentmere Hall, informed me he had an old pram. I made my first mistake in becoming too eager and spent most of the coins in my money box on buying the pram. I could not wait to bring the pram home, so after school was over, I went to Kentmere Hall, which meant I was late back for my tea – but I had not told my parents I would be late. As I was approaching Brow Top, I began to feel apprehensive. Although my father was a good and sensible man, he was also rather a strict disciplinarian. As I came through the front yard with the pram, he emerged from the gangway between the shippons under our barn, looking quite angry. "Heven't I telt thee to come straight yam fre school?" he said in rising fury. "Thy Mother hes been beside hersel wi worry." As quick as lightening, he took me over his knee and gave me two bats with the calf stick, which stung rather than hurt. He told me in no uncertain terms that he "would bensel (thrash) my arse" with his belt, if I did that again. He did not usually swear, so it was a surprise to me and a lesson which I ensured did not happen again!

Figure 10.1. LH and friend Graham Barratt on my first pram wheel bogie in 1950

He did not confiscate the pram wheels but instead helped me to make a really good bogie and a sledge for winter at the same time. I sensed he regretted his anger, but he was a good man and straight. We had a strong bonding between us as I explained in my "Kentmer College" verse. He taught me how to do practical things.

In 1951 I made another bogie with a steering wheel from an old scrap car. The experiment involved wires connecting the steering wheel to the front axle. I remember the steering was not very positive and I had to use my feet in the end! It appears from the next photo that it had been necessary to revert to sheep rack wheels on the back.

When I was big enough to ride a bicycle, my brothers helped me to make one from their old bikes. In those days we had two cycle repairers in the valley: old George Leyland in the Nook and Jossy Cousins in Green Quarter. Jossy's son, Victor, was my contemporary at Kentmere School and became a lifelong friend.

I tended to buy things from George Leyland because he was nearer and he sold pop from his hut on "Brant Brow" (*brant*: Old Norse for steep). We also bought Robinson's barley water, which got us into trouble with George, because we always took a big sip from the bottle before leaving. We did it on purpose, as lads will, so as to hear him exclaim in a loud voice: *"What yer mon't drink it straight fre t'bottle! You've ta DILUTE it ta TASTE!"*

George's jacket bottom was burnt to a cinder along the edges. In winter or on a cold day he would stand over a high chimneyed paraffin stove, bent over like a question mark, so the heat went up between his jacket and his back. How he never burnt his hut down I don't know! He had oil and paraffin for sale and he did cycle repairs. "Health and Safety" would have closed him down today, but to us he was a good friend and provided a good service in the valley.

Figure 10.2. LH with my pet lamb on experimental bogie!

George had a very old motor car and an even older Indian bike and sidecar – like the one in the film, "The Fastest Indian". When George, riding too fast towards the top of "Sissy House Hill", met the school taxi in which my brothers, Gerard and Jack, were returning from school, he had to dive up the banking. Gerard put it to him later that he had had a "near do". *"Nay,"* said George, *"Thur wes plenty o room up under t'nut trees!"* So wheels even got old George into trouble too, but he was a good hand at building our bicycle wheels and supplying any spares we needed.

In a comparatively short time horses had been replaced by " horseless carriages"which, during the First World War and afterwards, were under continuing development. The wheels, gears and moving parts in the internal combustion engine brought new industries, new opportunities and new skills. My father brought the first tractor into Kentmere, a standard Fordson Reg. Number ETJ 464. See figure 1.14.

I grew up in a time of change during and after the Second World War. It is said: "The old order changeth and giveth way to the new." Oil and its by-products, as motive power allied to the wheel, changed almost everything. Water wheels and turbines went out of fashion, yet perhaps 'the wheel' has now turned full circle, with the emphasis today on green energy. The question is: how will we turn the wheels economically when the oil runs out? I must have been reflecting on these changes years ago when I wrote the following poem: "Father rode a motorbike, Grandad rode a horse."

Figure 10.3. My father, Joseph Hayton, on a Braithwaite Jap motorbike made by Braithwaite Brothers of Staveley

FATHER RODE A MOTOR BIKE

Reflections on Global Warming

★   ★   ★

Father rode a motor bike
Grandad rode a horse
Great-grandad walked a lot
I drive a car of course!

Father used a little oil
Grandad only grease
Great-grandad was fit and strong
I'm overweight and wheeze!

Father bought a motor car
When I was just a boy
Grandad scoffed and said
"Mi lad, it's just a nasty toy."

Grandad died and things were bad
World War Two was on
So Father bought a tractor
To help the war along.

Father started t'Fordson
Did it all by hand

Developed mighty muscles
Working on the land.

Now hydraulics lift the plough
We've air-conditioned cabs
Time to go to barbecues
Eat skewered scorched kebabs!

Father used less fossil fuel
Grandad hardly any
Great-grandad never heard of it
It cost him not a penny.

The world goes on in cycles
As from centuries before
Survival of the fittest
Was always Nature's law.

Generations mark the milestones
Along Man's road endeavour
But have we kept the balance
Or are we just too clever?

For Father rode a motor bike
Grandad rode a horse
Great-grandad he walked a lot
I drive a car, of course!

c. LH. 29.6.1978

Figure 10.4. Martin and Penny with LH's Jaguar in 1987

MY EARLY MOTOR CYCLING DAYS

When I graduated to riding my brother Gerard's 250cc B.S.A. motor cycle, I drove straight into the wall at Brow Top on the first attempt – a good lesson on clutch and brake co-ordination! Fortunately I was not hurt.

My brothers had friends with motor cycles who congregated at Brow Top, because Gerard had incredible skills with engine tuning and mechanics. We also had hilly land and tracks to ride on. Gerard was mainly self-taught, though he took every opportunity to discuss all things mechanical with the best engineers he could find, and he read a great deal about his favourite interest. He enjoyed calling on and learning from Willie Storey in Staveley, who was a master craftsman

Figure 10.5. Kentmere Motor Cycle Club – Jack, Gerard, Derek Elvey and Tom Bland at Brow Top

and engineer. Willie, like the Braithwaite Brothers, was an engineer who kept the mills around Staveley running and serviced.

In later life Gerard became the "Fred Dibnah" of Kentmere. He drove the Kentmere school bus for many years to augment his farming income, and when he retired, his ex-passengers, then all grown up, came from far and near to a party in the Kentmere Institute to celebrate his 70th birthday. They also presented him with a full day's visit to Fred Dibnah's home to see his collection of memorabilia. Like-minded, Fred and Gerard had a wonderful day together.

Gerard taught me to ride a 250cc B.S.A., then his 350cc Sloper-Panther, which ran like clockwork, even on TVO: tractor vaporising oil! Later, with a trials-type Honda and joined by friends, I rode the tracks and passes in Kentmere, when we still had the freedom to do so. I have even

Figure 10.6. LH on the pillion with Jack on his New Imperial – long before crash helmets became compulsory

done the Kentmere Horseshoe on a 250cc Honda trials bike, which of course, would be frowned upon today.

For those who are interested in motorcycles, I had a series of Velos – starting with a GTP two stroke Velocette. In my last year at Windermere Grammar School I used to go to school on it and leave it at Geoff Braithwaite's house in Windermere. By that time I could do my own

maintenance, but try as I might, the flange on the GTP two stroke tended to unscrew with the vibration on the journey so that the exhaust pipe would come loose. Ignited gas flamed from the cylinder in a colourful array! I eventually cured it, but today we have no such problems with modern bikes.

Figure 10.7. LH in leather cap and army great-coat with my school friend, Iain Johnston, on my 2 stroke GTP Velocette

After I started work in Kendal in 1957, I used to go to work with my brother Jack. But when I was based at the Milnthorpe office, I travelled on my KTS Velocette. When I started my intermediate exam course at Blackpool Law College, I went on the Velocette. It was reliable and always easy to start.

By then I had graduated from the GTP model to a 250cc overhead valve MOV, then a 350cc MAC, but my favourites were my models KTS and KSS camshaft Velocettes. Of all the Velocettes I found these were the best starters and the most reliable. Later in life I owned a Velocette Viper and then a Venom. Both handled well on bends and were a joy to ride, but there was a definite procedure one had to follow to start the engine! No press button starters then!

Figure 10.8. My Velocette Viper

★   ★   ★

MY PENNY FARTHING
or High Bicycle or Ordinary

Historical notes

The Penny Farthing was first invented in 1871. It was a development from the earlier Velocipede or boneshaker. As early as 1819/20 a London coachbuilder had invented a "Pedestrian Accelerator" which was a "hobby horse" with two wheels and a seat between, astride of which the rider ran, and no doubt rode between bouts of running or down-hill travel.

The Penny Farthing was originally called the "High Bicycle" or the "Ordinary" because it was the ordinary bicycle of its day before the safety bicycle was invented in 1885. Penny Farthings were very popular in the 1870s and 1880s, and in that period over 250,000 were made. Bicycle clubs sprang up and races were held, attended by large numbers of people. H.L. Cortis was the first man to cover twenty miles in one hour on a High Bicycle. It is reported that travelling one hundred miles in a day on a Penny Farthing became common place, even on the road surfaces of that time. The biggest problem then, as today, when riding a Penny Farthing is "the header or imperial crowner" when you go over the handle bars if your passage is obstructed! Fortunately I have not yet done so.

I first saw a Penny Farthing in Kentmere. It belonged to my friend Martyn's mother, Jane Wrathall. The Wrathalls had an antique shop in Kendal. Their home was Capplerigg, which had been the Kentmere vicarage, built when my great great grandfather was the Parson. We learned to ride the Penny Farthing in Kentmere. On pages 46 to 47 I described my ride on the Wrathall's Penny Farthing to school in Windermere for the Speech Day in 1955.

The radius of a Penny Farthing wheel should normally equate to the length of the cyclist's inside leg measurement. The wheel on the Wrathall's cycle was much smaller than my present cycle and thus enabled me as a teenager to ride it comfortably. On this occasion I was dressed as a Mad Hatter and our form master asked me to do a demonstration ride around the cricket field, which was then in the centre of the school grounds. Figure 10.9 shows me on my return from Windermere with Gerard and Father inspecting the machine. Figure 10.10 shows the radius of the wheel in relation to the length of my leg.

Figure 10.9. LH as the Mad Hatter, 1955

Figure 10.10. LH on Penny Farthing at Pumple Syke

I have described in the Round Table years my five mile charity ride from Bowness Pier to Waterhead Pier in 1973.

When a heat of a national cycle race was held in Bowness, Reg Gifford, David Matthews and I were asked to entertain the crowd with a demonstration Penny Farthing race during an interval. This faced me with a dilemma because I had always mounted and dismounted my Penny Farthing from a wall. The race was to be from a standing start on level ground on the Glebe car park at Bowness, which meant that I had to use the small mounting step on the machine – difficult if one's toe obstructs the movement of the wheel!

When I bought my own Penny Farthing from my friend, Tom Potter, at Kirkby Stephen, the main wheel of the bicycle was slightly larger in radius than my inside leg. As a consequence it was difficult to mount because my trousers were prone to catch the seat! To get some practice in mounting the bicycle, I took it on to the lawn at Reg's hotel, Michael's Nook in Grasmere. The lawn was bowl shaped, circling round the tennis court with a six feet drop at one end to the tennis court below.

As I mounted the bike, my trousers got stuck with my private parts under the edge of the seat, and the bike careered down the lawn towards the drop to the tennis court below. I flung myself off just in time and landed on the grass with a bump. I had been suffering from back pain for some months, but when I hit the ground, it jolted my spine and

I have never had any such pain since! The fall was a blessing in that sense but it was a different story, however, for the tenderest part of my anatomy! The swelling lasted for over a week!

Nevertheless, I kept practising and as the picture below shows I succeeded in finding a technique to mount on the race day. David did a header over the top at the starting line but he was protected by his large colonial hat. He picked himself up and finished the race.

Figure 10.11. Reg and LH at the starting line on the Bowness Glebe

Reg, with his long legs and larger wheel, had the advantage at the start of our first heat round the circuit, but I caught him up. I passed him when he hesitated at the top of the hill from the cemetery down to the coach park and past Alec Santamera's café on the way back to the Glebe. So I won the first race but Reg did not make the same mistake the second time. He won the second race by a clear margin. Our races were always highly competitive!

Figure 10.12. David Matthews, Reg Gifford and LH, with Geoff Jones serving champagne at the Windermere Festival

★   ★   ★

A Century Old Flyer recalls the delightful experience of riding my "High Bicycle". Sometimes I would take an early morning spin from Pumple Syke to Millriggs or to Sawmill Cottage to visit Gordon and Barbara Fox. The poem also reminds me of my ride with Reg Gifford from Grasmere through Rydal to Ambleside on a beautiful morning with our friends. A High Bicycle was called an "Ordinary".

A CENTURY OLD FLYER
"High above the ground"

Gliding happily along five feet from the ground
No chain wheels, no rattles nor mechanical sound
A fresh wind on my face and blowing through my hair
On that sunny spring morning I abandoned all care.

I observed from my perch there high above the ground
Cud-chewing cattle and sleepy sheep in fields all around
On that lovely fine morning, oh the birds they did sing
And church bells in the distance I could hear faintly ring.

Though precariously seated so far from the ground
My passage no longer obstructed by stones or a mound
I was thrilled by the freedom, the gliding, the grace
As over smooth modern tarmac I sped at gazelle-like pace.

I saw in the hedgerows from my perch above ground
The birds building nests in safe places they'd found
And into hedge bottoms the rabbits did scurry
As my ancient invention caused panic and flurry!

The spoon brake is useless, so an uphill must be found
To slow down my progress and alight on the ground;
Oh the thrill and elation feels truly extra-ordinary
When I glide through the lanes on my century-old "Ordinary"!

LH 17.11.1999

I did a number of runs for charity over the years on my Penny Farthing. Figure 10.13 recalls an Ambleside event the purpose of which I cannot remember, but I do recall gliding through Ambleside on the early morning ride with no traffic to get in the way of progress!

One event better recorded is when Reg Gifford, proprietor of Michael's Nook Country House Hotel at Grasmere, and I did a charity ride early one Sunday morning for the Round Table on our Penny Farthings from the Travellers Rest, Grasmere, through Rydal to the White Lion, Ambleside. Our friends, Andrew Taylor, John Wood

Figure 10.13. LH riding past Ambleside market cross

and Tony Sansom, accompanied us as an escort in my car with a sign "Caution! Penny Farthing riders ahead!" Tony still has a video of this ride. Annabel Williams took the pictures of our practice run at Grasmere and Rydal which appear in the colour section.

Figure 10.16. "Doing a Header!" The Knutsford Great Race Programme 2010

We needed an escort and we did the run in the early morning because of holiday traffic. The problem was that our 130 year-old spoon brakes were ineffective when people overtook us and then slowed down suddenly to stare at the old bikes! A "header" was a distinct possibility, so we had to be careful.

Penny Farthing races are still popular. In September 2010 Reg invited my new wife, Jean, and me to accompany him to the Knutsford Great Race 2010. This event is held every 10 years in Knutsford in Cheshire and the race lasts for exactly 3 hours. Riders of all ages took part from all over the world and the day had a festive spirit with craft stalls and food stands and vintage cars and bicycles on display. The winners were those solo riders or relay teams who completed the most number of circuits in the time – it was a case of fortitude and stamina! The crowds of people there certainly entered into the fun of the day.

⋆   ⋆   ⋆

LIFE ON TWO WHEELS WITH ROARING COMBUST!

There are things in life one should not miss
A first embrace and a tender kiss
The discovery of love, those nights of passion
When youth excels, no bounds, no ration!

Likewise when we lift the clutch and grip the throttle
Courage supplants fear; have we got the bottle?
The balance, the thrust, with the freedom to fly
All this we learn fast as the hedges shoot by!

The bumps, the scrapes of the learning curve
The going too fast; can we keep our nerve?
This maiden on wheels is so lithe and so lissom
To our wise inner voice we need to listen!

For all such sensation can lead to temptation
Though sometimes it feels good to give in
Nothing can compare to the fresh morning air
When over Shap we're out for a spin!

The ecstatic thrill as we crest Huck's Brow hill
With high velocity coming up on the dial
To a man growing old who won't be told
It gives rise to a satisfied smile!

My Yamaha was smoother by far than any car
Her brakes and the steering were fine
She was good for the thrills over Lakeland hills
And the ride: well, it was just divine!

And this is still so on my Moto Guzzi
For though I am older my head's not yet fuzzy
I can glide with my Jean, my wife, my soulmate
And feel like a young man fresh out on a date!

Revised 2011

I obtained my motor cycle provisional licence on the 5th April 1956 and passed my motor cycle test on 13th June 1956. For most of the 55 years since then I have owned and ridden a motor cycle to blow the cobwebs away when time allowed. I have not had long safaris or ridden much in groups, except on a few Vintage Motor Cycle Club (VMCC) rallies.

My favourite rides are relatively local. In the 1970s the late Peter Robinson and I used to power to the top of Shap for 6 a.m. and then over Orton Fell to Appleby and Knock. I had a Triumph Trident three cylinder then, which was followed by a Norton Commander Interstate in June 1976.

From Knock we rode to the top of great Dun Fell where we had wonderful views over the Eden Valley. Peter was the son of J.C. Robinson, our past chairman of the Lakeland Dialect Society.

Figure 10.17. LH on Triumph Trident 3 – top of Shap fell at 6 a.m.in 1975

Peter was a chief engineer on a merchant ship. He was sadly killed, not on a motor bike, but in an accident on board ship heading to Egypt.

The run from Orton to Appleby, when the blossom is out in the spring, is always a joy to me. Sometimes I went on to Melmerby for breakfast, or called on Tom Potter and family at their garage in Kirkby Stephen. After Tom's day, I helped his family: Richard, John, Sheila and Bryan in arranging their first reduction sale of Tom's collection and more recently the rest - see colour section. I used to visit Tom on my Vincent Comet BEC 692, which I bought originally in 1966. Now it has been restored by Bill Bewley to perfection.

Perhaps by some hefting instinct, I always loved the wild open country of north Westmorland and the sense of freedom it gives. The Hayton family came from Orton and before that Great Asby near Appleby in the 1600s. See *"Poken Aboot Amang Papers"*. We had the same feeling of freedom and refreshment when we took the family to Islay. The one thing common to both places is the influence of the Norsemen and the Scots! See *"My Viking Trail"*.

When the British motor cycle industry collapsed, Norman Rowlandson and his brother, David, of Sapphire Motors, Staveley, suggested I try a second-hand Yamaha 600 Diversion, which was a pleasure to ride. David and Martin test my 1928 Sunbeam and LE Velocette each year. David is a fine engineer. His workshop and way of working is the tidiest I have seen in the business. He builds engines and motorcycles and then rides them in competition. He knows his subject and has the technical and engineering skills needed to provide a good service for our local community and other motor cycle riders around. My father's Braithwaite Jap motor cycle, figure 10.3, was built in Staveley in the late 1920s. Who knows, one day we might have a "Rowlandson Sapphire" marque motor cycle!

As already stated my friend Bill took restoring motor cycles to perfection as a hobby. He bought my Vincent Comet BEC 692 and completely dismantled it, replacing any worn parts and anything with even a blemish. The bike was rebuilt as good as, if not better than, new. Bill won Best in Class with the Vincent Comet: see colour section, figure 10.18. He went on to win the Best in Show with a Vincent 1000 at Stafford, plus many more top awards. As a result he has been appointed a judge - possibly to give others a chance! He applies similar standards in his business affairs.

Bill is Chairman of Bowness Bay Boating Company, which purchased the steamers to add to their fleet and now owns Windermere Lake Cruises. I have enjoyed a happy professional and business working relationship for many years with these companies. The directors and their families, who have worked in and developed these businesses, have always been 'hands on', serving visitors to Lakeland as well as providing employment. Above all, they are always going forward, honing their business skills and looking at new opportunities. By appointing and acquiring the skills of Nigel Wilkinson as their very able Managing Director, they have had more time to look at new ventures, one of which was the recent opening of the new Lakeland Motor Museum at Backbarrow.

Leslie Micklethwaite and Bill Bewley with Edwin Maher, the Museum Manager, and his team have produced another valuable attraction for visitors and locals. The same standards of excellence, which have been achieved by Bill with his motorbikes, have fed through into the museum, as he has taken a hands-on approach helping with this new project. It is highly acclaimed for the excellent and imaginative way in which the exhibits are displayed and it is well worth a visit.

Now Jean and I can trundle to the museum in the MG or on the motorbike have a look around and a light lunch there by the river. My motor cycling has always been a gentle pleasure, not all-consuming but I have ridden or tinkered with bikes, when time allowed. I would feel lost without one because to glide along the highways and byways of this lovely part of England is one of the golden threads running through the tapestry of my life. That Jean enjoys it with me is a new delight.

MANX RALLY ON MY 1928 SUNBEAM 2002

"Ballacraine to Ramsey"
A parade on the T.T. course
Isle of Man
(To be read out loud in a lively style!)

She was born in the "Roaring Twenties"
In those Charleston frenzied times
She is lacquered black and lined in pure gold
She has hand-change on the tank
And cost seventy guineas at the bank
Now my Sunbeam's rising seventy-four years old!

Well, I joined the Bewley Five
And my Old Lady came alive
I blew her cobwebs out at Union Mills
Then we powered up Helen Glen
Through those bends that come again
And rediscovered all our boyhood thrills.

Though a novice on the track
My technique was coming back
I'd learned to take a really good racer's line
Well, Bill & Sam, they've more power to go fast
So they both flew by and powered past
But my old flat-tank Sunbeam girl was doing fine!

Flat out down Sulby Straight
For a Scott she couldn't wait
And the oil drip I adjusted as I rode
When I approached a bridge left-hander
I tucked in right and took a gander
Then swept down through the bends in racing mode!

Well to the ton-up kids she's not so fast
But she's not there to come in last
And she seemed to have a spirit of her own
I was so thrilled and so elated
Like a fellow who's just been mated -
The miles to Ramsey, how they all had flown!

But when I arrived upon the Green
Feeling great and so serene
She missed and spluttered did my poor old pet
So I stripped the Amal down
'Twixt happiness and a frown
And I blew through the blocked-up jet.

Using all the original Sunbeam tools
Following time-tested simple rules
I rolled out my leather tool kit on the grass
I used them to disassemble
Then of course to re-assemble
And then the most unexpected came to pass.

Well I keep my Sunbeam clean
But "concours" is not my scene
The bike is just original every part
Most of her paintwork shines like new
And rusty spots are very few
The antique patina thrills my beating heart.

So pre-occupied with my task
I never heard the judges ask
When the prize-giving was getting underway;
As usual my good pal Bill
Had received the First Prize thrill
But Second Prize – "Len Hayton" did they say?

Figure 10.20. Manx Rally with Sunbeam, Bill, and Friends, 2002

Figure 10.18. The Potter family: Brian & Sheila in 1902 9hp Darracq with John and Richard in 1899 5hp Marshall two-seater Phaeton

Figure 11.9. Jean after her first ride on the Moto Guzzi

Figure 10.25. LH on Banbury Run 2009

Figure 10.26. Bill with my old Vincent BEC 692 which he restored to perfection

Figure 10.27. Frank Brown and LH with my MG on my 67th birthday

Figure 11.1. Mike and Kate Winkley in Inverewe Gardens

Figure 11.2. Finn and Reg Ashworth in County Donegal

Figure 11.6. Kayleigh on her High School Graduation Day

Figure 11.10. Martyn and Pam Wrathall with LH and their horse

Figure 11.10a. Mark and my daughter Penny at Wendy's party, 2010

The collage of wedding pictures on our Christmas card 2010 – front

The collage of wedding pictures on our Christmas card 2010 – back

Figure 1.13. Peter and Joan on Wedding duty!

Figure 11.15. LH and Jean with Jackie Jones and Lucy – See *"Sparkle Rhythm"*. Gordon Fox is church doorway

Figure 11.14. Jackie arriving with Millie and Jennie. For picture of Jackie with her husband, Gordon, see Christmas card collage on previous page

Figure 11.17. LH and Jean with Derek and Edna, Jan, Bill and Jenny

Figure 11.18. Jean with friends Jennifer and Ramon Vilbo from Oslo. See Barbara Fox, Shona Kerray, Edna Steel and Clive Davies also in the picture

Figure 11.19. LH & Jean with grandchildren: Front row, left to right: Michaela, Jennie, Millie, Sarah and Kieran. Back row: Rebecca, David, Christopher and Gareth

Figure 11.20. David & Annabel, Lucinda, Gil & Sam with Jean and LH

Figure 11.21. Keith Wood, Andrew Bromley and John Geldard with Christine Sutton, Rona Bromley, Christine Wood and Rachel Geldard

Figure 11.22. LH and Jean at Natland Mill Beck Ice Cream Parlour with Louise's display of knickerbocker glory and milkshakes! Photo: Louise Gardner

Figure 11.23. Jean with Bernard
and Marie-Françoise at
Wastwater

Figure 11.24. LH and Jean
enjoying the magic of marriage

Figure 11.25. Jean and LH with Bay Farm Tours holiday group in the Grand Canyon

It seems the votes had all been cast
By fellow-riders walking past
The approval of my peers 'chuffed' me so
Bill said: "There's no excuse now not to clean her
But it's not the Sunbeam's paint patina
It was the scarce original tool kit, don't you know?!!!"

LH 2002

I used to visit the Isle of Man with Bill Bewley and a quartet drawn from a variety of our friends: Alan Wilson, Douglas Tyson, Sam McGhee, Keith Coates, Alec Edmundson, Frank Brown, Ernie Shields and Malcolm Tyson. It was always an exciting and enjoyable holiday. Bill and Jenny have an apartment in Port Erin, where we used to stay. Bill had made an arrangement to use a workshop and store where we could secure our bikes, and that worked well. As usual he was always well organised with transport to the Isle of Man and for our stay there. We also had time to visit places of interest on the island.

Sadly, our chums Alan Wilson, Sam McGhee and Alex Edmundson have all died since those halcyon days. They are sorely missed not only for their humour and great company but they also drove the recovery and refreshments vehicle and even acted as Marshalls on the Vintage Rally. Alan was our top cook and provisions man. Sam on his Velocette, and I on the Sunbeam, did our best to keep up with Bill powering ahead on either his Sunbeam or on one of his Vincents. Douglas acted as our chief engineer at the depot and in the recovery vehicle but we rarely broke down. Mike Rocco and his wife, Norma, always made us welcome at their motor cycle and antiques shop in Port Erin and we all had great times together. I took part in the 2002 Manx Rally on the Sunbeam. See figure 10.19 in colour section. I did the Manx Rally again in 2003 on

Figure 10.19. LH's KTS Velocette at Manx Rally 2003

my KTS Velocette, which I had bought at the Stafford Auction but later sold to Michael Rocco on the Isle of Man.

NOTES ON MY 1928 Model 8 SUNBEAM

When my late brother Jack died in December 1967, he left me his 1928 Model 8 Marston Sunbeam 350cc. He had bought it about four years earlier from a George Huddleston at Windermere, who was an engineer. I knew George worked at Fells Engineering works at Troutbeck Bridge near Windermere, but some more information emerged out of the blue recently. I have had the old bike 43 years, so it is like an old friend, as is my old TF MG, which I have enjoyed for 28 years.

Figure 10.21. George Huddleston on his Sunbeam

Christine Wood, the wife of my law partner Keith Wood, telephoned me one day. Her mother's cousin, Leslie Phillips, had requested Christine to pass me a copy of a receipted bill and a picture of George Huddleston. George was the first owner of the Sunbeam in 1929, and Leslie thought I might still have the old bike. The registration number and photo are clearly correct but the receipt is for a lesser sum than the list price of the bike in 1929. It seems likely that a large deposit had been paid on the order and the receipt was for the balance payable on delivery. I have the original price list for all models manufactured in 1928. My Sunbeam is a model 8 manufactured by John Marston Ltd of Sunbeamland, Wolverhampton. *The price was £66 guineas plus £5 guineas for the Lucas Magdyno electric lighting outfit.*

After Jack died in 1967, I did not have much time to ride the Sunbeam,

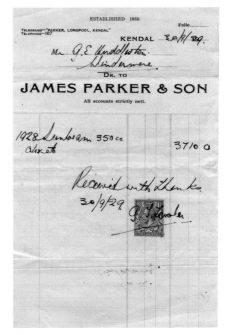

Figure 10.22. Bill of sale

but either on Boxing Day or New Year's Day each year, Gerard and I used to start it and give it a clean to keep it in order. We used to ride it down the lane and back, in memory of our brother. In the last 20 years, however, I have ridden the Sunbeam more often. As well as riding it locally for my own enjoyment, I occasionally went to the meetings of the Lakeland section of the Vintage Motor Cycle Club (VMCC) when time allowed.

Bill and I also completed the VMCC 61st Banbury Run in 2009. It was great fun bonking along through the lovely villages around Banbury. Given fresh petrol and clean points, my Sunbeam still starts at the first kick! See figures 10.24 and 10.25 in colour section.

Figure 10.23. Catalogue extract 1928 Model 8 Marston Sunbeam

Figure 10.24. LH and Joy on a Harley Davidson motorbike

In 2004 Joy and I accompanied my daughter, Ingrid, and family to South Dakota, U.S.A. when they were looking for a suitable site for their dairy farm. The weather was glorious and we decided to hire a Harley Davidson Kingsway motorbike in Sioux Falls. The roads were straight and we longed for some bends. It seems that the Harley was designed for cruising along the likes of Highway 29. If we had kept going north, we would have been in Canada! See figure 10.26 in colour section.

TO FRANK BROWN ESQUIRE
A Master Craftsman of Ambleside

Now it could be in the water
Which flows down through Skelghyll Beck
That provides the nutrition for perfection
To embue you with ability and feck.

For Ambleside folk are not ordinary folk
"Aut optimum aut nihil" a must
You can be sure they know their subject
Their skill and ability we can trust.

Malcolm Tyson first set the standard
The flag of excellence he raised on high
But many who sought to emulate him
Could only admire him and sigh.

Until there came the trio
Bill Bewley, Douglas Tyson, Frank Brown
Then the pursuit of super excellence
Spread outwards, away beyond the town.

Round the halls of a thousand motor bikes
In competition they gleam and glow
Because the finish achieved in Ambleside
Is the very best: as all judges know!

And behind the quintessence of finish
Is our chief master-craftsman in town
He's a jolly good chap with a smile for all
Our "no-shortcuts-perfectionist" Frank Brown.

This maestro has "painted my wagon"
My model TF, fifty three year old MG
It's better than new is the finish
And I'm over the top in my glee!

And when I arrived to collect her
Birthday balloons were attached for "Our Boy"
And you said the job was all paid for
A wonderful present from Joy!

So thank you Frank and Ken for all you've done
My car shines perfectly in the April sun
Your attention to detail and skill put in
To the base coats and finish –no wonder
your customers win!

LH 5.4.2007

See LH and Frank in figure 10.27, colour section

★NOSTALGIA AND MY OLD MG

Those times in youth we treasure still
When on a sunlit day
With oil up to the elbows
Beneath some sump we lay.

Perhaps we bought our pride and joy
From Andy Murphy's yard
Scrap cars were limousines to us
We'd labour on them hard.

At first no thought of women
Obscured our concentration
Every minute then was spent
To improve the acceleration!

We did overtime with constant zeal
To pay for our jalopy
Mention then of courting
Was thought a little soppy!

But from time to time some girl would come
Perhaps to help in cleaning
Maybe we noticed now and then
When she was closely leaning –

That she had curves and headlamps too
Perhaps acceleration
Then our feelings for the car
Were tinged with a new sensation –

As in those lowly parts of man
Where passion ebbs and flows
And love, confused with nature
Overcomes the doubts and no's.

So then: how to impress her?
Let's find a red MG
To speed through blossomed lanes in spring
Just my lovely girl and me.

Do you remember those happy times of youth?
Yes, the images are clear and strong
Nights of stars and moonlight
As enraptured we bowled along.

She was a car and she was a girl
We were out in our old TD
Yes me with my arm round her shoulder
And she with her hand on my knee.

Now you with your cars historic
Which you cherish as I would too
Give some thought to this conundrum:
Was it the car, or was it the girl,
Or the memory of the two?

* Lake District Historic Car Club. LH 24.01.1983

I bought my present 1954 model 1250 TF MG on the 5th April 1983 in very good condition. Mostly I did my own MG maintenance, but in recent years I have put its care in the capable and professional hands of Automobile Engineer, David Atkinson. David is well qualified and experienced in maintaining all ages of motor car. It is always a pleasure to call at Halhead Garage at Bonningate on the Crook Road, when test time comes, or if the MG needs some repair. He and his colleagues are up-to-date with all the technology, but they have time for a chat while getting on with their work. David's garage is in a quarry, but like 'the best clockmaker who was hidden in a wood,' there is a worn pathway of satisfied clients to his door. David runs the same friendly sort of business, which flourished in the hamlets of Lakeland when I was a boy.

CODE NAME PEGASUS

On the 28th and 29th of September 1994, at the request of Eric and Anne Hadwin, the proprietors of J.F. and E. Hadwin Ltd. of Torver, near Coniston, I addressed their guests on the launch of a new Range Rover - code name Pegasus. Our firm had done work for Eric and his brother, Jack, and I had bought my vehicles from them over the years. Jack had retired but was interested in old motorbikes and had his own museum for a while.

There were two days of the launch of the new car and three presentations per day: at breakfast, lunch and dinner in the evening. I was asked to entertain the evening guests each day. Joy and I stayed overnight and during the day had a sail on the Gondola on Coniston Lake with Richard Ransome, who was a friend from our Windermere Grammar School days.

Richard gave us a comprehensive account of the workings of the steam engine powering the Gondola. It was clearly his pride and joy for it was well maintained and shone. It was wonderful to watch and to note how little noise it made on its progress around Coniston Lake.

A very large marquee had been erected and tables were laid out and adorned in a grand manner. Eric wanted a Lakeland theme with some dialect and some historical snippets, so I skipped light-heartedly through my chronology of types of travel in the Lake District from Roman times to the launch of the new Range Rover, interspersed with "Tales of a Lakeland Lad". I concluded with:

TOAST TO PEGASUS THE NEW RANGE ROVER

When you have arrived in your calling
Or you have the where-with-all
There's many a way of saying it
But there's one way beats them all.

If you want to sit high in a cockpit
With power at your feet
If you want a clear view around you
From a design which is clean and neat;

When you have dismissed all imitations
And discarded the second rate
And your blood is inflamed for a four wheel drive
As it was when you chose your mate;

If you can perceive perfection
Which puts Rolls Royce in the shade
If you are full of desire, with a wallet on fire
Now buy the best one ever made.

Pegasus the new Range Rover
Must be your running mate
And Eric can supply you with one
On this, the launching date.

Pegasus, the steed of the fountain
In legend the wonder horse
Performed such feats for her rider
That this code-name is apt of course.

They say it is higher and wider
And aimed at the luxury class
You can glide fleet-of-foot on the highway
Or traverse a mountain pass.

Where the packhorse climbed and the cog-wheel cart
Struggled to make their way
You can sit in comfort protected
And never get tired all day.

With air conditioning and cruise control
And upholstery fit for a queen
It's a very far cry from the models gone by
When we hosed the inside clean!

So I give you the toast to perfection
Raise your glasses to Eric and Co.
To "Pegasus the New Range Rover"
We look forward to having a go!

TOAST TO THE NEW RANGE ROVER
Coupled with the names of
Eric and Anne Hadwin
and
Lakeland Land Rover

28th September 1994

In 1998 Eric and Anne Hadwin decided to purchase a site on the outskirts of Kendal on Shap Road to build a new garage and showroom which they called Kentdale Land Rover. They made a sound choice when they appointed Colin Shepherd as the Managing Director of the new arm of their business, which opened on the 1st August 1998. He is still there, as obliging and "on the ball" as ever, as are the service and sales staff who, together with reception and accounting staff, make up a happy and efficient team.

The two businesses operate as friendly rivals: perhaps in itself, an incentive to do well. However, having purchased vehicles from both outlets and done business with them over the years, I can say that the sales, servicing and after sales attention to detail and to customer satisfaction at both sites is second to none. In fact Kentdale Landrover has won regional and national awards almost every year since 2001 and has been National Dealer of the Year four times.

This is a Lakeland family business which has evolved on a sound basis and expanded in the pursuit of excellence. There are two teams of competent and friendly staff, properly trained and sincere in their desire to keep their customers happy.

Figure 10.28. See page 432 of "Nostalgia and my old MG". My Girl and the MG with tin cans – courtesy of our guests – which jangled all the way home after the wedding!

11

THE MAGIC OF THE INTERNET

MOVING ON

The opening weeks of 2010 brought sorrow and sadness. The sudden death in January of Michael Winkley, my law partner for 35 years and great friend of 52 years, was a profound shock to all of us who knew him – but the shock galvanised me into action in the spring.

Mike's lovely wife, Kate, asked his good friend, Peter Marshall, and I to do a eulogy for Mike at his Thanksgiving Service in Kendal Parish Church. Though a sad occasion, I have a wonderful, lasting memory of that day. As I stood in the pulpit, I beheld a full church of radiant faces, smiling up from the congregation like a garden of flowers in bloom. Shafts of sunlight beamed through the mullioned windows and played on the "garden" of Mike's family and friends. All had gathered to pay their respects, reflecting the esteem in which he was held. The sunshine of their smiles reminded me of the warmth and humour generated by Mike when telling his stories. Mike was a true family solicitor, a friend and a rock to rely on. His humour was a tonic and his grin infectious.

In the summer of 2009 Mike, Kate and I had a lovely holiday together, based at Poolewe in the north west of Scotland. We went to Inverewe Gardens and visited our friends, Peter and Margaret Dover, who live at Melon Udrigle in a beautiful area near Laide in Ross-shire. Though the Inverewe Gardens lie so far north in Scotland, they benefit from the influence of the Gulf Stream, and a wide variety of beautiful plants grow there.

Mike had always been healthy and strong and his death, after only six weeks of illness, had a profound effect on me. Like so many of my good friends, Mike and Kate had given me great support after Joy died at Christmas in 2007. Joy recognised that it would be hard to live alone and before she died, she advised me to look for a companion. However, it was difficult for me to consider such a thing for a long time.

I decided to pursue my interest in the Viking influence on Lakeland and its dialects, as well as investigating my family history and riding my motorbikes. I had an enjoyable holiday in Ireland with my friends, Reg and Finn Ashworth, in County Donegal.

For company I went with Bay Farm Tours to Russia. We visited St Petersburg, Moscow and Suzal. It was a wonderful experience. In St Petersburg we marvelled at the vast collection of treasures in the Hermitage Museum and admired the beautiful Summer Palace with its fountains and gardens. We visited an interesting fish farm. In Moscow we were treated to a circus performance, had time in the Kremlin, and enjoyed an evening cruise on the river. We also visited a horticultural farm there. I have never seen so many cucumbers, courgettes and tomatoes in my life! We had a wonderful trip to Suzal Monastery. In sharp contrast to the advanced horticultural farming we had seen near Moscow, the farming practices near Suzal, a long way out in the country, were primitive and fascinating. The farm trips were just a small part of the Bay Farm Tour itinerary, but they provided an opportunity to meet the people and see how they live.

Mike's death made me think again. After losing Joy, my friends had all encouraged me to "be positive". *Dum vivimus viviamus et gaudeamus:* while we live, let us live and be joyful. So I took a deep breath and decided to try the internet. I joined the Guardian Soulmates dating website.

After entering my profile and a description of the person I was looking for, I pressed the key for the best matches. Jean's profile came to the top with a 91 per cent match – and she was living only 18 miles away in Ulverston! Perhaps the missing nine per cent compatibility was due to her vegetarian preferences at that time! I found out that Miss Dorothy Jean Couper, known as Jean, was a retired nurse (a continence and urology nurse specialist) and a former teacher. She had recently lost two elderly friends, both of whom had been very precious to her. One of Jean's good friends, Jackie Jones, encouraged her to join Guardian Soulmates to cheer her. When I contacted Jean through the internet, her great friend, Jan Tomson, was staying with her for a few days, so we were delayed a little before meeting. However, eventually we met for our first date … and the rest, as they say, is history!

★   ★   ★

A WHIRLWIND ROMANCE WITH MY JEANIE

I saw your smile on "Soulmates"
And I hoped it wasn't too late
Over 90% compatible,
Your credentials were impeccable
… And so we arranged a date.

At Fountain Street I met you
The fifteenth of March to vet you
Then via Baycliffe, off to Lindal we went to dine
Captured by your smile, the twinkle in your eyes
I saw your character and honesty on the line!

Wow! Since then the world has altered
My will has never faltered
You occupy the centre of my world
You warm me to my toes like sunshine upon a rose
Stirs its petals to be so gloriously unfurled.

From Walney's sands to Melmerby
From Cartmel Choir to Asby
We have linked our hands in happiness every day
This warmth, this wholesome feeling has sent my senses reeling
And ever let it be so: Yes, I say!

Words cannot en-capture the ecstasy or rapture
We shared together through those lovely sunlit days
Your sweetness and your gentleness
The quiet application of your loveliness
Expressed beautifully in so many ways!

Then on the pillion of my Moto Guzzi
Not weak-willed, lily-livered or fuzzy
You're a natural cuddly biker kind of Gal!
With your gentle arms around me
In our "Seventh Heaven" you have found me
You're my Angel, you're my Baby, you're my Pal!

LH 6.40 a.m. 22nd March 2010

There were so many lovely coincidences and favourable omens. We knew that our whirlwind romance would create some astonishment, even concern, because it took everyone by surprise, ourselves included! I have always been a cautious country lawyer who normally digs for the facts and weighs all the pros and cons, so it came as rather a shock to many of my friends – until they met Jean! Michelle, the daughter of my friend Bill Bewley, was genuinely concerned about "Uncle Len", because it was so out of character! She made her own enquiries among her nursing friends and came back to Bill with glowing reports.

The second week of our romance we went down to the Cotswolds and Bath. Joy and I used to go and stay with our friend, Chris Sutton, in Cirencester and we would all go to see a play at the theatre in Bath. Chris invited the two of us to do the same, but due to the sudden illness of her young granddaughter, Chris had to go to London. She suggested we should use the theatre tickets; so Jean and I drove down to Bath.

We had a lovely time in the city and a very special experience in Bath Abbey. We had lit candles for Joy and Michael and Jean's parents and were sitting quietly together in the beautiful abbey church, reflecting on our lives, past and present. Just then a retired lady vicar, part of the Abbey's pastoral team, stopped to speak to us. We told her about our sad losses and how we came to meet. About ten minutes later the same lady minister appeared in the pulpit to say a few prayers, whilst all the tourists stood quietly and listened. To our great surprise she finished by giving us a special blessing from the pulpit.

Jean and I discovered that we were interested in many similar things. We found ourselves warmly amused by each other and were often in tucks of laughter. There seemed to be a kind of magic in the air, as if some influence was guiding us. I know this must all sound like a candy floss romance, but it was nothing of the kind. We got on so well that long weekend and enjoyed our journey together so much that we became engaged in Ludlow on our way home – exactly two weeks to the day since our first date! We arranged to meet Jean's friend, Jan Tomson, in Sandbach in Cheshire the same day. Jan was genuinely delighted for us because she could see how happy we were together.

When we got home from Ludlow, we decided to arrange our wedding for four months hence on Friday the 23rd July and to ask Jan to be Jean's matron-of-honour. Jean was overjoyed when her cousin, Derek Steel, who lives in Los Angeles, agreed to fly over with his wife, Edna, to "give her away" at our wedding. We enjoyed working together on the preparations for the wedding ceremony at St John the Evangelist Church in Levens and the organisation of the reception at the Heaves Hotel. The time fairly flew!

Jean has no brothers and sisters but she has several cousins, to whom she feels very close. It was lovely to meet them and gradually fit the faces to the voices I had heard and spoken to on the telephone! Jean's

cousin, Barbara Thomas, and her daughters, Sue and Val, and Val's husband, Clive Davies, were the first of her family I was pleased to get to know. We had a good get-together here in Levens and they enjoyed a swing in the front garden, as the photos show. Later on, Jean and I met her Scottish cousin, Shona Kerray, and her husband, Cameron, whilst they

Figure 11.3. Jean's cousins, Barbara and Sue

were staying in Keswick. Apart from Cameron, who was unable to come, they were all with us for our wedding in July.

In early May we decided to have a short break on the Isle of Arran. On the way to the ferry at Ardrossan in Ayrshire, we stopped to visit Jean's cousin, Ronnie Andrew, and his wife, Fiona, near Kilmarnock. Ronnie was waiting for a serious operation that July, but he was determined to attend our wedding afterwards, which he bravely did, with Fiona and their two daughters, Lindsey Farmer and Wendy.

We stayed in a delightful B&B on Lamlash Bay. Arran is like a miniature Scotland on an island with stunning scenery of mountains and

Figure 11.4. Val and her husband Clive on the swing

coast. Like a youthful couple we explored the island and revelled in the delights of each other's company. We took the short ferry crossing from Lochranza to the Mull of Kintyre and drove down the peninsula

Figure 11.6. LH and Jean at Carradale, Mull of Kintyre

through Carradale and on to Campbeltown. The sea was sparkling and the views were magnificent.

We stayed one night at the end of the Crinan Canal. The evening was memorable for its tranquillity, while a wonderful sunset reflected in the still waters of the bay. There is no age limit to happiness on a lovely walk together on a beautiful evening. The next day we enjoyed a leisurely drive across Scotland to visit Jean's cousin, Margaret Couper, near Dundee. Jean has Scottish family connections on both her mother and father's sides: both of her grandfathers were Scottish, but I don't know whether she has any Pictish or Viking ancestry! What I do know is that she has the character and grit of a good Scot. Jean has a lovely timbre in her voice, memorably so when we sang together, driving along the lochs and through the glens of Scotland.

Figure 11.7. Margaret and Jean

We knew that Jean's cousin, Margaret, would not be able to come to the wedding, so I was looking forward to meeting Margaret and giving her the chance to vet Jean's future husband! All was well and we were given a joyous welcome and had a happy time with Margaret. It was clear she was delighted with our engagement and gave us both her love and support.

Figure 11.5. Sea crossing to Arran

SPARKLE RHYTHM
My Internet Girl

Jean's chosen internet name was "Sparkle Rhythm". Her friend, Jackie, and daughter, Lucy, were staying with Jean at the time and Jackie suggested "Sparkle" to start with. However, this was rejected by the dating site, as no doubt someone else had already adopted the name. Jackie suggested that because Jean was musical and sang in Cartmel Choral Society, she had rhythm! And so "Sparkle Rhythm" was adopted. The title caught my eye and I liked the sound of "Sparkle Rhythm". I was not to be disappointed when we met! This poem was written for Jean a few days after we got engaged.

★   ★   ★

Somewhere up there, above the Cosmos
Somewhere there is a guiding hand
But when cancer took my Jollity from me
I was sorely tried to understand.

Yet through all the pain and grief
Throughout the loneliness and sorrow
My Family, my Friends and Jesus
Brought me hope of a new tomorrow.

Now that new tomorrow is here today
My Jean has consented to be my Wife
Loving, caring, selfless and sincere
Jean brings her special sparkle to my life.

LH 2010

Shortly after our return from Bath, Jean introduced me to her "Chums" in the Ulverston area, all of whom made me welcome and inspired me with their intellect and bright approach to life. It quickly became clear to me that my fiancée was held in high esteem by those who knew her, and that her work as a specialist nurse in South Lakeland was very highly regarded.

Although I enjoy much of the same music as Jean, I discovered that she has a wider knowledge and appreciation than my own and she has delighted in introducing me to music that is new to me. As well as her involvement with choral music, she especially loves the music of Beethoven and Chopin, as I do too.

Jean has a great experience of learning, reading and the enjoyment of the English language and our culture. Her steady hand and dogged perseverance in the editing and indexing of this book has been fundamental to its completion. We have gathered together the jottings and verses I have done over the years. I have never worked with anyone with such determination. She inspires me. I could not have achieved this without her.

Jean's background and professional life:

Jean was the daughter of Harry and Dorothy Couper (née Steel), who were both Barrovians by birth. Harry was a first class, mechanical engineer and was the Materials Inspection Officer for British Rail. Dorothy was a dressmaker and a gifted singer. They were married in 1944 and Jean was born the following year. In 1961 the family retired from Derby to live in the village of Baycliffe on the coast road between Ulverston and Barrow-in-Furness on Morecambe Bay.

After teacher training in Manchester, Jean taught in Manchester, Paris and Liverpool, before returning to live in Baycliffe with her parents. After another

Figure 11.8. Jean's parents, Harry and Dorothy Couper

four years teaching in Barrow and Dalton-in-Furness, she decided to make nursing her career, qualifying as a state registered nurse in 1982. She loved nursing, the camaraderie and the sharing of knowledge and skills between fellow nurses and the special relationship which nurses have with their patients and families. Her father was pleased to see her qualify and begin working as a staff nurse in the hospital before he died in 1983. Ten years later Jean and her mother moved to live in Ulverston.

Working at Furness General Hospital in Barrow, Jean developed an interest in the promotion of continence and the treatment of incontinence. She developed a new role as the Continence Advisor for South Cumbria Health Authority, which was a community nursing post. It involved having her own caseload, as well as advising and teaching other health workers: district nurses, health visitors and school nurses as well as staff in residential and nursing homes. Her work involved helping men and women with continence problems (both bladder and bowel) as well as children with enuresis (daytime and bedwetting problems) and encopresis (faecal incontinence).

Jean greatly valued her years of working with the highly dedicated doctors at Furness General Hospital, who were closely involved with her line of work: Mr Richard Wilson, Consultant Urologist, and Mr Prabas Misra, Consultant Obstetrician and Gynaecologist. They were greatly supportive of her role and very inspiring to work with. Mr Wilson encouraged her to take up the new hospital post of Urology Nurse Specialist, so her work covered both hospital and community patients and staff. She was delighted when other nurses showed an interest in the promotion of continence and she was able to pass on her knowledge and skills to them. Jean took early retirement in 2002 to look after her mother until she died aged 99 (in her 100th year!) at home the following year.

From time to time we have bad press about the National Health Service, but Jean has nothing but praise for the dedication and hard work of her colleagues in the N.H.S. They focussed on the highest standards of professional conduct and care of patients. Jean particularly enjoyed a special relationship with some of the other specialist nurses and they formed a unique teaching group called the SOS Team: Cynthia Crawshaw, Diabetes Nurse Specialist; Pam Dilks, Macmillan Nurse; Mary Harrison, Respiratory Nurse Specialist; and Ruth Hogg, their secretary. The team went on to become the runners-up at the N.H.S. Team of the Year Awards 1999 held at Loughborough University, which was a great delight. Three of them, including Jean, have retired but they have all remained friends and meet to catch up with news, when they can.

Earlier this year there was a reunion of nearly 50 members of the community nursing and secretarial staff from the Furness area, and Jean said it was wonderful to be back with such lovely ex-colleagues once again. We both think nurses are very special people, and we are delighted that my eldest granddaughter, Sarah Jopson, has just qualified, gaining her degree in nursing and shortly to take up her first post. We look forward to her wedding to Nicholas Hall, in June, 2012 in St. Cuthbert's Church in Kentmere.

A "GORGEOUS" SPRING 2010
And An Easter Ode

In the spring and early summer of 2010 Jean and I were invited to meet her friends and mine. It was lovely to know that they all cared. Our match was celebrated and we were made welcome wherever we went. However, I had a clear impression from Jean's friends, and she likewise from mine, that we would be answerable to them if we were ever unkind to one another!

This was a period of getting to know each other and doing things together. Jean embraced my interests and I hers. I found I could take her anywhere. Her kindness and caring nature shone refreshingly like the morning sun wherever we went. At Easter I wrote this ode to Jean.

TO MY JEAN – AN EASTER ODE

Wherever I take you
Wherever I go
Your smiles are infectious
My friends they all know
That my heart is inspired
And my face is aglow.

Aglow with the love light
You spark in my eyes
Aglow with the knowledge
That you're gentle and wise
Yet teenage excitement
Thrills us all through
With wild wonderful thrills
In the things that we do.

Your kisses are gentle
Your kisses are divine
Like swift shafts of lightning
They thrill through my spine
You are young and so vibrant
My years melt away
As I awake in your arms
At the dawn of the day.

Selfless care you have given throughout your life
Selfless caring precluded your being a wife
Yet now in our autumn you come to me
A creature so perfect, yet you don't seem to see
How lovely you are
How attractive your ways
That I just want to love and protect you
For the rest of my days.

Jean you are special
Jean you are great
We must not waste a moment
Our love it won't wait
It is twenty one days since we first met
And each new day is better yet!

LH Easter Day 2010

★   ★   ★

During the period from Easter until our wedding, we attended a variety of meetings in which I am involved, including the Lakeland Dialect Society. Jean was a member of Cartmel Choral Society and we enjoyed their performance with their gifted Musical Director, Adrian Self, of Sir Arthur Somervell's "The Passion of Christ" in Cartmel Priory, as well as the International Music Festival concerts in Ulverston, directed by the renowned pianist, Anthony Hewitt.

I introduced Jean to motor cycling. She had reservations at first because of her experience of nursing young men on the orthopaedic ward after fracturing their femurs in motorbike accidents and I found that she rode pillion on my Moto Guzzi as a natural. The sense of freedom and the sensation of the open air seemed to thrill her and she glowed with the new experience.

We visited the VMCC Motor Cycle Show in Stafford where Bill won "Best in Show" again! This time he won with his Vincent Black Shadow. When I rang the next day to congratulate Bill on his achievement, I said that Jean and I thought we must have brought him good luck, because I had introduced Jean to Bill and Jenny in their home on our second date and we had our first kiss beside his highly polished motorbike in the garage. Bill asked me if we had noticed the bike's registration number: LOV 579. Quick as lightning, Jean responded by adding the 5, 7 and 9 together to make 21, which two numerals added together make 3. She laughed as she pointed out that 3 is a backwards E, thus making the LOV into LOVE! That really was fun with numbers!

In May 2010 we helped together on the gates of the showground at the WCAS "Country Fest" - a lovely day. We attended other agricultural events, farm meetings and the Geldard's Barbecue at Low Foulshaw Farm – all of which Jean took in her stride. We also had an enjoyable day at Chester Races with Reg Gifford.

In June 2010 our friends Jenny Bewley and Jen Sansom held a joint birthday cruise on Windermere. The evening was warm with just a light rain and the lake was calm. The guests had a wonderful time with an excellent buffet on board. There was a jazz band playing, so Jean and I did a "Kentmere Reel" on the boat. It was lovely for me to introduce her to so many old friends but hard for Jean to remember everyone's names!

We attended Levens Church where Jean was made very welcome and we joined other church members at a service in Carlisle Cathedral. Jean accompanied me and helped with my talks at various celebration events. She was supportive, not only on happy occasions, but sad ones too. When my old friend, Ernest Shepherd, died Wendy, his widow, asked me to do the eulogy at his funeral. We visited Wendy on the day he died and Jean was a real comfort and help to both of us.

In June Jean and I wrote and performed together "A Prayer for Today" for the Lakeland Dialect Service in Levens Church and later that month we helped with the Levens Open Gardens Day.

Between organising our wedding and attending many social events, we had an enormously happy and busy time. I remain totally amazed that my fiancée Jean took up the mantle so completely and enriched both our lives with quiet accomplishment in such a short period of time. It seemed magic and still does.

PRAYER FOR TODAY, LAKELAND DIALECT SERVICE
St John the Evangelist Church, Levens, 20th June 2010

PRAYER FOR A BALANCE IN AGRICULTURE & CONSERVATION
Introduction

In certain areas around the coast of the UK, which include Witherslack, Meathop and Foulshaw Moss, the European policy is to make wetlands in these areas. If this policy is implemented, it will also affect the lower reaches of and other parts of the Lyth Valley. At the same time the drainage pumps, which help to lower the water table in the valley, need repair and maintenance but there is apparently insufficient money to do this and one pump is already out of action now.

The Cumbria Wildlife Trust wants to fell 80 hectares of woodland (97,755 trees – as stated in the felling licence application) to extend the wetland and sphagnum moss areas. However, the woods form a wildlife corridor and habitat for Red Squirrels, Deer, Badgers, Birds, Bats and Insects. The Forestry Commission has requested an ecological assessment.

These policies are causing controversy among farming and country people who are affected.

The loss of productive farm land in Britain, at a time when food security for our nation is in question, is causing concern.

Hence this prayer for today.

Len

Noo Jeanie, bonnie lass, mi bride ta be
In this prayer fer taday we mun esk guidance ta see
Hoo common sense, love en reason be sure ta prevail
In this hubbyshoo aboot pumps that drain oor dale.

T'authorities tell us that t'brass hes run oot
But fer moss restoration thur seems plenty aboot!
Noo we're o' interested in wildlife en God's creation
But balanced wi t'need to feed oor nation.

We nobbut grow aboot two thirds o oor baggin
En we'll hev ta be careful when oor pund is saggen.
Aboot oil runnen oot thur's turble consternation
En t'main o oor planes grunded bi volcanic detonation.

Ye'll knaa t'Heversham Inclosure of 1815
Med way fer land drainage o oor meeders sae green
Two hundred eer sen ta feed a growen nation
Oor for'elders had vision en determination.

Nut lang efter that they built this varra Levens Kirk
Fer they were turble God-fearen – nut flayt o work
Noo don't git ma wrang, because noo we leeve gay weel
But we're sadly oot o balance – Well, that's hoo I feel.

Jean
Now dearest Len, don't you get so distraught
For it was love, reason and kindness that Jesus taught
Civilised debate: faith in facts and reason
Will probably bring balance by this time next season.

Now I'm looking forward to being your wife
For I've taught and I've nursed folk for most of my life
I know you worry about food security and farming
You love nature and wildlife: you are so, so charming!

The Red Squirrels, Badgers and Deer who live in the wood
We worry for their shelter – as "English Nature" should
Let us pray for the flora and fauna on the farms in our dale
For the mammals and insects, lest their habitats fail.

Let us pray for our farmers, the wisdom and work they apply
To their own love of nature and the variety of food they supply.

Len
Aye – but Jeanie mi lass, as wise as ye be
It's them duffers in Brussels need tellen – dote yer see?
Fer thur wanten mayer wetlands en o' sick like
Mappen t' brass will run oot ta clean oor main drainage dyke!

This marpment caps langcrown en puddles me hee-ad
As at same time they tell farmers to increase thur food yield.
Mi fadder hed nobbut a lile Lakeland farm
Wi mixed stock en free-runner poultry which did wildlife nay harm.

We hed birds roon t'buildings en roses roon t'dooer
Hedges teamen wi birdlife en butterflees galore
O' oor becks en oor dykes were o' runnen clear
Wi brown trout en crayfish en lile voles sae dear.

Thur's o'er many theorists wain't listen ta us country folk
They lecture us o' wi fine words en wemly, unbalanced talk
So let us pray fer common sense en t'meeting o minds
Fer fair income fer farmers producen food of o' kinds.

Jean & Len: alternate lines
LH: So let us pray fer God's guidance in a civilised way
JC: In oor arn country talk let them hear what we say
LH: Farmers en country folk as many o ye ken
JC: Knaa a deal aboot wildlife like oor for'elders lang sen.

LH: Thur's plenty o bogland en plenty o moss
JC: Widoot takken farmland ner causen habitat loss
LH: Thur's birds en thur's bees, thur's insects galore
JC: En wi true balanced farming God brings even more.

LH: So pray let us alain ta oor arn country ways
JC: To admire damson blossom through lovely spring days
LH: We'll repair o' t'pumps at a fraction o t'cost
JC: Clean oot o' t'dykes so nay farmland is lost.

LH: En here in oor Dales en oot on the Plains
JC: We'll live here in harmony free from bureaucrat pains
LH & JC: Wid o' nature aroond us en God in his heavens
Let us pray fer peace a-plenty – in oor Village of Levens.

Len Hayton & Jean Couper, June 2010

"BRIGHTLY DAWNED OUR WEDDING DAY"
23rd July 2010

Jean and I had great fun together preparing for our Wedding Day. The helpful guidance from the Reverend Ruth Crossley and from Miles and Catherine Whitelock, the proprietors of the Heaves Hotel in Levens, where we were to have our reception, made everything run smoothly.

Having rained for days, the dark clouds gave way to a lovely dawn with the sun shining brightly through the bathroom window as I dressed for our wedding. The sun continued to shine all day as our photographs show. The collage of wedding pictures, which I prepared for our Christmas card in 2010, records the happy day and is reproduced in the colour section.

We were delighted when Jean's cousin, Derek, arrived with his wife, Edna, from Los Angeles to give her away at the wedding. We are grateful to our friends, Jenny Brown and Mary Orr, who did the readings at the ceremony. Jenny read the poem, "Epithalamium", a celebration of marriage, by the Scottish poet, Aonghas Macneacail. Mary read the First Letter of John, chapter 4, whose theme is: "God is Love". We also thank Robin Orr for beautifully playing our chosen music: Trumpet Voluntary by John Stanley, the blind English composer (1713-1786); Ave Verum

Figure 11.11. Jean with her cousin, Derek Steel, and Jan Tomson, matron of honour, arriving at Levens Church

by W.A. Mozart; Air from Suite No. 3 by J.S. Bach; theme from the 4th Movement of Beethoven's Symphony No. 9.

My niece, Annabel Williams, kindly took our pictures as a wedding gift to us, which was very much appreciated. Annabel succeeded in not only getting everyone in the photographs, but also portraying the happiness of the occasion. I do not propose to bore readers with a full description of the day because the selection from our wedding album speaks for us.

Our Vicar, the Reverend Ruth Crossley, conducted our ceremony in a meaningful way, which was thoroughly in tune with the spirit of our lives together. The goodwill around us in church carried through to the reception and throughout the whole day. The gorgeous arrangements of flowers by Ruth Martin, Averil Mason and Marjorie Dobson enhanced the simple beauty of Levens Church.

We recall our Wedding Day as full of laughter and smiles. Our guests were relaxed and our friends and families intermingled in an informal and pleasant way. Peter Brown provided a gentle medley of piano music in the background. Jean's friend, Eileen Parkinson, an expert in the skill of sugarcraft, made our wedding cake and decorated it with the most exquisite hand-made roses. My three Best Men, Bill Bewley, Tony Sansom and Peter Matthews, pulled my leg as usual, producing peals of laughter, as the above picture shows.

Figure 11.12. Best Man Bill Bewley's humorous address

I had suggested to Jean that she could also make a speech, but she said that it was not her forte. Instead she surprised me by singing Elton John's "Your Song", which she had adapted to include references to riding pillion on my motorbike and sitting in the MG! When everyone joined in the chorus after each verse, I was quite overcome. I never realised that I have "the sweetest blue eyes" until she sang this to me! As many of our guests said afterwards, it was a most enjoyable wedding, which is remembered as much for the brilliant sunshine and blue sky as the good humour and friendly atmosphere throughout the day.

We stayed at Leeming House on the edge of Ullswater on our wedding night, and the next day we had a delightful lunch with our friends, Bill and Isabell Broach, at Loch Maben on the way to Tynron, north of Dumfries. Jean's great friend, Helen White, had very kindly given us three days there in her lovely old cottage. By an amazing coincidence my old friends, Martyn and Pam Wrathall, live only a few miles from Tynron, so they invited us to a convivial lunch with their daughter and grandson whilst we were there.

We crossed the Irish Sea to Larne and stayed for two days on the beautiful Antrim Coast, watched the puffins on Rathlin Island (a Viking site!) and then travelled on to Glenties in County Donegal, where we enjoyed a lovely four days with Reg and Finn Ashworth. Fine weather accompanied us all the way.

On our return home, more invitations followed from our friends: the musical "Les Miserables" with Paul and Sue Baker at the Lowry Theatre; a holiday on the Isle of Man with Bill and Jen Bewley; Knutsford Great Penny Farthing Race with Reg Gifford – see "*Two Wheels and Four Wheels*". We attended the Westmorland County Show, when the sun shone all day. Jean's friend, Jan Tomson, was staying with us when their friends from Paris, Bernard and Marie-Françoise Autrand, came on holiday. We were lucky that we were able to take them to the Show and round the Lake District in bright sunshine and they were able to see the scenery in the best light.

Before I met Jean, I had intended to go to the Grand Canyon with Bay Farms Tours and visit my daughter, Ingrid, and Moss and the family in South Dakota. Jean and I decided to adopt this as our plan for our main honeymoon tour in October, touring California for ten days, before finishing the holiday in Las Vegas. The holiday started in San Francisco and included a visit to a vineyard in the Napa Valley. Then we moved on to Sacremento, the capital city of California, before spending a night in the beautiful Yosemite National Park. We visited film studios in Los Angeles and spent a night on the Queen Mary in Long Beach. We invited Jean's cousin, Derek, and Edna and family to join us for dinner, which was a very happy reunion for us all. Later that night, while fast asleep on the ship, we were awakened by a lady's voice telling us through the loudspeaker that there was a fire on the ship and we must assemble on deck! It was interesting to see how folk behave in an emergency – everybody was actually very calm. It turned out to be a false alarm, caused by some young people having a prank with the fire extinguishers!

We stayed in good accommodation everywhere. As well as visiting all the usual tourist attractions, we had farm visits in the San Joaquin Valley, being transported on open trailers through the fruit and nut orchards and enjoyed our first taste of plumcots (apricot/plum cross) – juicy and delicious! We also visited a cotton plantation and various cattle ranches. From there we drove to San Diego and flew to Las Vegas for three nights. Our helicopter flight to Grand Canyon with a champagne breakfast at the bottom of the canyon and a tour of the western rim was a wonderful experience. See colour picture figure 11.

The helicopter took us to "The Skywalk", a glass platform suspended 4000 feet above the Colorado River. Jean and I did a dance there, but it is not a desirable experience for anyone who has vertigo!

Figure 11.16. Isabelle aged 1 year old

We flew from Las Vegas to stay with Ingrid, Moss and family on their dairy farm, 30 miles north of Sioux Falls in South Dakota. They kindly drove us 400 miles across South Dakota to the Black Hills to see Mount Rushmore and the Crazy Horse Memorial. The colours of the trees in the fall (autumn) in Custer National Park were magnificent. We saw buffalo, bears, coyote and a variety of other wildlife.

On our return to Moss and Ingrid's farm, it was lovely to spend some time with my grandchildren, Nick, Kayleigh and Michael. Nick is engaged in the family farming business, Kayleigh is at university, and Michael was then in his last year at high school, now also at university.

Kayleigh and her fiancé, Mark Lee, have a beautiful little daughter, my great-granddaughter, called Isabelle. At that time she was only nine months old and it was a delight to watch her standing up and attempting to walk as well as trying to talk!

We want to say a big thank you again to all our family and friends who contributed to this wonderful holiday of a lifetime.

CREATING THIS BOOK TOGETHER

To my Wife and Editor Jean

When you read fifty years of my jottings
Then collected them all in a pile
When you had seen my attempts to write a book
You beamed with your wonderful smile.

"We're too old to create our own family
But I've got an idea," you said
"We'll collate all your verses and stories
And make a lovely big book instead!"

★   ★   ★

And so began nine months of collating and linking my stories and verses to create this book for browsers. All the unseen essentials in order to produce and publish a book have had to be dealt with. Trying to think of a title, celebrating my family years and the ups and downs of a lifetime all take time and consideration, so as not to upset anyone. In this way the book became semi-autobiographical. However, it is not just a compilation of my writings, but also an expression of my immense gratitude to all who have enriched my life along the way – too many people to include by name. We hope those who know Jean and me, and those who do not know us, will enjoy what we have to say.

In conclusion I can emphatically confirm that without the enthusiasm, diligence and application of Jean, our book would not have been published in my lifetime. If ever a man was truly lucky in finding a "gem" like Jean, then I am he. So long as health permits we have proved that with a youthful spirit and determination, hope springs eternal.

The internet is a mixed blessing for humanity but the magic of the internet has truly blessed Jean and me. If this book encourages others to find happiness in this way then it will have been worthwhile. As in all things, we must proceed with caution and common sense. Then when you find a "gem", you must act decisively and sincerely so that the "Tide of Good Fortune" can run its course!

We are grateful to everyone who has made this possible. If you, the reader, have travelled this far with us: thank you too.

GLOSSARY
MAIN GLOSSARY OF DIALECT WORDS

Where known the origin of the word is shown by the following abbreviations:

Celt = Celtic
D = Danish
Gael = Gaelic
Ice = Icelandic
N = Norwegian
ON = Old Norse
OE = Old English
WS = West Saxon
F = Furness
C = Cumberland
W = Westmorland

Aboon = above
Aboot = about
A crack = a good talk or conversation
Afoor = before
Ahin or **ahint** = behind
Alain = alone
Ald = old
Allus = always
Amang = among
Angry = painful or inflamed (Ice)*angr*
Anudder = another
Ark = a chest, meal ark, the meal-chest (Ice) *örk*
Arn = own
Aroond = around
Arval = (adjective) anything connected with heirship or inheritance (Ice) *arfr*
Arval bread = cakes which each guest received at a funeral
Atween = between
Aw or **o'** = all

Ba-eth or **beath** or **beeath** = both
Baggin = food or provisions
Bairn or **barn** = a child; anything born (Ice) *barn*

Bane = bone
Barns or **bairns** = children
Bauk = Beam to support the roof of a house (Ice) *balkr* a beam, naval bulkhead
Be or **bi** = by
Beck (ON) *bekkr* = a river or stream
Bedivilled = bedevilled
Begat = begot
Begattings = generations
Behint = behind
Besom-stick = birch stick
Be-us = beasts or cows
Bid = to invite, bespeak attendance (Ice) *bjóða* – applied chiefly to marriage and funerals. The district within which all were invited to funerals was called a 'bidding'
Bigg = barley (Ice) *bygg*
Bigum = mild exclamation of surprise
Biken = biking
Blacken = to tell someone off
Black Nanny = the name for a kettle smoked black over the fire
Blaa = blow
Blaaen = blowing
Blarn = blown
Blea = lead coloured or blue (Ice) *blá*
Blest = blessed
Bobby = policeman
Boggle(s) = ghost(s) (ON and Celt)
Boo = bow
Borra = borrow
Bow en scrape = to pray
Brant = steep (ON) *brattr*
Brass = money
Brat = course apron – sackcloth (OE) *bratt*
Brossen = bursting with food
Browt = brought

Brutches = breeches
Bumly = bumble bee
Burra = burrow
Byre = shippen, shuppen or cow house (OE) *byre*

Cald = cold
Cam or **cam steeans** = wall topping stone(s) (ON) *kambr*
Canny = nice or considerable
Caps langcrown = is beyond belief or very puzzling
Causen = causing
Caw = call
Cem or **com** = came
Cem oot = came out
Chasser = a chaser was a defective male sheep much given to pursuing and annoying females; a man with a similar propensity towards women was so named
Chimley = chimney
Claggy = sticky (D) *kloeg*
Clapped = clapped out thin
Clarty = muddy, sticky, unclean
Clashy = blustery or showery
Clayuths = clothes
Clegg = a cleg or horsefly (Ice) *kleggi*
Clim = climb
Closet = toilet (usually outside)
Clowt = clout
Com = come
Commen = coming
Coo = cow
Coo band = rope neck collar for tying up a cow
Coo-claps = firm dung of the cow
Coppy steal = three legged stool, milking stool (N) *kubbe stol*
Coves = calves
Cowle = to rake towards oneself
Cowle-rake = long-handled rake designed to pull manure from a horse-cart into heaps when spreading manure
Craa = crow

Crack or **good crack** = a chat, talk or good conversation
Cragfast = stuck on the ledge of a crag
Crag Quarter = North West Quarter of the Valley- See Index Ref. to Border Tenure & Kentmere Quarters.
Craks = cracks or fractures
Cravacked or **cravick't** = stiff-backed or stiff-jointed (WS)
Creaked = crooked
Creel = peat basket (ON) *krili*
Cum = come
Cursmas = Christmas
Cush cush = call to cows for milking (Ice) *kussa*

Dadder = to tremble or shake
Dadderam shakkem = jelly
Dalt or **dote** = a share in an open field
Dee = day
Deead = dead
Deed = died
Deet = to dress or make clean; hence: to winnow corn
Deeter tray = winnowing tray which shakes the grain from the husk within the thresher
Deftly = quietly, silently
Dess = to pile up in layers (Ice)
Deleet = delight
Donk = to moisten or wet, as rain does
Doo-er = door
Doon or **dean** = down
Doot = doubt
Dord-damn = an epithet borne of upset or frustration
Dote = don't
Dowly = lonesome or dull (ON/Ice) *daligr*
Dowter = daughter
Dross = grossness, unwholesomeness
Drush = druf (Sc) fall to pieces or fall down.
Du or **dew** = do
Dub = a deep pool (ON/Ice) *djupr*
Dunnet = do not or don't

Dyke = ditch or water-course or drainage channel

Easings = eaves (Ice) *efesan*
Eer = year
Efta or **efter** = after (ON) *eftir*
Elding = fire or fuel (ON/Ice)
'Em = them
En = and
Er = are and or
Eshes = ash trees
Esk or **ex** = ask

Fadder = father
Fa' or **foe** = to fall
Fain = glad, anxious, fully disposed, joyful, willing (ON) *feginn*
Fair = quite, really, completely
Falderment = useless things, finery
Fash! = Bother!
Fash or **fashment** = to worry or bother
Fasht = weary or fed up
Fassen = fasten
Feckless = feeble and incompetent
Fell = mountain (ON) *fjeld* (Ice) *fjall*
Fella = fellow
Fend = to provide or earn a living (Ice) *fe'na*
Fer = for
Fergit = forget
Fer sham o thisel = shame on you
Fettle = order, condition, to fit (Ice) *fella* (ON) *fitja*
Feyten = fighting
Flacker = flapping of wings
Flayt = frightened or nervous
Flee = fly
Flit = to remove from one house to another, as of household goods and chattels (Ice) *flytja*
Flooers = flowers
Force = a cascade or waterfall (Ice) *fors*
Forrad or **for'et** = forward
Forelders = ancestors, parents (Ice) *foreldri*
Fowt = fought
Fratchen = disputing and disagreeing

Fre = from
Freet = fright

Gaa = go
Gaily weel = very well
Gallasses = braces or suspenders
Gang = go or going
Gang = feeding passage or gangway between two rows of a skel-boose
Garburn = Garburn Pass from Kentmere to Troutbeck
Garn = go or going
Garn a' bullin = going with or taking a cow to the bull when it is on heat
Garth = an enclosure, generally used in compounds; a garden, also a small enclosed field close to the farmhouse (Ice) *garôr* (ON) *gardr*
Gat = got
Gate = a thoroughfare, a way (Ice) *gata*
Gaum = sense or forethought (Ice) *gaumr* heed or attention
Gay = rather, quite, somewhat
Gay happy = quite happy
Geal = to ache or tingle with cold, sudden pain
Gavelock or **geavlock** = steel crowbar
Generally what = usually
Gill or **ghyll** = small ravine, deep gully with stream (ON) *giel* (Ice) *gil*
Gimmer = female sheep under two years. Ewe lamb; a gimmer or ewe that has not lambed (Ice) *gymbr*
Giss giss giss = the call to young pigs (ON)
Giss or **griss** = a pig or swine (Ice) *gríss*
Git = get
Gitten = getting
Gloo-ered = looked around hard to see
God-fearen = God-fearing
Gowk = cuckoo (Ice) *gaukr*
Graa = grow
Granbarns = grandchildren
Grave = (verb) to dig or break up the soil (Ice) *grafa*
Grave peats = to dig peats
Greans = groans

Greeap or **greup** = channel where dung and urine is dropped by the cow in the shippen

Green Quarter = South East Quarter of the Valley

Gripe = dung or manure fork

Gris or **grise** = swine, young pigs (D)

Growen = growing

Grunded = grounded

Gurnen = pulling a face, grumbling, being miserable

Gurt = great, big

Guss = grass

Gussins = grassings or pastures

Hansom = handsome

Hap up = wrap up

Happen = perhaps

Happenen = happening

Har'd or **hard** = heard

Harnted = haunted

Hasky = a Lakeland dialect word meaning a sharp, frosty morning, clear and bright

Haver = oats (Ice) *hafrar*

Hay bay or hubbyshoo = a commotion, disturbance, uproar

Hay moo = haystack in the barn

Heafed or **hefted** = pasture on fell where sheep are born and return to (ON) *hefda*

Heaten = heating

Hebben = Heaven

Hed = had

Heead or **heed** = head

Hes = has

Hest = a horse (Ice) *hestr*

Hetta = have to

Hev = have

Hev a good crack = to have a good talk or gossip (OE)

Hezzel = hazel bush

Hey = high

Hinder pap = last teat

Hippins = baby's nappies

Hisk = gasp

Hoaf = half

Hod = hold

Hollow-belly = severe hunger

Hoo = how

Hoo-al = hole

Howe = small hill or knoll

Howk = to dig or scoop out

Hubbub = loud discourse

Hubby-shoo = a state of confusion; trouble or controversy; a commotion, affray or noisy gathering

Hurpled = lame, stiff, limping

Hurplen = limping, stiff with age

If you would = if you understand

Insteead = instead

Intacks = high pastures walled in from the fell

I'se = I'm, I am

Ivver = ever

Jike or **gike** = knock, creaking sound

Keisty = picky over food

Kekt or **Keckt** = tipped up

Keld = a well or spring (Ice) *kelda*

Ken = to know, be acquainted with (Ice) *kenna*

Kent = knew

Kessen = lying flat on back with legs in air – may be kicking or dead

Ket = dead meat, foul-smelling rubbish

Kine = cows

Kirk = church (Ice) *kirkja*

Kissened = burnt or overcooked

Kist = a chest (Ice) *kista*

Kittle = finely balanced, excitable

Knaa = know

Knott or **knot** = small, peaked hill

Kytle = a smock or loose jacket worn by farmers

Laa = low

Laa groond = low ground or bottom fields

Laik or lake = to play as children do, to amuse oneself (Ice) *leika*

Laiked = played
Laiken or **laiken aboot** = playing (ON) *leika*
Lait or **late** = to search for, to seek (ON) *leyta* (Ice) *leita*
Lang or **lang sen** = long or long ago
Langer (Ice) *lang* = longer
Lant = landed or arrived
Lan't back = landed back or came back
Larn = learn
Larnin = learning or study
Larnt = learned
Lathe = a barn (Ice) *hlaôa*
Laylick = lilac
Leak or **leuk** = look
Leak efter = to look after, care for
Leaven = leaving
Lee = a lie
Leead = lead
Leet = light
Leeved = lived
Leeven = leaving or living
Ligs = lies
Ligged = lain or lay
Liggen = lying down
Likesear = likewise
Lile = little, small
Lile lasses = little girls
Lish = agile
Loave! = exclamation of surprise or delight
Lonnin = green lane, path or road, country lane (ON) *leyna*
Lontered = loitered or dawdled
Loosed doon mi galasses = unfastened my braces
Louked = hit or struck
Loup or lowp = jump
Lowe = flame, blaze
Lownd = calm, still, quiet (ON) *logn*
Lowped = jumped
Lowse and **lowse oot** = release harness or yoke (ON) *laus*
Lowsen = to loosen, untie
Lug = ear

Maaen guss = mowing grass
Maanders = meanders
Maazled = amazed or puzzled
Mainly what = usually or most times
Maist = most
Maister = master
Makken = making
Macks or **maks** = makes, kinds or sorts
Mannished = **managed**
Mappen = **perhaps, maybe**
Maapment or marpment = silliness
Marra = friend
Mair or **mayer** or **mear** = more
Mart = market
Mebbe = maybe
Meckins = profits
Med = made
Meedas or **meeders** = meadows
Mekken = making
Mendit = mended
Menny = many
Merry neet = merry night: a social gathering of country people, usually involving a hot-pot supper, the drinking of good ale with volunteers singing, telling tales and reciting verses, the proceedings gently guided by a jovial MC
Mi = my
Mickle or **muckle** = large, much, great (Ice) *mikill*
Midden = heap of farmyard manure
Milk be-us = milk beasts or milk cows
Milken side = space between cow and rud-stake where there is room to sit to milk
Moidered = bothered or perplexed
Mon't = mustn't or must not
Mooan = moon
Mowdy or **mowdywarp** = mole
Mudder = mother
Mun gang = must go

Naybody = nobody
Neb = beak
Nebbers = neighbours

Neet = night
Ner = nor
Neuk = nook or corner
Nicked in t'heed = wrong in the head
Nin = none
Nobbut = only
Noo = now
Nowder = neither
Nowt = nothing
Nut = not

O = of
O' = all
O'er = over
Oor = our
Oot = out
Owt = anything

Pap = teat
Parlish = remarkable, wonderful, noteworthy, extraordinary
Physic = medicine
Piggin = a wooden drinking cup (Gael) *pigeon* – not the bird!
Pike = hill-top (ON) *picke*
Pill-dill = a happy gathering
Poapen = walking in the dark
Poddish = porridge
Pow = wooden pole
Prop't = propped up
Proven or **proggin** = animal food
Puddles = (verb) muddles or confuses
Pund = pound

Rannel boak or **baulk** = large beam running across chimney nook (Ice)
Rader or **rayder** = rather
Raken = wandering, roving about
Reddy = ready
Reean (F) rein or **rane (C & W)** = head-rigg or unploughed area
Red drench = animal medicine or tonic
Reek = smoke (Ice) *reykr*
Reet = right
Renart = fox (F) *renard*
Ridge = ridge (ON) *rigg*

Riggen or **riggin** = ridge of a house
Ring widdy = a ring swivel ring to which the cow band was attached
Rive = to rent or tear asunder, to pull or tug violently (Ice) *rifa*
Roards = roads
Roon or **roond** = round
Rough brat = apron made from sackcloth
Rowentree = rowan tree or mountain ash (Ice/ON)
Rud = red
Rud-stake = post to which cows are tethered in a byre
Runnen = running

Sae = so
Saggen = sagging or dropping
Sammel = gravel
Sang = song
Sark = a shirt (Ice) *serkr*
Sarra = to feed or serve animal stock
Sarra t'coves = feed or serve the calves
Sarved = served
Sayem or **seam** = same
Sayen = saying
Scale = Scale Farm
Scales = hut or farm (Ice) *skali*
Scrammelled = scrambled
Scrowe = a state of disorder, untidiness or confusion
Scrowe of barns = a large number of children
Se-an = soon
Se-an on = early on
Seanest = soonest
Seeves = rushes (Ice) *sef*
Segg = a hard callous place on the hand or foot (Ice) *sigg*
Sen = since
Settlestean = bed where cow lies down
Shaken or **shaken** = shaking
Shuppen or **shippen** or **shippon** = cow-house or byre (OE)
Sham = shame
Sheep lots = enclosed sheep fields

Shipperd = shepherd

Shoppen = shopping

Sick or sec = such

Sid = saw

Sike or **syke** = a small stream or gutter, a wet ditch or drain (Ice) *siki*

Sile = to strain milk

Sindens = last morsels

Skel-boose = cow stall for a pair of cows (ON) *skelja*, division

Skoggerslops = untidy person

Slaa = slow

Slape = slippery (Ice) *sleipr*

Sleck = to quench, to extinguish (Ice)

Smit = sheep mark (Ice)

Smithfield = Smithfield Cattle Show and market in London

Snaa = snow

Sneck and **sneck possit** = door latch and latch wedged shut to suitor

Sneck-lifter fee = entry fee or loan fee

Soart = sort

Somehoo = somehow

Soo-al = soul

Soond = sound

Sowk = squeeze

Sowked en eased ut ivvery pap = squeezed and eased milk by hand from every teat

Spane = to wean lambs from their mothers

Spar = spare

Sparra = sparrow

Spelk = splint, a splinter or slip of wood (Ice) *spelkr*

Springen = sharp shooting pain in foot

Stan = stand

Stang = a post pole or shaft of a cart (Ice) *stöng*

Stangin = on evenings of Christmas Day and New Year's Day revellers would mount those they met astride a stang and carry them to a pub and compel them to stand drinks all round. Also note: **Riding t'stang** = when a man or woman of the village committed adultery they would be carried from house to house on a stang in disgrace (Ice)

Starved = frozen

Stayvla-Gayt = old name for Staveley* (*ref: See Blezzard's Westmorland Songs published 1868)

Stee = a ladder (Ice) *stigi*

Steean or **stean** or **stane** = stone

Steg = a gander (Ice)

Stown = stolen

Streea = straw

Straw-walkers = mechanism in the front of the thresher that throws the straw on to the ground

Strutchen = stretching

Strutches = stretches

Sud = should

Summat = something

Sump = mire, puddle, midden (D)

Swardle(s) = Swaledale sheep

Sweltered = overcome with heat (Ice)

Ta = to

Taday = today

Tak = to take

Takken = taking

Tan = two

Taneet = tonight

Tarn = small mountain lake (Ice)

Taty-pot supper = meat, potatoes, carrots, peas, black pudding, etc.

Teamen = teaming or overflowing

Teck or **tek** = take

Teckins = takings or receipts of money

Tellen = telling

Telt = told

Than = then

Thi = thy

Thisel = thyself

Thoo = thou

Thoosen = thousand

Thowt = thought

Thrang = busy, working hard (ON/Ice)

Thur = there or their or they're

Thur's = there is

Toon = town

Thwaite = a field or clearing; a piece of land cut off by a fence or enclosed (ON) *thveit*

Thyvel = porridge stick, stirring stick (ON)

Ticker = heart

Toon = town

Trantlements = playthings, odds and ends

Trunlins = sheep droppings or muck

Tull = until or till or to

Turble = very

Turble grand folk = very pleasant folk

Turble laa watter = downhearted, depressed, not very well or under the weather

Turnip tops = turnip leaves

Twinter = sheep over two winters old

Udder = other

Ullet = owl

Ut = at

Varra = very

Wad or wud = would

Wain't = won't

Wake = weak

Wanten = wanting

War = were

Wark = work

Warnen = warning

Warse = worse

Wat = what

Watter = water

Wedder = weather

Weel = well

Wemly or **wemmly** = wobbly or unbalanced

Wha = who

Whar or **war** = where

Whativver = whatever

Whenivver = whenever

Whisht = quiet or silent; quietly or silently

"White side oot" = white lining out

White-weshed = white-washed in traditional Lakeland style

Wi or **wid** = with

Widoot = without

Winda = window

Wo' or **waa** = dry-stone field wall

Woddent = wouldn't

Wo-en = walling

Woes = walls

Woo = wool

Worrits = worries

Wrang = wrong

Ya or **Yaa** = an, one

Yak = oak

Yak Bob Day = 29th May when the sprig of an oak leaf is worn

Yam = home

Yan = one – See Shepherd's Tally

Yance = once

Yans = ones

Yansel = oneself

Yat or **yeat** = a gate

Yek = oak (Ice) *eik*

Yer = your

Yowe(s) = ewe(s), female sheep

My father's Kentmere version of the Shepherd's Tally; see also Garnett's *Westmorland Agriculture* (1800-1900), page 166

1 Yan	11 Yan-a-dick
2 Tyan	12 Tyan-a-dick
3 Tethera	13 Tether-a-dick
4 Methera	14 Mether-a-dick
5 Pimp	15 Bumfit
6 Sethera	16 Yan-a-bumfit
7 Lethera	17 Tyan-a-bumfit
8 Hovera	18 Tether-a-bumfit
9 Dovera	19 Mether-a-bumfit
10 Dick	20 Gigget or giggot

HOW MANY OF THESE WORDS
OR SAYINGS DO YOU KNOW ?

ON = Old Norse; OE = Old English; AS = Anglo-Saxon; Icel = Icelandic Old Norse;
WS = West Saxon; Dan = Danish; Fr = French; Celt = Celtic; Gael = Gaelic

WORD & ORIGIN of word where known . . . .   ANSWERS

1 BRANT   ON *brattr* . . . .   Steep

2 BRAT   OE *bratt* . . . .   Coarse apron made of sackcloth

3 BOGLE or BOGGLE   Celt *bwgwl* . . . .   Ghost

4 BYRE   ON *byr* . . . .   Cowshed

5 CAM   ON *kambr* . . . .   Wall topping stone

6 CLARTY . . . .   Muddy, sticky

7 CLAGGY   Dan *kloeg* . . . .   Sticky

8 COPPY-STEAL or COPPY_STOOL . . . .   Milking stool, small round stool

9 T'HEV A GOOD CRACK OE . . . .   To have a good talk or gossip

10 CRAVICK'T WS . . . .   Stiff in joints / muscles

11 CREEL   ON   *krili* . . . .   Peat basket

12 CUSH CUSH   Icel *kussa* Calling what? . . . . .   Cows

13 GIS GIS   ON *gris* Calling what? . . . .   Pigs

14 DUB   ON /Icel *djupr* . . . .   Deep pool

15 DOWLY   ON /Icel *daligr* . . . .   Lonesome or dull

16 EFTER   ON *eftir* . . . .   After

17 EASINGS   Icel *efesan* . . . .   Eaves

18. ELDIN   ON /Icel. . . . .   Fire or fuel

19 FASH or FASHMENT Fr *facher* . . . .   To worry or annoy

20 FELL   ON/Icel *fjall* . . . .   Mountain

21 FEND   Icel *fe'na* . . . .   To provide or earn a living

22 GILL or GHYLL   ON/Icel *gil*. . . . .   Ravine with stream

23 HAY-BAY or HUBBYSHOO Icel . . . .   A commotion

24 HEAF or HEFTED   ON *hefda* . . . .   Pasture on a fell where sheep are born and return to

25 LAIKING ABOOT   ON *leika* . . . .   Playing

26 LANG or LANG SEN Icel . . . .   Long or long ago

27 LAIT   ON *leyta* . . . .   To seek or search for

28 LONNIN   ON *leyna* . . . .   Lane

29 LOWSE – LOWSE OOT   *ON laus*. . . . .   Release e.g. horse from a harness

30 PIGGIN   Gael *pigeon* (not a bird) . . . .   Wooden drinking cup

31 RANNEL BAWK   AS *balca* . . . .   Cross beam running across the chimney nook

32 REEAN, REIN or RANE   ON *rein* . . . .   Unploughed land around a ploughed field

33 REEK ON *reykr* Icel *reykja*	Smoke
34 ROWAN TREE	Mountain ash
35 SARRA	To serve or feed animals
36 SCALE or SCALES ON/Icel *skali*	Hut or shed on a farm
37 SHIPPEN, SHIPPON or SHUPPON AS *seypen*	Cow house
38 SILE Icel *sile*	To strain milk
39 SKOGGERSLOPS	Untidy person
40 SLAPE ON *sleipr* Icel *sleipur*	Slippery
41 SLECK ON *slueyka*	To quench
42 SMIT AS *smitta*	Mark of ownership on a sheep
43 SNECK & SNECK POSSIT	Door latch & latch wedged shut to suitor
44 SPRINGEN OE *sprenge*	Throbbing, sharp shooting pain

45 STANG   ON *stang* .... On the evenings of Christmas Day and New Year's Day revellers would mount those they met astride a pole and carry them to a pub and compel them to stand drinks all round. Note also RIDING T'STANG: When a man or woman of the village committed adultery, they would be carried from house to house on a pole or plank in disgrace.

46 STEG ON *steagn*	Gander or young game cock
47 SUMP Dan *sump*	Mire, puddle, midden
48 SWELTERED AS *swaloth*	Overcome with heat
49 THYVEL ON *thyvel* AS *thyfel*	Porridge stick
50 TARN ON *tjorn*	Small lake
51 THRANG ON *thraungr*	Busy
52 THWAITE ON/Icel *thveit*	Field or clearing
53 YAK Icel *eik*	Oak
54 YAK BOB DAY	29th May-Royal Oak Day
55 YAT or YEAT AS *geat*	Gate

What is the meaning of these sayings?

56 *It's a case of lile clogs makken bigens run!*... Putative (suspected) father runs away!

57 *A lee is hauf way roon t'world afore t'truth gits its clogs on* ... A lie travels faster than the truth

58 *I'se gay watter shaken* .... I'm nearly incontinent of urine

59 *What he's that tight that he can nayder stand, sit ner hod bit guss!*... Drunk!

60 *He's gitten t' wrang pig be t'lug* ... He's got the wrong idea or there is a misunderstanding

Total number of correct answers: ......

Source LH Ref	Date - Year		LH CHRONOLOGY COMPILED TO INCLUDE TIMELINE OF THE VIKINGS AND THEIR INFLUENCE ON CUMBRIA CIRCA 800 – 1250 AD
Pitkin Celts	c. 300 BC		Celts in England were creating mirrors, weapons and horse harness in La Tene style
Pitkin Celts	c. 55 BC		England found Celts ready for battle with Roman invaders
Oxford Eng Ref. Dict	55 – 54 BC	Julius Caesar tried to conquer England	England was twice invaded briefly, but not conquered, by Julius Caesar
	43 – 400 AD	Britain part of the Roman Empire	England was quickly conquered in 43 AD by Roman emperor, Tiberius Claudius, as far north as Fosse Way and eventually the frontier of the Roman province of Britain at Hadrian's Wall. Romans built and developed cities of London, York, Lincoln, St Albans, Chester and Colchester, etc.
Vik. Enc. JH	1 – 400 AD	Southern Scandinavia	Warrior aristocracy emerged and kingdoms began to develop in Denmark, Norway & Sweden
WR	78 – 84 AD	Gnaeus Julius Agricola	Roman general and governor of Britain
	122 AD	Hadrian's Wall begun	Built after emperor Hadrian's visit to defend province of Britain from invasions from the north
WR	197 AD	Hadrian's Wall breached	Claudius Albinus took most of garrison away
	c. 300 AD	Hadrian's Wall breached	But was re-built by Constantius Cholorius about 300 AD
	c. 300 AD	St Anthony – Christian Egyptian	Went into desert as a hermit to devote himself to prayer. Founded first community of follower monks
	367 AD	Hadrian's Wall breached	"Barbarian conspiracy" of Picts, Scots and Saxons
Barrow Library	c. 397 AD	St Ninian	St Ninian brings Christianity to south-west Scotland and Cumbria. Founded church at Whithorn
MacS p.12	400 – 550 AD	Early Iron Age	Scandinavians all spoke the same language
	400 – 800 AD	Dark Ages	So called because time of relative obscurity. Foundation of Christian monasteries kept scholarship alive
WR .p32	410 AD	Romans leave	Emperor Honorius, powerless to help, rejected British request for aid against "barbarians"
Vik. Enc. JH	c. 425 – 500 AD	Anglo-Saxon migrations	From Denmark and Germany to Britain
	Mid-5th century	St Patrick to soldiers	Of Romano-British parentage Patrick was captured by raiders and taken to Ireland. He condemned them and Coroticus for trafficking in Christian slaves. In Ireland was converted to Christianity. Escaped to Gaul
	5th century AD		Kingdom of Rheghed emerged in the North West between the Solway and Duddon
	c. 518 – 603 AD	St Kentigern, also known as St Mungo	Celtic saint. Founded monastery at Cathures (now Glasgow). In 543 AD was consecrated Bishop of Cumbria. Buried in Glasgow Cathedral, which is named after him as St Mungo's
	Mid 5th century	St Patrick ordained	After 6 years in Gaul, St Patrick returned to Ireland. Founded archiepiscopal of Armagh in about 454 AD
	550 – 1050 AD	Later Iron Age	West Scandinavia spoke Norwegian and Icelandic. East spoke Danish and Swedish
Eng H	563 AD	St Columba, Irish missionary	Founded monastery on Iona. Converted the Picts to Christianity. Died in 597 AD
WR p.33	574 AD	Siege of Lindisfarne	Island of Lindisfarne, then held by Angles, was put to siege by King Urien of Rheghed

WR p.57	593 - 616 AD	King Aethelfrith	Powerful King of Northumbria at this time
	597 AD	St Augustine landed in Kent	St Augustine landed in Kent with a group of monks sent by Pope Gregory the Great – made headquarters in Canterbury. Christianity first comes to Anglo-Saxon England
MacS p.32	600 – 700 AD	Norse developments	The Norse were developing improved tillage and methods of farming. There was improved iron production and weaponry. Shipbuilding methods improved with better design and clinker-built – using shaped, riven timber
JGC p.36-39	600 – 700 AD	Norse ships and shipbuilding	For design and sizes see "The Viking World" by James Graham-Campbell
	? – 651 AD	St Aidan's year of birth unknown	Monk from Iona. Summoned by King Oswald of Northumbria to evangelise the North. Founded monastery on island of Lindisfarne and became its first bishop
Kings & Queens	600 – 871 AD	Early Saxon Kings	Divided England into 7 kingships – Kent, Sussex, Essex, East Anglia, Wessex, Mercia and Northumbria
F Barnes Barrow Library	613 AD	Lancashire South Ribble	Area was wrested from Strathclyde, then 70 years struggle between English of Northumbria and Britons of Strathclyde
WR p.57	615 AD	Battle of Chester	King Aethelfrith and Angles of Northumbria forced wedge between the Cymry of Wales and the Cymry of Cumbria and thereby the Celts were driven out
	627 AD	King Edwin of Northumbria	Mightiest ruler was baptised by Paulinus (a Roman missionary) in 627 AD
	633 AD	King Edwin killed	Cadwalla of Gwynedd and pagan nobleman Penda defeated and killed King Edwin. Paulinus fled
	634 AD	Cadwalla defeated	Oswald, having spent time in exile on Iona, defeated Cadwalla and became ruler of Northumbria.
	c. 635 – 687 AD	St Cuthbert, English missionary	Journeyed all over north of England. Bishop of Hexham and Lindisfarne from 684 AD. Died on Farne Island
	642 AD	Oswald defeated and killed	By Penda – Bede says Penda devastated Northumbria
Eng Heritage	655 ADD	Battle of Winwaed	Oswy defeats Penda. Oswy is Oswald's brother and became King of Northumbria
Eng Heritage	657 AD	Whitby Abbey	King Oswy founded monastery at Whitby – mixed men and women. Abbess Hilda is Abbess of Whitby (Abbey later attacked by Vikings in 867 AD)
Eng H	680 AD	Bede joined Jarrow monks	St Bede became monk, historian, teacher and writer – "A History of the English Church and People"
F Barnes	684 AD	Carlisle burned	Carlisle burned and all East Cumberland submitted to Ecgfrith, King of Northumbria
WR p.57	685 AD	Anglian control of best land	King Ecgfrith of Northumbria granted Carlisle and 15 miles around to St Cuthbert together with Cartmel "et omnes Brittanos cum eo" – together with its British inhabitants. King Ecgfrith was defeated and killed by Picts at the Battle of Nechtansmere in Scotland.
Tullie House	685 AD	St Cuthbert	Visited Carlisle. Cuthbert journeyed far and wide, preaching as he walked
	Pre 700 AD	Norway in several kingdoms	Consolidation under King Harald Fairhair (formerly Harald Thickhair) 872 - 930 AD
Eng H	700 – 1100 AD	St Benedict's teaching	Teachings from his Abbey in Monte Casino, Italy, became popular in monasteries
DK Kings	731 AD	Bede	Bede completes writing his "Ecclesiastical History of the English People"
RF p.84	741 – 829 AD	Royal Frankish Annals	Chronicle events of Frankish rulers and Viking attacks

V Encl	c. 750 AD	Russia	Swedish Vikings established at Staraja Ladoga, Russia
MacS	750 – 800 AD	Earliest Vikings raids	Raids on Ireland at first were sporadic and confined to coastline
MDS	c. 760 AD	Anglian invasion	See MDS map
RW p.67	787 AD	Anglo Saxon Chronicle	King Beorhtric took Eadburgh, King Olaf's daughter to wife. Northmen from Hordaland (Danes) killed the King's Reeve
V Encl	c. 789 AD	Norwegian Vikings	Sack Portland in Wessex
MacS	793 AD	Raid on Lindisfarne	Also raids on Jarrow – these were Danish Vikings. Viking raids on Lindisfarne, Jarrow and Iona had devastating effect on the monastery system
RF p.70-73	795 AD	Raid on Iona	Viking longships arrived – ransacked the monastery (reference: Annals of Ulster)
RF p85	799 AD	Raid on Noirmoutier-Loire	First Viking raid. Charlemagne (Charles the Great of Franks) built ships to defend rivers
	c. 800 AD	Vikings settle	Vikings settled on Shetland and Orkney
	802 AD	Second raid on Iona	
	806 & 807 AD	Further raids on Iona	After these raids the remaining monks moved to safer refuge at Kells in Ireland
DMW p.23	807 AD	Monastery at Kells in Ireland	New Columban monastery founded at Kells in County Meath. Book of Kells written by monks in 8th or early 9th century
V Enc	825 AD	Faeroe Islands	Irish monks driven out of Faeroe Islands
V Enc	c. 825 AD	First Scandinavian coins	Hedeby was first town in Scandinavia to have a regular mint
	830s & 840s AD	Viking attacks	Viking attacks increase in southern England
RF p.9 & 10	c. 830 AD	Gokstad ship (excavated 1900)	Graveship unearthed at Sandar, Vestfold – see Prof Holck's findings (Oslo Anatomy Dept) 2007
RF & JGC	834 AD	Oseberg ship (excavated 1904)	Oseberg ship in Slagan in Vestfold – built from trees felled in 820 AD. Both ships in Bygdoy Museum, Oslo
	837 AD	Vikings invade deeper into Ireland	60 ships in River Liffey and 60 ships in River Boyne
	838 AD	Battle of Hingston Down	Egbert, king of Wessex, defeated a joint Viking-Cornish army
RF p.104	840 AD onwards	Paris attacked	Paris under constant attack by Vikings. First Danegeld paid by Franks
Vik. Enc. JH	841 AD	Dublin area	First Norse fortified settlements. Dublin became Viking raiding base and slave market
	850	Winter quarters	Danes began to overwinter in England, at first on island of Thanet
	851 AD	Danes seized Dublin	
	853 AD	Norwegians defeated Danes	Established mixed Norse kingdom in Dublin under Olaf, son of king of Laithlinde in western Norway
MDS	c. 850 – 900 AD	Ribblesdale Farmstead	See MDS sketch
S Dickinson	8th to 9th Cent	Bryants Gill Kentmere	Viking Longhouse excavated in 1985. Spinning whorls & wetstones found. Radiocarbon dated to 8th-9th century
	860 AD	Iceland discovered	Explorers find Iceland which they settle in 870s AD
Vik. Enc. JH	c. 860 AD	Kiev seized	Kiev, fortified Slav settlement, seized by Swedish (Rus) leaders, Askald and Dir

Source	Date	Event	Description
	865 AD	Great Viking army	Viking army from Denmark under command of brothers, Halfdan and Ingvar, attacked Britain
JGC	865 AD	Danegeld in England	First payment of Danegeld recorded. For the promise of peace the people of Kent paid the Vikings money
	865 Ad	East Anglia invaded by Vikings	The East Angles "made peace" with the great army (*Anglo-Saxon Chronicle* records)
	866 AD	Danish Vikings	Danish Vikings under Halfdan captured York and placed a puppet Anglo-Saxon king on throne of Northumbria. York became capital of Viking northern England between rivers Humber and Tees
WR p.60	867 AD	Luel - City of Carlisle sacked	An army under Halfdan the Dane overthrew and destroyed Carlisle (*Anglo-Saxon Chronicle*) but see "*The Making of Carlisle*" p.86
Eng Her bk	867 AD	Whitby Abbey	Whitby Abbey destroyed by Danish Vikings (Whitby Abbey was founded in 657 AD)
RW p.73-74	870 AD	Vikings controlled Firth of Clyde	Vikings plundered into Cumbria. In Norway, Harald Thickhair (later called Harald Fairhair) set about subjugation of all Norway – became King and plundered Hebrides – very powerful
Vik. Enc. JH	870 – 871 AD	Olaf plundered Dumbarton	Olaf, King of Dublin, probably killed whilst raiding Scotland, or maybe when returned to Norway. Ivar Imhar became king and his descendants until 1034 AD
Vik. Enc. JH	871 AD	Alfred became King of Wessex	Eventually became leader of all the English not under Danish rule. Responsible for beginning the *Anglo-Saxon Chronicle*. His reign marked the start of a national KINGSHIP
	872 – 930 AD	King Harald Fairhair	In Norway, King Harald Fairhair consolidated the small kingdoms and is credited with unifying Norway but many fled. It is believed this added to the migration to the Western Isles and southwards.
Ang. Sax Chro	873 – 874 AD	Viking winter camp in Repton	Great army earthworks and burial of coins found in Derbyshire - verified date of fort in *Ang-Saxon Chron.*
Ang Sax Chron	875 AD	Danish leader Halfdan	Halfdan attacked Carlisle and laid it waste
	877 AD	Halfdan died	Halfdan was probably killed in Ireland – disappeared from records
RF	885 AD	Siege of Paris	Danes under command of Sigfrid besieged Paris for 8 months but were driven away by the Franks
JGC p.27	886 AD	Treaty with King Alfred	Treaty with King Alfred settled extent of Danelaw – line from Chester to North London. He now controlled River Thames to prevent Viking port of entry into England
F.Barnes P18	c. 895 - 900 AD	King Harald Fairhair	Harald Fairhair purged Norse settlers in Isle of Man who fled for refuge to Cumberland and Lancashire
BJNE p.60	899 AD	King Alfred's reign ceased	King Alfred died. Acquired his title "the Great" in 16th century: only English king to be so distinguished
BJNE	899 – 905 AD	Cuerdale hoard found in 1840 on bank of Ribble near Preston	Anglo-Saxon coins of this period included – thought to be connected with Norse expulsion from Dublin in 902 AD. Large quantity of silver and some coins minted in York as well as Arabic coins
Tullie House	9th century	Ormside in Cumbria	Viking sword and shield boss found buried in Ormside churchyard in 1898
DMW	Late 9th /10th	Balladoole, Isle of Man	Boat burial excavated by Gerard Bersu in 1940s revealing much more information about

Source	Date	Event	Description
DMW p.43	century	Aspatria, Cumbria	people who lived on Isle of man in the Viking age. DMW refers to lost ornaments from Viking age burial mound at Aspatria (See Edwards BJN, 1992)
Sedgef.Int. xiv	Pre-900 AD	Norse settlement in Cumbria	Frequent use of word "beck" which was in use in Norway pre-874 AD and pre-colonisation of Iceland
	c. 900 AD	Greenland discovered	Vikings from Iceland discovered Greenland
RF p.9	c. 900 AD	Tune Ship (excavated 1867)	First graveship unearthed at Rolvsoy in Ostfold, south east Norway – man, horse, sword, spears and saddle
Barrow Library	c. 900 AD	Tunwini Cross – Anglian	Found in 1911 in Urswick, south Cumbria
Sedgefield	Early 10th century	Mixed pop. of Britons and Angles	In early 10th century Cumbria was under Welsh kings and part of Strathclyde
	900 – 943 AD	King Constantine II of Alba	During his reign he fought Vikings and the English. Abdicated and retired to a monastery after 43 years
V Atlas. JH	902 AD	Irish expel Dublin Vikings	Influx of Norse-Irish settlers to northern England. Some settle in Cumbria
	911 AD	Normandy treaty	Charles the Simple settled Normandy on Viking leader Rollo. Rollo was baptised in 912 and the Vikings established themselves and remained there, becoming assimilated to French culture and language
V Enc. JH	917 AD	Vikings recaptured Dublin	The Norse led by King Sihtric Caech held Dublin and briefly became power to be reckoned with in York
V Enc. JH	924 – 939 AD	Athelstan, King of all England	First Anglo-Saxon king of whole of England, son of Edward the Elder, King of Essex.
	927 AD	York seized from Vikings	When Sihtric Caech died, King Athelstan seized York and marched into south-west Cumbria, so completing West Sussex take-over of England and becoming King of all England (except north Cumbria)
MDS	c. 930 AD	Norse people arrived in Lakeland	Fleeing "en masse" from the Isle of Man
	934 AD	Olaf, son of Guthfrith	Became King of Dublin ready to avenge his father's expulsion from York by Athelstan. Olaf allied himself with King Constantine II of the Scots, whose lands had been ravaged by Athelstan. They also joined with King Owain the Bald of the Strathclyde Britons. This formidable alliance aimed to bring down Athelstan and invaded England.
Enc Vik. JH S. Harding Viking Mersey	937 AD	Battle of Brunanburh	Thought to be near Bromborough on the Wirral – note conflicting claims as to site of battle. Crushing victory by King Athelstan over coalition of Dublin Vikings, Scots and Britons of Strathclyde. Britons were led by Olaf Guthfrithson of Dublin – purpose: to kerb Athelstan and recapture York but they failed
	939 AD	Athelstan died	He never married. Succeeded by his half-brother, Edmund. Norse army took York soon after
Eng H p.34	940 AD	Rebirth of English Monasteries	King Edmund I made Dunstan Abbot of Glastonbury – revival spread and 100 monasteries established
	943 – 54 AD	Malcolm I, King of Scotland	
Sedgefield	945 AD	Cumbria laid waste	English King Edmund granted Cumbria to Malcolm I, King of Scotland, on tenure of

xi			military service
MDS	945 AD	Scottish border then	See MDS map
V Enc. JH	946 AD	Edmund died	Murdered by an exiled criminal. Succeeded by his brother Eadred (King of England 946 –955 AD)
	946 – 966 AD	Short reigns by English kings	Accompanied by discontinuance of Viking activity but Cumbria seems to have been in Norse hands
RW p81	c. 954 AD	Eric Bloodaxe killed. He was also King of Norway c. 930 – 936 AD	Eric Bloodaxe (son of Harald Fairhair), last Viking King of York from 948 AD, was killed in an ambush at Stainmore in Yorkshire. With Erik's death, Northumbria was brought permanently into England by Eadred
MDS	c. 960 AD	Gosforth Cross, Cumbria	Carved scenes from life of Christ and from pagan Norse mythology in Irish monastic design
RF	978 – 1016 AD	Aethelred the Unready	Aethelred II as King of England was a competent ruler and skilled administrator
V Atlas. JH	980 AD	Viking raids recommence	England under Aethelred faced repeated well-organised attacks and paid larger and larger amounts of Danegeld. Aethelred was no warrior and failed to give his forces decisive leadership
	991 and 994 AD	King Olaf Tryggvasson of Norway	Attacked England but was bought off each time with Danegeld. Promised Aethelred never to attack again
RF	1000 AD	Cumberland	Aethelred marched north to Cumberland "and laid waste very nearly the whole of it" (Anglo-Sax. Chron.)
Tullie House	10th century	Cumwhitton finds in Cumbria	Norse cross still being investigated. In 2004 six Viking graves found, buried east to west – may indicate those buried were on cusp of conversion to Christianity but they were buried with their weapons
RH p.53	10th century	Hesket-in-the-Forest, Cumbria	Site of a cremation burial found in 1822. Contained Viking collection of objects including a sword, two spearheads, an axe-head, shield boss, spurs, a whetstone, antler comb, horse bit, various buckles, etc.
BJNE	Undated	Kentmere, Cumbria	Two Viking spearheads found in Kentmere in 1942; now in Kendal museum
BJNE	Undated	Esthwaite, Cumbria	Esthwaite and Lancaster Viking spearheads in Lancaster Museum
BJNE	Undated	Nan Bield Pass, Kentmere, Cumbria	Viking spearhead found on Nan Bield Pass
BJNE	Undated	Ormside churchyard, Cumbria	Shield boss found on grave dig in 1898 plus skeleton and small knife and sword (4m SSW of Appleby)
BJNE	Undated	Orton Scar, Cumbria	Brooch found in crevice on Orton Scar in 1847
BJNE	Undated	Bryants Gill, Kentmere, Cumbria	Viking farmstead site found in 1985 by S. Dickinson and team. They found whetstones and spindle whorls
JGC		Plan of Norse Settlement	See plan which shows settlement of Norse – Vikings in pink including Shetlands, Orkney, Ross, Hebrides, Iona, Jura, Islay, Kintyre, Coast of Northern Ireland, Larne, Dublin area, Coastal area of Galloway, Cumbria, Lancashire and Cheshire. The Danelaw. The Dane law occupied area with York. The capital is shown in yellow on the east of the Pennines stretching south from Jarrow to North London bounded by the King Alfred 886 AD treaty line, Chester to London
JGC p.157	Undated	Bridekirk Church font,	Has a line of Norse runes

Reference	Date	Event	Description
JGC p.181	Undated	Cumbria Thor Fishing Stone at Gosforth	Gosforth stone with Thor fishing – similar story found on stone at Altuna in Sweden
V Enc. JH	1013 AD	Danish King Svein Forkbeard	Aethelred fled to Normandy when Svein Forkbeard invaded. Svein was King of England for only 5 weeks
	1014 AD	Death of Svein Forkbeard	Aethelred invited back to England and drove out Cnut, son of Svein, back to Denmark
SP p.103	1014 AD	Battle of Clontarf, near Dublin	Celtic Irish fought a great battle against Vikings but it had no long-term consequences
	1015 – 1028 AD	King Olaf Haraldsson of Norway	Forced Christianity on Norway but was forced into exile in Russia in 1028
V Enc. JH	1016 AD	King Edmund Ironside	Became King of England on his father Aethelred's death. Edmund died in the same year
SP p.178	1016 – 35 AD	King Cnut (Canute, Knut or Knud)	Cnut assumed Kingship of England as well as of Denmark and Norway. Taxed the English heavily but was remembered as a just and pious ruler. In 1028 AD he added Norway to his dominions and by 1030 AD was overlord of Sweden also
V Enc. JH	1030 AD	King Olaf Haraldsson of Norway	Died at Battle of Stiklestad trying to win back his throne. Became patron saint of Norway in 12th century
Wiki Int	1035 - 1047 AD	Magnus the Good, King of Norway	Magnus was the son of Olaf, who in turn was succeeded by King Harold Hardrada (Hard Ruler) in Norway
V Enc. JH	1035 AD	Harold Harefoot, King of England	Harold Harefoot, illegitimate son of Cnut, usurped the throne from his half-brother, Harthacnut, the rightful heir and died in London in 1040 AD
	1040 AD	Harthacnut acceded to throne	Died in 1042 AD and was succeeded by Edward the Confessor, son of Aethelred II
V Enc. JH	1042 AD	End of Danish rule in England	With death of Harthacnut
	1052 AD	Last independent King of Dublin	Expelled by Dairmait
	1066 AD	Battle of Stamford Bridge	The last great Viking leader, Norwegian King Harald Hardrada (Hard Ruler,) invaded England to claim the English throne after Edward the Confessor had died. He was killed and his army routed by King Harold Godwinson at Battle of Stamford Bridge
	1066 AD	Battle of Hastings	King Harold marched army to Hastings (3 weeks after Stamford Bridge). English King Harold was killed at Battle of Hastings by William of Normandy, who had a claim on the English throne. Note: the Normans were originally Vikings who settled in north-west France in the early 10th century
Chron of Man	1070 AD	England ravaged to Cleveland	By Malcolm III Canmore, King of Scotland (1058 – 1093)
	1075 AD	Last Danish invasion of England	After several attempts.
	1085 AD & 1086.	William I, King of England - Commissioned the Domesday Book Christmas 1085	Manorial system and Domesday Book survey imposed – In Cumbria: Only Bootle, Millom, Kirksanton and Witham appear in Cumberland. In Westmorland only Kendal, Levens, Barbon, Beetham, Bothelford (lost in Helsington), Burton, Casterton, Dalton Old Hall, Farlton, Helsington, Heversham, Hincaster, Holme, Hutton Roof, Kirkby Lonsdale, Lupton, Mansergh, Middleton, Mint, Old Hutton, Patton, Preston(now

VIKING TIMELINE 473

Source	Date	Event	Description
MDS	1080 AD	Scottish border has moved	Preston Patrick), Stainton and Strickland appear. See MDS map
	1087 – 1100 AD	King William II, William Rufus	William Rufus became King of England after his father, William I, died
	1093 AD	Battle of Alnwick	Malcolm III Canmore, King of Scotland, killed whilst invading Northumberland
Sedgef Int xii	1097 AD	King William Rufus at Carlisle	William Rufus drove out Dolfin and made Carlisle part of English kingdom
V Enc. JH	1098 – 1103 AD	King Magnus III "Barelegs" of Norway	Led last major Viking expeditions in Irish Sea. Established direct royal control over Orkney and the Isle of Man and ravaged the Western Isles of Scotland but spared Iona. Basing himself on Isle of Man, he went on to capture Dublin and exacted tribute in Galloway and Anglesey. He defeated Norman earls, Hugh of Chester and Hugh of Shrewsbury. He was killed in a skirmish in northern Ireland in 1103
WR p.47	1106 – 1112 AD	Wetheral Priory, Cumbria	Ranulph de Meschines established Benedictine Priory
WR p47	1120 AD	St Bees, west Cumbria	Ranulph de Meschines' brother William, Lord of Copeland, founded St Bees as a Benedictine priory
WR p47	1122 or 1123 AD	Augustinian house, Carlisle	Thought to be founded by King Henry 1
WR p47	1127 AD	Abbey of St Mary of Furness	Founded by King Henry's nephew, Stephen, Count of Boulogne – later to become King Stephen
WR p47	c. 1134 AD	Rushen Abbey, Isle of Man	Rushen Cistercian Abbey is founded by Furness Abbey
WR p47	c. 1134 AD	Calder Abbey, west Cumbria	Established as daughter abbey of Furness Abbey in Calder Valley
WR p47	1150 AD	Holm Cultram Abbey, Cumbria	Cumberland was part of Scotland at this time and the abbey was founded by Prince Henry, son of King David I of Scotland. Holm Cultram was founded as a daughter abbey of Melrose Abbey in Roxburghshire
WR p47	1166 AD	Lanercost Priory, Cumbria	Augustinian priory established by Robert de Vaux, Lord of Gilsland
V Atlas. JH	1170 AD	Anglo-Normans take Dublin	
R McD	1176 AD	Cardinal Vivian visits Isle of Man	Caused King Gudrodd of Isle of Man to marry Olafr's mother
R McD	1187 AD	St Patrick's Isle, Peel, Isle of Man	Rognvaldr's father, Godredr Olafsson, died here in 1187 AD
R McD p70	1187 AD	Gudrodr Olafsson died	Buried in Iona – Olaf only 12 years old – Isle of Man people ask Rognvaldr (Reginald) to be King
R McD	1187 – 1229 AD	Internecine War	Between King Rognvaldr and his brother Olaf over Kingship of Isle of Man
WR p47	c. 1199 AD	Shap Abbey built	Premonstratensian house – originally to be at Preston Patrick but Thomas, son of Gospatrick, moved the community to Shap – Shap Abbey owned land on fells, east of Ullswater
	1204 AD	King John of England	Lost Normandy
R McD p129	1205 – 1210 AD	Visits to England	Rognvaldr visited King John. Rognvaldr got grants of land in Lancashire

Source	Date	Event	Description
R McD p17	1212 AD	King John of England	Received homage and fealty from King Rognvaldr of Isle of Man at Lambeth
	1215 AD	Magna Carta	English King John seals the Magna Carta giving power to the barons
R McD	1223 AD	Olaf killed Rognvaldr's son	Captured at St Columba's Isle – Skye and mutilated by Olaf
R McD	1229 AD	Holm Cultram Abbey	Rognvaldr granted fishing rights round Isle of Man to the Abbey
R McD	1229 AD	King Rognvaldr burned Olaf's ships	Night time raid by King Rognvaldr and killed nobles on St Patrick's Isle, Peel, Isle of Man
R McD	1229 AD	King Rognvaldr of Isle of Man	Rognvaldr (Reginald) buried at Furness Abbey – killed by his step brother Olaf on 14th February 1229
R McD	1229 AD	St Bees Abbey	Olaf granted licence to purchase 60 head of cattle or equivalent
R McD	1237 AD	Olaf, Rognvaldr's brother	Buried at Rushen Castle, Castletown, Isle of Man
	1237 AD	Treaty of York	The frontier question between England and Scotland was settled by Treaty of York to run between the Solway Firth in west and the mouth of River Tweed in east
KH	1263 AD	Battle of Largs in Scotland	Norwegian fleet, led by King Haakon of Norway, was defeated (mainly by weather) and Haakon died later of illness on Orkney
R McD	1265 AD	Castle Rushen, Castletown	Last King of Isle of Man, Magnus Olafsson, died here in 1265 AD
KH	1266	Treaty of Perth	The treaty ceded the Western Isles by Haakon's successor, Magnus VI of Norway, to the Scottish Crown for a payment of 4000 marks over the next 4 years with an annual sum of 100 marks to be paid to Norway in perpetuity. This ended the Norwegian control of Scotland and the Western Isles
R McD	1292 AD	Isle of Man under English control	Lead mining in the Calf of Man
	1397 – 1814 AD		Norway was under Danish rule which affected the Old Norse language. The Icelandic language is consequently nearer to Cumbrian dialect words
	1539 AD	Whitby Abbey on east coast	Suppressed by King Henry VIII
Shap LHS	1540 AD	Shap Abbey, Cumbria	Abbey was surrendered to commissioners for the Dissolution of the Monasteries on 14th January 1540

MERCHANTMEN
Trade & towns

he image of a Viking as a trader rather than a raider may be unfamiliar, but the achievements of the Vikings in this sphere are among their most dramatic and enduring. Piracy was all very well, but could scarcely ensure a regular income of the kind that might be had, for instance, by supplying the Arabs with slaves in exchange for their excess wealth of silver.

The first small trading centres in Scandinavia had been established before the ninth century, but with the great growth in trade during the Viking Age larger towns came into being. Many were royal foundations such as Hedeby in Denmark and Bergen in Norway, for the Scandinavian kings were naturally anxious to control trade, since taxation of merchants produced a substantial revenue.

Trade around the Baltic had been stimulated by the establishment of Swedish settle-

VIKING TRADERS
Viking merchants travelling along the great Russian rivers penetrated far to the east. Here they joined the international caravan routes and met foreign traders with goods from such distant countries as China and Persia. In the West other Vikings traded with England and the Frankish Empire.

▬▬▬
Viking sea and river routes

▬▬ ▬▬ ▬▬
land routes used by the Vikings

▬▬▬
international trade routes

Figure 8.9. Map of Viking Merchantmen – Trade and Towns. © James Graham-Campbell and Francis Lincoln Ltd.

KENTMERE TARN APPENDIX

Part One

Diatoms of the Kentmere Diatomite Deposits

JOHN CLEGG

Windrush, Carter Road, Grange-over-Sands, Cumbria, LA11 7AG

ELIZABETH Y. HAWORTH

Freshwater Biological Association, Far Sawrey, Ambleside, Cumbria, LA11 0LP

Summary

Kentmere, Cumbria, was the site of the only industrial diatomite deposit in England; dredging ceased there in 1977. The diatom-rich material is part of the sediment accumulated on the bed of a small lake formed at the end of the last ice-age. This forms part of the environmental record of the lake and its catchment. A list of the diatom taxa is included.

Introduction

THE MAIN deposits of diatomaceous earth, or diatomite, were formed under marine conditions during Miocene times, 35 to 15 million years ago, but after subsequent earth movements they now exist as hard rock-like material on land, often overlaid by lava, volcanic rock or other geological formations. Among the largest are the Californian deposits which exceed 1,000 feet in thickness and cover a very wide area. Large deposits also occur in Germany, Algeria and Kenya.

Diatomites have also accumulated at other times in both marine and freshwaters, e.g. the fossil deposits in the French Massif Central. Microscope slides of diatomaceous earth from Richmond, Virginia and Bermuda occur in most old collections of slides and are prized for the variety and beauty of the diatoms they include.

It has been estimated that a single cubic inch of diatomite contains between 40 million and 70 million diatom frustules or fragments. When dry the substance usually resembles a greyish chalk but it is much lighter in weight and more porous. Its properties of chemical inertness, low thermal conductivity and porosity have made it an important commercial commodity and it is sold as sawn blocks, as a powder and as a crushed aggregate.

Its main uses are as a filtering medium, especially for sugar refining and in the clarification of beer and other fermented liquor. Another important use is for insulation for furnaces, ovens, boilers, refrigerators and in sound-proofing. As a mild abrasive it has been used in metal polishes and toothpastes.

The ability of diatomite to absorb substances led to its use in two very different fields: to absorb the nitroglycerine in the original form of dynamite, thus making it safer; and to carry the essential pigments and perfumes in face powders.

The Kentmere Diatomite

The only freshwater deposits of diatomite that have been exploited commercially in England have been those in Kentmere, eight miles north of Kendal in Cumbria. The original lake, Kent Mere, receiving the waters of the river Kent which rises in the High Street fells, was formed behind a dam of moraines deposited during the retreat of the glacier which occupied the valley in the closing stage of the Ice Ages. A peculiar feature which bears on the purity of the diatomite deposit was the presence, a little above the main Kent Mere, of another lake basin also formed behind moraines which marked a later stage in the retreat of the glacier. Sediment brought down by the river was deposited in the upper lake so that purer diatom deposits accumulated in the main lake.

The lake was drained in 1876 to provide more grazing land but the operation was not a success and only a few acres of poor, boggy land were gained. About 1928 samples of the earth from the old lake bed were sent to the National Physical Laboratory for examination and it was confirmed that these were deposits of diatomite. A lease was taken on the old bed of the lake and a small company, Porosity Ltd., was formed to exploit it. Later the Leeds Fireclay Co. Ltd., became interested and formed a subsidiary company, the Kentmere Diatomite Co. Ltd. In 1943 the Cape Asbestos Co. Ltd., took over and completely mechanised the workings.

The deposits occupy about 64 acres and the thickness varied between 5 ft. and 35 ft. due to the shape of the original lake basin. For ease of working the area of operation was flooded and the water level maintained artificially. The diatomaceous earth was excavated by a dragline excavator operating over a 555 ft. radius, dredging wet material from the old lake bed up to a depth of 30 ft. This was then conveyed by an aerial ropeway to weathering dumps some distance away and left for several weeks during which most of the water drained away. It was then dried in a rotary kiln at a temperature of 1,000°C, calcined and pulverised into a fine powder, weighing 18 lb per cu.ft.

Some 10,000 tons of lake bed deposits were processed annually and the works employed about 25 people on average over the years when in full production.

The grade of diatomite at Kentmere was too low to permit the more traditional uses of the substance mentioned earlier and its main use has been as a major ingredient in heat insulation compositions. British Industrial Sand Ltd., who took over the plant in 1974, developed a granular form of diatomite which was mainly used for mopping up oil or other toxic liquid spillages but they also produced a fine powder to be used as a filler in the rubber industry. The production of diatomite, however, ceased in 1977 and the area is now a fishing lake and nature reserve.

Skeggles water, a small tarn on higher ground about two miles to the east of Kentmere, contains deposits of diatomite that are believed to be of better quality than those of Kentmere. An application to work the deposit was, however, refused some years ago on amenity grounds. The area is within the Lake District National Park.

The site of the Kentmere diatomite is currently owned by Mr. Leonard Hayton of Kentmere and the authors are grateful to him for all his information and advice, as well as access to his excellent record of this interesting deposit.

The Diatomaceous Deposits
The terms 'organic lake mud', 'diatom-gyttja' (a Scandinavian word), 'diatomaceous earth', and 'diatomite' (Kieselguhr) are all descriptions of

286

freshwater, or marine, sediments and are indicative of an increasing siliceous diatom content. Diatomite itself varies from dark-brown organic and diatom silica mixture to a white chalk-like rock that is almost purely diatomaceous. All these terms apply to material deposited on the lake or sea-bed from the water above. Diatomite is not necessarily homogenous, as is often implied by the microscope slides labelled *Diatomaceous Earth from* . . . ., but may contain the successive record of both climatic and vegetation changes including a series of differing diatom assemblages. It is, in truth, the environmental history book for a water-body and its catchment.

The diatom deposits in Kentmere are not of the highest grade but of the dark organic mud and silica variety, which can be treated by burning of the organic part. Accumulation of these deposits began after deglaciation of the last ice-age, about 14,000 years ago according to the radiocarbon age of a similar section in Windermere nearby (Pennington 1977). Analysis of the diatom stratigraphy was made by F. E. Round (1957) and has been reviewed in comparison with records of other Cumbrian lakes (Haworth 1985). Round recognized six different layers of diatom assemblages within the organic sediment that overlies glacial clays. Two of these were included within an early section related to the first period of warmer climate known as the Late-glacial Interstadial (*c.* 15,000 - 11,000 Before Present). This period ended when the climate became colder and local glaciers were again present in the Cumbrian uplands, depositing further glacial clay in lowland lakes, including Kentmere.

Four diatom assemblages were recognized within the post-glacial sediment that accumulated post-10,000 B.P. (the defined end of the Ice Age). The lowest is similar to those of the Late-glacial period being dominated by the small *Fragilaria* spp. and containing that large and unusual *Melosira teres* (Haworth 1985). Not only are there different taxa in the upper section but the diatom concentration is much greater, *i.e.* there are more diatoms per gram dry weight of sediment and less organic or mineral matter. Whilst the lowest of these sections also contains *Fragilaria* and *Epithemia* spp., it is characterized by the genus *Cyclotella* and while the latter remains in the middle section, the others are replaced by taxa more typical of more acidic waters such as *Achnanthes, Eunotia, Gomphonema* and *Cymbella*. *Cyclotella* is not typical of the uppermost section.

The overall picture is of a lake whose waters become less alkaline once glacial debris is weathered and vegetation cover creates organic deposits. Centric planktonic diatoms indicative of life in open waters at least several metres deep only flourish in the lower of the Post-glacial sections. They are seldom present in abundance in the earliest glacial sediments for reasons not fully understood but here they were probably excluded from the upper sections when the lake became shallow. Walker (1955), in his analysis of higher plant remains, found abundant evidence of such aquatic plants as *Potamogeton* spp., *Najas flexilis* and *Nymphaea alba* which thrive in shallow areas. Epiphytic diatoms, which live attached to such plants, make up the majority of the forms in the upper sediments. The shallow, weedy lake that existed for several thousand years provided an excellent site for diatomite accumulation.

The earliest study of these diatoms is reputed to be by a Dr Stolterforth of Chester (Strahan 1888) who listed nearly seventy species but no record of publication can be found. Both Neaverson (1933-34) and Stiles (1934) listed diatom taxa found in samples of the Kentmere diatomite but neither was aware of the stratigraphy. Stiles clearly fractioned his sample as his taxon list is mainly composed of the larger forms; some of the names are rather outdated.

Samples studied by the present authors include material collected (by E.Y.H.) from the diatomite works area; a slide made by the late R. I. Firth; and one of selected taxa made by Thomas Smith (Kendal) labelled *Kentmere Deposit,* lent by Dr N. Birkett. The taxa in these slides suggest that the diatomite is collected principally from the three upper layers, which constitute the bulk of the deposit, and these have become mixed during the extracation process so that *Eunotia* and *Epithemia* appear together. The illustration shows some of the larger forms which are considerably diluted by the smaller forms in raw samples.

The moral, therefore, is that there is far more to *Diatomite* than just a *Typical Assemblage* of larger, aesthetic forms. It represents some part of the environmental record of the locality or may be composed of an undefined mixture of several different diatom assemblages.

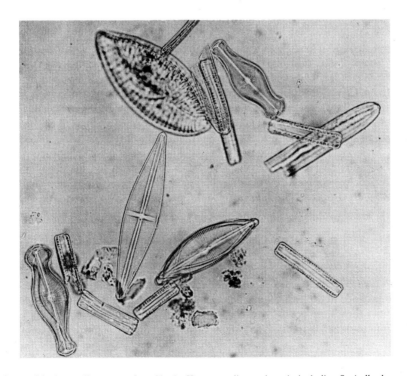

Some of the larger diatom taxa found in the Kentmere diatom deposit, including *Surirella elegans, Stauroneis phoenicenteron, Didymosphenia geminata, Cymbella ehrenbergii, Pinnularia maior, Eunotia formica, Epithemia turgida.*

Part Two
When was the Tarn drained?

The Rigmaden Estate Trustees sold some outlying farms from the Rigmaden Park Estate on 24th July 1919 by auction at Kendal. The Kentmere farms were: High Fold, Low Fold, Hayton Lot and Millriggs.

Lot number 28 described Millriggs and Longhouses farms. Plan no. 9, which delineates lot 28, shows the meadows east of the river Kent as part of Millriggs, stretching south from our Low Meadow. The land between the Kentmere road and the River Kent was later purchased by the Cape Asbestos Company.

The plan shows my grandfather, Gerard Hayton, as owning the field known as Low Meadow to the north of the Millriggs land. The Millriggs farm land stretched south along the river from there down to Waterford Bridge at the entrance to the Mill and Sawmill Cottage. No lake or tarn is shown on the plan in 1919 but the eastern bay, which has since been formed by dredging, is on part of the Millriggs land and what was Low Meadow.

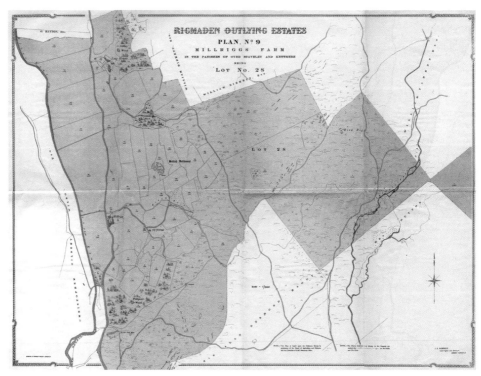

Figure 4.21. Millriggs and Longhouses Auction, plan 9, 1919

Joe Scott in *"A Lakeland Valley Through Time"*, published by the Staveley, Kentmere and Ings History Society, shows three maps of the River Kent and Kentmere Tarn on page 45 plus some good pictures and historical notes on pages 46 and 47. It is a very interesting book for anyone interested in Kentmere.

In addition to the above maps I have a copy map dated 1806, which is an extract from Mr Wilson's estate plan of Kentmere Hall.

This shows the tarn on a larger scale with boggy ground around it. The boggy ground and tarn is listed in the table of contents on the 1806 map as being 29 acres, 2 roods and 16 perches in customary measure and 40 acres, one rood and 14 perches in statute measure. The whole Kentmere Hall Estate at the time measured – in statute measure – 1098 acres, 3 roods and 5 perches.

The tarn has a similar shape to that shown on Hodgson's survey plan of 1824 and also on the Corn Rent map of 1836 referred to by Joe Scott in *"The Lakeland Valley through Time"*.

I attach a copy extract from the Corn Rent map and I have illustrated field no. 171 in white.

If we compare the shape of the tarn in 1806 in Figure 4.16 with field number 171 shown in white on the extract from the Corn Rent plan of 1836, we see that it has a similar shape.

The Schedule with the Corn Rent map lists Christopher Wilson as the owner of 171, William Martindale as the tenant and gives the name of this parcel as *Tarn Close*. However, it is described as pasture with an area of 24 acres.

This I find puzzling because:

a) My grandmother told me that her father, the game keeper at Kentmere Hall, used to fish in a boat on the tarn in the 1870s.

b) The tarn, as already stated and evidenced by the reports in the Westmorland Gazette, must have existed because it was not finally drained until 1876.

c) The boundaries of the field 171 shown on the Corn Rent map of 1836 equate almost exactly to the edges of the tarn shown on the estate plan of 1806 and it is referred to as Tarn Close.

I can only conclude that previous attempts at draining had not been wholly successful and that a stretch of water still existed in a boggy enclosure called Tarn Close.

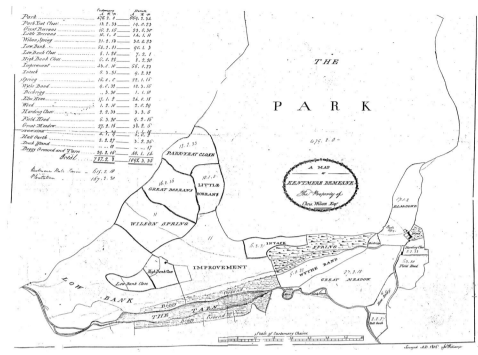

Figure 4.22. Wilson's Kentmere Hall Estate plan, 1806

Figure 4.23. Corn Rent map of 1836, Tarn Close – no. 171 shown in white.

Part Three
The Ecological Assessment of Kentmere Tarn and surrounding area

ECOLOGICAL ASSESSMENT OF KENTMERE TARN AND SURROUNDING AREA

INTRODUCTION

The following report details the findings of a botanical survey completed during July 1982, at Kentmere Tarn and adjacent shoreline. The survey was carried out at the request of the owner Mr Hayton as a preliminary step towards future discussions with the Board relating to tree planting in the area as well as assessing the possible impact of some agricultural reclamation work proposed for the eastern side of the site.

RESULTS OF BOTANICAL SURVEY

The main factor affecting the habitats present at Kentmere Tarn is the high water table relative to the presence of the tarn and also subsidence of areas due to land slip following excavation of the tarn.

The transition from open water to dry land (a hydrosere) can include a range of plant communities reflecting the gradually diminishing effect of the water. The best examples of a hydrosere shows a sequence from open water, through submerged and floating leaved plants, 'emergents' rooted in water but with the leaves projecting above the surface, wet alder/willow woodland ('carr') and finally into dry broadleaved woodland.

The development of a good hydrosere relies on a gradual slope. The eastern bank of Kentmere Tarn is steep and consequently plant communities typical of hydroseres are poorly developed. However some parts of the western edge of the Tarn do have gently shelving banks and it is here that the best examples of a hydrosere occur. The full hydrosere sequence is only present in the south west corner of the Tarn where open water grades into a wide strip of emergent sedges with a few willow shrubs passing gradually upslope into bracken dominated banks and finally into a small area of broadleaved woodland.

The ecological survey identified the following habitats at Kentmere Tarn (see map).

Tarn   included open water, floating and submerged plants, and the emergent fringe of rushes, sedges, reedgrass.

Wetland   included tall-herb communities, reed dominated communities and willow carr.

Dry Bankside   included various grasslands and the bracken dominated slopes.

Woodland   included broadleaved woodland, shrubs and hedgerows.

The following sections give a brief description of the above habitats and identify any species of particular interest associated with them.

1   TARN

No detailed survey was made of the submerged plants in the tarn but where visible the dominant underwater species appeared to be Canadian Pondweed. No floating leaved plants were found in the tarn but in the pools at the southern end of the former river channel Reddish Pondweed, Floating Pondweed, and Unbranched Bur-reed occurred with submerged Water Milfoil.

The emergent fringe includes reedgrass and various species of sedges and rushes. Mountain Water Sedge is dominant around approximately one quarter of the shoreline of the smaller tarn but in the larger tarn this plant only occurs occasionally. It is an unusual species more typical of the lochs of the Scottish Highlands, here it is at one of the more southerly points of its range. It is also common in the slumped area at the eastern edge of the smaller tarn where it grows with Meadow Sweet, Angelica and Monkey Flower and a solitary willow which is regenerating.

The sedge communities around the larger tarn are largely dominated by Bottle Sedge, with Bladder Sedge occuring less frequently. Two tussocks of another local species - Greater Tussock Sedge - which is an indicator of more base-rich or fen conditions, are present in the sedge fringe midway along the western bank.

Around much of the larger tarn there is just a narrow fringe of reed grass or rushes right at the water's edge, but both species extend into the land-based wetland habitats.

2   WETLANDS

The species composition of the large area classified on the map as 'tall herb communities' is very variable; it is best described as a matrix containing the following communities:-

a)   Herb-rich variants with rushes and sedges in the slumped areas around the tarn, species include Marsh Marigold, Valerian, Meadow-sweet, Ragged Robin, Cuckoo Flower, Lesser Water Forget-me-not and patches of Yellow Flag.

b)   Tufted Hair Grass is dominant in some areas notably along the eastern boundary of the site, where other species present include rushes, sedges and tall herbs such as Foxglove and Common Sorrel. Aerial photographs show that drainage ditches have been cut through this area in the past.

c)   Reedgrass is the dominant species in the tall herb community adjacent to the southern end of the tarn and former river channel.

d)   Some areas are dominated by sedges, predominantly Mountain Water and Bottle Sedge growing in bog mosses (Sphagnum and Polytrichum).

e)   The central zone has acidic grasses commonly tussocky Purple Moor Grass growing with Common Sedge, White Sedge and Wavy Hair Grass, all over hummocky bog mosses. Common Spotted and Heath Spotted Orchids are scattered through this area.

Reeds only occur in a small area of poor fen alongside Nuttera Beck. They are widely spaced and other species include Reed Grass, Bladder Sedge and taller herbs like Yellow Flag, Angelica, Meadow-sweet and Great Willowherb.

From an examination of aerial photographs it is clear that the area of willow carr has spread in the last nine years. Although still rather fragmented natural regeneration is occuring, particularly along the former river channel, so further development of the willow carr is likely.

3   DRY BANKSIDES

The dry bankside communities occur on the more freely drained land adjacent to the tarn. On the eastern bank this appears to be material excavated from the bottom of the Tarn.

The grassland communities consist of very few species and would appear to be of fairly recent origin, typically they contain species which are known to rapidly colonize disturbed areas (ruderal species) such as Oat Grass, Scented Vernal Grass or Creeping Soft Grass.

In certain places eg. on the peninsula projecting into the northern end of the main tarn, meadow species are present including Ox-Eye Daisy, Meadow Vetchling, Betony, Hardheads and another local species - Melancholy Thistle.

Nettles are another ruderal species characteristic of disturbed areas, they occur along the western bank adjacent to the car park and landing stage. Often other weeds and coarse grasses are present such as Cocksfoot, Goose Grass and Common Hemp Nettle.

4   WOODLAND

There is a small area of woodland in the south west corner of the site with a few mature oaks and a single mature sycamore, a few hawthorn bushes occur below the tree canopy. The ground flora is dominated by grasses with one or two typical woodland herbs including Red Campion and Enchanter's Nightshade.

South of the fence there is a small area occupied by shrubs of elder, hawthorn, guelder rose, blackthorn, and a single mature ash tree surrounded by several ash saplings. The ground flora below the shrubs is grass with bracken. There are also a number of hedgerow trees and shrubs along the western boundary of the site.

SUMMARY

The survey established that the ecological interest of the site lay in the complex of habitat types which include open-water, fringing vegetation at the edge of the Tarn, willow carr and a small area of broadleaved woodland - such diversity ensures that the site supports a wide range of plants, birds and invertebrates.

Of the various habitat types identified the communities of sedges, rushes and reed grass fringing the edge of the tarn were especially interesting - it is important that any land improvements should not affect these for this would certainly detract from the conservation value of the site.

One hundred and eighty-six plant species were identified on the site. Species of particular interest were Melancholy Thistle, Mountain Water Sedge and Greater Tussock Sedge.

The wet land on the east of the tarn, which is scheduled for agricultural improvement, supports tall herb communities of limited interest for nature conservation. Provided therefore that a wide margin (c. 25 m) is left to the east of the former river channel, then the conservation value of the whole site will not be seriously damaged by the proposed improvements.

The eastern bank of the Tarn appears to be little visited by fishermen, so is relatively undisturbed and it is suggested that this area be left alone to colonize naturally. However, in order to enhance the wildlife potential and improve the landscape, trees such as ash, birch, alder and oak and shrubs such as rowan, guelder rose, hawthorn and blackthorn could be planted at the northern end of the Tarn and in some of the nettle and bracken-dominated gaps along the western bank. Such planting would enhance the ornithological value of the site, without affecting the botanical interest.

COMPOSITE SPECIES LIST FOR KENTMERE TARN
COMPILED 8/9 JULY 1982

Acer pseudoplatanus	Sycamore
Achillea millefolium	Yarrow
Achillea ptarmica	Sneezewort
Agrostis canina	Velvet Bent
Agrostis stolonifera	Creeping Bent
Agrostis tenuis	Common Bent
Alchemilla glabra	Lady's Mantle
Alchemilla xanthochlora	
Alisma plantago-aquatica	Water Plantain
Alnus glutinosa	Alder
Alopecurus geniculatus	Marsh Foxtail Grass
Alopecurus pratensis	Meadow Foxtail Grass
Angelica sylvestris	Angelica
Anthoxanthum odoratum	Scented Vernal Grass
Anthriscus sylvestris	Cow Parsley
Arctium minus	Lesser Burdock
Arrenatherum elatius	Oat Grass
Athyrium filix-femina	Lady Fern
Bellis perennis	Daisy
Betonica officinalis	Betony
Betula pendula	Silver Birch
Callitriche spp.	Water Starworts
Caltha palustris	Marsh Marigold
Capsella bursa-pastoris	Sheperds Purse
Cardamine flexuosa	Greater Bitter Cress
Carex aquatilis	Mountain Water Sedge
Carex curta	White Sedge
Carex echinata	Star Sedge
Carex demissa	Low Sedge
Carex nigra	Common Sedge
Carex ovalis	Oval Sedge
Carex pallescens	Pale Sedge
Carex paniculata	Greater Tussock Sedge
Carex remota	Distant Flowered Sedge
Carex rostrata	Bottle Sedge
Carex vesicaria	Bladder Sedge
Centaurea nigra	Hardheads
Cerastium holosteoides	Common Mouse Ear
Chamanaerion angustifolium	Rosebay Willow-herb
Chrysanthemum leucanthemum	Ox-Eye Daisy
Circaea lutetiana	Enchanters Nightshade
Cirsium arvense	Creeping Thistle
Cirsium palustre	Marsh Thistle
Cirsium heterophyllum	Melancholy Thistle
Cirsium vulgare	Spear Thistle
Conopodium majus	Pignut
Cordyalis claviculata	Climbing Cordyalis
Corylus avellana	Hazel
Crataegus monogyna	Hawthorn
Crepis paludosa	Marsh Hawk's Beard
Cynosorus cristatus	Timothy Grass
Dactylis glomerata	Cocksfoot Grass
Dactylorhiza ericetorum	Heath Spotted Orchid
Dactylorhiza fuchsii	Common Spotted Orchid
Deschampsia caespitosa	Tufted Hair Grass
Deschampsia flexuosa	Wavy Hair Grass
Digitalis purpurea	Foxglove
Dryopteris dilitata	Common Buckler Fern

Dryopteris filix-mas	Male Fern
Elodea canadiensis	Canadian Pondweed
Endymion non-scriptus	Bluebell
Epilobium hirsutum	Great Willow-herb
Epilobium palustre	Bog Willow-herb
Epilobium parviflorum	Hairy Willow-herb
Equisetum arvense	Common Horsetail
Equisetum fluviatile	Water Horsetail
Equisetum palustre	Marsh Horsetail
Eriophorum angustifolium	Common Cotton Grass
Euphrasia sp.	Eyebright
Festuca pratensis	Meadow Fescue Grass
Festuca rubra	Creeping Fescue Grass
Filipendula ulmaria	Meadowsweet
Fraxinus excelsior	Ash
Galeopsis tetrahit	Common Hemp Nettle
Galium aparine	Goosegrass
Galium palustre	Marsh Bedstraw
Galium saxatile	Heath Bedstraw
Geranium robertianum	Herb Robert
Geranium sylvaticum	Wood Cransebill
Geum urbanum	Wood Avens
Glyceria fluitans	Floating Sweet Grass
Heracleum sphondyllium	Hogweed
Hieracium sp.	Hawkweed
Holcus lanatus	Creeping Soft Grass
Holcus mollis	Yorkshire Fog
Hypericum tetrapterum	Square-stalked St John's Wort
Hypochaeris radicata	Common Cat's Ear
Iris pseudacorus	Yellow Flag
Juncus acutiformis	Sharp flowered Rush
Juncus articulatus	Jointed Rush
Juncus bufonius	Toad Rush
Juncus bulbosus	Bulbosus Rush
Juncus conglomeratus	Common Rush
Juncus effusus	Soft Rush
Juncus squarrosus	Hard Rush
Lapsana communis	Nipplewort
Lathyrus pratensis	Yellow Meadow Vetchling
Leontodon hispidus	Rough Hawkbit
Lolium perenne	Rye Grass
Lotus corniculatus	Birds Foot Trefoil
Lotus uliginosus	Marsh Birds Foot Trefoil
Luzula multiflora	Many Flowered Wood-rush
Lysimachia nemorum	Creeping Jenny
Lythrum salicaria	Purple horsestrife
Matricaria matricoides	Pineapple May weed
Mecanopsis cambrica	Welsh Poppy
Mentha aquatica	Water Mint
Mercutialis perennis	Dogs Mercury
Mimulus guttatus	Monkey Flower
Molinia caerulea	Purple Moor Grass
Montia fontanum	Water Blinks
Montia sibrica	Pink Purslane
Myosotis caespitosa	Lesser Water Forget-me-not
Myosotis scorpioides	Water Forget-me-not
Myosotis sylvatica	Wood Forget-me-not
Myriophyllum alterniflorum	Alternate-flowered Water Milfoil
Nardus stricta	Mat Grass
Oenanthe crocata	Hemlock Water Dropwort
Oxalis acetosella	Wood Sorrel

Petasites hybridus	Butterbur
Phalaris arundinacea	Reed Canary Grass
Phleum pratensis	Timothy Grass
Phragmites communis	Reed
Plantago lanceolata	Ribwort Plantain
Plantago major	Great Plantain
Poa annua	Annual Meadow Grass
Poa pratensis	Meadow Grass
Polygonum aviculare	Knotgrass
Polygonum hydropiper	Water Pepper
Polygonum persicaria	Common Persicaria
Potamogeton alpinus	Reddish Pondweed
Potamogeton natans	Floating Pondweed
Potentilla anserina	Silverweed
Potentilla erecta	Tormentil
Potentilla palustris	Marsh Cinquefoil
Potentilla sterilis	Barren Strawberry
Prunella vulgaris	Selfheal
Prunus spinosa	Blackthorn
Pteridium aquilinum	Bracken
Quercus petraea	Sessile Oak
Ranunculus acris	Common Meadow Buttercup
Ranunculus flammula	Lesser Spear-wort
Ranunculus repens	Creeping Buttercup
Rhinanthus minor	Hay Rattle
Rosa sp.	Rose
Rubus fruticosus agg.	Blackberry
Rubus idaeus	Raspberry
Rumex acetosa	Common Sorrel
Rumex acetosella	Sheeps Sorrel
Rumex conglomeratus	Sharp Dock
Rumex crispus	Curled Dock
Sagina procumbens	Common Pearlwort
Salix caprea	Great Sallow
Salix cinerea	Common Sallow
Sambucus nigra	Elder
Sanguuisorba officinalis	Great Burnet
Sarothamnus scoparilis	Broom
Scrophularia nodosa	Figwort
Scutellaria galericulata	Skullcap
Senecio jacobea	Ragwort
Silene diocia	Red Campion
Sparganium emersum	Unbranched Bur Reed
Stachys palustris	Marsh Woundwort
Stachys sylvatica	Wood Woundwort
Stellaria alsine	Bog Stitchwort
Stellaria graminea	Lesser Stitchwort
Stellaria holostea	Greater Stitchwort
Stellaria media	Chickweed
Succisa pratensis	Devils Bit Scabious
Taraxacum officinalis agg.	Dandelion
Teucrium scorodonia	Wood sage
Torilis japonica	Hedge Parsley
Trifolium repens	White Clover
Trisetum flavescens	Yellow Oat Grass
Typha angustifolia	Reedmace
Ulmus glabra	Wych Elm
Urtica diocia	Nettle
Valeriana officinalis	Valerian
Veronica beccabunga	Brooklime
Veronica chamaedrys	Germander Speedwell
Veronica officinalis	Common Speedwell
Viburnum opulus	Guelder Rose
Vicia cracca	Tufted Vetch
Vicia sepium	Bush Vetch
Viola palustris	Bog Violet
Viola riviana	Common Violet

WESTMORLAND COUNTY AGRICULTURAL SOCIETY

PRESIDENTS

Kendal Agricultural Society

1799-1819	Daniel Wilson – Dallam
1826	George Wilson – Dallam

1864   Westmorland & Kendal District Agricultural Society

1881	Frank Atkinson Argles – Heversham
1895	Earl of Derby
1896	F. Punchard
1897	Capt. Bagot M.P. – Levens
1898	T. B. Tomlinson – Kirkby Lonsdale
1899	Lord Henry C. Bentinck. M.P.
1900	Victor Cavendish-Holker
1901	M. Bromley Wilson – Dallam
1902	J. G. Gandy – Heaves Levens
1903	Lord Hothfield – Appleby
1904	H. Goodwin
1905	Charles J. Cropper – Burneside
1906	R. W. Dent
1907	Colonel Bordrigge – North North – Thurland
1908	C. R. Rivington – Appleby
1909	R. Rigg
1910	J. Ranking
1911	J. W. Fothergill
1912	W. D. Crewdson – Kendal
1913	Col. Mason
1914	F. C. Danson – Grasmere
1915	R. Shaw – Milnthorpe
1916	War No president
1917	War No president
1918	War No president
1919	A. M. Sing
1920	A. M. Sing – Windermere
1921	G. H Pattinson – Windermere
1922	Lt. Col. Fothergill – Ravenstonedale
1923	R.D. Holt – Winster
1924	G.E. Thompson – Kirkby Stephen
1925	O.W E. Hedley – Windermere
1926	Sir Samuel Scott
1927	Major E.W. Hasell – Dalemain
1928	J.W. Cropper – Burneside
1929	F.R. Markham – Penrith
1930	Anthony Lowther – Penrith
1931	A.H. Willink – Burneside
1932	Major Wrigley – Windermere
1933	H. Oxley Ingham – Brough
1934	F.C. Scott – Windermere
1935	F.J. Milne – Windermere
1936	A.C. Somervell – Windermere
1937	H. Hornyold-Strickland – Sizergh
1938	H. Leigh-Groves – Windermere
1939	War
1940	War
1941	War
1942	War
1943	War
1944	War
1945	War
1946	
1947	
1948	Brig. General L.H. Wyatt
1949	Capt. R.R. Hewetson
1950	
1951	Robin Bagot – Levens
1952	
1953	
1954	
1955	
1956	Surg. Commander W.G. Thwaites R.N.
1957	
1958	R.A. Somervell – Kendal
1959	Capt. Michael Stanley – Witherslack
1960	
1961	Col. J.R. Danson
1962	
1963	
1964	
1965	Major T.W.I. Hedley M.B.E. – Windermere
1966	Sir Oliver Scott
1967	Captain Nigel Pease-Underley
1968	C.H.D. Ackland
1969	
1970	
1971	J.A. Cropper – Burneside
1972	T.M. Heaton
1973	Lt. Com. Hornyold-Strickland – Sizergh
1974	W.M. Dobson – Watercrook
1975	Major T.W.I. Hedley, M.B.E.-Windermere
1976	E. Ellis – Lane Foot
1977	E.N. Croft
1978	J. Procter
1979	C. Gibson
1980	J.W. Rutter
1981	S. Barrett
1982	G.E. Robinson – Moss End
1983	Nat. Bell
1984	W.H. Robinson – Holmscales
1985	Walter Martin – Helsington Laith
1986	Olive Clarke O.B.E., JP
1987	R. Dobson – Windermere
1988	Jim Johnson
1989	W.A. Robinson – Strickley
1990	Leslie Young – Kendal
1991	Brian Ellis – Lane Foot
1992	Hilda Gladstone
1993	John Fishwick – Staveley
1994	Vic Gregg – Langdale
1995	Tony Atkinson – Crosslands
1996	James Cropper – Burneside
1997	Derek Edmondson – Levens
1998	Lord Jopling of Ainderby
1999	Mrs D. Lambert

2000	Fred G. Martin – Lords Plain
2001	Fred G. Martin – Lords Plain
2002	Henry Willison
2003	Alan Thompson
2004	Tony Duckett
2005	George Procter
2006	Len Hayton
2007	Chuck Mason

2008	William Philip
2009	Doreen Galbraith
2010	Jim Dewhurst
2011	John Park
2012	(Hal Bagot, President Elect at time of writing)

PAST CHAIRMEN

1895	(C. Fell) Jacob Wakefield
1896	W. Atkinson
1897	W. Fulton
No Consistency of Meeting Chairmen	
1960-1962	
1963-1965	W. Dobson/Major W Hedley
1966-1968	
1968-1971	W. Dobson
1972-1974	W. H. Robinson
1975-1977	B. E. Ellis
1978-1980	W. A. Atkinson
1981-1983	F. W. Downham
1984-1986	J. L. Young
1987-1989	F. G. Martin
1990-1992	Henry Willison
1993-1995	Tony Duckett
1996-1999	George Procter
1999-2001	John Geldard
2001-2005	John Park
2005-2008	James Dixon
2008-2011	Judith Buckley
2011-	**Jonathon Mason**

SHOW FIELD DIRECTORS:

1979-1986   J. Leslie Young

1987-To date Stephen Procter 25 years to date

WESTMORLAND COUNTY AGRICULTURAL SOCIETY SECRETARIES

Honorary post for 80 years
1799	Dr Wm Briggs M.D. (Mayor of Kendal- 1801)
1811	Dr D Cambell M.D.
1811-1821	Wm Gray M.A. (Also Farmer & Conducted a School)
1821-1824	W & J Lawson
1824-1840	Edward Tatham
1840-1846	Reg. Remington
1846-1848	John Pickthall
1848-1868	William Longmire (Mayor of Kendal 1855)
1868-	

WESTMORLAND & KENDAL DISTRICT AGRICULTURAL SOCIETY

1868-1884	Jos Swainson
1884-1919	(George & Edwin Hoggarth, Major G. L. Hoggarth)
1919-1928	G. E. Thompson
1928-1935	G. Puncard
1935-1939	Michael Hodgson
1945-1946	G. G. Robinson (Temp. Hon)

WESTMORLAND COUNTY AGRICULTURAL SOCIETY

1946-1949	A. Whitwell
1949-196	Alan S. Thompson
1964-1966	John Williams
1966-1967	Brian Dakin
1967-1972	Robert W Sykes
1972-1998	Chris Lambert

WESTMORLAND COUNTY AGRICULTURAL SOCIETY LIMITED
Chief Executives

1998-2005 Rodger Read
2005 – To date Christine Knipe

TWENTY-ONE USES FOR A FARMER'S CAP

Being a farmer's son and having observed farmers, I have been amused at the variety of uses to which a farmer puts his cap. In particular I have observed the multiplicity of uses to which John Gardner of Natland Mill Beck Farm has put his cap! I don't claim this to be a complete list, because farmers are resourceful and I suspect new uses are found as time goes by. The following are some examples:

1. To protect and keep the head warm.
2. To collect eggs from the hen house.
3. To sit on a cold, hard rock.
4. To stuff with hay or grass and use as a cushion.
5. To carry a note or money inside the peak.
6. To extend the reach e.g. to catch a gate.
7. To pull up nettles or prickly things.
8. To remove briars from a sheep's wool.
9. To herd or turn cattle by waving arms and shaking cap.
10. To collect field mushrooms and carry them home.
11. To pick up icy cold things in winter.
12. To hold hot things e.g an exhaust pipe.
13. To wave at someone to get attention.
14. To dry an old wet tractor seat.
15. To put round an engine's starting-handle to protect the hand.
16. To demist windows in a vehicle.
17. To use as a shock absorber on a post-hammer shaft.
18. To collect wild berries and fruit.
19. To wipe a cow's teats.
20. To spin the cap while deep in thought.
21. To keck up the peak on the head when surprised.

DO YOU REMEMBER?

Answers to the quiz about the British currency pre-decimalisation

		£	s	d
1.	A stone (14 pounds)	14	0	0
2.	A bicycle (Penny Farthing)			1 ¼
3.	A male singer (Tenor)	10	0	0
4.	Part of the leg of a monkey (Ape knee)			½
5.	A man's name (Bob)		1	0
6.	A kind of pig (Guinea)	1	1	0
7.	The sun, moon and Mars (3 faraway things)			¾
8.	A leather worker (Tanner)			6
9.	50% of ladies' pants (Half a nicker)		10	0
10.	A royal headdress (Crown)		5	0
11.	To hit repeatedly (Pound)	1	0	0
12.	An unwell sea creature (Sick squid)	6	0	0
	Total	£ 32	17	8 ½

WINDERMERE AMBLESIDE AND DISTRICT ROUND TABLE 584

Formed 1959. List of Chairmen 1958-59 to 1990. WADRT continues to present day.

Date	No.	Chairman	Occupation
58-59	1	Cecil Barsby	Pharmacist
59-60	2	Tony Dobson	Shoe retailer
60-61	3	Colin Greaves	Auctioneer
61-62	4	Brian Whittaker	Banker
62-63	5	Kevin Ennis	Retailer
63-64	6	Ted Rothwell	Holidays Aft
64-65	7	Gordon Atkinson	Men's Outfitter
65-66	8	Alex M. Mann	Factory Manager
66-67	9	Peter Dover	Schoolmaster
67-68	10	Colin W. Tyson	Footwear Retailer
68-69	11	Alfred D. Mossop	Auctioneer
69-70	12	John A.E. Curtis	Co. Director
70-71	13	Brian Johnson	Stonemason
71-72	14	Bob Pennington	Dir. Sand & Gravel
72-73	15	Peter Matthews	Chtd. Surveyor
73-74	16	Keith Taylor	Lecturer
74-75	17	Leonard Hayton	Solicitor
75-76	18	David Richardson	Butcher
76-77	19	Jim Nelson	Dentist
77-78	20	Ron Perrygrove	Dentist
78-79	21	William J. Bewley	Co. Dir. Boats
79/80	22	J. Anthony James	Solicitor
80-81	23	John Wood	Pharmacist
81-82	24	Mike Hynes	Dentist
82-83	25	Bill Jackson	Co. Secretary
83-84	26	Tony Sansom	Vet. Surgeon
84-85	27	Dr John Farndale	G.P.
85-86	28	Robert Hughes	Surveyor
85-86		Andrew Taylor	First President
86-87	29	Paul Shingler	Retailer
87-88	30	Les Sutton	Local Govt.
88-89	31	Jeremy Smith	Mech. Engineer
88-89		Mike Hynes	President
89-90	32	Steve Dodwell	Vet. Surgeon

WADRT – MEMBERSHIP LIST 1974-75

In my Table Year as Chairman.

Allonby Paul W	Commercial Photographer	Nelson J.S. Jim	Dental Surgeon
Bewley W. J.	Company Dir – Boat Hiring	Perrygrove Ron	Dental Surgeon.
Chadwick Terry	Solid Fuel Merchant	Peters Chris	Schoolmaster
Clark Derek.	Banking	Richardson David	Butcher
Dawson Mike	Caterer	Sansom Tony J	Veterinary Surgeon
Edmundson Alec	Restauranteur	Sergeant John	Garage Manager
Harris Neil	Photofinisher	Taylor C.K. Keith	Lecturer
Hayton Len	Solicitor	Tebay Derek	Ph. Chemist
Holden Jim.	Bank Manager	Wagstaff Mike	Banking
Holt Mike	Insurance Broker	Wood D.W.E.	Hairdresser
Hynes Mike	Dental Surgeon	Wood John	Pharmacist
Jackson W. M.	Company Secretary		
James J. A. Tony	Solicitor		
Lowe A. B. Tony	Retail Jeweller	**Honorary Members:**	
Matthews P. G.	Chartered Surveyor	Curtis John A.E.	
Mossop Alfred	Auctioneer & Land Agent	Tyson Colin W.	

BIBLIOGRAPHY

BAILY, Leslie, *The Gilbert & Sullivan Book*, Cassell & Co., 1952

BARRATT, Stephen, *A Short History of Westmorland County Agricultural Society*, Westmorland County Agricultural Society, 1979

BINGHAM, Roger, *From Fell and Field: A History of the Westmorland County Show 1799-1999*, Cicerone Press, Milnthorpe, 1999

BINGHAM, Roger, *Kendal: A Social History*, Cicerone Press, 1995

BLEZZARD, T, *Original Westmorland Songs: relating to Scenes and Incidents in the Districts of Kendal and Windermere*, T. Blezzard and subscribers, 1868

BRENNAND, Mark & STRINGER, Keith J, *The Making of Carlisle: From Romans to Railways*, Cumberland & Westmorland Antiquarian & Archaeological Society, 2011

BULMER, J, *History, Directory & Topography of Westmorland*, T. Bulmer & Co., 1885; 1906

BULMER, J, *History & Directory of Furness and Cartmel*, T. Bulmer & Co., 1911

CALDWELL, David, *Islay, the Land of the Lordship*, Berlinn, 2008

CLARKE, Ken J, *The Brunskills of Sedbergh and Bowness-upon-Windermere: Victorian photographers and their studios*, Sedbergh Historian Vol. 5, No 5, Sedbergh & District History Society, 2008

CLARKE, Ken J, *The Brunskill family: Victorian commercial photographers of Sedbergh and Bowness-upon-Windermere. An end to operations*, Sedbergh Historian Vol. 5, No 6, Sedbergh & District History Society, 2009

CLEGG, John & HAWORTH, Elizabeth, *Diatoms of the Kentmere Diatomite Deposits*, Microscopy 35, July, December, 1985

DAVIES-SHIEL, Michael, *Wool is My Bread: The Early Woollen Industry of Kendal from circa 975-1575 AD*, Michael Davies-Shiel, 1975

DeVRIES, Kelly, *The Norwegian Invasion of England in 1066*, Boydell Press, 1999

DICKINSON, W, *A Glossary of the Words and Phrases pertaining to The Dialect of Cumberland*, Bemrose & Sons, London; Thurnam & Sons, Carlisle, 1879

DICKINSON, W , *Dialect of Cumberland*, Bemrose & Sons, 1899

DUMVILLE, David N, *The Churches of North Britain in the First Viking Age. (Fifth Whithorn Lecture)*, Friends of the Whithorn Trust, 1997

EDWARDS, BJN, *Vikings in North West England: The Artefacts*, Centre for North-West Regional Studies, 1998

ELLWOOD, T, *Lakeland and Iceland*, H. Frowde, Oxford University Press, 1895

FARRER, William & CURWEN, John F, *Records of Kendale, Volumes 1-3*, Cumberland & Westmorland Antiquarian & Archaeological Society, 1923

FERGUSON, Robert, *The Northmen in Cumberland and Westmorland*, Longman & Co., 1856

FERGUSON, Robert, *The Dialect of Cumberland*, (1873); Republished Llanarch, 1998

FERGUSON, Robert, *The Hammer and the Cross: A New History of the Vikings*, Allen Lane, Penguin Books, 2009

FOOTE, Peter & WILSON, David M, *The Viking Achievement*, Book Club Associates, 1970

GARNETT, Frank, *Westmorland Agriculture 1800-1900*, Titus Wilson, 1912

GIBSON, Alexander Craig, *The Folk, Speech of Cumberland: and some Districts Adjacent: Some Short Stories & Rhymes*, Bemrose & Sons, London; G. & T. Coward, Carlisle, 1880

GRAHAM, CAMPBELL, James, & BATEY Colleen E, *Vikings in Scotland: An Archaeological Survey*, Edinburgh University Press, 1998

GRAHAM-CAMPBELL, James, *Whithorn and the Viking World. (The Eighth Whithorn Lecture)*, Friends of the Whithorn Trust, 2001

GRAHAM-CAMPBELL, James, *The Viking World*, Frances Lincoln, 2001

GRAHAM-CAMPBELL, James & PHILPOTT, Robert, *The Huxley Viking Hoard: Scandinavian Settlement in the North West*, National Museums, Liverpool, 2009

GRIFFITHS, D, *Vikings of the Irish Sea*, The History Press, 2010

HALL, Richard, *Viking Age Archaeology*, Shire Archaeology, 2010

HARDING, Stephen, *Viking Mersey: Scandinavian Wirral, West Lancashire and Chester*, Countyvise Ltd., 2002

HAYWOOD, John, *The Penguin Historical Atlas of the Vikings*, Penguin, 1995

HAYWOOD, John, *The Encyclopaedia of the Viking Age*, Thames & Hudson, 2000

HOLGATE, Martin, *The Story of Appleby in Westmorland*, Hayloft Publishing, 2006

HOLMAN, Katherine, *The Northern Conquest*, Signal Books, 2007

JOHNSTON, Bob, *Dalriada: The Land that Scotland Forgot*, Ardminish Press, 2004

KERR, Gordon, *Timeline of Kings and Queens: from Charlemagne to Elizabeth II*, Canary Press, 2008

LEE, Joan, *The Place Names of Cumbria*, Cumbria Heritage Services, Carlisle, 1998

MacGREGOR, Lizzie, *Handfast: Scottish Poems for Weddings and Affirmations*, Scottish Poetry Library, 2004

MacSHAMHRAIN, Ailbhe, *The Vikings, An Illustrated History*, Wolfhound Press, 2002

McDONALD, R. Andrew, *Manx Kingship in its Irish Sea Setting 1187, 1229: King Rognvaldr (Reginald) and the Crovan Dynasty*, Four Courts Press, Dublin, 2007

MARSHALL, J.D. & DAVIES-SHIEL, M, *The Lake District at Work*, David & Charles Ltd., 1971

PREVOST, EW, *A Supplement to the Glossary of the Dialect of Cumberland*, Bemrose & Sons, London; Thurnam & Sons, Carlisle, 1905

RICHARDS, Julian D, *Blood of the Vikings*, Hodder & Stoughton, 2001

RICHARDS, Julian D, *Viking Age England*, The History Press, 2007

RICHARDSON, John, *Cummerland Talk: being Short Tales and Rhymes in the Dialect of that County*, Bemrose & Sons, London; G. & T. Coward, Carlisle, 1886

ROLLINSON, William, *A History of Man in the Lake District*, J.M. Dent & Sons, 1967

ROLLINSON, William, *A History of Cumberland and Westmorland (2nd Ed.)*, Phillimore & Co., 1996

ROLLINSON, William, *The Cumbrian Dictionary of Dialect, Tradition and Folklore*, Smith Settle Ltd., 1997

SCOTT, Joe (Editor), *A Lakeland Valley through Time: A History of Staveley, Kentmere and Ings*, Staveley & District History Society, 1995

SEDGEFIELD, WJ, *The Place-Names of Cumberland and Westmorland*, Longmans, Green & Co., 1915

TOWNEND, Matthew, *Language and History in Viking Age England*, Brepols, Turnhout, 2002

TOWNEND, Matthew, *The Vikings and Victorian Lakeland: The Norse Medievalism of W.G. Collingwood and his Contemporaries*, Cumberland & Westmorland Antiquarian & Archaeological Society, 2009

TUTU, Desmond M, *No Future without Forgiveness*, Rider, London, 1999

WHALEY, Diana, *A Dictionary of Lake District Place-Names*, English Place-Name Society, 2006

WHEELER, Mrs. Ann, *The Westmorland Dialect: in Four Familiar Dialogues with a Copious Glossary*, John Russell Smith, London, 1840

WHITNEY, William D, *The Century Dictionary in 16 Volumes*, The Times, London, 1900

WILLIAMS, Ronald, *The Lords of the Isles*, Chatto & Windus, 1984; House of Lochar, 1997

WILSON, David M, *The Vikings and Their Origins*, Thames & Hudson, 1970/89

WILSON, David M, *The Vikings in the Isle of Man*, Aarhus University Press, 2008

WRIGHT, Joseph, *The English Dialect Dictionary in Six Volumes*, H. Frowde, Oxford University Press, 1898

INDEX